P9-EAO-425

WITHDRAWN

The
Encyclopedia
of
Mummies

The
Encyclopedia
of
Mummies

Bob Brier

Facts On File, Inc.

For Ronald Wad
whose skill and knowledge made the
LIU-UMAB Mummy Project possible.

The Encyclopedia of Mummies

Copyright © 1998 by Bob Brier

All rights reserved. No part of this book may be reproduced or utilized in any form or by any means, electronic or mechanical, including photocopying, recording, or by any information storage or retrieval systems, without permission in writing from the publisher. For information contact:

Facts On File, Inc.
11 Penn Plaza
New York NY 10001

Library of Congress Cataloging-in-Publication Data

25245440

Brier, Bob.
   The encyclopedia of mummies / by Bob Brier.
     p. cm.
   Includes bibliographical references and index.
   ISBN 0-8160-3108-8 (alk. paper)
   1. Mummies—Encyclopedias.   I. Title.
  GN293.B75   1997
  393.3—dc21   97–16588

393.3
BRI

Facts On File books are available at special discounts when purchased in bulk quantities for businesses, associations, institutions or sales promotions. Please call our Special Sales Department in New York at (212) 967-8800 or (800) 322-8755.

You can find Facts On File on the World Wide Web at http://www.factsonfile.com

Text design and layout by Grace Ferrara
Cover design by M. P. R. Design

Printed in the United States of America

VB FOF 10 9 8 7 6 5 4 3 2 1

This book is printed on acid-free paper.

CONTENTS

ACKNOWLEDGMENTS

The study of mummies is interdisciplinary, and no one researcher can claim expertise in all the areas involved. My own specialty, Egyptian mummies, is but one corner of the picture, and I have had wonderful assistance from colleagues who are experts in areas where my knowledge is limited. They have read, corrected, and expanded many entries in this work and have supplied photographs to illustrate these entries. I have received so much help that it is impossible to name all who have improved this first edition of *The Encyclopedia of Mummies*, but several require special thanks.

Dr. Bernardo Arriaza, Department of Anthropology, University of Nevada, Las Vegas, read my entries on his specialty, the Chinchorro mummies, and furnished illustrations. Two Danish colleagues provided similar help: Dr. Christian Fischer, Director of the Silkeborg Museum, helped with photos and his expertise on the bog mummies, while Dr. J.P. Hart Hansen, Pathology Department, University of Copenhagen, gave advice and photos in his area, the Greenland mummies. Dr. Konrad Spindler of the Forschungsinstitut für Alpine Vorzeit supplied photos of Iceman, who is under his care. Dr. Gino Fornaciari, who has pioneered studies of mummies in church crypts throughout Italy, generously supplied numerous photos and de-

scriptions of his research. Dr. Ekkehard Kleiss repeatedly shared his vast knowledge of mummies derived from a lifetime of study and provided photos that I suspect are unavailable from any other source. Colleagues in China, such as Dr. Peng Lang-xiang, supplied photos of their research on the unique Chinese mummies. Dr. Félipe Cardénas-Arroyo of the Department of Anthropology, University of the Andes, Bogotá, not only supplied information on Colombian mummies and corrected my entries but also—and even more important—organized the Second International Congress on Mummy Studies in Cartagena that brought so many of us together for the first time.

My European, Asian, and South American colleagues have not been the only ones to contribute to this project. A special thanks is due to Jasmine Day of Australia. Closer to home, Eve Cockburn, who is now into her third decade of editing the *Paleopathology Newsletter*, supplied photographs of a wide range of mummies. Dennis Forbes, editor of *KMT* magazine, provided suggestions and photographs that greatly improved the *Encyclopedia*.

It is wonderful to have colleagues who are so knowledgeable and eager to help. It speaks well for the future of mummy studies.

INTRODUCTION

Mummies have always fascinated, but today the fascination goes well beyond the loyal fan's devotion of Boris Karloff's portrayal of Im-Ho-Tep in Universal Pictures' *The Mummy* or the modern reader who puts Ann Rice's *The Mummy or Ramses the Damned* on the best-seller list. In the past twenty years there has been a tremendous increase in scientific attention to mummies. Researchers are realizing that dead people do tell tales; there is an amazing amount of information contained in mummies, just waiting to be released by modern scientific techniques.

In 1857 August Mariette, the first chief of Egypt's Antiquities Service, discovered the mummy of the pharaoh Kamose, the great warrior who liberated Egypt from foreign domination. Strapped to the mummy's arm was a magnificent silver and gold dagger, now displayed in the Egyptian Museum in Cairo. As to the mummy of King Kamose, Mariette and his assistant, Heinrich Brugsch, threw it away! Today the Egyptian Supreme Council of Antiquities is so protective of the royal mummies that it is extremely reluctant to furnish even a single hair from the head of a pharaoh for research purposes.

Another great change in the study of mummies is the team approach. Scientific knowledge and techniques have grown so rapidly that no one scientist can have all the skills needed for a thorough investigation of a mummy. In research projects involving mummies, it is not unusual to have more than a dozen specialists—physicians, chemists, physicists, textile experts, forensic scientists, radiologists, etc. Studies on mummies have multiplied so much that mummy studies has become a significant discipline in itself. Twenty-four years ago the Paleopathology Association was formed to study diseases in ancient people. One of its chief sources of research material was mummies around the world. Just four years ago, the First International Congress on Mummy Studies was held in Tenerife in the Canary Islands, bringing together scientists from many countries to discuss techniques and research. The Second International Congress was held in 1996 in Cartagena, Colombia, and the variety of papers and research projects was astounding. One goal of *The Encyclopedia of Mummies* is to show readers the full scope of the research done on mummies today.

In an attempt to be as inclusive as possible, the word "mummy" has been used in its broadest sense. Mummification can be either artificial, as in the case of the ancient Egyptian mummies, or natural, as with Native American cave burials. Thus The Iceman, frozen in a glacier in the European Alps, is no less a mummy than the boy-king, Tutankhamen. But not every attempt at mummification was successful. There are many instances where the ancient Egyptian embalmer's art failed and the soft tissue crumbled, leaving only a skeleton. If such "mummies" are of particular interest, they have been included.

Because the range of mummies included in the *Encyclopedia* has been made as broad as possible, some readers may be surprised by some of the entries. Lenin, lying in his Kremlin crypt, is a mummy visited by millions each year, but American naval hero John Paul Jones is also a mummy, as is Eva Perón. For the true mummyphile, mummies in literature and film have also been included. *The Encyclopedia of Mummies* is intended both for the mummy researcher and the lay reader. This is the first edition, and there are undoubtedly mummies of which I was unaware that should have been included. If this volume is as welcome as hoped, later editions, enlarged to keep pace with the growing field and interest, will follow. As is the hope with mummification, this is just a beginning.

ABBOTT AND COSTELLO MEET THE MUMMY This brilliant 1955 spoof features a mummy named Kharis, played by stuntman Edwin Parker who appeared in three of Universal Pictures' previous mummy movies. Although the film focuses on the typical antics of Bud Abbott and Lou Costello, it introduces a mummy the audience can root for.

Abbott and Costello are stranded in Cairo and agree to bring a mummy back to the United States for an archaeologist. When they arrive at the archaeologist's home, they learn that he has been murdered and Kharis has disappeared. Soon they inadvertently become the possessors of a sacred medallion that, like the one in Universal Pictures' *The Mummy's Hand*, is the key to the buried treasure. The rest is almost history.

ACONCAGUA MUMMY On January 8, 1985, five mountain climbers attempting to scale Chile's Cerro Aconcagua, the highest mountain (22,834 feet) in the Western Hemisphere, discovered an undisturbed burial of an Inca prince. Buried in a stone circle at 17,400 feet, the body had quickly frozen in the cold, dry mountain air and was remarkably well preserved. Still bundled in the blankets in which he had been buried, the seven-year-old boy was carried down from the mountain and kept frozen until an international team of scientists was assembled to study him.

The prince had been painted red, the Inca color of life, and brought with him a small bag of cooked beans—his symbolic meal for the afterlife. Figurines of gold, silver-copper, and shell had been placed in the burial circle; some were human figures, perhaps companions for the boy's journey to the next world.

As the scientists worked on the boy's body, it became clear that he had been buried alive approximately 500 years ago. At this time it was common for the sons of Inca chiefs to be sacrificed to the sun god on high mountains. This established a link between the chief, the Inca emperor who was a descendent of the sun god, and the sun god himself. More than 100 of these burials above 1,500 feet have been discovered, and in most the bodies were naturally mummified by the atmospheric conditions.

ADIPOCERE The word *adipocere* comes from the Latin *adeps*, meaning "fat," and *cera*, meaning "wax." It is the gray-white substance, resembling bar soap, that forms in cadavers of obese people. The fat in the body combines with

Abbott and Costello Meet the Mummy When the popularity of Universal Pictures' mummy films waned, they turned to comedy and produced *Abbott and Costello Meet the Mummy.*

Advertising Palmolive ad from 1918 with mummy case in background.

water to produce fatty acids, the main component of adipocere. Adipocere draws out the water from surrounding nonfatty tissue, dehydrating it and retarding bacterial growth, thus preserving the body. The fatty acids also permeate the rest of the body, again retarding bacterial activity and preserving the body. With the right natural conditions (fat, water, temperature, etc.), enough adipocere can be produced to form a soap mummy, like the Soap Lady in Philadelphia's Mutter Museum. (See SOAP LADY.)

ADVERTISING, MUMMIES IN Because mummies—especially Egyptian mummies—symbolize endurance, permanence, and mystery, they have often been used in advertisements to associate a product with these qualities. At the turn of the century when the Palmolive Soap Company wanted to associate its soap with the beauty secrets of ancient Egypt, the advertisements often showed a mummy case in the background. The ads that included mummy cases all ran prior to the discovery of King Tutankhamen's tomb.

When Tutankhamen's tomb was discovered in 1922 and the general public came face to face with a real mummy in the newspapers, magazines, and newsreels, it was clear that mummies were not objects of beauty. Palmolive stopped using any reference to mummies or mummy cases in its

Advertising Ad for Delta bicycle lamp.

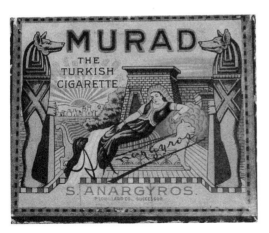

Advertising Two mummy amulets were important features in Murad cigarette ads.

ads, and Cleopatra became the Egyptian image used to sell its soap.

Palmolive was not the only company to use a mummy case to sell soap. Around 1900 Saites Soap produced a bar of soap shaped like a mummy that came in its own coffin-shaped soap dish.

In the 1920s the Delta Electric Company sold its new electric bicycle lamp with a marketing campaign that announced that there were "Some things which the Mummy Missed"—their lamps.

The Murad Cigarette Company often used Egyptian themes to advertise its cigarettes. Very often the boxes were decorated with mummies, mummy cases, and hybrid mummiform figures, all presumably denoting fine tobacco, which was misleading since no tobacco has ever been grown in Egypt.

AHMOSE, KING OF EGYPT, MUMMY OF (1575–1550 B.C.) This mummy is the first known to have had the brain removed during mummification. The founder of the Eighteenth Dynasty, Ahmose is generally credited with completing the expulsion of the Hyksos invaders from Egypt.

The mummy was found in the Deir el-Bahri cache (see DEIR EL-BAHRI) in its original coffin. On the inner wrappings, written in hieratic, a cursive form of hieroglyphs, was a note stating that Ahmose was embalmed and wrapped by order of his son and successor, Amenhotep I. The brain was not removed through the nasal passage—that technique would be developed later in the Eighteenth Dynasty—but rather by means of a unique operation. The uppermost vertebra on the spinal column, called the atlas vertebra because it supports the head, was removed via a postmortem incision in the left side of the neck to expose the foramen magnum ("large hole") at the base of the skull. The brain was removed through the foramen magnum, and the skull was packed with linen.

The mummy of Ahmose is the first indication that the Egyptian embalmers realized the brain, because it contains so much moisture, would decay if it were not removed during mummification.

AIR-DRIED CHAPLAIN, THE The Reverend Franz Xavier Sidler von Rosenegg was vicar of Saint Thomas on the Bladderstone in Upper Austria and died in 1746 at the age of thirty-seven. Approximately 200 years later his tomb in the churchyard was opened and his cadaver was found naturally mummified, probably because of the dry sand in the crypt that absorbed moisture. Since this discovery he has been irreverently called "the air-dried chaplain."

Today his mummy reposes in a wooden coffin with a glass lid. Many townspeople believe that the reverend has magical powers and that if a young girl wishes to marry, she has but to touch the mummy. This belief is possibly connected with an ancient cult stone (the "bladderstone") located nearby that may have been related to fertility rites.

ALEUTIAN MUMMIES The Aleutian Islands, off the southwest coast of Alaska's peninsula, have produced some of the most recent examples of artificial mummification in

North America. There are several theories about why the inhabitants of the Aleutian Islands began mummifying their dead sometime during the fifteenth or sixteenth century. One view is that at this time several family members of a wealthy chief named Little Wren were killed in a winter accident. The bodies were placed in a volcanically heated cave, and when the chief died of grief, he too was placed in the cave. The dry heat mummified the bodies naturally, and the custom began. Other theories suggest that the Aleuts mummified bodies because of reluctance to part with the dead or that the Aleuts in some way wished to use the power of the dead by preserving them.

The Air-Dried Chaplain The Reverend Franz Xavier Sidler von Rosenegg mummified naturally in his dry crypt and became known as "the air-dried chaplain." *Photo courtesy Dr. Ekkehard Kleiss.*

Mummification techniques depended upon the wealth and status of the deceased. Only leaders were eviscerated. The mummy was placed in flexed (fetal) position, dressed in its finest clothes, wrapped in furs, and placed in a cave. The practice of mummification ended in 1741 with the Aleuts' first contact with the Russians, which changed island society considerably.

ALEXANDER THE GREAT, MUMMY OF

(356–323 B.C.) King of Macedonia and conqueror of the Persian Empire. His mummified body has been the subject of an extensive search but remains undiscovered.

Alexander was the son of Philip II, king of Macedon. When Philip was assassinated in 336 B.C. Alexander succeeded his father and soon began a military campaign to dominate the world. Known for his bravery and skill as a military strategist, Alexander assembled an army of more than 50,000 devoted soldiers. Within ten years of becoming king, Alexander had defeated the Persians, controlled vast areas, including Egypt, Afghanistan, and Turkistan, and extended his reach as far as India. In India, after years of waging war, his soldiers would go no further, and they began the long journey home. On the way back in the summer of 323 B.C., Alexander contracted a fever and died in Babylon. Just before his death, his generals came to see their commander for the last time and asked, "To whom do you leave your kingdom?" Arrian, Alexander's biographer, recorded his whispered answer—"To the strongest."

Alexander's body was embalmed in Babylon, probably using a modification of the Egyptian style. The body lay in precious spices for two years, while Greek craftsmen prepared a gold coffin and the catafalque to carry Alexander to Aegae, the traditional burial place of Macedonian kings. The historian Diodorus describes the thousand-mile journey, which he heard from an eyewitness. The catafalque was a miniature temple of gold, with a vaulted roof supported by Ionic columns. At each corner of the temple, the goddess of victory held out a trophy. On the sides, painted friezes portrayed scenes from Alexander's campaigns. The entrance to the temple was flanked by two gold lions, while the gilded wheels of the catafalque had axles terminating in lions' heads holding spears in their mouths. The immense weight of this golden confection was pulled by sixty-four mules, each with a gold crown and a gold bell to announce Alexander's entrance to cities along the route. At each town, offerings were made and prayers said for the deified Alexander; it was a spectacle remembered for generations.

When the procession reached Syria, Alexander's faithful general Ptolemy, who now controlled Egypt, met the entourage with his army in order to hijack the body and bring it to Egypt. Had Alexander clearly designated a successor, such an event would never have occurred, and Alexander would have been buried in Greece. It was, however, appropriate that the mummy of Alexander be buried in Egypt. Alexander had always favored Egypt. When he freed Egypt from Persian domination, he immediately traveled to the remote Siwa Oasis in the western desert to consult the oracle at the temple of Zeus Amun. Alexander asked, "Who is my father?" The oracle replied, "The sun." Now that the oracle had established him as a god, Alexander could be crowned pharaoh.

Soon after becoming pharaoh of Egypt, Alexander planned the city of Alexandria with his architect Dinocrates, laying out the streets to take advantage of the sea breezes. Thus it was not inappropriate that Alexander was finally buried in the city that bears his name. Before the body was buried, it remained in Memphis for twelve years, while the tomb was being prepared at the crossroads of the two main avenues of Alexandria.

The mummy rested undisturbed in Alexandria for more than 150 years until Ptolemy IX, needing funds, exhumed the body in order to melt down the gold coffin and replace it with one of glass. Fifty years later Alexander's remains were shown to Julius Caesar by Cleopatra. As Egypt slipped from the control of the Ptolemies into the hands of the Romans, once-great Alexandria declined. Eventually even the location of the famous library of Alexandria was lost to history. Buildings collapsed or burned, and when the city was rebuilt centuries later, it no longer conformed to the original plan of Dinocrates and Alexander, and the crossroads of the two main avenues disappeared.

The search for Alexander's mummy has intrigued many scholars. Some believe that Alexander lies beneath the Nebi Daniel Mosque in Alexandria, at the intersection of Rosetta and Nebi Daniel streets. There are indeed caverns beneath the mosque, but while clandestine searches have been made, a proper excavation will be difficult because of the danger of undermining the mosque.

In February of 1995 the *New York Times* published a report stating that a Greek excavator working in Egypt claimed to have uncovered the tomb of Alexander the Great about twelve miles outside of the Siwa Oasis. Such a find was not totally implausible because one tradition states that Alexander had requested burial at Siwa, where he had been proclaimed a god. The excavator, Liana Souzaltzi, claimed to have found a tomb containing inscribed tablets written in Greek that established beyond doubt that this was Alexander's final resting place. One was supposedly written by Ptolemy, describing the transportation of Alexander's body—"light as a small shield"—to Siwa, with 30,000 soldiers standing guard. Souzaltzi also said she had found a tablet with an eight-sided Macedonian star, again evidence of Alexander.

When archaeologists were sent to the site to examine the finds, they concluded that the translations, done by Souzaltzi's businessman-husband, said nothing like her claims, and there were no Macedonian stars. They declared the tomb to be definitely of the later Roman period; the mummy of Alexander the Great remains undiscovered.

AMENEMOPE, KING OF EGYPT (933–984 B.C.) See TANIS, ROYAL MUMMIES OF.

AMENHOTEP I, KING OF EGYPT, MUMMY OF (1550–1528 B.C.) The only pharaoh whose mummy was not unwrapped in the nineteenth century—because of the beauty of the wrapping. The mummy was first wrapped in large linen sheets tied at the back. These were further secured by both horizontal and vertical linen strips that were also knotted at the back.

AMENHOTEP II, TOMB OF With the exception of the Deir el-Bahri cache (see DEIR EL-BAHRI), the tomb of Amenhotep II in the Valley of the Kings in Egypt is the only cache of royal mummies ever discovered. Unearthed in 1898 by Victor Loret, Director General of the Antiquities Service, a side room of the plundered tomb contained the mummies of Tuthmosis IV, Amenhotep III, Merenptah, Siptah, Seti II, Ramses IV, Ramses V, Ramses VI, and an unidentified woman.

Just as at Deir el-Bahri, these mummies had been gathered together by a Twenty-first Dynasty king to protect them from further desecration. An inscription written on the bandages of the mummy of Seti II explained that on the sixth day of the fourth month of winter, in the twelfth year of the reign of Pinedjem I, that king had the despoiled royal bodies rewrapped and placed in the tomb of Amenhotep II for safekeeping. In addition to the mummies in the side room, Loret also discovered, in other parts of the tomb, the mummy of Amenhotep II still in its sarcophagus and the mummy of a woman referred to as "The Elder Lady," later identified as Queen Tiye. (See TIYE, QUEEN.)

ANCON, PERU, MUMMIES OF Ancon is an ancient Peruvian cemetery that has produced a large number of mummies. Located on an isolated stretch of Peruvian coast, the Ancon necropolis is twenty-four miles north of the modern city of Callao. Because of its remoteness

Ancon was ignored by the Spanish when they conquered Peru, and it remained relatively untouched into the twentieth century. The tombs were unmarked shafts dug into the sandy soil, so they were not obvious targets for tomb robbers. Many of the tombs contained multiple burials and had been periodically reopened to accommodate new arrivals.

The mummies were almost always seated with knees drawn up in the Peruvian manner for embalming. The mummies were enveloped in cloth, so they resembled huge textile bundles. On top of the bundles rested false heads, fashioned out of cushions, often with eyes and noses made of shells and hair made of plant fibers, all capped by elaborate headdresses.

The inhabitants of Ancon were illiterate, so not much is known about their beliefs in life after death. The mummies, however, were buried with food, fishing equipment, and even mummified pets. All this suggests they believed that the next world would be a continuation of this one and they would need provisions and possessions.

ANENCEPHALIC INFANT, MUMMY OF Anencephaly is a condition in which an infant is born without a developed brain, often with only a brain stem. On January 9, 1826, a unique case of a mummified anencephalic infant was presented at the Académie des Sciences in Paris.

The mummy was found by Italian excavator and collector Giuseppe Passalacqua at the ancient site of Hermopolis in Middle Egypt. Passalacqua had originally come to Egypt as a horse dealer, but when the business failed he turned to excavating antiquities with the intention of selling them. In 1825 he brought to Paris an important collection of artifacts that he planned to sell to the French government. Among these antiquities was the mummy of an anencephalic infant.

The mummy was examined by the famous naturalist Geoffroy Saint-Hilaire, who had been one of the scientists on Napoleon's Egyptian expedition and thus had a special interest in Egyptian antiquities. Saint-Hilaire was especially qualified to examine the mummy because he was the founder of the scientific study of "monsters"—infants horribly deformed at birth. The modern term for such studies, *teratology*, was coined by Saint-Hilaire.

The mummy in question had been wrapped in a manner normally used for baboon mummies—in a squatting position. Near the mummy a small amulet of a squatting baboon had been found. In most cases of anencephalic births, the skull is severely deformed. The roof of the cranium is absent, the ridges above the eyes are exaggerated, and the palette is cleft, all of which could give the impression of a baboon. The ancient Egyptians may have believed that the mother had given birth to a nonhuman baby, a baboon, and had mummified it as such.

ANGELUS SOLIMAN (1721–1796) The son of an African prince, Angelus Soliman was mummified in Vienna by the orders of Emperor Franz II.

When he was seven years old, Soliman was abducted in a tribal feud and sold into slavery. Eventually he was sold to a marquis in Messina, Sicily. Given a good education and baptized Angelo (Latinized as *Angelus*) Soliman, because of his great intelligence and refined manners, he was introduced into society and made the acquaintance of Prince Lobkowitz, who lived in Sicily. Soliman was taught German and became the prince's servant, accompanying him on his travels and in war.

In 1755 Prince Lobkowitz died and left Soliman in his will to Prince Wenzel Liechtenstein. In the company of Wenzel Liechtenstein, Soliman attended the coronation of Josef II in 1765. In 1768, at the age of forty-seven, Soliman married and left Wenzel Liechtenstein to serve his nephew, Prince Franz Liechtenstein.

In 1783 Soliman became a Freemason and entered the "True Concord Lodge" to which Mozart and Haydn belonged, and during this same year, he retired. Soliman lived a peaceful, uneventful life until 1796, when he died of a stroke while taking a walk.

For some unknown reason the Emperor Franz II ordered that Soliman's body be mummified and displayed in the Royal Zoological Museum. The actual mummification was conducted by Franz Thaller of the Physikalische Kabinett of the Zoological Museum and took place in a coach house in the courtyard of the imperial library. Soliman's skin was flayed and then mounted on a wooden model so it could be displayed in a lifelike manner.

Standing with his right foot back, left arm forward, he was positioned inside a glass case covered with green material. He wore a belt and crown of red, white, and blue ostrich feathers; his arms and legs were decorated with strings of white glass beads. The room in which he was displayed was decorated like a tropical forest with reeds, pools of water, and stuffed birds and animals.

In 1802 the King of Naples donated a stuffed African girl to keep poor Soliman company, and later an African zoo keeper and an African hospital porter were added.

Soliman's daughter, distressed that her father was displayed as a public curiosity, repeatedly asked for the skeleton and skin of her father to be returned to her for burial, but her requests were ignored. She finally petitioned the archbishop of Vienna to intercede on her behalf, but even this did not help. Poor Soliman remained part of the imperial collections until 31 October 1848, when Prince Alfred Windischgratz's troops, attempting to restore order during a civil war, fired on the imperial castle and hit the attic where the collection was stored. Soliman and his three unfortunate mummified companions were totally destroyed.

ANIMAL MUMMIES The ancient Egyptians mummified all kinds of animals, from bulls to mice, literally by the millions. Pets were buried out of fondness; certain sacred animals were mummified when they died of natural causes; and

Animal Mummies   Some cats were raised in ancient Egypt to be sacrificed and mummified as offerings to the gods.   *Photo courtesy Museum of Fine Arts Boston.*

for years, so they were dispatched as soon as they were mature enough to be presentable.

The mummification technique for cats was relatively simple. The internal organs were removed and the body cavity stuffed with sand or some other packing material; then the animal was wrapped. For the more elaborately prepared mummies, faces were painted on the wrappings in black ink.

Ibis and falcon mummies were buried at Saqqara (see ANIMAL NECROPOLIS AT SAQQARA) as were the Apis bulls (see APIS BULL and SERAPEUM). Other sacred bulls were buried at Armant (see BUCHIS BULL) and Heliopolis (see MNEVIS BULL, MUMMIES OF).

ANIMAL NECROPOLIS AT SAQQARA

The most extensive animal cemetery in Egypt. Known in antiquity and commented upon by savants in Napoleon's expedition to Egypt, this vast cemetery was not systematically excavated until the 1960s, when Walter B. Emery, an excavator for the Egypt Exploration Society, began searching for the tomb of Imhotep, the architect of King Zoser's step pyramid.

Because Imhotep was an important official, Emery believed that his tomb would be near that of his pharaoh. More than 2,000 years after his death, Imhotep was deified as Aesculapius, the Greek god of medicine, and numerous ancient authors state that his tomb became a place of pilgrimage for the sick. Believing that pilgrims often broke pottery by accident along routes, Emery followed a trail of broken pottery at Saqqara in the hope of finding Imhotep's tomb. He found an entrance to the now-famous ibis galleries whose niches contained hundreds of thousands of mummified ibises that had been presented as offerings. Spurred on by the knowledge that the ibis was sacred to the deified Imhotep, Emery continued his excavations in search of the tomb and found a gallery of mummified baboons, each in its own coffin placed in a niche carved from the soft limestone. Both the ibis and baboon were forms supposedly taken by the god Toth, who was associated with Imhotep.

other animals were raised to be ritually killed and mummified as offerings to the gods.

Among the animals most frequently mummified were cats, ibises, and falcons, each having its own cemetery. The most famous cat cemetery was located at Bubastis (the city of the cat goddess Bast) in the Delta, but there were others at Dendereh, Abydos, and Giza.

In the 1980s the British Museum x-rayed its collection of fifty-three wrapped mummified cats. From this a picture of the animal mummy industry emerged: Of the fifty-three cats, forty-four were aged twelve months or less. The X rays also revealed that many had their necks broken. In the business of raising cats for sacrificial offerings, it was clearly not desirable to feed and care for them

Animal Mummies   The Egyptian god of mummification, Anubis, embalming a Nile perch. Tomb of Khabekhnet, Thebes.

In his six seasons of excavating at Saqqara, Emery discovered several other galleries, including one of mummified falcons. The galleries ran for miles and contained more than a million mummified animals, the largest concentration ever discovered. The tomb of Imhotep was never found.

ANNA OF HABSBURG (d. 1281)   Queen Anna, wife of King Rudolf of Habsburg, is one of the few examples of late medieval mummification for which we have a description of the procedure.

A history of the Basel Cathedral, where Queen Anna is buried, provides the details. Her internal organs were removed and the body cavity was filled with ashes, presumably to dehydrate the body quickly and avoid putrefaction. Her skin was then oiled and the body wrapped in waxed cloth. She was dressed in a silk robe and gilded crown, and a locket was placed around her neck. This was all done in Vienna, where she died, then the body was transported by forty horses from Vienna to Basel for burial. She was buried next to her son, Carolus, who died five years earlier at the age of six months.

Two hundred and thirty years after her mummification, the crypt of Queen Anna was opened by canons of the cathedral. The body of the queen was found to be in excellent condition, while the

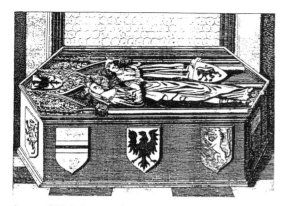

Anna of Habsburg The tomb of Queen Anna in the Basel Cathedral holds her mummy.

nonmummified body of the infant was merely bones. The queen's jewels were removed and placed with the cathedral's treasures.

ANTHROPOLITH   Petrified human remains.

ANUBIS   The Egyptian god of mummification, Anubis was represented either as a jackal or as a man with the head of a jackal. Anubis presided over the mummification process, and tomb paintings often show him leaning over the mummy as it rests on the funerary couch. During the actual mummification, a priest, representing the god, wore a jackal mask.

Because mummification took place out of doors, in a tent, one of the names of Anubis was He-Who-Is-in-His-Tent. Because the tents were often placed on top of hills to take advantage of the breezes, another name for Anubis was He-Who-Is-upon-His-Hill.

APIS BULL   A sacred bull, worshipped by the ancient Egyptians and mummified when it died. The cult of the Apis was central to Egyptian religion during the Late Period. According to one account the Apis was born when a bolt of lightning came down from heaven and impregnated the mother of the Apis. The Apis calf had special markings—it was black with a white diamond on its forehead, an eagle on its back, a scarab under its tongue, and its tail hairs were split.

There was only one Apis bull alive at any time, and when it died a search began for a new one. The Egyptians were resurrectionists and believed you only lived once, but their view of the Apis is very close to a belief in reincarnation. When alive, the Apis lived in a temple at Memphis and was perfumed and pampered. When it died it was mummified on huge alabaster mummification tables that can still be seen at Memphis. Then it was taken to its special burial place, the Serapeum at Saqqara (see SERAPEUM). The Apis was so important to the Egyptians that when the Persian king Cambyses invaded Memphis, he could think of no greater insult than to kill the Apis and eat it.

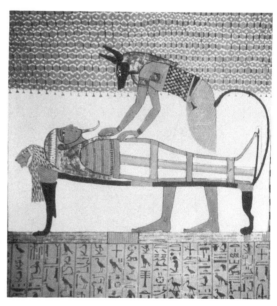

Anubis The jackal-headed Anubis was the god of mummification.

Apis Bull The sacred Apis bull was pampered while alive and when it died was mummified and given a burial appropriate for a god. *Photo courtesy Smithsonian Institution.*

APIS PAPYRUS The only papyrus discovered so far that described in detail the process of mummification and burial. It gives specific instructions for the preparation of the Apis bull.

The papyrus, discovered in the nineteenth century, instructs embalmers in preparing and wrapping the mummy, and priests in ritualizing the event. The papyrus states that when the bandages are cut, the priests "must raise a lamentation."

The Apis was not eviscerated; rather, the internal organs were dissolved by injecting certain fluids into the anus. This explains why no canopic jars, used to hold internal organs, were ever found in the Serapeum, the burial place of the Apis bulls. The bulls were mummified in a recumbent position, which is unnatural for a bull. To accomplish this, the embalmers had to cut the tendons in the bull's legs. The bull was then clamped onto a board approximately 2 ½ yards long and 1 yard wide with twenty-two bronze clamps. The head was plastered and then covered with gold leaf. A crown similar to the one it wore in life was attached between the horns. Stone or glass artificial eyes were placed in the sockets to give the bull a lifelike appearance. Finally, in a great procession, the Apis was laid to rest in the Serapeum.

ARAGONA, MARIA D', MUMMY OF (1503–1568) A noblewoman of the Italian Renaissance known for her beauty, her right arm had been bound with linen bandages intertwined with ivy leaves. Beneath the bandage was an ulcer and inside it was a poultice of vegetable fibers that had been dipped in sulfur—a common treatment for skin diseases during the sixteenth century. Histological tests revealed that the noblewoman had venereal syphilis, which was known during the Renaissance as the "Neapolitan disease." This is the first case documented from soft tissues of ancient human remains.

The research team also determined that both Ferdinando Orsini, Duke of Gravina in Apulia (d. 1549), and Ferrante I of Aragon, King of Naples (d. 1492), died of cancers similar to those found today.

ARCHIVE OF HOR A series of writings by a priest named Hor who worked in the ibis galleries of Saqqara during the second century B.C.

During the excavations of the sacred animal necropolis at Saqqara in the 1960s (see ANIMAL NECROPOLIS AT SAQQARA), several dozen pottery fragments were discovered that had been used as "scrap paper" for drafts of official documents concerning the administration of the animal mummy trade. These writings by Hor provide a unique glimpse into the activities of the ibis galleries at Saqqara.

Hor refers to the vast farms on which ibises were raised, eventually to be killed and mummified so they could be presented as offerings to the gods. He mentions an official called "the doorkeeper" who must be reliable, for he supervises the birds and their young. Several of Hor's records deal with reforms he urged for managing the mummy galleries. Apparently many of the cemetery officials who were supposed to be present at various ceremonies were shirking their responsibilities, and the pious Hor wanted to put a stop to this. In one memorandum Hor refers to cemetery procedures.

There was an annual mass burial of all the ibises offered over the course of the year. At this time the necropolis officials would gather in a procession terminating at a new gallery excavated to receive the burials. The procession included priests, the "servants of the ibises," as well as "the men who care for the bandages," and "efficient carvers"—probably the stonecutters who carved the galleries and niches to hold the birds. Hor wanted to ensure that everyone who should have been present in fact attended.

Hor was also concerned that pilgrims who purchased the mummified ibises were not cheated and says that there should be "one god in one vessel." Sometimes pilgrims were sold a few random bones wrapped to look like an ibis and placed in a pot.

From Hor's writings a picture emerges of an extensive trade in animal mummies. Not only were there keepers of the thousands of birds raised to be killed, but a major industry employing animal embalmers, potters, bandage merchants, etc. As the pilgrims made their way to the animal galleries, the route must have been lined with stalls selling the mummies. Hor merely wanted to make certain that the industry was regulated so the clients were not cheated.

ASTO VIDATU In Persian mythology the god of death and the personification of the disintegration of bodies.

ATACAMA DESERT Located in Chile near the borders of Peru, Bolivia, and Argentina, the Atacama Desert may contain more natural mummies than any other site on earth. The combination of soil conditions, dry air, and altitude has created ideal conditions for the natural preservation of human remains. For hundreds of years before the Spanish Conquest, the Indians buried their dead in chambers excavated beneath the desert. Provided with food and clothing for the journey to the next world, the bodies dehydrated naturally and remained untouched for hundreds of years.

Serious interest in the remains beneath the Atacama began in the 1950s, when Father Gustave Le Paige, a Belgian priest, established the San Pedro Museum to display these relics of Chile's past. Soon after the museum's founding, grave robbers realized that the tombs held valuable treasures that collectors and tourists would buy. During the last twenty years, the graves have been systematically plundered, leaving the surface of the desert littered with bones, textile and pottery fragments.

AUSTRALIAN MUMMIES Mummification was practiced by Aboriginal societies in Australia until the time of extensive contact with Europeans and the introduction of Christianity in the nineteenth century.

The purpose of Aboriginal mummification was not, as in the case of ancient Egypt, to achieve continued existence in the next world but rather to ease the grief of the deceased's family. Consequently interest in the mummy would rarely extend beyond a generation or two, then the mummy would be buried or disposed of in some other manner. For this reason the mummification techniques did not have to yield a permanent mummy.

In the Australian method of mummification, the corpse was tied in a flexed, sitting position, similar to South American mummies, and was then placed either on a specially constructed platform or in a tree until dehydrated by the sun. Sometimes the body's orifices were sewn shut, and the body was smoked. Occasionally the internal organs were removed through an abdominal incision to assist dehydration, then the opening was sewn shut. Once the body was dry, the epidermis was peeled off and all bodily hair removed. The mummy was then painted red and decorated with ornaments.

Relatively few Aboriginal mummies have survived, primarily because they were kept by the family for only a generation or so. One of the first examples was obtained in Adelaide by Sir George Gray and was given in 1845 to the Royal College of Surgeons in London. The mummification technique was not the central focus of early mummy studies, so this mummy was defleshed in order to study the bones. The fate of this unfortunate mummy was sealed when even the skeleton was destroyed by the German bombing of London during World War II. There are, however, several complete mummies in the Queensland Museum in Brisbane and in the South Australian Museum in Adelaide.

AUTOLYSIS The decomposition of tissues caused by enzymes within the body. During life these enzymes are bound to cells, but they are released at the time of death, causing decay.

B

BAB EL-GUSUS TOMB, THE   The most famous of all Egyptian mummy caches was discovered at Deir el-Bahri (see DEIR EL-BAHRI) in 1881 and contained the mummies of the kings and queens of the Eighteenth and Nineteenth Dynasties. In 1891 a second, even larger, mummy cache was found at Deir el-Bahri in a tomb called "Bab el-Gusus." The cache is also called "The Second Find at Deir el-Bahri."

One of the discoverers of the first cache, Mohamed Ahemd el-Rassoul, found the second tomb and reported it to the Egyptian Antiquities Service, who opened the unplundered find. The tomb had been carved out of the rock of Deir el-Bahri during the reign of the Twenty-first Dynasty pharaoh Psusennes to house the mummies of the high priests and priestesses of Amun.

The tomb contained an amazing number of mummies and funerary objects. Apparently, between 948 B.C. and 945 B.C., the mummies of the priests had been gathered from their individual tombs and placed in the Bab el-Gusus tomb for safekeeping. One hundred and fifty-three coffins, along with many smaller funerary statuettes, jars, etc., covered the tomb's floor. So many objects crammed the store rooms at the Egyptian Museum that between 1893 and 1894 the Egyptian government presented seventeen museums in Europe and the United States with sets of coffins and funeral objects.

Although many coffins and objects were given away, all the mummies remained at the museum. In May of 1891 George Daressy, a curator, began unwrapping them. His examinations confirmed what had been learned from the earlier Deir el-Bahri cache—that during the Twenty-first Dynasty there had been a change in mummification technique. Rather than placing the internal organs in canopic jars (see CANOPIC JARS) to hold them until the time of resurrection, the organs were dehydrated in natron and replaced in the body cavities. This change may have been instituted to prevent tomb robbers from stealing the canopic jars and thus depriving mummies of their internal organs and consequently their ability to resurrect.

The mummies of the high priests and priestesses of Amun are now stored in the Egyptian Museum, Cairo, and are not on view.

BELZONI, GIOVANNI BATTISTA (1778–1823)   An Italian circus strongman who became an early excavator of Egyptian antiquities and did much to popularize mummy unrollings. Belzoni was trained as a hydraulic engineer and first went to Egypt in 1816 to sell Mohamet Ali, the ruler of Egypt, a new irrigation pump. During the demonstration of the pump, an accident occurred and Belzoni's assistant's leg was broken, which discouraged Mohamet Ali from investing in the new invention. Forced into a new profession, Belzoni turned his attention to antiquities, his ability to move large objects gaining him commissions from Henry Salt, the British consul, who was building an Egyptian collection.

While excavating in the Valley of the Kings, Belzoni discovered the tomb of Seti I. When he returned to England to display a replica of the tomb, he also brought back a number of mummies that were later used at public unrollings. When he asked the English physician, Thomas Pettigrew, to examine several of the mummies,

Belzoni, Giovanni Battista Giovanni Battista Belzoni, an Italian circus strongman who removed a large number of antiquities from Egypt, stirred the public's interest in mummies by giving vivid accounts of his adventures.

Pettigrew became fascinated and began his career as the greatest of the mummy unrollers. (See PETTIGREW, THOMAS.)

BENES, BARTON LIDICE (1942–) An American contemporary artist who is best known for his series of collages using shredded and torn American dollars and foreign currency. In his later works Benes frequently focused on death themes and often incorporated fragments of Egyptian mummies in his art. In *The Cremated Ashes of Hans Schneider*, Benes enclosed the actual ashes of Hans Schneider in a miniature mummy case that he covered with ancient Egyp-

tian mummy wrappings. Another of Benes's works is a life-sized mummy made from sea shells. Inside the mummy are secrets written by the people who commissioned the statue.

BENTHAM, JEREMY, MUMMY OF (1748–1832) British philosopher, most famous as a champion of the doctrine of utilitarianism—the theory that consequences make an action right or wrong; thus one ought to do those actions that bring about the most good for the most people. To some extent Bentham's belief in utilitarianism led to his mummification.

Bentham's will stipulated exactly what was to be done with his body upon death. In accordance with the principle of utilitarianism, Bentham

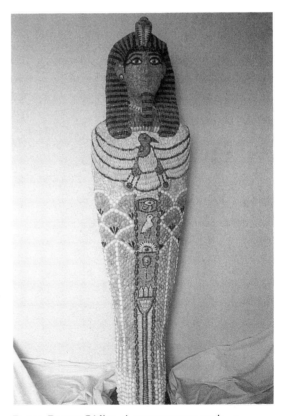

Benes, Barton Lidice A contemporary work—a mummy case made of sea shells.

thought that the most good would be achieved if his body were dissected as an anatomy lesson for medical students, and this, indeed, was done. Bentham's last instructions for his body, however, seem to go beyond utilitarianism. The head was to be preserved intact with glass eyes placed in the sockets, and the skeleton, wired together in anatomically correct configuration, was to be dressed in Bentham's clothes. The dressed skeleton surmounted by Bentham's head was placed in a chair and deposited at University College, London, with the instructions that it be brought to all the meetings of the Utilitarian Society.

In the twentieth century the head began to deteriorate and was replaced by a wax duplicate, but the mummy of Jeremy Bentham still attends meetings at London College.

BIRCH, SAMUEL (1813–1885) An important Egyptologist, responsible for unwrapping many mummies in England during the nineteenth century. Birch had an early interest in languages, mastering Chinese by the age of nineteen. In 1836 he joined the British Museum as an assistant in the department of antiquities and began a lifelong study of the Egyptian language. He was one of the strongest defenders of Champollion's decipherment of hieroglyphs, which was then being debated in England. Among his hundreds of published works is the first hieroglyphic dictionary (1867). As he advanced his position at the British Museum, he organized and increased the Egyptian collection. From 1866 to 1885 he was keeper of Oriental, British, and medieval antiquities at the museum and is generally credited with establishing the first careful cataloguing system for those collections.

Because of the wide range of objects for which Birch was responsible, he published in many areas but was an acknowledged shining light of Egyptology. As a result of his position, Birch was frequently asked to unwrap mummies. Unfortunately he had no anatomical training and was more interested in inscriptions than bones. He had the unique opportunity to unwrap the twenty mummies brought back from Egypt by the Prince of Wales in 1868, but in writing about this investigation, he mentioned much about the coffins and little about the mummies. On June 10, 1850 he unwrapped a mummy that had been provided with silver gloves.

During his long career Birch unwrapped many more mummies, but because of his lack of medical background, little was learned, and the unwrappings were often more social than scientific events. Because of the demands on his time made by his prominent position at the British Museum and his prodigious writings, despite his long career, Birch was never able to visit Egypt.

BLOOD FROM THE MUMMY'S TOMB (1971) Produced by England's Hammer Films, _Blood from the Mummy's Tomb_ is the last of their four mummy films—_The Mummy_ (1959), _The Curse of the Mummy's Tomb_ (1964), and _The Mummy's Shroud_ (1967).

Based loosely on Bram Stoker's novel _Jewel of the Seven Stars_, the plot centers around the evil Tara, Queen of Darkness, who was killed by ancient Egyptian priests. In an attempt to diminish her powers in death, the priests cut off her hand and threw it to the dogs before sealing her tomb. But the hand takes on a life of its own and crawls back to the tomb as all the priests are killed in a supernatural sandstorm.

The tomb remains untouched until discovered by an expedition led by professor Julian Fuchs. When the coffin lid is lifted, the queen (played by Valerie Leon) is found to be perfectly preserved, as beautiful as ever, but blood begins to flow from the stump where her hand was cut off. In spite of this omen, each member of the team takes an artifact from the tomb back to England. From the queen's severed hand, Dr. Fuchs removes a ring with a stone in which seven stars shine. Other members take a statue of a cat, a statue of a snake, and the skull of a jackal. While the coffin is being opened in Egypt, supernatural events occur in England.

At the moment the queen's body is revealed in the tomb, Dr. Fuchs's wife dies in childbirth, and their baby girl's heart stops beating for a moment, then begins again—a link between the child and the queen that will prove fatal. Margaret Fuchs matures into the image of Queen Tara, whose mummy her father sequesters in the basement. For her twenty-first birthday, Dr. Fuchs gives Margaret the ring, telling her never to take it off. The ring causes the supernatural bond between Margaret and the queen to become stronger, and the soul of Tara begins to possess Margaret, compelling her to visit the members of the expedition to retrieve the stolen antiquities. As each member is killed, the snake and cat statues and the jackal's head are placed in the basement tomb that has housed the sleeping Tara for twenty-one years.

The one member of the expedition who fully understands what is happening is the evil Corbek, who has the Scroll of Life that, when read in the presence of the queen and the artifacts, will resurrect the queen. As Corbek reads the scroll, Dr. Fuchs and Margaret realize the evil about to be unleashed and kill Corbek, just as he mouths the last words. It is too late. The reanimated Queen of Darkness kills Dr. Fuchs, and as Margaret plunges a dagger into Tara's chest, the queen grabs Margaret by the throat and tightens her grip. As the mirror images engage in the death struggle, the walls of the basement tomb begin to crack, and swirling winds bring the house down.

The final scene takes place in a hospital, where the viewer sees a woman lying in bed, heavily bandaged, looking much like a mummy. The nurse is explaining to a visitor that everyone but this woman was killed when the house collapsed, but it is never made clear whether it is the queen or Margaret beneath the bandages. The reason for the ambiguity may be that the director, Seth Holt, made significant changes in the script, and only he knew exactly how the film was to end. Just before the film's completion, he died of a heart attack on his way to the studio, and the film was finished by Michael Coreras.

BLUMENBACH, JOHANN (1752–1840) An eighteenth-century German physician and anthropologist who became the first expert on mummies. On a trip to England in 1792, Blumenbach unwrapped many mummies, both animal and human, including several now in the British Museum. He was one of the first to observe that some of the animal "mummies" sold to travelers were modern fakes.

BOGIES A term used to refer to mythical creatures that come out of the peat bogs of Europe. Variants include bogan, bogey beasts, boggle boos, buggane, bug-a-boos, and of course boogie men. Legends of these creatures are quite common in Ireland, Scotland, and England, where they are often tied to stories of the early Germanic and Celtic tribes' practice of burying human sacrifices in bogs. The tales of dangerous creatures from the swamps were undoubtedly fueled when several bog mummies were discovered with ropes around their necks.

The Isle of Man has produced many of these stories, perhaps the most famous of which concerns the Buggane of St. Trinians. There is, in fact, a roofless church in Marown, supposedly unfinished because a buggane opposed the church's construction. According to the legend, a tailor named Timothy was challenged to stay in the unfinished church overnight and make a pair of pants. As he worked on the trousers, the buggane—with thick black hair, glowing eyes, and long arms—rose from beneath the floor and destroyed the roof. The terrified tailor, pursued by the buggane, fled to the consecrated ground of a nearby church. The buggane, angry because he could not follow Timothy into a sacred place, ripped off his head and threw it at the man, breaking it to pieces among the gravestones. No one has yet dared to complete the roofless church.

Bog Mummies A nineteenth-century photograph of the discovery of a bog mummy in Denmark. *Photo courtesy the National Museum, Copenhagen.*

Perhaps the most recent story inspired by the bog mummies is the modern horror classic *The Creature from the Black Lagoon.*

"BOGMAN, THE" A short story (1990) by Margaret Atwood that has a subtle twist at the end. Julie is having an affair with a professor who is studying a bog mummy. As Julie's interest in the professor dwindles, she decides that the bog man is more interesting than the staid academic. In the end the professor, for a brief moment, becomes the bog man. Chasing Julie into a phone booth, he presses his body and face to the glass, desperately trying to reach his lost love. It is then that Julie realizes she has become the object of his studies, ". . . the squashed tip of his nose, his mouth deformed, the lips shoved back from the teeth."

BOG MUMMIES These naturally preserved bodies have been discovered primarily in the bogs of Denmark. When the bog plant sphagnum decays, it gives off humic acid in sufficient quantities to kill bacteria. The acidic bog water preserves both the flesh and bones if it is not too strong; if the acid is too highly concentrated, the bones dissolve but the skin is preserved.

For centuries peat has been cut from Denmark's bogs as a source of fuel. The first bodies found were so well preserved that often the peat cutters who discovered them believed they were murder victims. Actually most of the bog people lived during Denmark's early Iron Age, between 500 B.C. and 0 B.C. Many of the bog mummies seem to have been killed—some by hanging, some by knife wounds, and some by drowning. Severed heads have also been found. One theory is that these people were sacrificed to the gods, but this has not yet been established. (See TOLLUND MAN, GRAUBALLE MAN, LINDOW MAN, and LINDOW WOMAN.)

BOOK OF THE DEAD

During the New Kingdom (1570–1075 B.C.), the ancient Egyptians began to write magical spells on papyrus rolls with the intention of helping a mummy to resurrect. Although not a book in the sense of a coherent work with a beginning and an end, such a collection of spells, prayers, hymns, and rituals became known as the "Book of the Dead."

Preparation of these "books" was a major industry in ancient Egypt. Scribes wrote the spells on long papyrus rolls, and artists added illustrations. The completed papyri were sold to customers and were placed inside the coffin with the mummy. The actual title of the Book of the Dead was "The Going Forth by Day," which indicates that its function was to protect the mummy and enable it to regain power in its arms, legs, etc. Then, in the next world, the mummy could "go forth" into continued existence.

The Book of the Dead also told the deceased how to behave and what to say to the gods in the netherworld. On the day of judgment, it would be decided if the deceased would be admitted to the next world or if he or she would go out of existence, and it was the Book of the Dead that told the mummy exactly what to say.

BOOTH, JOHN WILKES, ALLEGED MUMMY OF (1838–1865)

American actor and assassinator of President Abraham Lincoln. Some believe that the man killed by federal troops and identified as John Wilkes Booth was someone else and that Booth escaped, lived until 1903, and was mummified after his death.

Booth was a staunch supporter of the South during the Civil War and on April 14, 1865, he slipped into President Lincoln's box at Ford's Theater and shot the president in the back of the head. Booth jumped onto the stage, fracturing his left leg, but still managed to escape, eluding police for twelve days. Finally, cornered in a barn in Bowling Green, Virginia, John Wilkes Booth was shot by federal troops.

Although historians generally agree that it was indeed Booth who was killed, there is a theory that Booth escaped before the troops arrived, and it was someone else who they found in the barn. The theory is based on a book, *The Escape and Suicide of John Wilkes Booth*, published in 1907 by attorney Finis L. Bates. Bates states that in 1877 a man he knew under the name of John St. Helen confessed that he killed Lincoln. Believing that he was dying, St. Helen gave Bates a picture of himself and asked that upon his death it be given to his brother, the actor Edwin Booth. St. Helen, however, recovered. In 1903 a man named David E. George, just before committing suicide, admitted to a friend in Enid, Oklahoma that he had killed Lincoln. Bates read a newspaper account of the suicide and, with the picture he had kept of St. Helen, went to Oklahoma to investigate. After showing the picture to friends of Mr. George, Bates became convinced that George and St. Helen were the same person—the real John Wilkes Booth.

Bates obtained the unclaimed body of David E. George and had it mummified so it could be preserved for history. When Bates died in 1923, the mummy was sold to a carnival and exhibited across the country as the mummy of John Wilkes Booth. In 1931 the body was examined by six doctors who said that it could be the body of Booth, but nothing conclusive was demonstrated. The mummy has since disappeared, but the theory has sufficiently impressed several descendants of John Wilkes Booth, who in 1995 requested that the court allow the body in the Booth family plot in Green Mount Cemetery in Baltimore to be exhumed and examined. With modern DNA tests, a relationship between the body and the descendants could be demonstrated and the issue would be settled. An examination of the left leg fractured in the jump to the stage could also end the controversy. The request was not granted.

BOUIN'S FLUID   A fixative used in the preservation of tissues for anatomical specimens. It is composed of picric acid and saturated aqueous solution, 75 milliliters; formalin (40% formaldehyde), 25 milliliters; glacial acetic acid, 5 milliliters.

BRAIN, REMOVAL OF   The most discussed aspect of ancient Egyptian mummification is the removal of the brain. Beginning in the Eighteenth Dynasty, in the better quality mummifications, the brain was removed through the nostrils with a hook. The delicate ethmoid bone, located at the front part of the skull base, was broken by probing through the nasal passage with the instrument, which could then be pushed into the skull to extract a small portion of the brain. The probing was repeated many times until the brain broke down into a semifluid mass that could run out the nostrils.

Of the few ancient references to internal organs in connection with mummification, none mentions the brain. It is probable that the brain was simply thrown away. Because it was removed piecemeal it would have been in shreds by the time the embalmers had finished their task.

BRAINS OF MUMMIES   It is extremely rare to find mummies' brains. The ancient Egyptians, who were the most prolific mummifiers, removed the brain via the nostrils. Because it was thus reduced to tiny pieces, it was discarded. Only the brains of mummies of the lower classes have been found intact, because having the brain removed was very expensive.

In places where the climate is not dry, enzymatic and bacterial decay begins soon after death, destroying the brain. High temperatures can also increase the rate of decay, so unusual conditions are needed if a mummy's brain is to be preserved.

Occasionally the brains of bog mummies (see BOG MUMMIES) have been preserved, primarily because the lack of oxygen in the bog water retards decay, the acid in the water preserves the brain, and the plants in the bog produce humic acid which tans the brain, keeping it intact.

In 1983 in the town of Dordrecht in the Netherlands, excavators of a monastery's ancient cemetery discovered a large number of bodies in which the skulls were damaged, but the brains were preserved. The reason for this curious phenomenon was purely geographical. Dordrecht is located in the delta of the rivers Meuse and Rhine, thus the soil is exceptionally moist. The bodies in question were buried at the end of the fourteenth century, and soon after the great floods of 1421 inundated the entire area, submerging Dordrecht. The water level remained high, covering and waterlogging the bodies, but the acid in the water shrunk and preserved the brains, as in the case of the bog mummies. A similar situation was discovered recently in Florida when a 7,000-year-old body was found in a swamp. The brain was

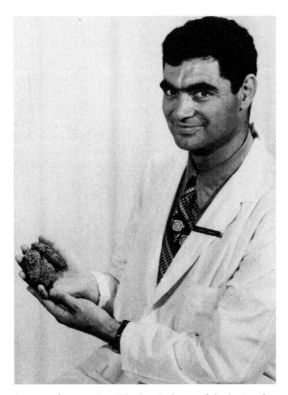

Brains of mummies The hemispheres of the brain of Nakht, a weaver who died in Egypt 3,000 years ago, have shrunk to approximately one-fifth their original size. *Photo courtesy Dr. P.K. Lewin.*

sufficiently preserved that DNA from it could be cloned.

BUCHIS BULL This sacred bull was selected by the ancient Egyptians for its markings, worshipped while alive, and mummified when it died. According to the ancient writer Macrobius, the Buchis changed color every hour and its hairs grew backward. The Buchis had its own cemetery at Armant in Upper Egypt, and the site, called the Bucheum, was discovered and excavated in the 1920s.

Similar to the Serapeum, where the Apis Bull was buried (see APIS BULL and SERAPEUM), long galleries were cut into the rock and the burial chambers were at right angles. After mummification, a bull was ornamented for burial. The eyes were inlaid with glass or painted stone, and the head was encased in a plaster mask covered with gold leaf. On top of the mask sat the crown that the Buchis had worn while alive—a solar disc with ostrich plumes flanked by two cobras.

C

CAILLIAUD, FRÉDÉRIC (1787–1869)

French mineralogist who was hired by Mohammed Ali, the ruler of Egypt, in 1815 to find the lost emerald mines mentioned by medieval Arab writers. Cailliaud became fascinated with the antiquities, and on his second trip to Egypt, in 1818, he discovered an intact mummy of the Greco-Roman period that he brought back to Paris. On November 30, 1823 Cailliaud performed one of the earliest public mummy unwrappings before a fascinated audience. The unwrapping was such a sensation that it was even reported in the United States in the *Salem Observer* of 19 June 1824.

A MUMMY UNWRAPPED

Two mummies lately brought from Egypt by M. Cailliaud, were opened at Paris. One of these had been remarked for its size and extraordinary weight. The head bore a crown, formed of plates and buttons of copper gilt, imitating the leaves and young fruit of the olive. Attention was also much attracted by the case, on which was painted figures resembling those on the zodiac of Denderah. A Greek inscription was also observed upon it, nearly defaced. The name of Pentemenon was found also on a bit of papyrus, which seemed to have been placed between the folds of the dress. Much curiosity having been excited respecting it, M. Cailliaud consented to open it. There were present a great number of distinguished persons. . . . an outer bandage was taken off, which confined to the body a cloth covered with paintings and hieroglyphics little observed in Egypt. Under this were other wrappings, soild, and forming the first envelop, which were easily removed. . . . The seventh and last envelop was saturated with black bitumen, and formed six different pieces, stuck together

with balsam. After which came the slender covering, and then the body. . . . The belly was filled with a black balsam. No MS (manuscript) was found, but large masses of black balsam were discovered on the legs. The unrolling the body took three hours, and 2800 square feet of cloth were taken off.—M. Cailliaud found several parts of the arms were also gilt. . . . Under the cloth which covered the face below each eye, on the ball of the cheek, a gold plate was found with the representation of an eye with the lids. On

Candy Mummies and Deadies are small hard candies shaped like human bones that appear in candy stores around Halloween.

Canopic Jars Set of four canopic jars used to hold the internal organs of the Princess Sit-Hathor-Yunet. *Photo courtesy Metropolitan Museum of Art.*

the mouth was another plate, with a representation of a tongue placed perpendicularly to the closing of the lips, which were fast shut.

CANDY Yummy Mummy candy sticks shaped like mummies in bandages were produced in the early 1990s by Sunmark Inc. The candy package showed an ancient Egyptian carrying one of the mummy candies. Basically

Candy Yummy Mummies Candies were fruit-flavored candies wrapped like mummies.

solidified Koolaid, the candies were not popular with the public. They were packaged five to a wrapper, and although each was a different color, the taste was much the same. It is interesting to note that all of the flavors—tropical punch, orange, green apple, cherry, and banana—were unknown in ancient Egypt.

Small boxes of mummy candy called "Mummies and Deadies" are produced by J. Fleer, the bubble gum company. The small hard candies are shaped like human bones.

CANOPIC CHEST A chest used to house the four canopic jars (see CANOPIC JARS) that, in turn, housed the deceased's internal organs. Normally a privilege of royalty or nobility, the earliest known canopic chest is that of Queen Hetepheres of the Fourth Dynasty (see HETEPHERES).

CANOPIC JARS A set of four jars, usually of stone or ceramic, used to hold internal organs removed at the time of mummification. Canopic jars, first used in the Fourth Dynasty, were un-decorated. Later the jars were made with lids in the shape of human heads, and still later, in the Eighteenth Dynasty, the lids were carved in the shapes of the heads of the four sons of Horus: Imsety (human), Hapi (ape), Duamutef (jackal), and Qebehsenuf (falcon). Each god was supposed to protect a different internal organ, and fre-quently a magical spell declaring the god's power was inscribed on each jar. A typical inscription would be:

Words spoken by Hapi: "I am Hapi, thy son, Oh Osiris. I have come to render thy protection. I bind for thee thy head and limbs, killing for thee thy enemies under thee. I give to thee thy head, forever."

The jars are called "canopic jars" after Canopis, whom Homer tells us was the pilot of Menelaus. Canopis was deified and worshiped in the form of a jar, so when early Egyptologists discovered jars with lids shaped like human heads, they called them "canopic."

In the Twenty-first Dynasty the practice of wrapping the internal organs and replacing them inside the body removed the need for canopic jars, but frequently a set of "false canopic jars"—with the lids and jar all of one piece—were carved and placed in tombs purely for ritual pur-poses, perhaps so that the sons of Horus would still protect the organs.

CAPUT MORTEM A brownish purple art-ist's oil color used during the Victorian era. One of its basic ingredients was burned Egyptian mummy wrappings.

CATACOMBS A series of underground rooms used as tombs for the dead. The word derives from the Latin *catacumbas*, which was used in the fifth century A.D. to describe the underground cemetery at the Basilica of St. Se-bastian on the Apian Way near Rome. The first catacombs were probably abandoned rock quar-ries reworked to form burial chambers.

The earliest catacomb burials were non-Christian, as were the Catacombs of Kom el-Choqafa in Alexandria, Egypt. These cata-combs were used for Egyptian, Greek, and Roman burials.

The Kom el-Choqafa Catacombs were dis-covered in 1900, when a donkey cart fell through the pavement into one of the rooms. The cata-combs consist of three tiers cut into bedrock, but because of the fluctuating water table, the lowest tier is now often filled with water.

The entrance is from a ground level staircase that winds around a large shaft through which the bodies were once lowered. The stairway ends at the top tier in a vestibule. There is a semicircular niche with a bench on each side of the stair, presumably where the members of the funerary party could gather while the mummy was being lowered by ropes through the shaft. Beyond the vestibule is a rotunda from which the family and friends of the deceased would enter the tri-clinium, or dining hall. The triclinium has large benches carved into three of its walls; a wooden table, long since disintegrated, would have stood in the middle of the chamber. The benches were fitted with cushions on which the family and friends of the deceased could relax as they enjoyed a final banquet in honor of their loved one.

The Catacombs of Kom el-Choqafa date from the second century A.D. and are unique both in their layout and their decorations. The cata-combs housed a mixture of Roman and Egyptian mummies, which seem to have been buried in designated areas depending on their religious affiliations. One room was dedicated to the god-dess Nemesis. In one of the loculi (cubicles in which the coffins were placed), the mummy of a priestess of Nemesis was found. She was adorned with a gold chain around her neck, which was decorated with the wheel of the goddess. The mummy's eyes were covered with gold leaf, as were her breasts, tongue, mouth, fingernails, and toenails.

Nemesis was the goddess of sports, and that may account for the numerous animal bones, mostly those of horses, that were found in another area of the catacombs. It is believed that horses famous for winning races in Alexandria were honored and placed under the protection of Nemesis when they died and were entombed in the catacombs.

A staircase descends from the rotunda on the first tier into a vestibule and the funerary chapel on the second level, which houses a fascinating mixture of Roman-Egyptian art. There are three niches in the chapel, each with a sarcophagus. The niches are decorated with scenes of ancient Egyptian gods in Roman costume—the composite style that developed from the two artistic traditions. A gallery around the chapel and vestibule has several loculi in its walls. Some spaces held several mummies.

The most famous catacombs are in Rome. They are located one above the other in orderly rows, but the long galleries in which they are found form a labyrinth of pathways. The passages are small for the most part, only about eight feet high and five feet wide, with niches for the bodies covering the sides. Occasionally a pathway expands into a large gallery, some of which are covered with fresco paintings. The early Christians used the catacombs as gathering places for worship and as hideouts during times of trouble.

It has been suggested that if the passageways of the Rome catacombs were placed end to end, they would extend to the length of Italy. Many of the tunnels have been destroyed, some from the passage of time and some deliberately. Even during medieval times the bodies of saints were removed from the catacombs and placed in churches for safekeeping. Catacombs also exist in Naples, Palermo, and Syracuse.

The stone quarries of old Paris became the city's catacombs, when in 1786 a Parisian official began to move the bones and bodies mainly from the cemeteries of Sts.-Innocents, St.-Eustache, and St.-Étienne de Gras. In order to avoid curious onlookers and to diminish the odor, the bodies were moved during the winter in the dead of

Catacombs Many European catacombs contain naturally mummified bodies.

night. The procession was accompanied by church officials chanting hymns and overseeing the orderly arrangement of the remains. All of the leg bones were placed together, as were the arm bones, and the skulls formed orderly rows nearby. It is estimated that the remains of between 3 million and 6 million Parisians were interred in the catacombs.

Catacombs can also be found in Cyprus, Israel, Greece, Iran, Syria, and Peru.

CAT SCAN   Short for Computer Assisted Tomography, a CAT scan is a series of X-ray cross sections of the body that provide a complete record of the subject. A computer can then image the subject from any angle. The first application of the technique with a mummy was on the brain of a fourteen-year-old weaver named Nakht, also known as ROM-I (Royal Ontario Museum mummy I). Although Nakht died approximately 3,000 years ago, the CAT scan showed the internal structure of the brain, including ventricles.

The most advanced stage of this technique is known as "axial X-ray tomography," and is a standard procedure in current research on mummies.

CATS, MUMMIES OF   See ANIMAL MUMMIES.

CEROPLASTY   The art of sculpting anatomical specimens in wax. Because it was difficult during the Renaissance to preserve cadavers for teaching purposes, the practice of crafting specimens became popular. These sculptures were often exquisite works showing the finest anatomical details. Ceroplasty flourished especially in northern Italy, and many of these creations incorporated actual bones as the substructures.

Perhaps the greatest of the ceroplasts was Abbot Felice Fontana (1730–1805), who under the patronage of the Duke of Tuscany, established a large workshop in Florence. In the shop, beehives were melted in hot water to obtain the wax needed for the sculptures. Pigments whose formulas were often kept secret were ground to render anatomical details in their true colors. Some anatomists also dissected cadavers to reveal the anatomical features that were to be reproduced. Plaster was placed directly on the cadaver, and when it hardened it was used as a mold for the molten wax. When the details were added, threads soaked in wax were used to represent the tiniest capillaries.

These artistic anatomical creations were first exhibited in 1780 at the Museo Reale di Fisica e Storia Naturale. When the emperor of Austria, Josef II (Marie-Antoinette's brother), saw the 486 sculptures, he made Fontana a knight of the Holy Roman Empire and commissioned him to create an extensive series of wax sculptures showing obstetrical complications. In six years Fontana's studio produced more than a thousand sculptures. These were sent to Vienna for the imperial school of surgery. Most of these models still survive in the Vienna Museum of Pathological Anatomy.

CHINCHORRO, MUMMIES OF   Named after Chinchorro Beach in northern Chile, the Chinchorro culture may have been the first culture to practice artificial mummification. The earliest known Chinchorro mummy, dating from approximately 5000 B.C., begins a pattern of mummification that lasted more than 3,000 years.

A great deal of what is known about Chinchorro mummies comes from a single discovery made in October of 1983, when the Arica Water Company was installing pipes along the northern coast of Chile on a bluff called El Morro. Approximately 40 inches below the surface, a cemetery filled with mummies was uncovered. The Archaeological Museum of San Miguel de Azapa inspected the site and, in an area of less than seventy-five square feet, discovered ninety-six mummies, all buried in an extended position on their backs. Whereas most previously discovered Chilean mummies had been naturally mummified by the dry air, these newly excavated ones were elaborately mummified.

The internal organs had been removed and replaced with straw. The brain was often extracted via the foramen magnum at the base of the skull or sometimes by cutting the skull in two, to be replaced with plant fibers. The limbs were either dissected or permitted to decay to the point that they became detached from the body. These early mummies were reassembled, with limbs tied to the body with plant fiber and the jaw fastened to the skull. The entire mummy was placed in an extended position then covered in black mud, giving rise to the name "Black Mummies." The facial details were painted and the genitals molded in clay, suggesting that a statuelike appearance of the deceased was the goal rather than preservation. Because the black mummies were produced during the preceramic period of the Chinchorro culture (5000–3000 B.C.), the clay which covered them was not fired, making them extremely fragile. The earliest of these mummies predates the first Egyptian attempt at mummification by 2,000 years.

Life for these early Chinchorro inhabitants was relatively easy by prehistoric standards. Food, water, and shelter were readily available, and there were few threatening predators, leaving them both time and energy to develop a cult of the dead. Examination of the mummies suggests that they were not buried immediately after preparation. Some had several coats of paint, suggesting wear and tear. Perhaps the mummies were set up in their households or paraded at feasts and festivals. When finally buried, a few possessions were included—a fishing line or perhaps a carved figure—indicating a belief in life after death.

Around 2800 B.C. the mummification technique became less elaborate, yielding the "Red Mummies," so called because they were painted red rather than black. These mummies were not thoroughly disarticulated, though wooden splints were used to stabilize the body. They frequently wore wigs and were bandaged.

Chinchorro, Mummies of This Chinchorro mummy of the black style may be one of the earliest artificial mummies in the world. *Photo courtesy Dr. Bernardo Arriaza.*

The last phase of artificial Chinchorro mummification began around 1700 B.C. and involved only a coating of mud. Because these later mummies are intact, a great deal of information about Chinchorro daily life has been learned. Although obtaining food and shelter was easy, the Chinchorro died young; the average life span was twenty-five. Of the mummies discovered in 1983, one-quarter were children who died before the age of one. One-fifth of the adults had tapeworms, the result of eating raw or partly cooked fish. Nearly half the mummies had infections so severe than their bones were damaged. These infections may have resulted from working with the decomposing flesh of bodies during mummification. Perhaps the most interesting findings is the earliest evidence of an occupational hazard. Many of the adult males' skulls had auditory exostosis—small bumps in the ear canal. These bony growths are stimulated by repeated exposure to cold water, such as divers experience when they go down with unprotected ears. The women too showed signs of their occupation—child bearing. Nearly one-fifth had osteoporosis, a weakening of the bones, to such an extent that their vertebrae fractured under the weight of the body. In our society osteoporosis is an affliction of the elderly, but young Chinchorro women were plagued with it, probably because of a combination of two factors. Starting in their teens, these women undoubtedly bore many children, which in itself extracts calcium and other minerals from the body. In addition, a low-calcium seafood diet left these mothers with no way of replacing the lost minerals.

In addition to the artificial mummies, there are numerous naturally preserved Chinchorro mummies of the later period, when artificial mummification had discontinued. Through all its phases, Chinchorro mummification seems to have been egalitarian, with all mummies, including those of infants, receiving equal treatment.

CHINESE MUMMIES Several remarkably well preserved Chinese mummies have been discovered in recent decades, the most famous in 1972 (see MARQUISE OF TAI). Subsequently several mummies were discovered in Xinjiang in northwestern China. The mummies of two females were said to be supple, the joints still flexible. All internal organs were in place and well preserved. Hair, fingernails, and toenails were complete. These mummies had not been placed in coffins and apparently had not been embalmed. They mummified because of tomb conditions.

Lacquer-mummification was practiced by Chinese Buddhist monks during the Middle ages and later. After a monk died his body was coated with numerous layers of lacquer, much like the lacquer used on Chinese furniture. These mummies then became objects of veneration, and poems were written about them.

PAYING MY RESPECTS TO THE MUMMY
OF THE MONK CH'ANG-ERH

The wheel of samsara has come to a peaceful
  halt;
the gleam of the lacquered body—
as fresh as a polished mirror!
I know that his soul has long since vanished,
but—amazing!—his nails and teeth are still here,
He is a Buddha of the Age of Adornment,
a human antique, who has lasted a thousand
  years.
So much for artifacts of bronze or iron—
by now, they would have turned to dust.
                              —Yuan Hung-tao

CHOACHYTES The term used in Egypt during the Greek occupation (332–30 B.C.) for the priests who performed the various ceremonies connected with mummification. These were not the men who cut open the bodies but rather those who wrapped them and recited the necessary prayers.

CHURCH OF SANTA MARIA DELLE GRAZIE, MUMMIES OF The Church of Santa Maria delle Grazie in Comiso, Sicily, houses the mummified bodies of more than fifty Capuchin friars and laymen connected to this order. The bodies lie in niches, many still in monastic robes. Some are labeled with the deceased's name and year of death, the earliest being 1742, the latest 1838.

The bodies were preserved by a combination of geography and burial practices. The climate of Comiso is hot and dry, which helped to dehydrate the bodies. This was assisted by the eighteenth- and nineteenth-century practice of placing the bodies of important people in seated position in the vault of the church for several months. Large vases (cantarelle) were placed under the cadaver to catch the body fluids as they ran out. After all the fluids had run out, the bodies were placed prone in tubs

Church of Santa Maria della Grazia   The mummies of more than fifty Capuchin friars in their niches in Comiso, Sicily.

and covered with soil, which completed the desiccation. Finally the bodies were dressed in their robes and placed in the niches.

The mummies were studied in 1988 by Dr. Gino Fornaciari, Professor of Pathology at the University of Pisa Medical School, who discovered that the friars suffered from a wide range of ailments, including varicose veins, tuberculosis, arteriosclerosis, and hernias.

CLAIRE OF MONTEFALCO, SAINT (1268–1308)   Saint Claire (Santa Chiara) is one of the few saints whose body was artificially mummified.

As a young child Saint Claire demonstrated advanced theological knowledge and piety. As a result of her piety, Saint Claire was permitted to join a group of recluses when she was only seven years old. At the age of thirteen, she joined her sister in a community that later became an Augustinian nunnery. When her sister died, Claire was made abbess, and her life of austerity is said to have inspired those under her charge.

When she died on August 17, 1308 at the age of forty, she was mummified by Sister Francesca who, without any medical training, slit Claire's body open from the back with a razor and removed the heart and viscera. It was said that when the heart was examined, the figure of the crucifix could be seen on it, formed of tissue. Also visible was the scourge with which Christ was tortured, which was said to have been formed of a "hard white nerve." This was almost expected by the sisters, as Saint Claire had often said, "The cross of our Lord Jesus is deep in my heart." The three gallstones found in her gall bladder were of equal size and were believed to represent the trinity.

Saint Claire's body is on view in her shrine at the Church of the Holy Cross in Montefalco, Italy. Part of her heart is enclosed in a statue of Saint Claire and can be seen through a crystal that is set into the chest. The gallstones are inside a jeweled cross, which also houses the other part of her heart.

CLAUDERUS, GABRIEL (LATE SEVENTEENTH CENTURY)

This seventeenth-century physician of Altenburg, Germany, developed a method of mummification that did not involve evisceration. He concocted "balsamic spirit" from one pound of cream of tartar and one-half pound of ammoniac dissolved in six pounds of water. The body cavities were injected with the balsamic spirit, then the entire body was immersed in the solution for five or six weeks. Finally the body was dried in the sun or in an oven. Clauderus was one of the few early embalmers to publish his technique.

CLONING

The reproduction of the genetic material of an individual. In 1985 Swedish scientist Dr. Svante Paabo became the first to clone DNA extracted from a mummy.

DNA, deoxyribonucleic acid, is the genetic material in every living cell. The molecule takes the form of a helix of two chains wound around each other—the famous "double helix." These chains consist of four kinds of links or units. The way these units are strung together, repeated, and alternated is the genetic code. In humans the genetic code is composed of approximately six billion such units.

After examining tissue samples from twenty-three Egyptian mummies, Dr. Paabo found that traces of DNA were still preserved in three. Using DNA extracted from the mummy of an infant stored in the Egyptian Museum in Berlin, he reproduced part of the genetic code. The technique, PCR (Polymerase Chain Reaction), involves two steps. First the DNA is extracted and the two strands of the double helix are separated. Next the single strands are immersed in nucleic

acid bases, whose enzymes reproduce the missing strand. The amount of DNA is thus doubled. This process can be repeated indefinitely until enough DNA is produced for analysis. Paabo grew more than 3,000 DNA units.

The cloning of DNA from an Egyptian mummy raises exciting possibilities that may be realized in the 1990s. Clonings so far have used mitochondrial DNA, which is found in the body of the cell and comes exclusively from the mother. Chromosomal DNA, however, is found in the cell nucleus and comes from both parents. In the near future it should be possible to clone chromosomal DNA to gain additional information, such as the parentage of royal mummies. The possibility of such a study is based on the fact that DNA varies among individuals as much as fingerprints do. (A child acquires half his or her nuclear DNA from each parent.) Extremely well preserved and uncontaminated DNA will be needed for parental identification, and this can be obtained by drilling into mummies' teeth.

COCAINE MUMMIES

A term applied to a group of Egyptian mummies in the Egyptian Museum in Munich that have recently been shown to contain traces of cocaine and nicotine.

The finding was first published in 1992 by Dr. Svetlana Balabanova, a forensic toxicologist at the Institute of Forensic Medicine in Ulm, Germany. The presence of cocaine and tobacco was shocking as cocoa leaves, the primary source of cocaine, and tobacco, the main source of nicotine, are both New World plants known to have existed in South and North America, but not in Egypt.

At first it was believed that the traces of the drugs were the result of contamination—perhaps the nineteenth-century Egyptologists who first examined the mummies had been smoking and had dropped ash onto them, for example.

To test the contamination theory, a hair shaft test for the drugs was performed. Hair from the mummies was washed in alcohol and the alcohol was tested for the presence of cocaine and nicotine. When this proved negative, the hair shafts themselves were tested, and evidence of the drugs was found. Because the cocaine and nicotine were inside the hair, but not outside, the substances must have been injested.

Mummies outside the Munich Museum were tested to find out if the phenomenon was widespread: of 134 natural mummies from the Sudan, one-third tested positively, as did mummies in the Manchester Museum's collection.

The interpretation of this finding is being debated today. One extreme view, held by only a few archaeologists, is that the ancient Egyptians obtained cocaine and tobacco from the Americas via a previously unknown trade route. The more conservative and widely accepted belief is that other plants that were known to the Egyptians and that contain traces of cocaine and nicotine (for example, beladonna, herbane, and mandrake) were the source.

COFFIN TEXTS Ancient Egyptian magical spells painted or carved on coffins during the Middle Kingdom (2040–1786 B.C.) were intended to protect mummies and assist their resurrection in the next world. There were hundreds of spells for various specific purposes, and the entire body of texts became known as the Coffin Texts. Spell 637 of the Coffin Texts was intended to open the doors of the sky to the deceased.

> These are the two doors which belong to
> He of the sky-window and which belong to He
>   who
> is under the tree in front. Oh Keeper of his
>   mooring post,
> prepare a path for the deceased so that he may
>   pass,
> being alive, prosperous, and strong. No one will
>   do evil against him.

COMIC BOOKS Most of the numerous comic books featuring mummy characters are based on mummy films. One four-part series called *The Mummy* (Monster Comics, 1991) is a takeoff of the classic 1932 film. It begins with a 1919 museum expedition. As in the film, nothing significant is uncovered until the last day, when an undisturbed tomb is found. The series is full of inside jokes—"I understand Howard Carter is planning an expedition to start sometime next year. . . . Perhaps he'll have better luck." (Howard Carter discovered Tutankhamen's tomb.) The mummy is even named Carloph after the film's star. The comic contains many idiosyncratic

Comic Books This comic book version of *The Mummy* combines the traditional film story and the names of real people to create a mummy named Carloph. *Illustration courtesy Scott Beaderstadt.*

details that appear in the film. For example, the Ardath Bey character, now called "Annubis-Rus," does not like to be touched ("an Egyptian prejudice"), and a pool of water is featured into which the characters peer to see the past.

As in the film, the plot revolves around the other characters defeating the mummy and freeing the heroine from his evil grasp. At times the series blends the classic film with an Anne Rice novel, *The Mummy or Ramses the Damned*—the 3,000-year-old Carloph is called "Carloph the Damned."

The Mummy or Ramses the Damned has its own twelve-part comic version (Millennium Publications, 1990). Here the art is the attraction, with the first four issues done in color pencil to create a pastel feeling in keeping with Egypt's subtle colors. The later issues were printed from acrylic paintings, using browns and antique colors to complement the Edwardian period theme. The series was followed by a sequel comic, *The Mummy Archives*, which discusses the Anne Rice characters and the comic book series.

While the 1932 film *The Mummy* inspired several comic book treatments, none has more faithful art than the series that appeared in *Monster World* magazine in the 1960s and was reprinted in *Famous Monster Magazine* in the 1970s. The November 1964 issue of *Monster World* introduced the series with a beautifully drawn version of the classic film, the characters being clearly recognizable as the actors in the film. Unfortunately the characters of Dr. Muller and Sir Joseph Whemple are confused. This was quickly followed by another beautifully drawn rendition, this time the sequel *The Mummy's Hand* (Monster World, January 1965). Here the mix-up is that scenes from *The Mummy's Curse* are included in the comic version.

In England, Hammer Films published comic versions of their mummy film series. Their remake of *The Mummy* (1959), which starred Christopher Lee as the mummy, appeared as a comic in Hammer's *Halls of Horror* magazine (1978). It

was followed by the comic version of *The Mummy's Shroud* (1967) in *House of Hammer* magazine (December 1977).

The most interesting of the various mummy comic book series is Marvel Comics's *The Living Mummy*, which appeared in the 1970s. This mummy, with his fully developed personality, has his adventures in modern times against Egyptian backdrops. He originally died buried alive—not unlike the mummy portrayed by actor Boris Karloff in *The Mummy* (1932). In the first issue we are told that N'Kantu was buried alive for the "crime" of freeing his people from the yoke of the Pharaoh Arem-Set. The series tells the tragic story of N'Kantu, who is controlled by four "Elemental Beings who held sway over Earth in Ancient Times." N'Kantu loathes being forced to do evil and struggles against his malevolent masters. The living mummy has only one ambition—to live again as a man.

Along with such satisfying treatments of mummies are quite a few superficial comic book characters. One four-part series, *The Mummy's Curse* (Aircel Comics, 1990), shows a mummy on the cover but inside is nothing more than a fiend performing sadistic acts.

COPPER MAN   The naturally preserved mummy of a South American miner who died around A.D. 800 while working in a copper mine. As he was removing the copper ore, the tunnel in which he was working collapsed, killing him. The dry air of the Chilean Atacama Desert, combined with the copper salts, preserved his body. As the copper oxidized it stained his body green, thus he is called "the copper man."

Discovered in 1899, the copper man wore only a loincloth and his hair was neatly braided. Next to him were the tools he was using when the accident occurred—four rope baskets for the ore, a stone hammer, and a rawhide bag. His body was exhibited in Chile, then bought and transported to the United States, where it now resides in the Museum of Natural History in New York.

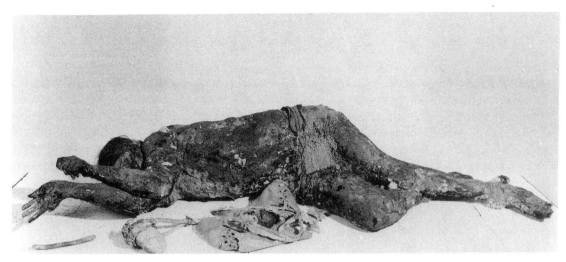

Copper Man The Copper Man's body was naturally preserved, and was stained green by oxidized copper. He was the victim of a copper mine cave-in around A.D. 800. *Photo courtesy Department Library Services, American Museum of Natural History. Negative No. 336628.*

CROCODILES, MUMMIES OF During the Ptolemaic period (332–30 B.C.), there were important crocodile cults at Kom Omboo in Upper Egypt and Crocodilopolis in the Fayoum. The crocodile god, Sobek, was worshipped, and crocodiles were kept in sacred pools.

Herodotus, a Greek who visited Egypt around 450 B.C., was amazed by the treatment the crocodiles received. "They are adorned and fed. Pendants made of artificial stones or gold are put in the ears of the crocodiles, and bracelets are put on their front feet. They are given special food and victims, they are cared for in every possible way during their lives and when they die, they are embalmed and placed in sacred coffins." Modern tourists can still see mummified crocodiles in the store rooms of the temple of Kom Omboo.

CRONOS PROJECT A major research effort to study the bioanthropology of Guanche mummies (see GUANCHE MUMMIES). Under the direction of Dr. C. Rodríguez-Martín (Canary Islands Institute of Paleopathology and Bioanthropology), Dr. Rafael González (Museo Arqueológico de Tenerife), Dr. Fernando Estévez (University of La Laguna), and Dr. A.C.

Aufderheide (University of Minnesota—Duluth) existing Guanche mummies are being studied to determine who the Guanche were and how they mummified their dead. When a new burial cave is discovered, the site is mapped and photographed and the following data are recorded:

1. Name of the burial cave
2. Municipality
3. X, Y, Z coordinates
4. Exposure of the cave
5. Orientation of the cave
6. Type of cavity
7. Size
8. Geomorphological environment
9. Altitude
10. Climate level
11. Annual average temperature
12. Rain (outside the cave)
13. Insulation and humidity outside the cave
14. Temperature and humidity outside the cave
15. Vegetation around the burial

Many of the mummies have been both x-rayed and CAT-scanned. One interesting finding is that those mummies that were artificially

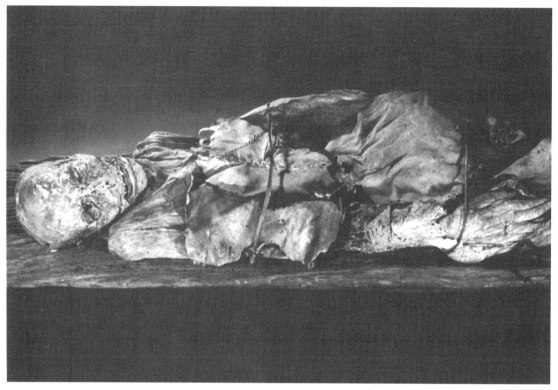

Cronos Project One of the Guanche mummies studied in the Cronos Project. It is on a funerary board called *chajasco* by the Guanches. *Photo courtesy Dr. Conrado Rodríguez-Martín.*

mummified rarely showed Harris lines. When these lines appear on X rays of the long bone, they indicate periods of malnutrition or illness during which the bones temporarily cease to grow. These lines appear in the skeletons of the Guanches who were not mummified but were merely placed in caves. This suggests that the upper class, who were mummified, had a better diet and less disease and illness than their lower-class counterparts.

By analyzing trace elements in 171 burials, the Guanche diet was reconstructed. A major source of protein came from pigs, sheep, and goats, and this was supplemented with dairy products. Relatively little fish was consumed.

CRYONAUT A slang term for one who has elected to be frozen after death.

CRYONICS A branch of the science of cryogenics (from the Greek *kryos*, "icy cold") that preserves tissues by freezing at extremely low temperatures. Although freezing of blood, sperm, and other human tissues has been utilized for many years, in cryonics the entire body is frozen.

The purpose of creating a frozen mummy is to preserve a person until science finds a way to reverse both the damage that caused death and the damage done by the freezing itself—a kind of technological immortality. The cryonics movement began in 1964 with the publication of *The Prospect of Immortality* by Robert C. Ettinger. Ettinger pointed out that clinical death is not necessarily irreversible. There are many cases of people who have been declared dead after their hearts stopped only to be revived later. Perhaps in the distant future virtually all cases of death will be reversible, and any damage to the body can be repaired. Thus the strategy is to preserve the body as well as possible to make future reanimation more likely.

With normal freezing, the water in the body crystallizes and expands, causing damage to the cells. But when tissues are frozen at extremely low temperatures—below -196 degrees Celsius—there is relatively little damage, and virtually all activity within the body, including decay, ceases. In this state the frozen person awaits the advances in science that will allow the body to be thawed and repaired.

One of the first human bodies to be frozen was that of Dr. James H. Bedford, a retired professor of psychology, who died of cancer in 1967. After he was declared dead, his heart was artificially kept beating so the cells would continue to receive oxygen and not die. At the same time his body temperature was lowered and his blood drained and replaced by glycerol, a cryoprotective agent, so damage caused by the freezing would be kept to a minimum. Then the body temperature was lowered to -190 degrees C (-310°F) by placing it into a capsule filled with liquid nitrogen. Dr. Bedford remains in the capsule in Phoenix, Arizona, looking very much as he did on the day he died.

The cryonics movement continued to grow throughout the 1970s and 1980s and several organizations were formed to place human bodies in "cryonic suspension." The process costs approximately $50,000, which includes an annuity to pay for the permanent storage of the capsule and periodic replacement of liquid nitrogen. Because of the expense and the advances in cloning techniques, in the 1990s several individuals have opted to have only their heads frozen. Thus they await the time when it will be possible to either perform a body transplant or regenerate the body by means of the genetic information contained in each cell.

Most proponents of cryonics agree that science is far from being able to revive those who are frozen. Many consider the possibility highly unlikely, but point out that the alternative, dying and not being frozen, is worse. Aside from the technological dif-

ficulties, there are considerable social obstacles. If, for example, 200 years pass before science progresses to the point that those who are frozen can be thawed, the company entrusted with storing and maintaining the capsules must remain stable for that period. This seems unlikely to some. Also, if reanimation ever became possible, those who were frozen might be ill equipped to deal with society as it had evolved. This theme is briefly explored in Woody Allen's comedy *Sleeper*.

CURSE OF THE MUMMY'S TOMB, THE (1964) One of the best Hammer Film Production mummy films, this one includes authentic-looking artifacts based on those from Tutankhamen's tomb.

A 1900 expedition discovers the tomb of Ra-Antef, one of the twin sons of Ramses VIII. While Ra was a "thinker and searcher for the mysteries of life," his brother was an evil pleasure seeker. As the brothers grew, the evil brother was favored, and finally succeeded in having Ra banished from Egypt. Found by a nomadic tribe in the remote desert, Ra was recognized for his abilities, made their leader, and given the Medallion of Life, which was used to revive the dead. As Ra was preparing to return to Egypt, his brother's assassins found and killed him,

The Curse of the Mummy's Tomb England tried to cash in on the mummy film craze with *The Curse of the Mummy's Tomb*, which featured a murdering mummy and artifacts based on those in Tutankhamen's tomb.

hacking off his left hand with its signet rings of authority.

Now Ra's intact tomb has been discovered by Dr. Eugene Dubois and his beautiful archaeologist daughter, Annette, and her fiancée, John. The tomb's priceless artifacts belong to the expedition's financial backer, Alexander King, an American businessman who refuses to sell the treasure to the Egyptian government for its museum. Rather, he intends exhibiting the artifacts around the world to raise even more money than he has been offered.

The first time Mr. King presents the opening of the coffin on a London stage, he explains that there is a curse, theatrically opens the coffin, and discovers that the mummy is gone. A series of deaths of those who had been involved in the excavation of Ra's tomb ensues, and the mummy is the murderer. Even the mysterious, handsome Englishman Adam Beecham, who has befriended Annette and John, is attacked but narrowly misses death. Annette is puzzled why Adam, who was not involved in the excavation, has been attacked by the mummy. Adam, now in love with Annette, reveals that he is the evil brother of Ra. When his father, Ramses VIII, suffered a stroke and was near death, he realized who had caused all the troubles and cursed his one remaining son with eternal life, unless he died at the hand of his brother Ra. Adam has suffered for 3,000 years, but on hearing of the discovery of his brother's tomb, realized that his chance for release had come. His brother has been brought to life by the archaeologists who read the Medallion of Life that was in the tomb, and he yearns to be his brother's next victim. But now he loves Annette and wants to take her with him.

In the end everything works out as expected. Adam is killed by his brother, the mummy perishes when a building collapses, and Annette is spared the mummy's wrath so she can marry John. *The Curse of the Mummy's Tomb* combines many of the elements found in previous mummy films—an ancient Egyptian who falls in love with a modern beauty; a medallion that brings the dead back to life; a curse on those who defile a royal tomb; and a murdering mummy—but blended in a thoughtful way.

CURSES, OF MUMMIES The idea of Egyptian mummies reanimating to destroy modern defilers of their tombs was made popular by films and novels; it was not a central part of the ancient Egyptian culture. The ancient Egyptians were more concerned with contemporary rather than future tomb robbers, but they did occasionally carve curses on the outside of tombs.

The vizier Khentika was an important official during the reigns of the pharaohs Teti (2345–2333 B.C.) and Pepi I (2332–2283 B.C.). He had great political power, and ordered that a magical spell be carved on his tomb at Saqqara to protect his mummy:

> As for all men who will enter this my tomb of the
> necropolis being impure, having eaten those abominations
> that good spirits who have journeyed to the West abominate . . . there will be judgment with them concerning
> it in the Western Desert in the Council of the Great God . . . an end shall be made for him concerning that
> evil . . . I shall seize his neck like a bird . . . I shall cast
> fear of myself into him. . . .

Instead of concern about tomb robbers in the distant future, Khentika's concern is about the priests who were to make the daily offerings for his soul. The priests were supposed to abstain from eating fish, which was considered impure for priests, before entering the chapel above Khentika's tomb.

A slightly earlier curse, written on the tomb of Ankhtifi (c. 2500 B.C.) states that if anyone did "evil and wickedness to the coffin and any stone parts of this tomb . . . may Hemen [a local God] not accept any of the offerings [that the robbers might offer for their souls] and may his heirs not inherit."

The most famous of all mummy curses is the supposed "curse of King Tut." When Howard

Carter and Lord Carnarvon discovered the tomb of Tutankhamen in the Valley of the Kings in 1922, the story quickly spread that there was a curse on all who defiled the tomb of the boy-king. Newspapers and other popular accounts even published the text of the curse: "Death shall come on swift wings to him that toucheth the tomb of a pharaoh." The truth is that there was no curse.

The story of a curse was fueled by the death of Lord Carnarvon in April of 1923. Carnarvon had cut himself while shaving and died of an infected mosquito bite, but the newspapers claimed it was the result of disturbing Tutankhamen's tomb. From this single death, the curse became established in the minds of readers around the world. Soon it was claimed that scores of people who had entered the tomb had died of mysterious causes.

There are several reasons why, in spite of the facts, belief in the curse grew. When Carter and Carnarvon first discovered the tomb, they decided they did not want the distraction of reporters. Consequently they sold the exclusive rights to the story to the *London Times,* so they would only have to deal with one person. The other papers, unable to get solid reports from the excavators, played up the curse aspect, as it was one of the few things they could write about.

Another reason the theory flourished was that the creator of the brilliant Sherlock Holmes, Sir Arthur Conan Doyle, publicly proclaimed his belief in the curse. Although he created a detective who was the paradigm of logic and rationality, Conan Doyle believed in all sorts of things, from fairies to ghosts. When Lord Carnarvon died, Doyle expressed the opinion that the death might have been caused by "elementals" created by Tutankhamen's priests to guard the tomb.

A careful analysis of those present at the opening of the burial chamber reveals the truth. Of the twenty-six people present, only six died within ten years. Of the twenty-two people present at the opening of the sarcophagus, only two died within ten years. Finally, of the ten who were present at the actual unwrapping of the mummy, none died within ten years. Indeed Dr. Derry, who conducted the autopsy on Tutankhamen's mummy, lived another two decades, and Howard Carter, the first to "defile" the tomb, died in 1939.

DAU PAGODA This pagoda, twenty-three miles south of Hanoi in the Ha Son Binh province of Vietnam, contains the unique mummies of two Buddhist monks. According to local tradition, two sixteenth-century superiors of the pagoda were mummified in seated position to serve as statues.

It is said that Superior Vu Khac Minh entered his hut, placed a jar of water on one side and a jar of burning oil on the other, and assumed the lotus position. He then told his disciples to open the door after three months and ten days. If no offensive smell was detected, they were to lacquer his body. If, however, maggots had infested his mortal remains, they were to fill in the hut with earth.

Recent studies have revealed the techniques used to mummify the two superiors. Vu Khac Minh was covered with a layer of soft earth, mixed with paint and sawdust. This was then coated with a resin to seal it; mixed with the resin was a thin silver sheet, which gives the mummy the appearance of a silvered statue. A coating of oil paint completed the process. Recent X rays have shown that although the bones of the hands and feet are perfectly articulated, all the vertebrae, ribs, and collarbones have separated, collapsed, and now lie in a pile in the abdominal area. Unlike Egyptian mummies, it appears that no attempt was made to preserve the soft tissue, and the brain remains inside the skull. The mummy weighs only fifteen pounds, so evidently dehydration took place over the centuries even though the body was sealed.

The second mummy, that of Superior Vu Khac Truong, was completed somewhat differently. It is painted white with red lips and decorated eyebrows. These mummy-statues of the two Buddhist monks are the only ones known in Vietnam.

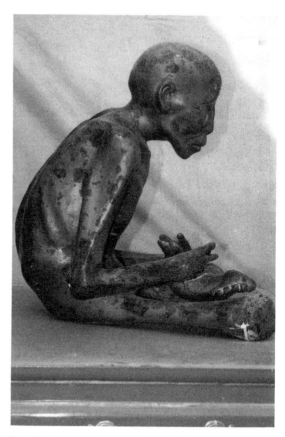

Dau Pagoda The mummy of Superior Vu Khac Minh was preserved in lotus position to serve as a statue in the Dau Pagoda, Vietnam. *Photo courtesy Dr. Nguyen Lan Cuong.*

Decorative Arts and Mummies   Mural designed by Giambattista Piranesi for the English coffeehouse in Rome.

DAWSON, WARREN R. (1888–1968)
English historian who became one of the leading authorities on Egyptian mummification and medicine. In 1924 he published with Sir. G. Elliott Smith *Egyptian Mummies,* the first scientific book on the subject of mummies since Pettigrew's *History of Egyptian Mummies* nearly a century earlier.

DECORATIVE ARTS AND MUMMIES
The mummy became a popular image for illustrators and artists after Napoleon's expedition to Egypt in 1798. The French savant Dominique Vivant Denon, who had accompanied Napoleon on his Egyptian Campaign, provided a wealth of new ideas for the decorative arts with his publication *Voyage in Upper and Lower Egypt* as did the impressive volumes of the *Description de l'Égypte* commissioned by Napoleon.

One of the greatest eighteenth-century designers to use the mummy as a decorative motif was Giambattista Piranesi (1720–78). He published *Diverse maniere di adornare i cammini* in 1769, which combined accuracy with fantasy and contained the largest group of Egyptian designs ever compiled, including motifs for such daily objects as fireplaces and furniture. One of Piranesi's extraordinary chimney pieces included two large wrapped mummies that served as pillars for the ornamentation above their heads. Some of

Piranesi's designs for wall paintings were executed at the Caffe degli Inglesi in Rome. The coffeehouse was a meeting place for British travelers, but the walls were decidedly Egyptian, with mummiform figures everywhere.

In England Thomas Rolandson used the mummy as a theme in his cartoons and ridiculed the current fashion of keeping a mummy in the parlor. These amusing illustrations did much to spark Europe's interest in all things Egyptian.

When the designer Thomas Hope redecorated his house on Duchess Street in London, the Egyptian Room became the most spectacular example of the new Egyptian style ever seen, and created an interest in and desire for Egyptianized art that has continued to this day. Amidst the clutter of carefully arranged Egyptian motifs in Hope's fabulous drawing room was a mummy in a glass case, and the ceiling motifs were derived from a mummy's coffin.

As Egyptian motifs were reinterpreted to fit the design needs of the day, so too was the figure of the mummy. Josiah Wedgwood, the ceramist, experimented with Egyptian themes in the 1770s. A mummiform vase appeared in the Wedgwood and Bentley catalog along with his other Egyptian designs.

During mummification the internal organs were removed and placed in canopic jars, resembling a shorter fatter mummiform shape. The Romans, fascinated with Egypt, copied Egyptian designs of all sorts including canopic jars. Later, in 1719, Bernard de Montfaucon illustrated the Roman canopic jars in his publication *L'Antiquité Expliquée.* These carefully detailed renderings later inspired the Wedgwood canopic vases,

Decorative Arts and Mummies This canopic vase drawn by Bernard de Montfaucon later inspired several Wedgwood designs.

which were designed without an opening at the top, making them purely decorative. Later some of the canopics were fitted with a nozzle so they could be used as candleholders. These mummiforms were a favorite design in the Wedgwood collection and continued in production until the 1970s.

Wedgwood and Bentley produced one particularly curious piece: a glazed ceramic blancmange (pudding) mold in the shape of a canopic jar that was intended to leave the imprint of its mummiform on the pudding. The artists at Wedgwood and Bentley also used the design of the mummy's head to create an inkwell that was quite popular.

Another figure in the decorative arts derived from the mummy is the ushabti, or servant statue. Each mummy was buried with approximately 365 of these mummiform figures that were intended to accompany him or her to the next world. Ushabtis were often made of faience, and their shape refers to the mummiform figure of Osiris, the god of the dead. When Baron Denon returned to France with his drawings from Egypt, he urged the Sèvres porcelain factory to produce a small ushabti as an item for their collection.

After the Wedgwood and Sèvres designs appeared, all of Europe caught the mania, and mummies could be spotted everywhere. As the popularity of Egyptian motifs grew, the mummy-inspired shapes began to appear in all areas of design, and decorative mummies became a popular element in English Regency furniture design.

No longer confined to the decorative arts, mummies were incorporated into architectural design as minor elements to complement the major components—the pyramid, obelisk, and sphinx. They were seen in theater and set designs, often as hybrids of the original canopic jar and ushabti shapes. As Egyptian motifs became commercialized, the mummy appeared in various forms as an icon to promote products.

One of the most curious Egyptian forms from the late 1700s is one of what was a pair of decorative mummies, now in a private collection in Paris. Made of painted and gilt wood and measuring approximately six and one-half feet, the size suggests an architectural context and the design seems to be derived from the Piranesi drawings.

Egyptian motifs found their way into the repertoire of nineteenth-century artists, as death became a theme for painting. The Dutch painter Sir Lawrence Alma-Tadema (1836–1912) produced over twenty paintings with Egyptian themes, his most famous being *An Egyptian Widow*, in which the grieving wife kneels at the foot of her husband's mummiform coffin.

Charles Sprague Pearce (1851–1914), while studying in Paris, was inspired by Alma-Tadema's *Egyptian Widow* to paint *Death of the First Born*, showing distraught parents mourning over their son whose ornate mummiform coffin lies between them. On the floor around the coffin are faience ushabtis, the servants of the dead.

The artists of the nineteenth century transformed the popular image of the mummy in the decorative arts, as they reinterpreted the powerful icon to represent the mystery of death.

The opening of the Suez Canal in 1869 generated a wave of Egyptomania, and the mummy became a popular motif on decorative mantle clocks that were produced to commemorate the occasion.

The discovery of King Tutankhamen's tomb in 1922 by the British Egyptologist Howard Carter made King Tut a household name and created an explosion of "Tutmania." Egyptian themes dominated the design and fashion worlds and mummy motifs appeared regularly in jewelry and textiles.

DEIR EL-BAHRI A site on the west bank of the Nile opposite Thebes. (Arabic for "place of the northern monastery" because a Coptic monastery was once situated there.) Sometime during the 1870s the Abd el-Rasoul brothers, members of a family of grave robbers, discovered a cache of royal mummies and began selling antiquities from the tomb. By 1881 enough important royal

Deir el-Bahri The huge coffin of Queen Ahmose-Nefertari, found in the Deir el-Bahri cache, contained not only the mummy of the queen but also the mummy of Ramses III.

artifacts had appeared on the antiquities market that the director of the Egyptian Antiquities Service, Gaston Maspero, went to Luxor to investigate. Two of the Rasoul brothers, Ahmed and Hussein, were sent to Qena for questioning by Daoud Pasha, the local governor. Though one of the brothers limped for the rest of his life after the interrogation, neither revealed the location of their find. Later the oldest of the Rasoul brothers, Muhammed, revealed to Daoud Pasha the site of the tomb.

Because Maspero was in France, his assistant Émile Brugsch came to investigate. He was taken on a narrow path up the cliffs of Deir el-Bahri where, behind a chimneylike outcropping of rocks, he was shown a shaft eight feet by ten feet that descended forty feet. The shaft led to the entrance of a tomb consisting of a seventy-foot corridor terminating in a room seventeen feet square. All along the corridor were funerary objects bearing the names of kings and queens of the New Kingdom Dynasties. In the room were the coffins containing numerous kings, including Amenhotep I, Tuthmosis I, Tuthmosis II, and Tuthmose III of the Eighteenth Dynasty. Inside other coffins lay Ramses I, his son Seti I, and Seti's son Ramses II, all of the Nineteenth Dynasty.

Behind this room was a larger chamber, where the mummies of the royal family of the Twenty-first Dynasty lay. These included Pinedjem I, Pinedjem II, Queen Henettowy, and many others. All these royal mummies had come to be buried together as a result of the declining powers of the pharaohs at the end of the Twentieth Dynasty. With the loss of power, guarding the royal tombs in the Valley of the Kings became more difficult. An inspection of the valley during the Twenty-first Dynasty revealed that nearly all the tombs had been violated. Rather than attempting to protect the individual tombs, the bodies were rewrapped, labeled with dockets, placed in new coffins when necessary, and removed to safer tombs in the Valley of the Kings. Inscriptions on the bottom of the shaft of the Deir el-Bahri tomb record the last burial of these mummies. This secret tomb was considered sufficiently safe that the priest-king Pinedjem II chose it for his own resting place. On his burial day the bodies of Seti I and Ramses II were also interred, and remained undisturbed for 3,000 years.

All the coffins and mummies were removed by Brugsch and transported to the museum at Boulaq, a district of Cairo. No photographs or drawings of the objects in situ were ever made, and there is still doubt about their original positions in the tomb and about the identities of some of the mummies.

DESCRIPTION DE L'ÉGYPTE Published by the scientists who accompanied Napoleon Bonaparte to Egypt in 1798, this was one of the greatest publications ever on any subject. The eleven huge volumes of illustrations and twenty-two smaller volumes of text described every aspect of Egypt. The nearly 1,000 copper engravings depicted the ancient temples, modern crafts, and the flora and fauna of Egypt. They also provided the European world with the first accurate illustrations of mummies. The scientists sent the heads of two mummies, a male and a female, to France, where they were drawn and illustrated in color for the first edition. The empress Josephine was given the head of the woman, and when her Malmaison collection was sold in 1814, the head was bought by Dominique Vivant Denon, the first director of the Louvre, who had been with Napoleon in Egypt. The *Description de l'Égypte* also included illustrations of animal mummies such as crocodiles, cats, and ibises. An essay by P.C. Rouyer, a pharmacist who accompanied the French expedition to Egypt, is one of the first scientific descriptions of the mummies and the process of mummification. (See ROUYER, P.C.)

DESPELLOJADOS   Spanish term for "flayed men." Between the sixteenth and eighteenth centuries, this was a common technique for preserving human cadavers as anatomical specimens. The skin was removed to reveal musculature, veins, and arteries, and the body was placed in a natural posture.

DESTESTANDAE FERITATIS ABUSUS Latin for "an abuse of horrible savagery." The papal bull issued in 1299 by Pope Boniface VIII to stop the practice of dividing the bodies of miraculously preserved saints for distribution to churches. It stipulates:

> . . . we have thought it fit to abolish that abuse of detestable savagery which certain of the faithful imprudently practice in accordance with a horrible custom, less this abuse should continue to lacerate human bodies and still the minds of the

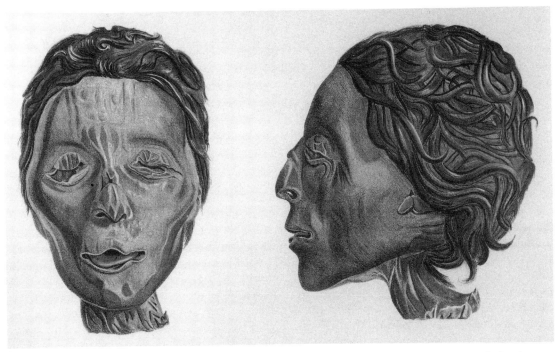

Description de l'Égypte   One of the first accurate drawings of a mummy was made for Napoleon's *Description de l'Égypte*. The actual head used for the drawing was given to Josephine.

faithful to horror . . . for the aforesaid faithful, intent upon this vicious and reprehensible custom, at the death of any one among their kinsfolk who may be illustrious for nobility of race or dignity of rank (especially if he have the debt to nature beyond the limits of his own country), when he has chosen to be buried in his own parts . . . truculently disembowel them, divide him limb by limb or gobbet by gobbet, and seethe him down in a cauldron.

The bull did not stop the division of saints' bodies, which continued into modern times.

DE VELASCO, JULIAN (19TH CENTURY)

Nineteenth-century physician and professor of anatomy at the Complutense University in Madrid, Spain. He was an avid collector of anatomical specimens, many of which he prepared himself. One technique of this period was to remove the skin of the deceased in order to reveal the muscles, veins, and arteries. The cadavers were then placed in natural postures. Several are still on display in the university's anatomical collection. It is said that Dr. de Velasco mummified his own daughter.

DIODORUS SICULUS (c. 80–20 B.C.)

A Greek writer who visited Egypt in 59 B.C. and recorded his observations in Book I of his *Library of History*. Diodorus's account of mummification is an important ancient source on the practice, second only to that of Herodotus (see HERODOTUS OF HALICARNASSUS). Diodorus repeats many of the observations of Herodotus but adds numerous details indicating independent knowledge. He mentions that one embalmer drew the length of the incision on the left side of the body and then a second embalmer, called a "slitter," made the incision with a sharp Ethiopian stone (obsidian). Having opened the body, the slitter ran away while those present threw stones at him—probably a ritual to indicate a prohibition against damaging the body. Diodorus was the first to mention (correctly) that the slit was made on the left side of the abdomen.

Diodorus was also the first to discuss what happened to the internal organs during mummification. He mentions that all but the heart and kidneys were removed and that the organs were washed with palm wine and spices, indicating that he knew they were not discarded. He also mentions that the body was treated with spices for thirty days, not the seventy of Herodotus.

While Diodorus's account of Egyptian mummification is accurate and reasonable, his account of Ethiopian mummification is pure fantasy. He states that after the body was embalmed, it was covered with gold and then glass was poured over it before it was finally placed in the tomb.

DISPLAY OF MUMMIES

Conservation is an important issue whenever museum objects, including mummies, are displayed. Mummies must be protected from biological attacks by living organisms such as bacteria, fungi, and insects, and from environmental hazards, such as humidity, light, and pollutants.

In 1987 the Getty Conservation Institute was asked by the Egyptian Antiquities Organization to design display cases for the royal mummies that would protect them, permit tourists to view them easily, require minimal maintenance, and be relatively inexpensive to construct.

It was decided that to keep maintenance to a minimum, the display cases would be hermetically sealed. Thus, once desirable conditions inside the cases had been achieved, no maintenance would be required for about twenty years.

To destroy the bacteria, fungi, and insects that might damage the mummies, the cases were filled with nitrogen, which is inert and invisible. Nothing can live in an atmosphere of nitrogen (when it was first isolated in the eighteenth century, nitrogen was called "azote" by the French—without life), thus the mummies would remain free of biological infestations. The goal was to reduce the amount of oxygen to less than 1 percent, so nothing could live inside the cases, and the relative humidity to between 30 and 50 percent, so the mummies would not expand or contract by absorbing or giving off moisture. These factors are especially important in a city like Cairo, which lies near the Nile and experiences great fluctuations in humidity, and whose museum is not air-conditioned. In addition the temperature had to be controlled, so that the mummies would not expand and contract with temperature variations and thus be damaged.

The basic task, then, was to meet all the above requirements and still produce low-maintenance, inexpensive cases. A prototype was constructed of five pieces of glass and an aluminum base, all held together by an aluminum frame. Nitrogen was introduced through one of six small ports that are used for introducing nitrogen, taking samples, etc. The nitrogen was carefully humidified so that when it was piped into the case, the desired humidity was established. Through a larger port, a commercially available product called "Ageless" was introduced, which absorbs oxygen. Small amounts of silica gel were placed in the case to absorb moisture.

Initial tests showed that the prototype case was extremely tight. Oxygen leaked into the case at the rate of less than ten parts per million in a day. Thus the oxygen would remain at the desired level for eleven years with no maintenance. With the oxygen scavenger Ageless, the case would not require maintenance for twenty years.

DUAMUTEF One of the four sons of the Egyptian god Horus. Duamutef was associated with the east and protected mummies' internal organs. He is represented as having the body of a man and the head of a jackal but should not be confused with Anubis, the jackal-headed god of embalming.

Frequently, magical spells were inscribed on the four jars holding a mummy's internal organs (see CANOPIC JARS). On the jar with the lid in the shape of Duamutef's head, a typical spell would read:

Words spoken by Duamutef:
I am thy son Horus, loving thee.

I come to avenge my father Osiris.
I do not permit destruction to be
done to thee. I place it under thy
feet, forever.

DUCH, MUMMIES OF The mummies from the necropolis of Duch in the western desert in Egypt are an important source of information about the general health of the ancient Egyptians. This Egyptian/Roman town was occupied between the first century and the fifth century A.D., and the cemetery has provided a wealth of material about the lives and deaths of its citizens.

An examination of 200 mummies showed that nearly everyone suffered from some medical complaint. That the population was afflicted with so many ailments seems to have been the result of the hard labor they endured as well as a lack of medical attention. In the first century A.D. in Egypt, the average life span was about forty years, providing one lived to adulthood. Deaths at childbirth were common and the infant mortality rate were very high.

When the teeth of the Duch mummies were examined, widespread abrasion was discovered, a result of the course ground flour (which contained sand), from which bread was made. As the teeth were worn down, the gums were damaged and abscesses developed. There was little evidence of tooth decay, for sweets were not a part of the diet.

When the mummies at Duch were x-rayed, they frequently showed Harris lines, the striated marks that appear on the long bones indicating malnourishment or long periods of illness. Sometimes a specific cause of death could be determined from the X rays and an examination. Such was the case of a seven-year-old girl, who succumbed to typhoid and was buried with a small wig because the illness had caused her hair to fall out. Another child had clearly died from a fractured skull. Bone fractures were common, and many of the mummies showed signs of osteoarthritis and scoliosis, all maladies common to those who labored in the fields or stone quarries.

When one of the mummies was being prepared for X ray, a small bundle was found between the legs. It was determined that the mummy was a castrated male and the bundle contained a mummified frog. The ancient embalmer had carefully place the symbol of rebirth, the frog, between the man's legs so that when he reached the next world, his body would be complete.

ÉCORCHÉ French term for cadavers that were skinned in order to reveal the muscles, veins, and arteries for anatomical displays. These bodies were often placed in naturalistic poses.

EDMUND, SAINT The supposedly incorrupt body of this ninth-century saint may actually be a bog mummy. According to Abbo, who in 986 wrote a life of the saint, Edmund was King of East Anglia in 869, when the Danes attacked. Refusing to surrender, Edmund was captured and tied to a tree. While arrows were shot at him, he continued to profess his love of Christ. As special punishment his head was cut off and buried in a wood, apart from the rest of his body, but his followers found it. When the head was brought to the body, it miraculously reunited with it. It was said that the body did not putrefy, and only a red scar, like a scarlet thread, could be seen around the neck. Around 945 the Bishop of London checked the body and attested that it had not decayed. One hundred years later, Leofstan, Abbot of Bury Saint Edmunds, decided to see if the head and body were truly united. While a monk held the feet, the abbot pulled on the head, but it did not yield. The abbot's hands, however, became paralyzed. In 1198 Abbot Sampson, in the presence of sixteen monks, inspected the body and declared it uncorrupted.

Sometime during the following centuries, the body of Saint Edmund disappeared and was rumored to have been taken to France. Modern scholars have suggested that the reports of the incorruptibility of the body may have been accurate, but the body may not have been that of Edmund, King of East Anglia, but that of a bog mummy. The story of Edmund's martyrdom takes place on the edge of the bogs, so it is quite possible that when a bog body was found, it was said to be Saint Edmund. Bog bodies have been found with strings and ropes around their necks, and to those searching for Saint Edmund's head and body it would have been an attractive option to claim that they had found him when they discovered a complete body with the required markings. Thus the descriptions of the incorrupt body of Saint Edmund may be the earliest records we have of a bog mummy.

EGTVED GIRL, THE One of the best preserved of the mound people (see MOUND PEOPLE), the discovery in 1921 of this young woman caused a sensation in Denmark, not because of its remarkable preservation but because of the way it was clothed.

This Bronze Age (c. 1100 B.C.) burial was discovered by a farmer in central Denmark, who unearthed a coffin made of a hollowed oak tree trunk. He immediately notified the National Museum in Copenhagen, so the burial was carefully excavated and recorded, and the finds were preserved. The coffin, made from a six-and-a-half-foot-long tree trunk, had been buried under a huge earth mound, around which the soil had formed a hard crust, protecting its contents from the effects of oxygen. The only thing that seemed to have reached the contents during its 3,000-year burial was water. When first uncovered, water poured out, but this too had preserved the contents. The water had leached the tannic acid from the oak coffin, tanning the skin of the young woman and preserving her clothes and the artifacts with which she had been buried. Even so, the coffin and contents had to be handled very carefully.

When the lid of the coffin was removed, the remains of a woolen blanket were revealed, but little else could be seen except a small bucket made from the bark of a lime tree. This was the extent of the on-site examination. The remains were carefully covered with straw, the lid replaced, and a large crate was constructed so that everything could be sent in toto to Copenhagen for study and conservation.

In the laboratory at Copenhagen, the wool blanket and a large rug both made of sheep wool, were rolled back, and for the first time in 3,000 years the Egtved girl came into view. Her shoulder-length hair had been blond but was stained dark by the acid water that had filled the coffin. Her teeth were well preserved, and the condition of her molars suggested that she was approximately twenty when she died. Like most of the mound burials of Denmark, she had been buried with jewelry, a comb, and other small items. She wore a tunic gathered at the waist by a belt with an elaborate tassel at the end. Her waist was 23½ inches, she stood 5 feet 3 inches tall, and her fingernails were well cared for. The lower part of her body was covered by the Bronze Age equivalent of the miniskirt. Made of corded sheep wool, the 16-inch garment resembled a grass hula skirt. Women previously discovered in such burials had worn hair nets and full length skirts, and this had given the conservative Danish public the image of the modest proper Bronze Age Danish woman. The Egtved girl did not fit this mold. One archaeologist, protecting the modesty of the Egtved girl, suggested that it was an undergarment. German archaeologists drew it in their publications as a garment worn over a longer skirt.

Even more sensational than her skirt was a bundle found in the coffin. It contained the burned human bones of a nine- or ten-year-old. The twenty-year-old Egtved girl was too young to have had the child, and it has been suggested that the child was a servant sacrificed to accompany her mistress into the next world.

EKIMMU   In Assyrian mythology, the spirit of an unburied body.

ELLING WOMAN   The body of Elling Woman was found in 1938 in the Bjaeldskovdal peat bog, near the Danish town of Silkeborg. Like many of the bog mummies (see BOG MUMMIES), the body was discovered by a peat cutter. The body was removed along with the surrounding soil, placed in a large crate, and sent to the National Museum, where it was then excavated from the peat.

X rays revealed that the woman was approximately thirty years old at the time of her death. Still visible on her neck was an indentation made by the rope with which she was hanged. After she was hanged her body was placed in the bog. Elling Woman was clothed in a sheepskin cloak that had been made by sewing rectangular pieces of sheepskin together. Around her waist was a belt woven from sheep's wool. She wore her hair in a single braid, about one meter long.

Twelve years after the discovery of Elling Woman, Tollund Man (see TOLLUND MAN) was found less than one hundred yards away from where the woman had been found. Radiocarbon dating of some of their clothing indicated that they lived at approximately the same time, about 210–70 B.C. Tollund Man had also been hanged, perhaps as a sacrifice, and it is even possible that they knew each other.

Elling Woman and Tollund Man reside in the Silkeborg Museum, near the area where they lived and died.

EMBALMERS' ARCHIVE   A collection of twenty-five papyrus rolls and fragments written in demotic (late Egyptian language) around 50 B.C. that deal with the daily business of a group of embalmers. These papyri were discovered in the northern town of Hawara, in the Fayoum district about fifty miles from Cairo, and were purchased in 1935 from a Cairo antiquities dealer by the famous Egyptologist, Sir Alan Gardiner. Gardiner later gave them to Oxford University's Ashmolean Museum, where they are currently kept.

Although the papyri do not give any information about the actual practice of mummification, they offer valuable insights into how the mummification industry was organized in ancient Egypt. The documents include oaths taken by members of an embalmers' guild, deeds to tombs, and contracts for tomb maintenance and inspection. Members of the guild were known as "men of Anubis" in reference to Anubis, the jackal-headed god of mummification (see ANUBIS). The largest group of funerary priests were the sealer-embalmers. Their duties were to go to the village and collect the deceased; perform the religious rituals associated with embalming; perform the actual mummification; and anoint the mummy after embalming. Overseeing every ten sealer-embalmers was a god's sealer-embalmer, who had the ultimate responsibility of ensuring that all aspects of mummification were conducted properly.

EMBALMERS' CACHES   Collections of rags, linen, jars, and tools buried by ancient Egyptian embalmers.

Frequently the materials used in a mummification were buried in pits, perhaps because they had been in contact with the body of the deceased and thus had acquired religious status. One Middle Kingdom cache discovered by Herbert Winlock at Deir el-Bahri contained sixty-seven sealed jars, which held soiled rags, packets of natron, sawdust, and oils. Winlock also discovered the embalmers' cache from the mummification of Lady Henettowy of the Twenty-first Dynasty. Although a thousand years younger than the Middle Kingdom cache, it was remarkably similar.

The most famous of all embalmers' caches was that from Tutankhamen's mummification. The cache was buried in a pit six feet long, four feet wide, and four feet deep. Discovered in 1908

about 100 yards from the then undiscovered tomb, the excavator, Theodore Davis, believed the contents to be a reburial of Tutankhamen's plundered tomb. The dozen jars taken from the pit contained the usual embalmers' equipment—packets of natron, linen, etc.—some with Tutankhamen's name written on them. The linen, mostly torn into long strips from sheets, had been rolled so it could be used in the same way that bandages are today. About fifty of these rolls were finished on both edges, indicating that they had been woven specifically for wrapping Tutankhamen's mummy. Some of the packets of natron in the cache were so small that they could not have had any practical use. These may have been created as amulets to invoke the magical properties of natron. The cache is now in the Metropolitan Museum of Art in New York.

EMBALMING   The process of chemically treating a cadaver to reduce the presence and growth of microorganisms and to retard organic decomposition in order to preserve the body.

Prior to 1880 few Americans were embalmed. Preservation of the dead was a novelty usually reserved for the famous. The bodies of common folks were packed in ice until the time of burial. There were some patented "preservers" that were basically rectangular ice boxes with a glass window so the face of the deceased could be viewed. A hose in the bottom drained the melted ice.

Prior to embalming it was not unusual for airtight lead coffins to explode soon after burial because of the gasses that developed from the cadaver. If a coffin began to bulge before burial, it would be tapped by drilling a small hole to let out a jet of gas. This would be ignited and could burn for as long as thirty minutes.

Before the nineenth-century embalming was attempted only when a body had to be transported great distances. Two early pioneers in embalming were the surgeons, John (1728–93) and William (1718–83) Hunter. They injected a mixture of vermilion, turpentine, and oil of lavender into the arteries of their cadavers—an early example of arterial embalming. The brothers would vigorously massage the corpse so the mixture would diffuse into the tissues. An even earlier attempt at embalming was made by the famous seventeenth-century English chemist Robert Boyle, who preserved animals by injecting wine into their arteries.

In the United States a patent was granted in 1856 for a method of preserving human bodies for transportation. The body was washed with a mixture of arsenic and alcohols, then electrically charged. Finally, it was covered in oils and sealed in a coffin filled with alcohol. This was merely to preserve the body for transportation and did not permit viewing.

During the Civil War so many bodies had to be transported that embalming became a necessary and common practice. It was only at the beginning of the twentieth century that formaldehyde, the chemical essential to modern embalming, became inexpensive enough to be widely used.

Today when a body is embalmed, it is washed first with a disinfectant to kill any insects, then with a germicidal solution. The procedure used in modern funeral homes is arterial embalming. Three or four gallons of embalming fluid are injected into a major artery, often the carotid in the neck or right femoral in the groin. At the same time the blood is drained by way of the veins.

The two basic chemicals used in embalming—formaldehyde and wood alcohol—change the proteins in the body so they will not putrefy. Once the chemicals have circulated through the body, the muscles begin to stiffen, and after twelve hours the position of the arms and legs cannot be changed.

ETEMMU   In Babylonian mythology, the soul of an unburied body.

ETHICS AND MUMMIES   The question of whether mummies should be displayed has often been debated by museum curators, but no general consensus has been reached. The changing attitudes toward displaying mummies can be seen in the way the collection of royal mummies in the Egyptian Museum in Cairo has been moved on and off display. The royal mummies were brought to the museum when it opened in 1902 and were displayed until 1929, when out of a feeling of reverence for the former heads of state, Egyptian officials decided the royal mummies should no longer be displayed.

In 1959 the mummies were returned to public display in Room 52 (Royal Mummies Room). In the 1970s, however, President Anwar Sadat had the mummies removed from public view, stating that it was an indignity for former rulers of Egypt to be gaped at and photographed by thousands of tourists every year. In 1995 the mummies were again put on display, and can still be seen today.

Although many emotional issues arise when the subject of displaying mummies is discussed—"It's disrespectful," "It's an indignity," "It's disgusting," "It's ghoulish," etc.—these beliefs differ from the ethical question, "Is it right to display mummies?"

One of the fundamental issues in this question is whether the dead have rights. Just as it is often argued that future generations have a right to clean air and water, so might it be argued that past generations have rights. Just because Ramses the Great is dead does not mean that he no longer has rights. Indeed, he might still retain his right to privacy, thus his mummy should not be displayed without his permission.

But does Ramses have rights? It could also be argued that only living beings have rights, and certainly Ramses is no longer alive. While we may call the mummy in Room 52 of the Egyptian Museum in Cairo "Ramses," certainly it is not; it is only his body. The person called Ramses ceased to exist more than 3,000 years ago, thus an entity called Ramses does not exist, so cannot have any rights. Therefore we may do with his body what we choose—display it, perform an autopsy on it, or even rebury it.

There may, however, be other reasons for honoring what Ramses would have wanted done with his body. When a person dies and leaves a will, we honor it by following the conditions it contains, not necessarily because the deceased still has rights, but because we as living persons have an obligation to follow such requests. This might be viewed as keeping a promise. If we promise to keep a secret, then we are obliged to keep that secret. If we apply this line of thinking to the display of mummies, then it becomes important to know what the deceased would have wanted. If, for example, we somehow knew that Ramses would not have wanted his body displayed, then perhaps we have an obligation (not that Ramses has a right) to honor his wishes, as if he had left a will. We, of course, do not know what Ramses's wishes would have been. Certainly when he was placed in his tomb in the Valley of the Kings with all of his treasures, he did not want his body to be disturbed. But Ramses's body was disturbed, when his tomb was discovered and looted thousands of years ago, his body being rediscovered in 1881. It might also be pointed out that the ancient Egyptians believed that to say the name of the dead was to make him or her live again. To display Ramses's mummy is surely to invite the repetition of his name, something he would undoubtedly have wanted.

Yet another aspect of the question is who ought to decide what is done with Ramses's mummy? In everyday situations it is the "next of kin" who has the right to decide, but clearly Ramses has no known next of kin. Should Anwar Sadat, just because he was president of Egypt and believed it was undignified to have the mummies on display, be able to take them off display? One can ask what special ethical expertise made his decision the correct one. Merely being in a position of power does not mean that one has expert status. This is why presidents and kings do not make decisions about scientific research. They don't decide how to cure cancer or whether nuclear energy is safe. They leave such decisions to the experts.

The ethical question of whether it is right to display mummies was discussed for years by non-experts, and however strong these opinions and feelings may be, they are not reasoned philosophical positions based on an analysis of the issues. Only recently have professional philosophers begun to discuss the question, so it is still far from settled.

In the meantime The International Council of Museums (ICOM) in its "Code of Ethics" includes a paragraph stating its position with regard to mummies.

> Where a museum maintains and/or is developing a collection of human remains and sacred objects these should be securely housed and carefully maintained as archival collections in scholarly institutions, and should always be available to qualified researchers and educators, but not the morbidly curious. Research on such objects and their housing and care must be accomplished in a manner acceptable not only to fellow professionals, but to those various beliefs, including in particular members of the community, ethnic or religious groups concerned. Although it is occasionally necessary to use human remains and other sensitive materials in interpretive exhibits, this must be done with tact and with respect for the feeling for human dignity held by all peoples.

ETHMOID BONE   Located in the front of the skull behind the nasal passages, the ethmoid bone, because of its many perforations, derives its name from the Greek *ethmos,* meaning "sieve." It was intentionally broken by Egyptian embalmers so they could remove the brain with a wire hook, which they inserted through the nostrils and into the cranium.

EYES OF THE MUMMY MA, THE   This 1922 German film (*Die Augen der Mummie Ma*) was the first mummy film in which major stars appeared. The plot revolves around a modern Egyptian dancer (Pola Negri), who is priestess of a sect of mummy worshipers. When she leaves Egypt with a German painter with whom she has fallen in love, she is followed by Radu (played by Emil Jannings), the high priest of the sect.

Directed by Ernst Lubitsch, with a script by Hanz Krali, this film paved the way for the long string of mummy films that was to follow in the United States and England.

F

FACE TO FACE WITH YOUR PAST An exhibition held from August 2, 1996 to October 31, 1996 at the Silkeborg Museum in Silkeborg, Denmark. This unique exhibit brought together twenty bog mummies from museums across Europe. Already at the Silkeborg Museum were Tollund Man and Elling Woman, two important bog mummies who date from approximately 210–70 B.C. They were joined by Huldremose Woman and Haraldskjaer Woman from Denmark, Worsley Man from England, and Gallagh Man from Ireland. From Germany came Damendorf Man, Windeby Girl, and Bernuthsford Man, among others. In addition to the mummies, many artifacts associated with their lives were on display.

FALCON MUMMIES See ANIMAL NECROPOLIS AT SAQQARA.

FAYOUM PORTRAITS Hellenistic portraits that were painted on Egyptian mummies in place of traditional mummy masks. Mummies with portraits were found more than 100 years ago in the Fayoum, a lush farming region southwest of Cairo. The Fayoum portraits began to appear when Egypt, ruled by Rome, was culturally influenced by the Greek population.

When Alexander the Great conquered Egypt in 336 B.C., Greeks were encouraged to settle in Egypt. After Alexander's death his general, Ptolemy, came to power and thus began 300 years of Greek rule and Hellenistic influence in Egypt. When Cleopatra VII, the last queen of Egypt, died in 30 B.C., Egypt became a Roman province. Greek traditions were perpetuated under the Romans who admired the Hellenistic culture, and Greek became the language spoken by anyone who had social aspirations.

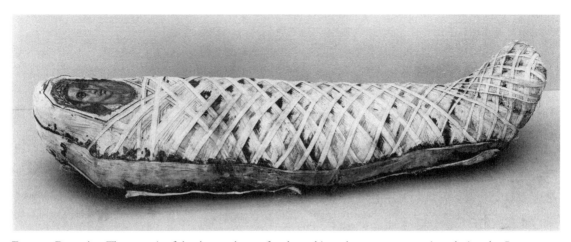

Fayoum Portraits The portrait of the deceased was often bound into the mummy wrappings during the Greco-Roman Period. *Photo courtesy Metropolitan Museum of Art.*

The Fayoum mummy portraits are an excellent example of how aspects of two cultures joined to produce a unique icon. Mummification was unique to Egypt and was a tradition that, once developed, remained relatively unchanged for 3,000 years. The mummified body was placed in a coffin that included a stylized funeral mask as part of its decoration, and it was this mummy mask that was replaced by the Fayoum portraits.

Egypt had four cities that were predominantly Greek—Alexandria, Naukratis, Ptolemais, and Antinoopolis. The upper classes lived very comfortably in town houses of two or three stories and often owned a country house as well. The wealthy Greeks were landowners, bankers, importers, and merchants.

Slaves did the work in Greco-Roman homes, with every upper-class family having several slaves to attend to the daily chores of running a large household. Slaves were often freed after their owners died; indeed, there is a mummy portrait of a freed slave named Eutyches.

In addition to the Greeks many other foreign groups settled in Egypt—the Libyans, Jews, Syrians, and Asians—who brought their own traditions and religions, creating a very cosmopolitan society. Most of the finest mummy portraits were painted during the second century A.D. when this culture flourished.

Society was made even more complex in Greco-Roman Egypt by the variety of religious beliefs. While the Egyptian culture was not embraced by the Greek upper class, Egyptian religion, because of its ancient origins, was highly revered. The Greeks and Romans adopted many Egyptian deities, and outsiders were often surprised that Greek, Roman, and Egyptians gods could represent the same pantheon. A god could, for example, be known by his Roman name, his Greek name, or his Egyptian name. The Serapis-Isis cult was most important because it combined elements of the ancient Egyptian religion and the Greek religion. The Egyptian cult of the dead centered on Isis and her husband, Osiris, the god of resurrection, who became the Hellenized Sera-pis. Egyptian mummies were objects of veneration because of their association with Osiris/Serapis, and the Fayoum mummies also became objects of veneration. Deceased men were imbued with the divinity of Osiris, and deceased women with the divinity of Isis. The Jews and the Christians were two notable groups in Egypt whose culture was Hellenistic but who did not permit the assimilation of foreign deities into their religions.

Painting was highly regarded in Greco-Roman Egypt, with the best painters and sculptors being Greek. Generations of Greek artists had developed great skill in portrait painting, and some time during the reign of the Roman emperor Tiberius (A.D. 14–37), naturalistic portraits of the deceased began to replace traditional mummy masks on the coffins of the wealthy. The bodies were still mummified, wrapped in linen bandages, and decorated with Egyptian religious motifs, but mummy masks were replaced with beautiful, lifelike portraits. The artists portrayed their subjects in the current fashions, with great attention to the details of jewelry and hair styles. Men, women, and children are depicted, and the Fayoum portraits are some of the earliest true portraits that have survived from antiquity. Most of them date from the first two centuries A.D. and are painted on rectangular cedar or cypress boards over a layer of white gesso. The best of these portraits were done by mixing pigments with beeswax and applying them with a brush and spatula—a technique known as encaustic. When an artist completed a portrait, it was given to the embalmers. The painting was secured to the mummy with linen bandages carefully wound around the head, then the bandages and sometimes the portrait were embellished with gold leaf. These portraits had a great influence on the later Byzantine icon painting.

The Fayoum mummies may not have been placed in tombs immediately after mummification. From the findings of archaeologists and the comments of ancient writers, it seems that at least some of the Fayoum mummies were returned to

Fish Mummies Mummified *Bagrus bayad* fish, one of the fish that devoured the phallus of Osiris, the Egyptian god of the dead.

their families and kept in the home as objects of veneration. The Greek historian Diodorus Siculus (80–20 B.C.) mentions that in Egypt the bodies of ancestors were kept in costly chambers, and family members would gaze upon the faces of those who had lived generations before them.

When the famous British Egyptologist Flinders Petrie examined a cache of Fayoum mummies in 1881, he found that the beautifully wrapped and decorated mummies often showed signs of wear; they appeared battered or as if they had been exposed to the elements for a long period of time. He concluded that the mummies were kept by families in their homes until such time as their memory had passed out of existence, and then they were buried. Whatever the actual practice, these unique and hauntingly beautiful portraits give us a rare glimpse into the past.

FISH MUMMIES Hundreds of fish mummies have been found in their own special cemetery at Esneh, but it is not certain why they were mummified. Most of the fish mummies are Nile perch, *Lates niloticus.* A painting in the Theban tomb of Khabekhnet shows a huge Lates being mummified by Anubis, the god of embalming.

Although the reason for mummifying this species is uncertain, it is possible that a different species, the *Bagrus bayad,* was mummified because it was sacred. In Plutarch's version of the myth of Osiris (see OSIRIS) the author says that when Osiris was cut into pieces by his evil brother Set, his phallus was thrown into the Nile and eaten by three fish of different species. One he calls the "phagros," which is probably our modern "Bagrus." Thus this fish may have been revered because of its association with Osiris and perhaps was mummified for this reason.

FIXATION The stage in the artificial preparation of tissues that renders enzymes inactive, neutralizes bacteria and thus prevents decay. The most commonly used fixative is formalin, a saturated solution of the gas formaldehyde. The aim when fixing a specimen is to permeate all cells as quickly as possible to stop decay. Several methods are used.

1. Immersion—The specimen is soaked in a solution of formalin (often approximately 10 percent). This technique is particularly effective for thin specimens, as the solution can quickly permeate all the cells. It is also helpful if the soaking is done at a low temperature since this retards putrefaction. Frequently the temperature of a refrigerator is used; that is between 1° and 5°C (33.8° and 41°F).

2. Injection—The fixative is injected into the specimen via the vessels, normally the arteries rather than the veins. A small plastic tube is inserted into an artery, and the fixative is injected. Prior to injecting the fixative the vessels are usually flushed with saline to remove any blood. This technique is particularly suitable for preserving entire bodies since immersion will not reach the innermost cells quickly.

3. Perfusion—This is the continuous flushing of the vascular system. As mentioned above the blood vessels are frequently rinsed, or perfused, with ordinary saline. They can then be perfused with the fixatives. The perfusion with saline is necessary in order to remove any blood clots in the vessels that might block the perfusion of the fixative.

4. Infiltration—The direct injection of the fixative into the specimen's tissue. This technique is used when a specimen is too thick for immersion or when the vascular system has been damaged and injection is not possible.

5. Dilation—A hollow organ is distended (inflated) by forcing the fixative fluid through it under hydrostatic pressure. The fluid permeates the walls of the organ and fixes it in its normal distended shape. Thus hollow organs like the heart can be preserved in a noncollapsed shape.

FORMALDEHYDE The chemical most used in preserving bodies today was independently discovered by two scientists, Alexander Butherov (1828–66) and August Wilhelm von Hofmann (1818–92). Butherov was the first to make the discovery (1859). In 1868 von Hofmann prepared formaldehyde by passing methanol vapors and air over a heated platinum coil.

The effectiveness of formaldehyde as a preservative for tissue was discovered accidentally in 1893 by a German physician, Ferdinand Blum (1865–1959). Blum was working on a project using a 4 percent solution of formaldehyde and noticed that his wet finger became stiff. He published his findings, and formaldehyde began to be used as an embalming fluid. In the early twentieth century, it was discovered that metals such as arsenic that had previously been used for embalming were poisonous, and formaldehyde became widely used.

The way formaldehyde preserves tissues involves complex chemistry because two reactions are involved. First methylene glycol is produced, then formaldehyde reacts with oxygen to yield formic acid.

FORMALIN   A chemical used in the preservation of animal tissue. Formalin works by "denaturing" the protein molecules that make up animal tissue. Once the protein molecules have been so altered, the body's natural enzymes cannot act on the tissue, and decay is arrested. Once used for preserving scientific specimens, it is now used extensively by morticians to preserve human bodies for viewing at funerals.

FOUR SONS OF HORUS   The Egyptian falcon god, Horus, was said to have four sons: Duamutef who had the head of a jackal, Qebhesenuef who had the head of a falcon, Hapi who had the head of an ape, and Mesti who had a human head. Each of these sons was responsible for protecting one of the mummy's internal organs (stomach, liver, intestines, kidneys). Other internal organs were removed by embalmers (spleen, gall bladder, etc.), but for some reason these are not mentioned by the ancient Egyptians.

FRAGONARD, HONORÉ (1732–1799) An anatomist who trained to be a surgeon, Fragonard spent the later years of his life making sculptures out of human and animal cadavers.

Born in Grasse, France, at the age of thirty-three Fragonard became director of the world's first veterinary school, the École Royal Vétérinaire in Lyons. (Today it is the École Nationale Vétérinaire.)

Soon after entering the school, Fragonard began dissecting cadavers at the rate of two a week and developed his unique technique for preservation. Cadavers were soaked in a mixture of alcohol, pepper, and herbs, and some arteries were injected with the mixture. The bodies were then skinned and posed in the desired position, and finally were injected with colored wax mixed with turpentine. The "sculptures," without skin and with their exposed organs and discolored blood vessels, are truly macabre.

Working late into the night, Fragonard became obsessed with his anatomical preparation and ultimately produced nearly 3,000 specimens. In 1771, at the age of thirty-nine, Fragonard was fired from his position at the school on the grounds that he was insane.

His cousin, Jean-Honoré Fragonard, the famous painter, had many connections in French society and introduced Honoré Fragonard to the aristocracy, who for twenty-two years purchased his creations. During the French Revolution he resumed working at a medical school and died in 1799. The school that dismissed him for insanity now houses a small collection of his work. (See FRAGONARD MUSEUM.)

FRAGONARD MUSEUM   Located in the École Vétérinaire d'Alfort in Paris, its three rooms house the anatomical preparations of Honoré Fragonard (see FRAGONARD, HONORÉ). By far the most dramatic exhibit in the museum is a horse in midstride. It has been flayed and injected with chemicals so its ligaments, veins, and arteries are all clearly visible. Astride the horse is a human cadaver, also skinned, grasping the reigns and staring into space. A rumor once circulated that the rider was Fragonard's fiancée who died the day before their wedding and was skinned and preserved by Fragonard (the rumor is false; the rider is a male). A skinned bust of a man and an antelope have been prepared in a similar way.

The museum is open to the public but has so few visitors that a sign at the entrance reads, "Unfortunately, we have too few visitors. If you enjoy the museum, why not send us your friends—if not your enemies."

FRANCIS XAVIER, SAINT, BODY OF (1506–1552)   Saint Francis Xavier was canonized by Pope Gregory XV on 12 March 1622 as a result of his exceptional missionary works. Born an aristocrat, he met St. Ignatius Loyola at the University of Paris and became one of his original seven followers. He did his missionary work in India and Japan and had even hoped to continue on to China but died on December 3, 1552 soon after his arrival in that country. He was buried in a coffin packed with lime to accelerate the decomposition of the flesh, a frequent practice with the cadavers of saintly people, so that later the bones could be distributed as relics.

On February 17, 1553 a ship bound for Malacca, where St. Francis was especially venerated, retrieved his body. Upon arrival, although packed in lime the body was found to be in "perfect" condition and was subsequently buried at the Church of our Lady in Malacca. Five months later the body was exhumed and taken to Goa, India, where St. Francis had experienced an extremely successful missionary stay and was revered. His body was viewed by thousands in the Basilica of the Bom Jesus.

In 1614 the body was examined and found to be miraculously well preserved. The right forearm was amputated and sent to the Jesuits of Il Gesu in Rome, where it remains today. In 1619, when Catholics were being cruelly persecuted, the Jesuits asked for a relic of the beloved St. Francis Xavier. The upper arm was amputated and sent to them. In the 1620s the left hand was divided in two, half going to Cochin and the other to the College of Malacca. So great was the demand for relics, that in 1636 St. Francis's internal organs were distributed to religious centers throughout the world.

In 1648 there was a secret exhumation to examine the state of preservation. The report stated "The eyes are black, lively and sweet, with so penetrating a glance that he would seem to be alive and breathing. The lips are of a bright reddish color and the beard is thick . . . The tongue is quite flexible, red and moist, and the chin is beautifully proportioned. In a word, the body has all the appearance of being that of a living man."

The body was last publicly displayed from November 1974 to January 1975 at Goa with more than half a million faithful paying their respects. *Newsweek* for December 30, 1974 described the body as "surprisingly well-preserved." The body now rests in the Basilica of the Bom Jesus in Goa, India.

FRANKINCENSE The spice frankincense was used by ancient Egyptian embalmers during the mummification process. Frankincense is the resin of the *Boswellia* tree, which grows in the Sudan and in Yemen. The fragrant resin no doubt helped to reduce the odor caused by the embalmer's work.

FRANKLIN EXPEDITION In 1845 two ships under the command of Sir John Franklin left England to discover a passage through the frozen waters of North America to the riches of China and East India. The expedition was equipped with the finest provisions and scientific equipment in the history of Arctic

Franklin Expedition Frozen mummy of John Torrington, a twenty-year-old member of the Franklin Expedition who died in 1846.

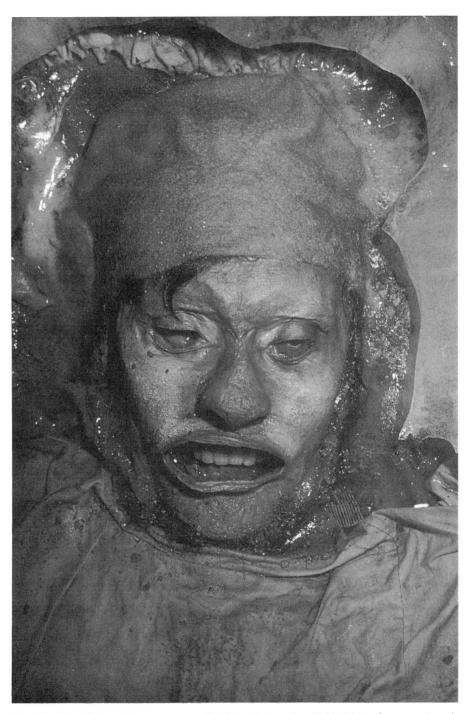

Franklin Expedition Frozen mummy of William Braine, who died in 1846 of pneumonia and tuberculosis as a result of his weakened condition due to lead poisoning.

Franklin Expedition   Frozen mummy of John Hartnell. Weighing less than ninety pounds, it indicated a lengthy illness before he died. (*Photos courtesy Dr. Owen Beattie, University of Alberta, Canada.*)

exploration, but none of the 129 men ever returned. More than a century later, the frozen mummies of three of its crew members provided the clues of the mystery of what happened to the Franklin Expedition.

For 300 years before the Franklin Expedition, various nations had sent ships to find the Northwest Passage, but all had failed. The territory from North America to the North Pole is dotted with islands, providing only narrow passages for ships. In addition, in winter when the passages are frozen, the ships can be trapped then crushed or upended by newly risen icebergs. Franklin's two ships, the *Erebus* and the *Terror*, were fitted with iron planks to protect the bows. Every modern scientific innovation was available to the expedition. A steam engine was installed in each ship to supply emergency power. Steam and

hot water were forced through a one-foot diameter pipe hidden beneath the deck, to heat the cabins below. The expedition was the first to carry a camera to the Arctic, and a library of nearly 3,000 books was available to the men who could read. For those who could not, school supplies were brought to teach them.

The expedition brought huge quantities of food—enough for three years. More than sixty tons of flour, 16,000 liters of liquor, 9,000 pounds of chocolate, and a ton of tea would feed these "iron men in wooden ships." Aware of the effects of scurvy on earlier expeditions, 10,000 pounds of lemon juice were also included in the rations. Tinned food, a recent invention, was the most important of all the provisions, and 8,000 tins of meat, soups, and vegetables were loaded on the two vessels before they departed from

England. Thus on May 29, 1845 there was great optimism that the Franklin Expedition would finally discover the Northwest Passage.

John Franklin's last contact with the outside world took place in Baffin Bay on July 9, 1845, when the expedition encountered two whaling ships. Franklin told the captain of one of the whalers that he had enough provisions for five years and could stretch them out over seven if necessary. Whenever possible he intended to supplement his stock by killing birds and game. With this comment the expedition sailed north, never to be seen again.

At the end of 1847, when no word of the expedition had been received, people began to feel that something might be wrong. Three separate relief expeditions were sent to make contact, but when they returned without having even sighted Franklin's ships, it became clear that something was seriously wrong. The fate of the Franklin Expedition became a national cause for Victorian England, and Her Majesty's government offered a twenty-thousand-pound reward for anyone who could find and assist the expedition. By 1850 a fleet of ships was searching, and in August the first traces of the men were found. On Devon Island, empty food tins, old clothing, and trash marked the men's winter quarters. Then on nearby Beechey Island, three graves marked with tombstones were found. The first read:

Sacred
to the
memory
of
William Braine, R.M.,
H.M.S. Erebus
Died April 3rd, 1846
aged 32 years
'Choose ye this day whom ye will serve'
Joshua, ch. XXIV., 15.

The second read

Sacred to the memory of
John Hartnell, A.B. of H.M.S.

Erebus
died January 4th, 1846
aged 25 years.
'Thus saith the Lord of Hosts, consider your ways.'
Haggai, i, 7.

The last said:

Sacred
to
The memory of
John Torrington
who departed this
life January 1st A.D. 1846,
on Board of
H.M. ship Terror
aged 20 years.

Although arctic expeditions normally experienced deaths, three fatalities was unusual so early on. Hope remained, however, and, in 1851 twenty-eight sleds were sent to search for survivors. Only more empty tins and discarded clothing were found. Nine years after the expedition had first set out, searchers still hoped to find some of the men alive. In 1854 a local Inuit reported that Franklin's party had been seen years earlier attempting to walk out of the area after its ships had been crushed by the ice. Mutilated corpses were also seen, indicating that the men were starved and had resorted to cannibalism. In spite of the depressing news, Lady Franklin had still not given up. More than a decade had passed since she last saw her husband, but she used her private fortune to fund another search.

In 1858 Captain Francis M'Clintock of the Royal Navy found more traces of the expedition, and on May 25, 1859 he found a human skeleton in a steward's uniform on the ground near the Peffer River. Next to the body he found a notebook—the only written notes of the expedition ever recovered. One scrawled entry read "Oh Death whare is thy sting, the grave at Comfort Cove for who has any doubt now . . . the dyer sad." Later a lifeboat from the expedition was discovered; it held two human skeletons, still in their clothes, holding loaded double-barrelled guns. In their demented state the crew had brought books, toothbrushes, soap, and other items unnecessary for survival and had attempted to pull them in the lifeboats across the ice to civilization.

Over the years additional skeletal parts and discarded tins were found, but the question of what caused the demise of the Franklin Expedition was never answered. In 1981 forensic anthropologist Owen Beattie attempted to solve the mystery. By surveying areas where traces of the expedition had been found, he recovered bone fragments from expedition members and from some Inuit of the same period. Laboratory analyses of the fragments revealed that there was ten times the lead content in the expedition members' fragments as in the Inuit samples, suggesting lead poisoning. Lead accumulates over many years in bone, so it could not be conclusively shown that the lead was accumulated during the expedition; for that soft tissue would be needed. The final answer to what happened to the 129 men lay in the three graves that had been found more than a century earlier. Beattie realized that if the graves of the three expedition members had been frozen for all this time, then soft tissue would remain and be available for analysis. In 1984 Beattie and a team of researchers flew to Beechey Island to exhume the bodies of John Torrington, John Hartnell, and William Braine.

The first body to be examined was that of John Torrington, but after the gravel covering the coffin had been removed, the task became excruciatingly difficult. The coffin was frozen solid into the permafrost. Hot water had to be poured over the coffin to free the lid, but even then the team could not see the body, which was covered by a blue cloth that was frozen to it. More hot water was applied, and when researchers peeled away the cloth with large surgical tweezers, they came face to face with John Torrington. The twenty-year-old seaman looked as if he had

died yesterday, not 138 years ago. The ice-coffin had preserved him perfectly; indeed his hands looked as if they could still be warm. When the entire body was freed from the ice, it was placed on a tarpaulin, the clothes were removed, and beneath the arctic sky the autopsy proceeded.

There were no signs of violence or an accident, but Torrington's emaciated appearance indicated that he had been ill for quite a while before his death. For more than four hours, the team worked on the mummy, first making large incisions in the abdomen and chest to reveal the organs. Each organ had to be thawed with hot water so tissue samples could be taken. Specimens of the right thumbnail, hair, a rib, and the brain were also taken. When the intestines were examined, no traces of undigested food were found, confirming that he had been ill before he died. The uncovering of the grave and autopsy had taken far longer than expected, and the team had to return to Canada without examining the other two bodies.

Laboratory tests showed that the level of lead was indeed high. The hair samples were long enough to show that the lead had been ingested during Torrington's time with the expedition. One surprise was that although the mummy of John Torrington seemed perfectly preserved, microscopic examination of the tissues told a different story. Many of the cell structures were unrecognizable, the result of damage done when the water inside his body froze, expanded, and destroyed the cells' integrity. If the bodies of the other two expedition members showed high levels of lead, it would be confirmed that somehow the men died of complications associated with lead poisoning. Thus in 1986 Beattie and a team that included a radiologist returned to complete the job begun two years earlier.

The job of exhuming John Hartnell was difficult, as expected. Again water had to be heated and poured on the coffin and body. The radiologist, Dr. Derek Notman, had brought a portable X-ray machine and set up a darkroom in which the films could be developed. When the films of the abdominal area were exposed, however, the organs could not be discerned. When Hartnell's clothing was removed to take another set of X rays, the explanation became clear. Running from Hartnell's hips and up his chest was an inverted Y incision. In 1846 the ship's surgeons had conducted an autopsy to see if they could determine the cause of death. They had removed the organs for inspection and had placed them in a pile in the abdominal cavity and sutured the incision closed. Beattie's team merely reopened the incision, took their samples, and resutured the inverted Y.

The last mummy to be examined was that of William Braine, and his proved to be the most difficult to extricate, since it was buried six feet down. For an entire day the team took turns with pick axes and hot water until finally they came face to face with Braine. Unlike the other two, he was not perfectly preserved, his body showing signs of decomposition. For some reason, still unknown, he was not buried immediately after death. Like Torrington, Braine was emaciated, weighing less than ninety pounds. The samples taken from his body along with those from Hartnell were kept frozen and flown to the University of Alberta Hospital for analysis.

The final tests confirmed that lead poisoning was a main cause of death. All three bodies had high lead levels. Both Hartnell and Braine had tuberculosis and died of pneumonia as a result of the weakness brought on by the lead poisoning. The last question to be answered was the source of this poisoning, and the answer was the discarded tins.

The tins had been made from wrought iron cylinders soldered on both the inside and outside seams. The solder was 90 percent lead, and many of the seams were incompletely soldered. Thus the food had spoiled and lead had seeped into it. Each sailor would have been rationed approximately one-quarter pound of tinned food each day, thus they were regularly consuming lead, which poisoned them. One of the effects of lead poisoning is impaired reasoning, and this explains why the men tried to walk out with useless items.

The careful autopsies of the frozen mummies of John Torrington, John Hartnell, and William Braine enabled modern scientists to solve the mystery of the Franklin Expedition. After the autopsies all three mummies were replaced in their coffins and reburied in their graves in the permafrost. The stones were carefully replaced in the same positions on top of the graves. Today the three men still lie in their icy graves on Beechey Island.

FURTA SACRA Latin for "stolen relics," this term often refers to the theft of portions of the miraculously preserved bodies of saints that were stolen during the Middle Ages so other churches could share the glory of having a saint buried within their grounds.

Around the year 1200, Hugh, bishop of Lincoln, visited the arm of Mary of Magdalen that was buried in the abbey at Fecamp in Normandy. The arm had been sewn into a protective cloth. Hugh had been refused permission to view the arm, but with a knife he cut open the wrappings. He then tried to break off a few of the fingers so he could return with the relics, but they would not yield. Finally he bit them off with his teeth.

GANNAL, JEAN (1791–1882) An apothecary who served in Napoleon's medical unit and in his later years was asked by the French government to devise a better method of preserving cadavers for medical schools. Many of his innovations made embalming techniques available to the medical community at large. Gannal's *History of Embalming* covers mummification practices of all kinds.

GAUTIER, THÉOPHILE (1811–1872) French pioneer of mummy fiction and writer of romantic novels and short stories. Gautier is known for exotic stories such as "One of Cleopatra's Nights." His novel *The Romance of a Mummy* and short story "The Mummy's Foot" are among the earliest mummy stories, and both involve love between modern mortals and mummies. (See THE ROMANCE OF A MUMMY AND "THE MUMMY'S FOOT.")

Several years after having written *The Romance of a Mummy,* which describes a mummy unwrapping. Gautier actually participated in such an event at the Universal Exposition of 1857. He was not disappointed and indeed reveled in the odor of ancient spices that filled the room as the bandages were unwound. Even gold jewelry was uncovered, but the mummy of Lady Nesikhonsu was not beautiful like the mummies in Gautier's stories.

GINGER This Egyptian predynastic mummy has been on exhibit in the First Egyptian Room of the British Museum for nearly a century. The mummy was discovered at Gelelein 100 miles south of Luxor, along with five others, all dating prior to 3000 B.C. Typical of burials of this period, the body of this male was not artificially mummified but was merely placed in a fetal position and buried in the sand. The warm sands rapidly dehydrated the body, preserving it.

Soon after the mummy was placed on display, it was nicknamed "Ginger" because of its red hair. In 1985 Ginger was taken off display for conservation. The skin, particularly around the face, was cracked, and the hair was brittle and in danger of falling out. The skin was gently heated to make it more pliable, and an adhesive was brushed on that penetrated the skin, adhering it to the bone beneath. The hair was brushed with a solution to strengthen the strands, then loose tufts were attached with an adhesive called Mowilith 50. Ginger is again on display in the British Museum in London.

GLUTARALDEHYDE A chemical used in preservation of tissues, especially in embalming. Glutaraldehyde was first used in embalming in 1955 and reacts with tissue proteins even more strongly than formaldehyde (see FORMALDEHYDE). It has not replaced formaldehyde as a preservative, however, because it is five times more expensive to produce.

GOOSEBUMPS A series of children's books produced by Scholastic Inc. and written by R.S. Stine. Two of the most popular books in the series *The Curse of the Mummy's Tomb* and *The Return of the Mummy,* deal with mummies and capitalize on the idea that kids are fascinated with mummies and love to be scared. The back covers of the books (rated at reading level 4) include the warning, "Reader beware you're in for a scare!" The

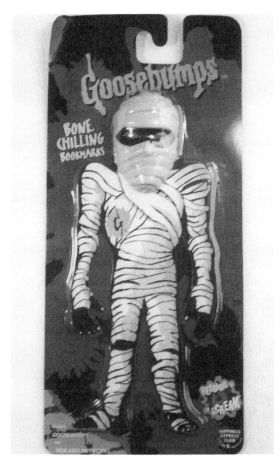

Goosebumps A mummy bookmark that encourages reading—"Reading is a scream."

stories are narrated by Gabe, a very Americanized 12-year-old Egyptian who lives in the United States and carries a fake mummy's hand as a good luck charm. In *The Curse of the Mummy's Tomb* he is visiting Egypt with his parents, and his first scare comes when he is alone in a Cairo hotel room, and a ghoulish mummy appears at the door.

When Gabe's parents must make a quick trip to Alexandria, Gabe is left in the care of Uncle Ben, a famous Egyptologist, who has just discovered a new chamber in the great pyramid. When Uncle Ben takes his daughter, Sari, and Gabe into the pyramid with him, the adventures really be-

gin. Sari teases Gabe into exploring the newly discovered tunnel, and they become separated and the lights go out. Gabe finds an ancient coffin and is terrified when the lid begins to slide open, only to realize that the body inside is Sari, playing one of her many mean tricks on him. The story is full of surprises, mummies, coffins, and curses. In the end Gabe makes a fabulous discovery, mysteries are solved, and the whole family celebrates.

The Return of the Mummy is the second in the series of Gabe's adventures in Egypt. A year older and a year wiser about the mysteries of Egypt, he is to spend this vacation with his uncle and Sari, living at the excavation site near the great pyramid.

During his flight to Cairo, Gabe notices that his good luck charm, a plastic mummy's hand, seems to be giving him a warning. He remembers the practical jokes that his uncle and Sari love to play and is determined not to fall for every trick this year. When they arrive at the pyramid, Uncle Ben

Goosebumps A mummy flashlight for young explorers.

has a gift for Gabe, a 4,000-year-old scarab preserved in amber for him to wear around his neck for good luck. Gabe needs good luck, for as soon as he enters the pyramid, he loses his way and falls into a secret passage full of spiders. His luck seems to change when Uncle Ben opens the newly discovered tomb and finds it filled with more treasures than King Tutankhamen's tomb. A curse also comes with the tomb, however, and gives the story plenty of twists and turns. In the end it is up to Gabe and Sari to save the tomb, treasure, and Uncle Ben from the wrath of the mummy.

The Goosebumps books have become so popular with young readers that a fan club has been started, with members receiving all sorts of creepy gifts and a quarterly newsletter that is full of spine-tingling news and hair-raising puzzles. In addition, Goosebumps markets a line of mummy toys and accessories including a mummy flashlight for young explorers, a necklace with a mummy hologram, a mummy and coffin attached to a pencil, a mummy's head bookmark, and a plastic mummy's head filled with yellow mummy matter, which includes the warning, "Not a food item."

GRANVILLE, AUGUSTUS (1783–1872)
English physician who published the erroneous theory that wax was the main ingredient in mummification and that to preserve the bodies of the deceased, ancient Egyptian embalmers immersed them in a solution of wax and resin and cooked them slowly over a fire for several days. In spite of these errors, Granville greatly furthered the study of mummies by his exemplary scientific investigation of a female mummy purchased for four dollars in Thebes in 1819.

Granville's dissection of the pelvic area alone occupied two hours a day for a week and enabled him to conclude that the probable cause of death was uterine disease. Recent research, however, suggests that the tumor Granville found was in fact benign. The Granville mummy disappeared for quite a while but was rediscovered in 1992 in a storage room of the British Museum. Granville's "An Essay on Egyptian Mummies,"
published in 1825 in the Philosophical Transactions of the Royal Society, is remarkable for its time, reviewing the known literature on the subject and carefully describing the details of the autopsy.

GRAUBALLE MAN
One of a series of mummies found in the peat bogs of Denmark, dating from the early Iron Age (500–0 B.C.). Grauballe Man was found on April 26, 1952 in Nebelgard Fen, just south of the village of Grauballe. Like most other bog mummies, he was uncovered by peat cutters and, because of his excellent preservation, was first believed to be a recent murder victim. Indeed, his skin was so well preserved that his fingerprints could easily be seen, and he retained his hair. Grauballe Man had been killed, his throat slit from ear to ear.

An analysis of his stomach contents indicated that his last meal was a vegetarian gruel of more than sixty different grains. There was, however, no trace of autumn or summer fruits or greens, thus the death probably came during winter or early spring. Grauballe Man may have been a midwinter sacrifice.

The acidic bog water had partially tanned his skin and preserved his body, but once removed from the protective waters, he would have begun to decay. To preserve the body permanently, the tanning process was completed by immersing Grauballe Man in a solution of oak bark from November 1952 to June 1954. He is now displayed in the Museum of Prehistory at Aarhus, Denmark.

GRAVE WAX
A soapy substance that forms in the body under certain conditions of moisture and warm temperature. (See ADIPOCERE.)

GREENHILL, THOMAS (1681–1740)
An English physician who wrote the first book of mummification. He was the youngest of thirty-nine children, all born alive to one mother. This remarkable achievement was commemorated in

NEKPOKHΔEIA:
OR, THE
Art of Embalming;
Wherein is ſhewn
The Right of Burial,
AND
FUNERAL CEREMONIES,
Eſpecially that of
Preſerving Bodies
After the EGYPTIAN Method.

TOGETHER WITH
An Account of the *Egyptian* Mummies, Pyramids,
Subterranean Vaults and Lamps, and their Opinion of the *Me-
tempſychoſis*, the Cauſe of their *Embalming*.

AS ALSO
A Geographical Deſcription of *Egypt*, the Riſe and
Courſe of the *Nile*, the Temper, Conſtitution and Phyſic of the
Inhabitants, their Inventions, Arts, Sciences, Stupendous Works
and Sepulchres, and other curious Obſervations any ways rela-
ting to the Phyſiology and Knowledge of this *Art*.

PART I.

Illuſtrated with a Map and Fourteen Sculptures.

By T H O M A S G R E E N H I L L, *Surgeon.*

L O N D O N: Printed for the Author, M DCC V.

Greenhill, Thomas Title page of Thomas Greenhill's
NEKPOKHΔEIA, the first printed book on
mummification (1705).

1698, when the family was permitted to make an
addition to the family arms noting this fact.

In his book, *NEKPOKHΔEIA*, or *The Art of
Embalming* (1705), Greenhill recounts the descriptions and observations of the classical
authors, such as Herodotus and Diodorus, and
mentions that he does not believe Herodotus's
account of how the brain was removed with a
hooked instrument. Greenhill believes that Herodotus did not supply the details of this procedure
because it was not possible, ". . . the thing being
in itself impracticable and ridiculous; which any

one skill'd in Anatomy will readily agree to."
Greenhill believed that even if the brain could
have been removed with a hooked rod, it would
have destroyed the cartilage and deformed the
face. He suggests that the brain was removed by
injecting corrosive liquids that dissolved it.

GREEN KNIGHT, THE The Green Knight
in the story of *King Arthur and the Knights of the
Round Table* may well be a reference to bog
burials in general and Lindow Man in particular.

According to the legend, Arthur's court was
celebrating New Year's Eve when the Green
Knight, carrying a bundle of holly and a great axe,
entered the banquet hall on horseback. Both his
skin and garments were green, and he offered the
assembled knights a challenge. If anyone dared to
take up his axe and strike a blow with it, that brave
knight could keep it, but one year and a day from
that time, the Green Knight had the right to return
the blow. With Guinevere at his side, Sir Gawain
took the challenge and with a single blow decapitated the challenger, whose head came to rest at the
foot of the banquet table. But the Green Knight
dismounted, retrieved it, and told Gawain, "To the
Green Chapel go thou and get thee a nimble knock
in return on New Year's morning."

On November 2, after the Feast of All Hal-
lows, Gawain began his search for the Green
Chapel. Traveling through the mythical realms of
Logres and the Wilderness of Wirral, in northern
Wales, he came upon a castle where he was given
a green ribbon for protection. On New Year's Eve
he tied the ribbon to his waist and set out for the
Green Chapel. The chapel was a "worn borrow
on a brae by the brink of a water"—a traditional
burial place. When Gawain was greeted by the
Green Knight, he was told to place his head down
so the knight could have his blow. When the axe
finally descended, it only nicked Gawain's neck,
and he was saved, protected by the green band.
There is a great deal to link this legend with the
bog mummies that were ritually killed.

The greenness of the knight suggests fertility, and the fact that the wielding of the axe is

reenacted almost exactly one year later empha-
sizes the cyclical nature of growth. Gawain may
well represent the sacrifice to the gods to assure
a good harvest—undoubtedly the function of
some of the mummies found in the bogs. It is also
significant that he wears a green band. Several of
the mummies wore bands—Tollund Man on his
waist and Lindow Man on his arm. Even the
beheading of the Green Knight and near decapitation of Sir Gawain have their parallels with the
bog mummies. Lindow Woman and several other
bog mummies were beheaded. Thus the Arthu-
rian legend may contain distorted memories of
ritual bog killings enacted centuries before the
stories were first written.

GREENLAND MUMMIES   On October 9,
1972 two brothers hunting near the abandoned
settlement of Qilakitsoq in Greenland came upon
the undisturbed burial of eight Inuit Indians, who
had died around 1475. The brothers reported the
find to the authorities but otherwise kept the
location secret. Thus the finds remained intact
until they were officially investigated in 1978.

The cold and dry Arctic air had freeze-dried the
bodies in the two graves, so they were remarkably well
preserved. The larger of the two graves contained five
mummies, piled on top of each other. Uppermost
was a six-month-old boy and beneath him was a
four-year-old boy and three women ranging in age
from twenty-five to forty-five. The second grave
revealed three women, two approximately fifty years
old and one no more than twenty-two years old.

The Inuit of Greenland believed that upon
death the deceased would make their way to the
Land of the Dead, so they were buried with the

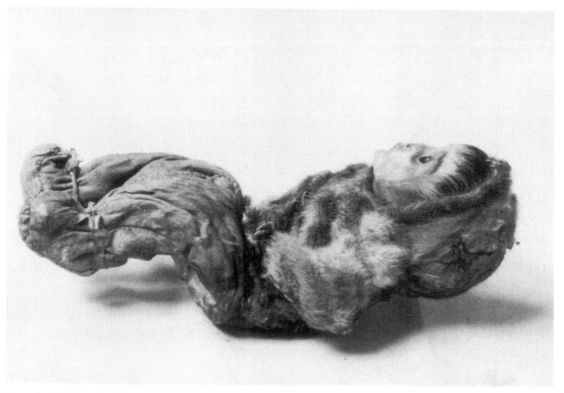

Greenland Mummies   The mummy of a six-month-old boy, buried during the fifteenth century in Greenland.
Photo courtesy Dr. Jens Pederhart Hanson.

clothing, tools, and implements they would need. The eight Qilakitsoq mummies all were fully clothed for the journey, but no items were buried with them.

When finally investigated, the mummies were sent to the Department of Conservation at the National Museum in Copenhagen. To determine if the mummies were related, tissues samples from each were typed, in a manner similar to blood typing, which revealed that they were from two families, one family in each grave. The grave that contained five mummies may well have held three generations—a grandmother, two daughters, and two grandchildren. The smaller grave probably held two sisters and one of their children.

All the adults were women, and their teeth indicated the kinds of activities they had been involved in. Some of the teeth had grooves across their surfaces caused by pulling animal sinew across the teeth to make thread. Some teeth were extremely worn down by years of chewing sealskin to soften it for clothing. The mummies literally provided a frozen glimpse into Inuit life in the fifteenth century, ranging from the details of their clothing to an elaborate tattoo on one of the women's forehead.

Investigators were intrigued about when and how the six women and two children had died. Perhaps a natural disaster like drowning or disease had killed them. Although careful examination of the mummies revealed that they had suffered from scalp lice, no evidence of a common fatal disease was found. It was hoped that analysis of the fruits and grains in the stomachs and intestines might have shown that all died during the same season, but only one mummy had sufficient contents to determine that her death was during or near the month of August. This question may be settled by future research. Four of the mummies are now on permanent exhibition in the Greenland National Museum.

The cold dry Greenland climate preserves not only tissue but also machinery. In 1947 a B-29 Superfortress plane was forced to land on a frozen lake bed 950 miles above the Arctic Circle. The crew of the *Kee Bird*, as the plane was named, was rescued, but the 85,000-pound bomber was left behind. For nearly half a century the *Kee Bird* remained exactly as it had landed—in a sense a mummy of a plane. In 1995 a team headed by plane restorer, Darryl Greenamayer, was able to repair the damage done on landing and fire up the plane's four engines and taxi for takeoff. Just as takeoff speed was approached, a fuel line broke, and the plane burned for four hours, fire destroying what the Arctic cold had preserved.

GREW, NEHEMIAH (1641–1712) An English physician who studied mummies and made early suggestions about the methods used by ancient Egyptian embalmers.

Grew's main area of study was plant physiology, and in 1671 he was made Fellow of the Royal Society. In 1681 he published a catalog of oddities in the Royal Society's collection in London. In this work he describes a mummy "taken out of the Royal Pyramids" that had been given to the society by Prince Henry, Duke of Norfolk. Grew carefully observed that the cloth in which the mummy was wrapped was of three qualities, the finest on the interior. He even mentioned that the outermost was like "Flaxen Cloth of two shillings an Ell."

After describing the painting on the outermost layer, he described the bones as black, as if they had been burned. Not realizing this was probably due to a chemical reaction, Grew concluded that the Egyptians mummified their dead by boiling the bodies in balsam to dissolve the flesh.

GROTTAROSSA MUMMY, THE The only known Roman mummy in existence, this well-preserved eight-year-old girl was found in Rome in the northern district of Grottarossa.

The mummy was discovered on February 5, 1964 by construction workers who were removing rubble from a building site. Inadvertently the mummy and its sarcophagus were loaded along with rubble on a truck for disposal, but when the driver realized he had a human cadaver on board, the police were called in. Eventually the mummy was sent to the Institute of Forensic Medicine at La Sapienza University in Rome.

The sarcophagus was made of white marble, carved with hunting scenes that show deer, lion, and boar. Such a sarcophagus indicates that the young girl came from a wealthy family, and this is confirmed by the jewelry with which she was buried—gold earrings, a gold necklace with sapphires, and a gold ring. The jewelry style indicates that the girl lived and died during the second century A.D., perhaps at the end of the Emperor Hadrian's reign. The Romans of this period did not practice mummification, so this mummy is an anomaly. In 1585 another mummy was discovered five miles outside Rome near the Via Appia. It too was a girl and was exhibited near the capitol in the Palazzo dei Conservatori. Pope Innocent VIII, afraid that there would be unruly demonstrations, had the mummy buried in a secret location, so it is lost to history.

Because the Grottarossa mummy is unique, a team of scientists investigated it in the 1990s. The mummy was x-rayed and CAT-scanned, which enabled the scientists to determine the girl's age at the time of death. This was confirmed by several different measurements. Her teeth indicated an age of approximately eight years and this was confirmed by the body height and by the body itself. The X rays of the girl's legs showed that she had suffered periods of severe infection or malnutrition. During such times the bones stop developing, and this is shown as a line (Harris line) on X rays. CAT scans of the chest and biopsies suggested that the young girl had suffered a severe infection in both lungs.

In a strict sense the young girl was not mummified but embalmed. Balms, or oils, were used to preserve her body. The surface of the entire body was dark brown, and analysis showed that this was because resin, probably from the juniper tree, had been applied. Pollen grains from myrrh

were also found, so this too may have been used to preserve her body.

When she died her family buried her with an ivory doll and some small amber objects, suggesting a belief in life after death. Because mummification was so unusual for a Roman, and because some aspects of the burial are consistent with Egyptian beliefs about life after death, it was suggested that perhaps the girl died in Egypt and was reburied in Rome. Analysis of the clothes disproved this theory—the cloth was woven in a manner specific to Italy. Perhaps her parents were Romans who believed in the Egyptian religion and who had once lived in Egypt.

One unusual aspect of the mummy is that eyewitness accounts say that when the mummy was first discovered, it had a lifelike appearance, but soon became wrinkled and turned dark brown. This may have been due to rapid dehydration when it was first exposed to the air.

The Grottarossa girl is now in the "caveau" of the new Museum of the Roman World in Rome.

GUANCHE MUMMIES   The inhabitants of Tenerife, the largest of the seven Canary Islands off the northwest coast of Africa, are called Guanches. Descended from Berber tribes of northwest Africa, these people practiced mummification. In some cases natural mummification also occurred on the island.

The mummies were first commented on by the Spaniards of the fifteenth century, who found them in a remarkable state of preservation. Unfortunately most of the well-preserved mummies have been destroyed, and researchers are now trying to piece together details of how the Guanche mummified their dead.

The burials were usually located in caves or other inaccessible places and were often protected from the elements by dry stone walls. In some cases the dryness of the caves naturally preserved the bodies. Sometimes pieces of wood or reed mats were placed on the ground, and the deceased were placed on them. Thus there was no

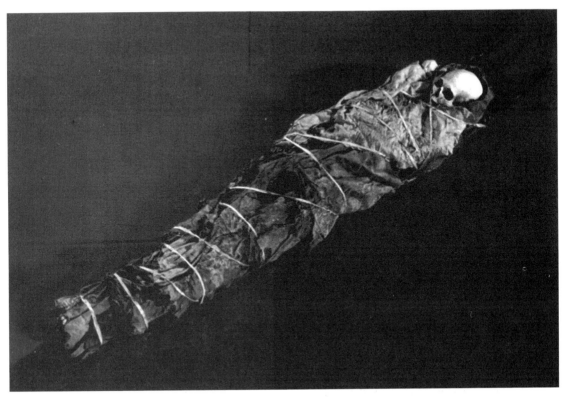

Guanche Mummies A typical Guanche mummy from the Canary Islands. *Photo courtesy Dr. Conrado Rodríguez-Martín.*

contact with soil, so these were not "burials" in the strict sense.

Only upper-class Guanches were artificially mummified. This involved removing the internal organs and, at times, packing the abdomen and thorax with stones, goat skins, solid fats, and occasionally soil. In one case sand was placed beneath the skin to "flesh out" the mummy.

A report of an early discovery appeared in the January 1773 issue of *A Monthly Chronicle or Historical Register.*

FRIDAY JANUARY 8TH

An account of the extraordinary MUMMY brought to England by Capt. Young, Commander of his Majesty's sloop the Weesel, in October, 1772.

Capt. Young, Commander of the Weesel sloop, having touched at Tenerife in his return from the coast of Guinea, had the curiosity to ascend the pike with a guide; whereon, in a cave (the burying-place of the ancient pagan inhabitants) he discovered several bodies sewed up in goats skins, one of which he opened, and discovered a body perfect, fresh, and the features not in the least mutilated; Some were seven feet long, and others five feet three inches. He expressed a great desire to obtain one of those bodies; but the Romish Priest made many objections. Those, however, a little gold removed, and he procured him a female Mummy. The body is perfect in every particular, the bowels are extracted, and the skin appears of a deep tanned copper colour. The hair is long and black, and retains a curl; and the teeth and nails of the toes and the fingers are fresh. According to the tra-

Guanajuato, Mexico, mummies of The mummies of Guanajuato are now housed in a modern museum with festively painted display cases. *Photo courtesy John Mahoney.*

dition of the priest, and the extinction of the inhabitants it cannot be less than 500 years since the decease of this body. Indeed, it may be as probably 1000; for, according to its appearance, it may as well continue ad infinitum, as remain one year in its present condition. It looks like a tanned hide, and consists of bone and skin; the nerves, tendons, veins, and arteries, appear distinctly like strings.

It is deposited in Trinity College, Cambridge.

That mummy is now in the Department of Biological Anthropology at Cambridge University. Although the accounts says the body is a female, it is, in fact, a male.

GUANAJUATO, MEXICO, MUMMIES OF

Guanajuato, a mountain city fifty miles north of Mexico City, has an extremely dry climate that causes natural mummification. For centuries the inhabitants have placed their dead in above-ground crypts, where they dehydrate naturally and are preserved with no special preparation. Because space in the above-ground crypts is in demand, after a period of time, if the body is unclaimed by a relative, it is placed in an underground crypt. There the bodies are propped up against the walls, where they can be seen by the curious. "The Next in Line," a short story by science fiction writer Ray Bradbury, describes these mummies. (See "THE NEXT IN LINE.")

h

HAMMER FILM PRODUCTIONS   A British motion picture company specializing in horror films. They produced a series of mummy movies, beginning with a remake of the 1932 classic, *The Mummy* (1959) and continuing with *The Curse of the Mummy's Tomb* (1964) and *The Mummy's Shroud* (1967), and finally *Blood from the Mummy's Tomb* (1971).

HAMRICK, GRAHAM H.   Hamrick was a late-nineteenth-century amateur embalmer who claimed he had discovered, from a careful reading of the Bible, how the ancient Egyptians mummified their dead. As a farmer he first tried his methods on animals but later mummified the remains of two inmates of the Barbour County, West Virginia, insane asylum when they died. Hamrick took the results of his work to the Smithsonian Museum in Washington but refused to reveal his process. Hamrick died without ever telling his method, but the bodies can be seen today, as they are on display at the Barbour County Historical Museum in Philippi, West Virginia.

HAPI   One of the four sons of the Egyptian god Horus. Hapi was associated with the north and protected mummies' internal organs. He is represented as a man with the head of a cenocephalic (dog-headed) ape. Often magical spells were inscribed on the four jars that held a mummy's internal organs (see CANOPIC JARS). On the jar whose lid was shaped like a Hapi's head, a typical spell reads:

Words spoken by Hapi:
I am Hapi, thy son Osiris.
I have come. I exist to
protect thee. I bind for thee
thy head and limbs.
I smite for thee thy enemies
beneath thee. I give to thee thy
head, forever.

HARVEY, WILLIAM (1578–1657)   English physician who discovered the circulation of the blood and published his findings in 1628. This discovery made arterial embalming possible. Harvey was especially interested in preparing anatomical specimens, and it is said that he autopsied and preserved the cadavers of his own father and sister.

HATSHEPSUT, POSSIBLE MUMMY OF
The mummy of Queen Hatshepsut, the only Egyptian queen ever to rule as king, may have recently been rediscovered.

In 1989 researcher Dr. Donald Ryan, working in the Valley of the Kings, reopened Tomb 60 and encountered the mummy in question. Tomb 60 was first uncovered in 1903 by Howard Carter, who was later to become famous as the discoverer of Tutankhamen's tomb. Carter noted that the uninscribed tomb had been plundered but contained the bodies of two women, one in a decorated coffin. The inscription on the coffin indicated that the occupant was Sitre, royal nurse to Queen Hatshepsut. The second mummy lay on the floor, its left arm bent at the elbow, the clenched hand over the center of the chest, and the extended right arm rested against the side.

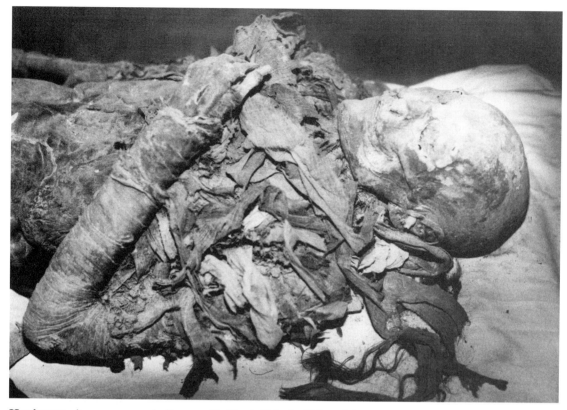

Hatshepsut A mummy recently discovered in Tomb 60 in the Valley of the Kings may be Queen Hatshepsut. *Photo courtesy Dr. Donald Ryan.*

This is a typical pose for mummies of royal women of the era of Hatshepsut and has given rise to the suggestion that this may be the missing mummy of the queen. It is known that Hatshepsut's original tomb was robbed in antiquity, and it is possible that her damaged mummy was reburied in her nurse's tomb.

The hypothesis that the mummy in Tomb 60 is Queen Hatshepsut has yet to be tested, but this could happen. The mummy of her father, Tuthmosis I, and her half brother, Tuthmosis II, are in the Egyptian Museum in Cairo, so DNA testing on the three mummies may some day establish if there is a relationship.

HAXEY HOOD GAME This ceremony, still practiced at Haxey, Humberside, an English vil-

lage, has origins going back to the ritual bog burials of antiquity.

The Hood Game is associated with the medieval legend of the Lady de Mowbray, whose hood blew away as she was riding to church on Christmas day. Twelve gallant men rushed to retrieve the hood, and the thankful Lady de Mowbray left a parcel of land—Hoodland—as an endowment, so its rent could pay for a hood to be used in an annual contest between twelve villagers dressed in scarlet tunics and capes.

The current Hood Game takes place on 6 January, "Old Christmas Day," and involves twelve boggans (bog people) whose leader is King Boggan. The week before the game, the participants go through the town collecting money for the ceremony. On the day of the contest, a character called the Fool delivers a speech in the center of town. He holds a stick with a bran-filled stocking tethered to it by a leather strap. Parts of his clothing are set on fire in the phase called "smoking the fool" that is the signal for him to deliver his final, cryptic speech:

Hoose agen hoose, toone agen toone.
If thou meets a man knock him down,
but don't hurt him.

King Boggan brandishes a wand made of thirteen sticks of "celery" willow bound together by a cord wrapped thirteen times. In the field where Lady de Mowbray lost her hood, he throws twelve false hoods into the air. If a villager catches one and can get it to one of the village inns before being tackled by a boggan, he is entitled to free drinks. But this is just the prelude to the main event, which involves the Sway Hood, a leather-bound piece of rope twenty-five inches long and nine inches in circumference that is treated much like a rugby ball. Teams comprised of patrons of the different taverns form a giant scrum—the Sway—and try to capture the hood for their pub. The pushing and shoving usually lasts for several hours with great honor going to the pub that becomes the custodian of the hood for the year. In 1985 the hood was stolen during the game and has not yet resurfaced.

There are obvious parallels between the Haxey Hood Game and the bog burials of Europe. The game takes place on the border of the bogs that have produced the greatest number of mummies, who were naturally preserved by the bogs after being ritually killed. The game takes place in midwinter, the traditional time of sacrifice, so perhaps when the fool is being "smoked," he is being sacrificed. The sticks that King Boggan holds may be a remnant of the sticks frequently found alongside bog mummies. The fact that the game centers around a leather hood may be the most significant connection to the ancient bog burials. Several bog mummies were found with hoods tied to their heads; indeed, a hood was the only article of clothing that Tollund Man was wearing. (See TOLLUND MAN.)

HEANEY, SEAMUS   Contemporary Irish poet who feels a close kinship to the bog mummies and whose poetry describes his adoptive family.

Heaney traces his attachment to bogs and bog mummies to a single childhood incident. "I believe my betrothal happened one summer evening thirty years ago, when another boy and myself stripped to the white country skin and bathed in a moss-hole, treading the liver-thick mud, unsettling a smoky muck off the bottom and coming out smeared and weedy and darkened. We dressed again and went home in our wet clothes, smelling of the ground and standing pool, somehow initiated."

The closeness to the bog mummies eventually grew to the point that Heaney suspected he was actually related to them, with Tollund Man (see TOLLUND MAN) his uncle. Writing of this mummy, whose capped head with a noose around its neck had captured the imagination of the public, Heaney described Tollund Man as the bridegroom of the Bog Queen.

She tightened her torc on him
And opened her fen,
Those dark juices working
Him to a saint's kept body.

Heaney's poetic descriptions of his centuries dead family are not always flattering. Of Grauballe Man he says:

The grain of his wrists
is like bog oak,
the ball of his heel
like a basalt egg.
His instep has shrunk
cold as a swan's foot
or a wet swamp root.

HEART   The heart was the only internal organ left in the body by Egyptian embalmers at the time of mummification. This may have been because the Egyptians believed that the heart managed the body—it is your heart that beats quickly when you are excited, not your brain. The word for heart, pronounced "haty," also meant "foremost one," and biblical phrases such as "Pharaoh's heart was hardened" attest to the crucial role attributed to the organ by the ancients. It was probably left in the body so the deceased would have the ability to think when he or she arrived in the next world; thus the spells required for full activity could be spoken.

HERODOTUS OF HALICARNASSUS (c. 484–430 B.C.)

Greek historian who visited Egypt around 450 B.C. and left the earliest written description of the mummification process. The travels of Herodotus are divided into nine books, the second of which is devoted to Egypt. It is doubtful that Herodotus ever saw a mummification, so his account must be viewed as secondhand. Much of what he says, however, has been confirmed by modern research.

Herodotus tells us there were three different prices for three different levels of mummification. Of the highest quality mummification, Herodotus mentions that the brain was extracted through the nostrils with an iron hook; what was left inside was dissolved with drugs. He notes that the flank was slit open with an obsidian blade and the internal organs removed. The body cavity, after having been washed out with palm wine and spices, was filled with aromatic spices except frankincense (see FRANKINCENSE). The incision was sewn up and the body placed in natron (see NATRON) for seventy days. Finally the embalmers washed the body, wrapped it in linen, and returned it to the family of the deceased.

Herodotus's descriptions of the lower priced techniques are more brief. In the medium quality mummification, the internal organs were not surgically removed; rather, cedar oil was injected into the body via the anus, which was plugged to prevent the oil from running out. Then the body was placed in natron for seventy days, the plug was removed so that the oil and dissolved organs could run out, and the body was wrapped. In the least expensive method, even less attention was given to the body, and no expensive cedar oil was used. After seventy days it was wrapped and returned to the relatives.

HERTZOG, CHRISTIAN European apothecary who wrote one of the earliest accounts (1718) of a mummy unwrapping. The mummy was headless, but its thirty-five layers of bandages contained seventy-four amulets.

HETEPHERES Queen of Egypt during the Fourth Dynasty and mother of Cheops, builder of the Great Pyramid of Giza. The mummy of Queen Hetepheres is important to the history of mummification but also presents an unsolved mystery.

Her sealed burial chamber near the Great Pyramid was discovered in 1925 by the Harvard–Boston Museum Expedition. Inside the chamber was the queen's alabaster canopic chest (see CANOPIC CHEST) that contained four packets of her internal organs, which had been removed at the time of mummification. The packets lay in a yellow liquid that chemical analysis revealed to be a 3 percent solution of natron. This discovery led some researchers to conclude that when mummified the entire body of the deceased was immersed in a solution of natron, rather than in dry natron. This is probably incorrect, as it would have been a far more time-consuming and complicated process than immersion in dry natron. Also Herodotus (see HERODOTUS OF HALICARNASSUS) clearly states that the body cavities were packed with spices before the corpse was placed in natron. This would not have been practical if the natron were in solution.

The mystery connected with Queen Hetepheres's mummy is that when discovered, her tomb, canopic chest, and sarcophagus were sealed, but when the sarcophagus was opened, it was empty. This led Dr. George Reisner, the tomb's excavator, to speculate that this was a

Higham, George *The Negative Confession in the Temple of Maat* is a contemporary work inspired by the mummified fetuses found in Tutankhamen's tomb.

reburial and that Hetepheres's original tomb had been plundered and her body destroyed. Reisner went on to suggest that the vizier, afraid of telling the pharaoh that his mother's body was gone, told Cheops that the robbers had been interrupted in the act of desecrating the tomb and that the queen's mummy was intact in its sarcophagus. The king, believing that his mother's body was still in the sarcophagus, reburied it, along with the canopic chest, in the chamber near his pyramid for protection, where it remained for 5,000 years.

HIGHAM, GEORGE A   contemporary sculptor, who also is a forensic radiologist for the New York City Morgue. Higham's sculptures of mummies frequently have an Egyptian theme. One recent piece, *The Negative Confession in the Temple of Maat,* was inspired by the recently rediscovered fetuses originally found in Tutankhamen's tomb.

HOLMES, THOMAS H. (FL. 19TH CENTURY) The father of American embalming. During the Civil War he served with the American Medical Corps even though he had been expelled from New York University Medical School for leaving cadavers in inappropriate places. He made a fortune during the war embalming the bodies of dead officers so they could be sent home. Holmes charged $100 for each cadaver and is said to have embalmed more than 4,000 soldiers in his four years of service. He claimed that his technique—injecting zinc chloride with an arsenic base—would preserve the bodies "forever, or at least as long as stone."

Holmes provided a tremendous boost to the practice of embalming when in May of 1861, he prepared the body of the war hero Colonel Ellsworth, which was later displayed at the White House, New York's City Hall, and the State Capitol in Albany. The body was viewed by thousands who wondered at its lifelike appearance. Holmes requested that when he died he not be embalmed.

HUNTER, DR. WILLIAM (1718–1783)   A

Scottish anatomist who is generally considered the father of modern embalming techniques. Before Hunter, many who practiced embalming kept their techniques secret; Hunter was one of the few to make his method public.

Hunter was also one of the first to successfully inject chemicals into the arteries to preserve human bodies. Via the femoral artery he injected oil of turpentine, oil of lavender, oil of rosemary, and vermilion. He permitted the chemicals to diffuse throughout the tissues for several hours, then removed all the internal organs. The viscera were soaked in the same chemicals he had injected into the femoral artery, then were replaced in the body cavities and covered with camphor, resin, and dehydrating salts. Powdered camphor, resin, and salts were packed in the mouth, nose, ears, etc., then the body was placed on a bed of plaster of paris to absorb the fluids.

There are remarkable parallels between Hunter's techniques and those of the ancient Egyptian embalmers. Both eviscerated, and in the Late Period of Egyptian history (after the Twenty-first Dynasty), the organs were returned to the abdominal cavity, just as in Hunter's method. While the Egyptians placed the body on a bed of natron (see NATRON) for dehydration, Hunter merely substituted plaster of paris.

William's brother, John, a leading physician, used this technique to embalm the wife of the prominent Englishman Martin van Butchel. Van Butchel was so impressed with the result that he had his wife dressed in her finest gown and placed in a glass case, where she was displayed in the parlor. When van Butchel remarried, his second wife objected to the presence of another woman and the first Mrs. van Butchel was donated to the Royal College of Surgeons in London, where she remains today.

IBIS, MUMMIES OF See ANIMAL NE-CROPOLIS AT SAQQARA and ARCHIVE OF HOR.

ICEMAN, THE Highly publicized mummy found on September 19, 1991 in the European Alps on the border between Austria and Italy. At first it was believed to be the body of a modern mountain climber and thus for several days was mishandled, which damaged the left hip and thigh. The man actually died about 3300 B.C. during the Late Stone Age and is the best preserved European body of antiquity. Six days after the recovery there was a heavy snowfall that would have covered him again, perhaps forever.

At the time of death, which was probably during early winter, the body rapidly dehydrated and was subsequently covered by snow and then preserved in ice when it froze. As a result

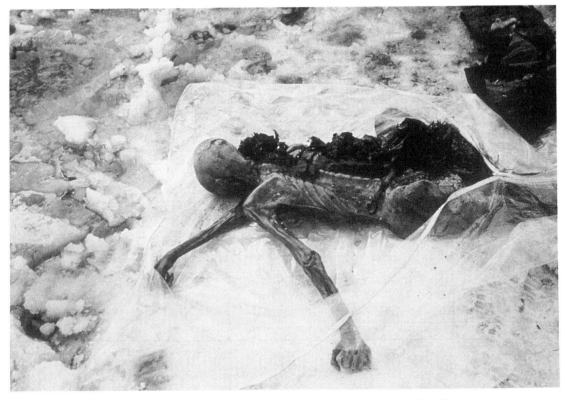

The Iceman The Iceman as first found, frozen in a glacier. *Photo courtesy Dr. Konrad Spindler.*

of the natural freeze-drying process, the iceman weighed approximately twenty-eight pounds at the time of his discovery.

Studies of the body indicate that the man was five feet two inches tall and between twenty-five and forty-five years old when he died. He carried a copper axe with a wooden handle, a quiver of fourteen arrows, and a small flint knife with a wood handle. In a pouch he carried a flint scraper, a flint, and a tinder fire lighter. In spite of these tools, he seems too unprepared to have been hunting. Twelve of his arrows were unfinished, and he carried an incomplete bow made of yew wood. He also had fragments of stag antlers that he may have intended to fashion into arrowheads. X rays of his body show that he had fractured ribs. Why was this injured man with incomplete hunting equipment on a high mountain in winter? One theory is that rather than hunting, he may have been fleeing pursuers.

The Iceman had numerous tattoos made up of simple lines and crosses on various parts of his body. One series of four short lines was at the base of his spine, where he could not have seen them, and where they would rarely have been seen by others. There were three lines on his right ankle and seven on his right calf. X rays revealed that the tattoos were in places where he suffered from arthritis, so the tattoos may have been applied for therapeutic reasons such as pain relief.

The clothes of The Iceman are the only complete garments that we have from the European Neolithic period. He had goatskin leggings held up with a belt. His feet were covered with bearskin shoes, laced together with threads made of animal sinews and stuffed with grass for insulation. Close to his body he wore a goatskin cape and over this he had an outer cape made of plaited grass. Repairs to these garments were made with animal-hair threads.

In 1994 DNA samples from The Iceman's muscle and bone were analyzed by laboratories in Munich and Oxford. Both laboratories agreed that the mitochondrial DNA—genetic material passed down on the maternal side—showed The

Iceman to be closely related to modern central and northern Europeans, which is not surprising since Stone Age people did not travel widely. Because of the mummy's importance, a normal autopsy will probably never be performed, and only relatively nondestructive tests will be conducted. The Iceman remains, still frozen, in a laboratory in Innsbruck, Austria.

INDIVIDUUM Latin for "undivided one." This medieval phrase referred to the bodies of saints that were said to remain intact, miraculously preserved. When in the Middle Ages the demand for relics became so great that the bodies of saints were divided so that many churches could have pieces, it was believed that a portion of a saint represented his or her entirety.

So great was the desire for saintly relics that frequently crypts containing the bodies of saintly persons were secretly opened, and pieces of the saints were hacked off. The monks of Conques in France kidnapped the body of Saint Foy "for the health of the area and for the redemption of its inhabitants."

INDONESIA A group of hundreds of islands stretching across more than 3,000 miles of sea, the Republic of Indonesia includes diverse cultures. More than 85 percent of the people are Muslims, but scattered throughout the islands are Buddhists and Hindus. Indonesia also includes the western half of the island of New Guinea, which is called Irian Jaya. (The eastern part is Papua New Guinea.) In Irian Jaya the local aboriginal population practiced mummification of deceased family members until fairly recently. The purpose of the mummification was usually to keep the deceased relative with the family to minimize the sense of grief.

The basic mummification technique was to place the body in a seated flexed position and place it in a tree in the sun to dehydrate. Sometimes the body was smoked to aid the process. After the body was dry, it was decorated with paint and shells.

Indonesia Mummy from Irian Jaya (western New Guinea). *Photo courtesy Dr. Michael Gunn.*

INTERNATIONAL SOCIETY FOR PLASTINATION

This is a multidisciplinary organization dedicated to the promotion and advancement of plastination. Plastination is the process by which specimens are impregnated with polymers and resins to preserve them for teaching and research purposes in the fields of medicine, dentistry, veterinary, and other health-related sciences. Membership consists of individuals in the fields of anatomy, biology, pathology, radiology, botany, and related sciences.

The aims of the society are:

1. to provide for and maintain an international association for individuals who perform plastination techniques or are interested in plastination preservation methods.
2. to define plastination as a specialty area of professional activity, to encourage other institutions to adopt plastination preservation methods, and to invite individuals to learn and practice plastination as a career in the sciences.
3. to regularly publish the *Journal of the International Society for Plastination.*
4. to maintain a record of member institutions and individuals performing or interested in plastination.

The society holds a biannual conference on plastination and publishes the *Journal of the International Society for Plastination.* Inquiries can be sent to

Ronald Wade, Treasurer
International Society for Plastination
c/o Bresler Research Building, Room B-024
655 West Baltimore Street
Baltimore, MD 21201-1559

INVADERS OF THE MUMMY'S TOMB
A solar-powered handheld video-game produced by Bandai Electronics Company in the 1980s. The goal of the game is to enter the pyramid and steal the mummy's treasure. To enter the tomb the explorer must avoid scorpions and snakes. Once inside the burial chamber, he or she is confronted with an angry mummy attempting to protect the treasure. The player controls the explorer's movement by pushing "left" and "right" buttons.

IRAS, A MYSTERY A novel by H.D. Everett, *Iras, A Mystery* (1896) is an early example of the mummy as an object of love rather than a fearsome creature.

The mummy in question is Iras, an ancient Egyptian beauty who was placed in suspended animation by a wicked priest when she refused to marry him. It is predicted that she will have a lover "not of this land or generation." The priest can claim Iras only if he defeats her future lover.

The future lover is interested in rediscovering the chemical used in ancient mummification, and he smuggles the mummy of Iras into England in a crate of sponges. In her coffin, Levenham, the scientist/future lover, finds a tablet that reveals Iras's state. She awakens and, despite their age difference (2,000 years), they fall in love.

There are some humorous episodes in which Levenham explains Iras's presence to his landlady and finds suitable Victorian clothes for his bride-to-be. The couple take the train to Scotland, where they are married, but the ancient priest, in spirit form, follows them and attempts to kill Iras by removing beads from her magical life-giving necklace. As beads are destroyed Iras fades away until only Levenham can see her. Every trace of her begins to evaporate, including her signature in the marriage register. In the end Levenham finds the clothes Iras wore, intact in their chest, as if she had never existed.

ISKANDER, NASRI Dr. Nasri Iskander, General Director for Conservation of the Supreme Council of Antiquities, is responsible for the mummies in the Egyptian Museum, Cairo. In 1994 he supervised the refurbishing of the Royal Mummies Room in the Egyptian Museum and built the new cases in which the mummies are displayed.

In 1974 Dr. Iskander restored the mummy of Queen Henettowy of the Twenty-first Dynasty. The skin beneath her face had been packed by the ancient embalmers to give it a lifelike appearance, but the packing material absorbed moisture from the atmosphere, expanded, and burst the skin. Dr. Iskander removed the cheeselike packing and reattached the skin to the skull. Material inside Queen Henettowy's body had also expanded, and this too was removed. This is the only mummy in the Egyptian Museum's collection to have been restored.

I WAS A TEENAGE MUMMY Produced by Ghost Limb Films (1992), this black-and-white low-budget production features Raymond, a demented high school student who has waited centuries to be reunited with Isis, another student who lived in ancient Egypt. The ancient duo take bloody revenge on a gang of toughs who tormented them. Not for those with either a weak stomach or a sense of taste.

JACKAL   In ancient Egyptian religion and mythology, the jackal was connected with death and mummification. The association was made because of the jackal's unique digestive system. Jackals cannot easily digest protein, so they prowl cemeteries in search of already decayed meat. Thus, to the Egyptians, the jackal was connected with cemeteries and mummies.

Several Egyptian gods are depicted as jackals, but they have distinct attributes. Anubis was the god of mummification and presided over the procedure. Duamutef, one of the four sons of Horus, protected the internal organs of the mummy until it resurrected. Wepwaat, whose name means "Opener of the way," led the deceased into the next world.

JACOB, CALLED "ISRAEL," MUMMY OF
One of the only two characters in the Old Testament said to have been mummified was the patriarch Jacob.

Jacob's youngest and favorite son, Joseph, was sold to Egyptian slave traders by his jealous brothers. Because of his intelligence and ability to interpret the pharaoh's prophetic dreams, Joseph was made vizier of Egypt and was responsible for planning for the famine he foresaw. By stockpiling grain during Egypt's seven prosperous years, Joseph was able to prevent famine during the seven lean years that followed. Because he heard that Egypt had grain, Jacob sent Joseph's brothers from Canaan to Egypt to trade for grain. Joseph forgave his brothers their sins, and the entire family settled in Egypt under his protection. Thus, when Jacob, who was called Israel, died at a venerable age, he was mummified according to the Egyptian custom. The Bible states, "And Joseph commanded his servants the physicians to embalm his father. And the physicians embalmed Israel. And forty days were fulfilled for him, for so are fulfilled the days of those who are embalmed. And the Egyptians mourned for him for seventy days." (Genesis 50:1–3)

The biblical account of mummification is important because it explains a disparity between the account of Herodotus and other sources concerning the period of embalming. Herodotus says that the body remained in natron for seventy days, but Egyptian sources indicate a thirty-five-day period. The shorter period is supported by modern researchers. The reference of Jacob's mummification explains the confusion. The mourning period was seventy days, not the embalming period.

Jacob's son, Joseph, is the only other Old Testament character said to have been mummified, but the Bible gives no details of the procedure.

JADE SUITS   During the Han Dynasty (206 B.C.–A.D. 220) the Chinese emperors and members of their families were buried in suits made of jade plaques, which were intended to preserve their bodies.

Ancient Chinese records mention these suits and indicate that only the emperor could grant permission for burial in one. The eunuch Zhao Zhong buried his father in a jade suit without the emperor's knowledge. Upon hearing of the secret burial, officials opened the tomb, removed the body of Zhao's father, and imprisoned the entire family.

Some emperors sent jade suits to foreign rulers as imperial gifts. Presents of these suits were made to the kings of Fuyu (modern northeast China) and to others, but although these suits are mentioned in numerous ancient accounts, no complete suit was found until the 1950s. One reason is that the plaques comprising the suits were drilled at the four corners and sewn together with gold thread—a great temptation for tomb robbers. Only three years after the Han Dynasty collapsed, the Emperor Wen of Wei noted in A.D. 223 that every royal Han tomb had been looted, with the robbers burning the jade suits to extract the gold more easily. Wen decreed that no more suits were to be produced, and all indications are that his order was followed.

In 1954 archaeologists excavating a looted Han tomb in Suining found 229 jade plaques but

Japanese Mummies The priest Tetsumonkai assisted his own mummification by altering his diet for the last three years of his life.

did not realize that they came from a suit. In 1968 excavators uncovered two unplundered tombs of the Han Dynasty, one of Prince Liu Sheng and the other of his consort, Dou Wan. Their bodies had decayed, and the suits had collapsed upon them. The excavators painstakingly recorded the position of each plaque and removed the suits on wire mesh passed beneath the plaques. Liu Sheng's suit was composed of 2,498 plaques that had been held together with more than two pounds of gold thread. The suits were sewn in sections—helmet, mask, tunic, pants, armlets, gloves, and boots. Care had been taken to match the shades of the jade in the different sections. The tunic was blue-green, while the pants were yellow-gray.

Jade was believed to have spiritual properties that would preserve the body and assure a successful afterlife. Jade suits may have been viewed as the ultimate armor for the next world.

JAPANESE MUMMIES The practice of mummification in Japan has been closely tied to Buddhist principles, so almost all Japanese mummies are of priests.

In a history of Japanese Buddhism called the *Genko-shakusho* it is recorded that when the monk Zoga died in A.D. 1003 at the age of eighty-seven, his body was placed in a large barrel and buried for three years, then exhumed. The same work also mentions that the priest Rinken was mummified in A.D. 1150 and placed in a shrine at Mount Koya. Thus as early as the twelfth century the mummies of holy men were objects of veneration in Japan.

The priests who were mummified believed in the Maitreya-bodhisattva—a Buddha who would appear on earth exactly 5,670,000,000 years after the first Buddha achieved enlightenment. When the Maitreya comes, he will save all intelligent creatures from suffering and illusion, and the mummified priests wished to assist him in this task. Thus their bodies had to be preserved so they would be on earth when the Maitreya appeared. To achieve this goal the priests prepared

for mummification while alive, and the process was completed by their fellow monks after death.

Toward the end of their lives, the priests began a process of self-mummification. They greatly reduced their food intake and abstained completely from eating the five grains (rice, barley, corn, millet, and beans). One priest, Tetsumonkai, abstained from eating cereals for three years prior to his death in 1829. They believed that this ascetic diet made the body resistant to decomposition. This self-mummification was called *nyujo*—"entering into Heaven." A mummified priest was called "a Buddha of the body." After death, the fellow priests concluded the process by gathering around the holy man's corpse with great candles to dry it out. Sometimes a corpse was smoked, giving it a black coating.

The only nonpriestly mummies in Japan are of the powerful Fujiwara family. This clan created a great empire in a remote region of northeastern Japan that rivaled the capital. During the twelfth century, four family leaders—grandfather, father, son, and grandson—were mummified and are preserved in the Golden Hall of Chuson-ji Temple in Hiraizumi City, which is in the Iwate prefecture of Japan. It is difficult to determine what mummification procedures were performed on these four mummies, as the bodies have been damaged and the internal organs eaten by rats.

JESUS, EMBALMING OF Although the early church fathers spoke against mummification, it is clear from the New Testament that Jesus' body was embalmed according to Jewish tradition. We are told that Nicodemus brought a large quantity of myrrh to use in the preparation of the body. "And there came also Nicodemus, which at first came to Jesus by night, and brought a mixture of myrrh and aloes, about a hundred pound weight. Then they took the body of Jesus, and wound it in linen clothes with the spices, as the manner of the Jews is to bury." (John XXIX: 39–40)

The use of linen and spices in preparing the bodies of the dead was not an attempt to preserve

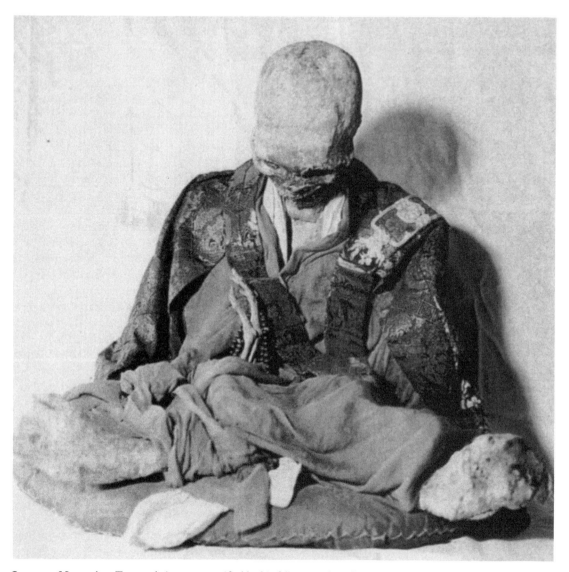

Japanese Mummies Tetsuryukai was mummified by his fellow monks, who removed his internal organs, packed the abdominal cavity, and closed the incision with thread. *Photos courtesy Eve Cockburn.*

the deceased for an afterlife, as Jews do not believe in life after death. Rather, the spices may have been used for ritual or sanitary purposes.

JEWEL OF THE SEVEN STARS, THE Written by Bram Stoker (1847–1912), the author of *Dracula,* this is the first story to connect reanima-

tion of an ancient Egyptian queen with a living contemporary heroine. Published in 1906, *The Jewel of the Seven Stars* provided the inspiration for later novels and films.

In the story a queen's tomb is discovered in Egypt, and its contents are transported to England. Although the queen had made plans to resurrect, her *ka*, or soul, in the meantime dwells in the body of the Egyptologist/adventurer's beautiful daughter. The key to the queen's reanimation is the jewel of the seven stars—a ruby containing seven seven-pointed stars.

The novel itself was resurrected on the screen in the 1980s under the name *The Awakening*, which starred Charlton Heston. The poorly scripted film lasted one week in the theaters then became part of mummy history.

JOHANN PHILIPP OF HOHENSAX, MUMMY OF (1550–1596)

Johann Philipp of Hohensax is well known in the history of Switzerland, but modern investigations have raised numerous questions about his death and mummification.

The Hohensax family was prominent in eastern Switzerland during the Middle Ages. According to the official reports, on May 4, 1596 Johann quarreled with his nephew in a public drinking place and was stabbed in the head and chest with a hunting knife. He was brought to his castle, where three days later he wrote his report of the incident for the police, and on May 12, he died and was buried in the family vault at Sennwald. In 1830 a fire damaged the crypt and workmen found the baron's body in a remarkable state of preservation. When news reached the neighboring Catholic town of Vorarlberg, the inhabitants assumed that the baron was a saint and at night stole the body as an object of veneration. Only when it had been explained that the baron was a Protestant, and thus could not be a Catholic saint, was the body returned.

In 1979 the body was examined by Dr. B. Kaufmann of the Natural History Museum in Basel. It was then that several questions emerged. The preservation was excellent with the skin dark and leathery, the face virtually intact. During the examination an abdominal incision was made, and it was established that all the internal organs were present. On the top of the head were two deep gashes that were so extensive they could not have been caused merely by a knife, as was re-

ported. An X ray of the skull showed fractures so severe that it would have been impossible for Johann Philipp to write his own account of his fight with his nephew. Further, there was no evidence of knife wounds to the chest as officially reported. Either the official report is wrong or the body in the family crypt at Sennwald is not that of Johann Philipp of Hohensax.

The other question concerned the method of mummification. The internal organs had not been removed, and there was no evidence of salts or spices on the skin. The answer may have to do with the indentation and bulges found on the mummy's neck. It had been a practice to hang a body in a windy dry place—frequently a church tower—to dehydrate it quickly and thus preserve it. This may have been how Johann Philipp of Hohensax was mummified.

JONES, JOHN PAUL, MUMMY OF (1747–1792)

After a highly successful career in the Revolutionary War and the United States Navy, Admiral John Paul Jones accepted an offer in 1788 from Catherine the Great to join the Russian navy. After moderate success he retired (1790) and went to Paris, where he died on July 18, 1792. Because he was an American and not a French hero, his grave in Paris was untended and soon forgotten. The location of John Paul Jones's grave was unknown for more than a century, before it was discovered in 1906 by General Horace Porter, U.S. ambassador to France. Porter searched for five years before finding the body in an unmarked grave in a cemetery in Paris. "The body was marvelously well preserved, all the flesh remaining intact but slightly shrunken and of a grayish-brown or tan color . . . The face presented a natural appearance. . . ."

An autopsy was performed at the Paris École de Médecine. When an opening in the back was made to examine the thoracic cavity, a quantity of alcohol ran out. John Paul Jones had been mummified in whiskey. The body was returned to the United States, and in 1913 it was buried in the U.S. Naval Academy Chapel.

Jones, John Paul American naval hero John Paul Jones was mummified in whiskey. *Photo courtesy Horace P. Mende and U.S. Naval Historical Center.*

JOSEPH, MUMMY OF Along with his father, Jacob, Joseph is the only person in the Old Testament said to have been mummified.

> "So Joseph died being a hundred and ten years old; and they embalmed him, as he was put in a coffin in Egypt." (Genesis 50:26)

Orthodox Jews generally oppose any kind of mutilation of the body, including autopsies, so the mummification of Joseph and Jacob is most unusual. There is no firm belief in life after death in the Jewish religion, so mummification was not considered necessary. The mummification of the two patriarchs may have been the result of their having lived in Egypt for so long, or perhaps they were mummified so their preserved bodies could be taken back to Israel.

JUANITA, THE ICELADY Discovered at 20,700 feet on a Peruvian mountain, Juanita, as researchers have named her, may be the most important mummy of all time. Frozen by the snows on Mount Ampata, she is the only continuously frozen mummy in scientific hands. Even Iceman (see ICEMAN), discovered in the Alps in 1991, thawed out considerably before being refrozen by scientists.

Approximately 500 years ago, the young Inca woman was brought to the top of the snow-clad Andean mountain as a sacrifice to the sun god. The Incas frequently made such sacrifices of young boys and girls, drugging them, wrapping them in bundles of textiles, enclosing statuettes of gold, silver, and bronze, and leaving them to freeze to death.

Juanita was discovered in September 1995 by Dr. Johan Reinhard, an American anthropologist and mountain climber. She was bundled and completely frozen when discovered. Reinhard carried the mummy down from the mountain on his back as his climbing companion, Miguel Zarate, cut steps in the ice for the descent. Once at the bottom, a thirteen-hour trip by mule brought the mummy to the village of Cabanaconde, where a bus took it and the mountaineers to Arequipa on the coast of Peru. There the mummy was placed in a freezer borrowed from a local appliance store.

An international team of researchers, headed by Dr. Sonia Gullen, assembled at Santa Maria Catholic University to study the mummy. Working with hair dryers and soldering irons, they carefully thawed the knot that held the bundles of cloth around Juanita's body and the fabric slipped off to reveal a remarkably well-preserved mummy.

One of the unique aspects of this mummy is her clothing, which includes some of the finest Incan textiles ever found. The richly patterned garments are woven of the best alpaca wool and include a red and white shawl of the finest weave. A cocoon of textiles was wrapped around the body to complete the garb.

One of the notable features of this mummy is that she is frozen but not freeze-dried. Normally with Andean mummies, a great deal of water leaves the body by sublimation—going directly into the gas state, similar to the way ice cubes shrink in the tray in a freezer. Juanita merely froze, retaining much of the water in her body, and this presents unusual possibilities for research. She is probably the closest thing to a living Inca that modern people will ever see.

The team hopes to be able to extract DNA from the skin and hair and thus learn something about the connection between the current inhabitants of Peru and their ancient Inca ancestors. The frozen blood in the veins and arteries will be tested for antibodies and may reveal what bacteria and viruses the young Inca woman fought off during her brief life. Intestinal contents can be examined to determine her last meal and what parasites plagued the Incan population 500 years ago. The complete research project is expected to take ten years and involve more than a dozen experts in various fields.

Most recently Juanita, still frozen, was flown to the United States where Dr. Elliot Fishman, Director of the Division of Computed Body Tomography at Johns Hopkins Hospital in Baltimore, CAT-scanned her. The images re-

vealed that the young girl had been killed by a powerful blow to the head, making it possible to reconstruct the last days of her life.

The girl, a "capochoca," meaning "chosen for the gods" had been selected as a sacrifice to the mountains. An entourage of priests, using llamas as pack animals, began a procession from the girl's village to the summit of the mountains. The trip took several days, and when the travelers were 16,000 feet up the mountains, they made a base camp of simple stone structures with an enclosure for the llamas. The next day they climbed to 19,000 feet, where another camp was established. The air is extremely thin at this height, and the climb would have been slow and difficult. Perhaps the group was stimulated by chewing coca leaves as they made the journey. When they awoke in the morning at this campsite, Juanita was given her last ritual meal, perhaps including the highly alcoholic drink, chicha. Dizzy from the lack of oxygen and the intoxicating drink, Juanita was led the final 1,200 feet to Ampata's summit. When the group reached the top of the mountain, Juanita, cold and drugged, was probably placed in a seated position before one of the priests struck the death blow that ended her long journey and her short life. The priests dug a grave and placed Juanita in it, along with pots, statues, and offerings to the gods, where she rested undisturbed for 500 years.

K

KARLOFF, BORIS (1887–1969)   Born William Henry Pratt in London, Karloff is most remembered for his portrayal of the monster in Universal Pictures' *Frankenstein* (1931) and as the mummy in *The Mummy* (1932). In *The Mummy* he plays two roles—the wrapped mummy, Im-Ho-Tep, and the mummy's resurrected alter ego, Ardath Bey.

Eight hours of preparation were required to transform Karloff into the mummy. At 11:00 A.M. all his facial skin was covered with cotton strips. When this had dried, it was covered with beauty mud, into which, when hardened, wrinkles were carved to produce an ancient look. Finally Karloff's body was wrapped with acid-died linen. When he stepped on the stage at 7:00 P.M. for shooting, the entire crew gasped.

Karloff did not appear in any of the sequels to *The Mummy*.

KHARIS   The name by which most people remember the mummy in various films. Kharis actually appeared in four films produced by Universal Pictures—*The Mummy's Hand* (1940), *The Mummy's Tomb* (1941), *The Mummy's Ghost* (1944), and *The Mummy's Curse* (1944).

Contrary to popular belief, Boris Karloff never played Kharis. Karloff appeared in only one mummy film, the original version of *The Mummy* in 1932. Here the mummy was Im-Ho-Tep. The actors who played Kharis were Lon Chaney, Jr., and Tom Taylor.

In *Abbott and Costello Meet the Mummy* (1955), the mummy is named Kharis.

KID MILLIONS   This is by no means what one would normally call a "mummy movie," since only the final half-hour of the film actually takes place in Egypt or involves any Egyptian themes for that matter. The plot loosely revolves around the star, Eddie Cantor, inheriting an Egyptian treasure. Various thugs and greedy types try to trick lovable Eddie into either losing or giving up his inheritance. Wackiness ensues.

Being a vaudevillian Eddie winds his way through more than enough dance numbers and

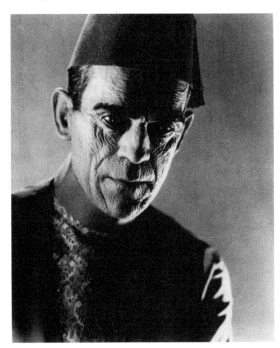

Karloff, Boris Boris Karloff played two roles in *The Mummy*—the wrapped mummy, Im-Ho-Tep, and Ardath Bey, the everyday form of the mummy that pursues the heroine, Helen Grosvenor.

avoids death on many occasions, particularly on the boat ride to Egypt. This part of the film includes an entertaining dance piece by the Nicholas Brothers, as well as some off-the-deep-end black humor. Eddie was a lot funnier on stage, and his true talent is somewhat lost in this film.

Upon arriving in Cairo, Eddie and Louie (a greedy thug claiming to be his long lost brother) watch a magician in the street turn a boy into a dog. Not believing it, Louie insists on the magician doing the same to him. He crawls into the basket only to be dropped into a secret chamber below, knocked unconscious by two turban-wearing criminals, and have his wallet taken. Meanwhile, a prop dog jumps out of the basket and scampers off. Thinking the dog is Louie, Eddie chases it through the streets of Cairo, until it jumps into the lap of a woman being hauled through the street in her carriage. Eddie snatches the dog up, thus saving the woman from the "vicious creature." She instantly falls in love with him and reveals herself to be the daughter of a sheik—the very sheik who is currently in possession of the infamous treasure.

The scene then shifts to the sheik's palace. Here we learn that the sheik has sworn to kill the heir to the treasure, whomever that may be. Eddie is treated like a prince until the sheik learns of his heritage. He is then sentenced to be cooked in a broth. Despite all of his misfortunes, Eddie still finds plenty of time for singing and dancing with the sheik's numerous wives (who look an awful lot like the dancing girls on the boat).

The craziness continues until eventually Eddie, the thugs, and greedy-types are individually sneaking around the dark underground tomb below the palace, trying to steal the treasure. Soon the sheik and his assistant (who looks like Gandhi) arrive, and all are forced to hide in sarcophagi lining the walls of the chamber. (Luckily they were incorrectly buried standing up.) In one of the film's funnier moments, our mummies sing a soulful chorus of "Let My People Go."

Eddie happens to stumble upon the treasure and a convenient biplane, which has just enough gas in it to fly back to New York. This is where the movie gets really bizarre.

After seeing Eddie's biplane sputter across the New York skyline, we learn via a spinning newspaper that he opens a gigantic ice-cream factory—and quite a sight it is! This grand finale is one long musical number, complete with the ever-present dancing girls (now in the form of factory workers donning sparkling jumpsuits and roller skates). The factory comes complete with a four-story-high singing plastic cow, which the gals elegantly milk while roller-skating. To add to the surrealism, this is the only scene in the entire movie that's in color! And what color it is—Easter egg green, Pepto Bismal pink. You name it, they used it.

This final scene does present one particular delight. There's a shot in which the gals are carrying giant chocolate bars up a staircase to a giant mixer. One of the girls is Lucille Ball in a very early appearance.

It's quite a strange film, but the mummy scene is very funny and the ice-cream factory is truly a sight to behold.

KIEVO-PECHERSKAYA LAVRA, MUMMIES OF   A monastery in the Russian city of Kiev; its crypt contains ninety-six naturally mummified bodies of monks.

The monastery was founded in the eleventh century and remained an important religious center until the Russian Revolution of March 1917. It is most famous as the home of the monk Nestor (d. 1115), the author of some of Russia's earliest histories.

When the monks died they were buried in the dry crypt, deep beneath the monastery. Because of soil and atmospheric conditions, the bodies dehydrated quickly, creating the mummies. Most of the mummies date from the twelfth to fourteenth centuries, and aside from the bog mummies, they are the oldest European mummies.

For centuries the monks' bodies were objects of veneration by the faithful, who considered their incorruptibility to be miraculous. Today the monastery is a state-run institution, and the monks are on display in modern glass-topped coffins as part of an official tour of the facility.

KIM IL SUNG, MUMMY OF Leader of North Korea until his death in 1994. Kim's cult included a story of his divine birth, and when he died experts from Moscow's Center for Biological Structures were hired to mummify his body. As of 1997 no Westerners have been permitted to see the body, and details of the mummification process have not been revealed.

L

LEEDS MUMMY, THE The first mummy examined by a team of scientists. In 1828 the Leeds Philosophical Society enlisted the aid of physicians, anatomists, and a chemist to examine a mummy that had been given to the society's museum.

The mummy had come to Leeds by a rather circuitous route. The mummy and its coffin were discovered in 1823 by Giuseppe Passalacqua, an Italian horse dealer who turned to excavating when business was bad. Digging in an area near Queen Hatshepsut's funerary temple at Deir el-Bahri in Thebes, Passalacqua found "two remarkably fine mummies" and sent them to Trieste for sale. Eventually they were sent to London, with one going to the Leeds Philosophical Society.

The Leeds mummy is that of a priest named Natsef-Amun, who lived during the Twenty-first Dynasty. The inscriptions on his coffin mention that he was a Scribe of Accounts of the Cattle of the Estate of Amun and also held the offices of Incense-bearer and Scribe in the Shrine of Montu.

The mummy was stuck to the bottom of its decorated coffin by the bitumen that had been used in its mummification, but when freed and the unwrapping began, a floral pectoral was discovered around the neck, exactly like the one painted on the coffin. Within the bandages and filling the body cavity were spices that when placed in water gave off the odor of myrrh. The brain had been removed through the nostrils. The internal organs had been taken out via an incision in the left side of the abdomen, dehy-drated, wrapped, and the returned to the abdomen. This is all in agreement with the early account of mummification given by the Greek traveler Herodotus. Thus the examination was an early scientific confirmation of the accuracy of Herodotus. (See HERODOTUS OF HALICARNASSUS.)

The pamphlet describing the results of the unwrapping—"An Account of an Egyptian Mummy Presented to the Leeds Philosophical and Literary Society"—contains an appendix giving the first careful chemical analysis of a mummy. The chemist E.S. George reported that although he was aware of the theory that wax was used in mummification, this was more likely adipocere, a fatty substance produced by dead bodies. The pamphlet also presents the first drawings published of the internal organs removed from a mummy.

The Leeds group's contribution to the study of mummification was considerable and exhibited a remarkable degree of sophistication for its time. In 1931 and 1964 Natsef-Amun was x-rayed and given a dental examination. (His teeth were considerably worn down because of diet.) A more recent study by the Manchester Museum's team showed that the Leeds group was correct in identifying adipocere in the mummy. Microscopic examination of tissue taken from the groin by the Manchester group revealed a worm. The priest of Thebes suffered from filariasis, a disease that blocks the lymphatic channels, creating fluid buildup (oedema) and causing tissue swelling, commonly called elephantiasis.

In 1992, using modern forensic techniques, the face of Natsef-Amun was reconstructed from measurements obtained by CAT-scanning his skull. A computer-controlled milling machine carved the polystyrene replica of the mummy's skull that would form the core of the sculpture of Natsef-Amun's head. Twenty-one wooden pegs were inserted into the plastic model to indicate the thickness of muscle tissue at these points. With these as guidelines the sculptor, Richard Neaves, reproduced in clay what Natsef-Amun probably looked like thirty centuries ago.

LEEK, FRANK FILCE (d. 1985)   British dental surgeon who conducted many examinations of Egyptian mummies, specializing in dentition. In 1968, along with Professor R.G. Harrison, he examined the mummy of Tutankhamen.

LELLI, ESCALE (18TH CENTURY)   Commissioned by Cardinal Lambertini to produce a series of wax anatomical sculptures for the Bologna School of Medicine, Lelli produced two life-sized sculptures, one male and one female, which showed extraordinary anatomical detail. As an armature for the wax, he used real skeletons, and more than fifty cadavers were dissected to supply the necessary detail. The sculptures are on display at the Institute of Anatomy of the School of Medicine in Bologna.

LENIN, VLADIMIR ILICH, MUMMY OF (1870–1924)   Russian revolutionary leader and creator of the Soviet Union. When Lenin died his body was preserved and placed on display in the Kremlin in Moscow.

As a young man Lenin was greatly influenced by Karl Marx's *Das Kapital* and converted to Marxism. Lenin spent much of his life in exile in Europe but returned to Russia just after the czarist regime was overthrown by the March 1917 revolution. He subsequently became leader of the new government.

In the 1920s a series of strokes incapacitated Lenin, and when he died on January 21, 1924,

he was considered a national hero. His body was mummified and placed in a specially built crypt in Moscow's Kremlin, so the people could view it forever, giving rise to the popular Russian saying, "Yesterday, today, and tomorrow, Lenin is always with us." The body appears to be well preserved, but many have commented that the face looks waxy. This could be the result of the use of wax in the embalming procedure, but there is also an unsubstantiated rumor that the body was damaged when sewers backed up and flooded the tomb, and that it was replaced with a wax duplicate. The Russian government has never released information about the method used to prepare Lenin's body, but the basics of the technique are known. Every eighteen months Lenin's body is removed from its mausoleum and immersed in a vat of glycerol, potassium acetate, and other preservatives. After the bath the liquid is permitted to drip off, and the body is wrapped in rubber bandages to retain the remaining preservatives. The head and hands are bathed with embalming fluid twice a week and are checked for bacteria.

Moscow's Institute of Biological Sciences, which is responsible for the preservation of Lenin's body, sells their services for $250,000 to those who wish similar treatment. With the change in government in the former Soviet Union, it is possible that Lenin's body will be buried.

LINDOW MAN   One of the best preserved bodies ever discovered in an English bog, Lindow Man was found on August 1, 1984 by commercial peat cutters of Lindow Moss. The first trace was a human foot found in the already cut peat stacks. Archaeologist R.C. Turner was called to the site, and the next day he found a flap of skin protruding from the uncut peat. The police, remembering that the murdered woman for whom Lindow Woman had been mistaken had never been found, agreed to a rapid excavation of the area. (See LINDOW WOMAN.)

A block of peat containing the body was taken to Macclesfield District General Hospital. Excess peat was removed so a smaller mass containing the body could be placed in the mortuary's low-temperature storage room. X-rays revealed that the body was almost certainly ancient. There was no metal at all, and almost all modern bodies have metal fillings in their teeth. Further, the bone had dissolved, and the remaining tissue resembled that of the Danish bog mummies. When it was determined that the body was more than 1,000 years old (A.D. 410–A.D. 560), it was transferred to the British Museum, where a team was assembled for the final examination.

While the body was kept at a low temperature (4 degrees Celsius [39.2°F]), excess peat was removed with wood and plastic implements. When the body was visible, gentle jets of water were used for the final cleaning. An arm emerged first and then the upper torso, followed by the ribs and head. Finally the second arm and the upper torso came into view, but that was all; Lindow Man's lower body was missing. The most striking revelation was a cord around Lindow Man's neck. He had been strangled.

From his remains it was determined that Lindow Man was between the ages of twenty-five and thirty when he died and was approximately five feet, seven inches tall, muscular, and had a beard and moustache. The skin was broken in two places at the top of his head, the result of powerful blows to the skull. Because other bog bodies have been found with cords around their necks, Lindow Man may have been ritually killed by being first struck on the head, causing a loss of consciousness, then strangled.

As with many other bog mummies, the acid in his stomach served to fix the stomach's contents so decomposition was stopped, and it could be determined that his last meal was primarily bread. His intestines also contained eggs of two parasites, the human whipworm and maw worm—parasites found where there are no sewage systems.

"LINDOW MAN" A short story (1990) by Richard Selzer in which Lindow Man has a fatal impact on the life of an American archaeologist. The story first appeared in the collection *Imagine A Woman* and is one of the better recent pieces of mummy fiction.

Frederick Nolan visits Lindow Man on display at the British Museum and envies the mummy's placid countenance. Nolan has recently smothered his wife, who was dying of Lou Gherig's disease, and longs to escape his depression by joining Lindow Man. In the end Nolan journeys to Lindow Moss, stands at the edge of the bog, and calmly steps in. As he slowly sinks deeper and deeper, Nolan has second thoughts.

LINDOW WOMAN One of two important bog finds from Lindow Moss in England, the head of the Lindow Woman was discovered by peat cutters on May 13, 1983. The head was turned over to the Forensic Science Laboratory at Southport, and the coroner determined the remains to be of a European female between the age of thirty and fifty. The left eyeball was still intact, and some hair was still attached to the skull.

At first police believed the skull to be that of a woman murdered by her husband, Peter Reyn-Bardt, in 1960. While in prison for another crime, Reyn-Bardt had told his cell mates that he had killed his wife and buried her body in the garden. When police questioned him, he denied the killing, and a search of the garden revealed nothing. The skull of Lindow Woman was found less than a quarter of a mile from where the couple had lived, and when confronted with the new discovery, Reyn-Bardt confessed to the murder.

Suspicious of the age of the skull, the police had it radiocarbon-dated, which revealed that it was nearly 2,000 years old (A.D. 245, ±80 years) In December 1983 Reyn-Bardt was convicted of his wife's murder, even though her body has never been found.

LITTLE ALICE One of the best-preserved Native American mummies, found in Kentucky in 1875.

The naturally desiccated mummy was discovered in a cave by two local men in an area now known as Mummy Valley. The limestone tablet they placed in the cave where the body was found reads:

Sir I have found one of the Great wonder of
the World in this cave Whitch is a muma "Can All
 Seed hear after" found March the 8 1875
T.T. lee J l lee "an Wd Cutliff" discuvers

No recording of the original body position or accompanying artifacts was made, so all that is known comes from a newspaper article of the time that states that the body was lying on a ledge protruding from a wall of the cave with ashes and charred sticks in front of it. There was a bowl, pipe, arrow points, and several pairs of moccasins.

The body was bought by a man named Morrison who described it as, "The little girl turned to stone, the most interesting and wonderful of all cave phenomena" and named it Little Alice. Little Alice was displayed commercially for more than a century in tourist caves and at fairs. In 1958 the mummy was scientifically examined for the first time by a team of scientists at the University of Kentucky. It was discovered that Little Alice had a phallus and was actually a boy who was between nine and ten years old at the time of death. Renamed Little Al, the body was radiocarbon-dated, and was found to date back only to the beginning of the nineteenth century. Little Al was probably a member of the Woodland Indians, who occupied the cave during that time.

LIVING MUMMY, THE   This 1910 novel by Ambrose Pratt attests to the public's fascination with mummies even before the discovery of Tutankhamen's Tomb some twelve years later. Set in Egypt and London, the novel reveals more about the social and racist views of the time than about mummies.

The tale begins, as so many mummy stories do, with an earnest Egyptologist, Dr. Pinsett, who in this case is the narrator of the story. While working on his manuscript in Egypt, Pinsett is interrupted by a noted Egyptologist and his bright and beautiful daughter who arrive at the doctor's camp to ask for help. The world-renowned and wealthy Egyptologist Sir Robert Ottley has found several papyrus scrolls that reveal the location of the tomb and treasure of Ptahmes, High Priest of Amen in the Eighteenth Dynasty. Ottley has just discovered the tomb and needs Pinsett's "Arabs" to help raise and open the sarcophagus of Ptahmes.

The mummy is not found and in a scuffle Ottley is wounded when the "Arabs" steal all the treasure found in the sarcophagus. Miss Ottley seeks help, and Pinsett rushes to help the pair. The story unfolds in the rather quaint dialogue popular at the turn of the century, but many of the exchanges are both racist and chauvinistic, and some of the Egyptological references fictional.

When Pinsett arrives at the Ottley camp, there are problems. Ottley is near death from a bullet in his shoulder, which Pinsett removes with his pocket amputation knife, and the "curse of Ptahmes" has been activated, as is demonstrated when the mummy appears in the tomb as a ghost. The physical mummy has not yet been found, and the ghost of Ptahmes is scaring everyone away.

It seems that for political reasons, Ptahmes, the high priest of Amen, committed suicide in the Eighteenth Dynasty, leaving complete instructions on the papyrus scrolls found by Ottley as to how his body should be prepared, as well as directions on an ivory stela about how he can be awakened centuries later to resume his position of High Priest of Amen.

While Pinsett is waiting for Ottley to recover from his field surgery, and when he is not arguing with or insulting the beautiful Miss Ottley, he discovers that the sarcophagus in which the treasure was found has a false bottom, and he unwittingly releases an ancient and powerful toxic perfume, which causes everyone to be out of sorts and act strangely. Two of Ottley's colleagues arrive from London, one of whom is Miss Ottley's fiancé, who appears only briefly in the plot before his demise, and the other is the mysterious Dr. Belleville. Ottley, in spite of his promise to include Pinsett, and in spite of the noxious fumes, secretly opens the sarcophagus in the presence of his colleagues. The mummy is found in the hidden compartment and thus released roams around the Ottley and Pinsett camps trying to strangle everyone. Ottley, having lost all sense of propriety, presumably from inhaling the noxious fumes, secretly arranges for the mummy to be shipped to England.

When the characters and the mummy arrive in England, it becomes clear that Ottley's fiendish colleague, Belleville, is in possession of the supernatural powers described in the papyrus scrolls and intends to cruelly murder everyone involved except Miss Ottley, whom he plans to marry. When Pinsett tries to rescue her, he is captured and held in the same laboratory as the mummy, who is now under Dr. Belleville's evil power. The mummy, by writing hieroglyphs on a chalk board, communicates with Pinsett that he too is a prisoner and will help Pinsett kill the evil Belleville in order to prevent him from using his recently gained evil powers. There is much ado in the laboratory while Belleville and his prisoner, Pin-sett, scuffle about. Pinsett and Belleville become invisible, blows are struck, and a struggle ensues because Belleville is trying to mummify Pinsett while he is still alive. Miss Ottley swoons several times. Eventually a fire started in the laboratory rages out of control and burns the entire Ottley estate. The mummy, Ottley, and Belleville all perish in the flames; the servants, Miss Ottley, and Dr. Pinsett escape. Miss Ottley and Dr. Pinsett marry and live happily ever after.

"LOT NO. 249" (1892) One of two mummy stories written by Sir Arthur Conan Doyle (see THE RING OF THOTH), this may be the first fiction to use a sinister mummy as a character. The title refers to an auction lot consisting of a mummy in its case that is purchased by Edward Bellingham, an Oxford University student of Eastern languages. Bellingham reanimates the mummy and sends it out to murder his enemies. When Bellingham is caught, he is forced to cut the mummy's body into pieces and burn them. The secret of how he brought the mummy to life is never revealed, but reference is made to certain old plant leaves that he was forced to burn along with the mummy. These may be the prototypes of the tana leaves used in later mummy movies to bring the mummy Kharis back to life. (See TANA LEAVES.)

MACLEAY MUMMY, THE The Macleay mummy was collected on Darnley Island off of Papua, New Guinea, in 1875 by zoologist Sir William Macleay. It is an excellent example of mummification as practiced in Melanesia in the nineteenth century.

The body of the deceased was set aside for a few days and then taken out on the water in a canoe, where the internal organs were removed via an abdominal incision and thrown into the water. The abdominal cavity was then packed with vegetable fibers, and the incision was sewn closed. Removal of the brain was accomplished by forcing an arrow between the top vertebra and the base of the skull, so the foramen magnum ("large hole") at the bottom of the skull was accessible, and the brain could be pulled out through it. The brain was also thrown into the water.

When the canoe returned to land, the body was lashed to a stretcher made of poles and placed upright to dry. Holes pierced at the elbows, knees, hands, and feet permitted body fluids to run out. The corpse would remain upright on the stretcher for months until thoroughly dry so it could be decorated.

The Macleay mummy is an adult male with absolutely no hair on the body, a result of the Melanesian practice of removing all body hair at the time of death. The entire body has been painted with red ocher and the facial features carefully indicated. Inlaid artificial eyes made of shells stare straight ahead, with pupils created by black resin dots. Eyelids have been detailed to heighten the effectiveness of the eyes, and a hole in the nasal septum, where a nose plug had been worn in life, has been filled in. The skull, from the hairline to the nape of the neck, is painted black, probably to indicate hair. So that the head would not fall forward, it has been lashed to the crossbars of the stretcher in an upright, lifelike attitude. All the fingernails and toenails are missing—evidence of the custom or removing the nails and skin of the palm and presenting them to the deceased's spouse as totem objects.

The Macleay mummy was the subject of considerable debate, when in 1914 at a meeting of the British Association for the Advancement of Science, the anatomist, Grafton Elliot Smith, stressed similarities between the way it had been preserved and ancient Egyptian mummification practices. Smith went on to claim that the rest of the world learned mummification (and other important practices) from ancient Egypt. His diffusionist theory had a small following for a while but is now widely discredited.

The Macleay mummy is at the Macleay Museum, University of Sydney, Australia.

MAGIC MUMMY Tom and Jerry cartoon (1932). A singing mummy is stolen from the museum and policemen Tom and Jerry attempt to recover it. One of the earliest mummy cartoons.

MAMMOTHS, MUMMIES OF The wooly mammoth is an early form of elephant that has been extinct for approximately 10,000 years. Frozen mammoths are the earliest true mummies.

Until modern times the existence of the wooly mammoth had not been established. The earliest indication that such a creature existed was an unusual kind of ivory that appeared in China during ancient times. The Chinese were familiar with ivory from Indian and African elephants and the tusks of walruses, but this was a different kind of tusk. What the buyers didn't know was that these tusks were from frozen mammoths found in Siberia. To explain the source of the different ivory, stories of a huge slow-moving beast known as Fyn shu began to circulate. By the Middle Ages some of the mammoth tusks had reached Europe, where they were proclaimed to be unicorn horns.

When traders from the outside world reached Siberia in the seventeenth century, the flow of mammoth ivory into Europe increased greatly, but still the actual beast had not been seen. In 1692 Peter the Great sent his ambassador, Isbrant Ides, to China to explore trade possibilities. Learning that ivory was a valuable commodity, Ides found a trader who described having found the frozen head of a mammoth complete with tusks. This of course was still far from solid proof of the beast's existence. Something close to that proof came a quarter of a century later.

In 1724 a head and part of a hide were found near the Indigirca River. This find was important in establishing just what kind of creature the mammoth was. It had long been suspected that the mammoths may have merely been elephants, escaped from Hannibal's army around the time he invaded Rome (217 B.C.), that had wandered into Siberia. But the hide found was covered with hair, and both African and Indian elephants are practically hairless. In 1799 Johann Blumenbach, the German anthropologist and early expert on Egyptian mummies (see BLUMENBACH, JOHANN) declared it a separate species, naming it *Elephas primigenius.* But still no one had found a mummified mammoth, and the exact nature of the beast remained speculative.

Two years after Blumenbach pronounced the mammoth a separate species, an intact frozen mummy was found near the Lena River by the chief of the Siberian Tungus people, Ossip Schumakhof. Eventually Schumakhof cut off the tusks and traded them. Several years later, in 1806, the botanist M.F. Adams, traveling through Russia, heard about the mammoth and went to investigate. When he arrived at the site, he discovered that much of the carcass had been butchered to feed the Tungus's dogs through the hard winter. Still much of the mammoth remained, and Adams was able to describe the animal and bring a large piece of the hairy hide back to Europe. But again scientists had been cheated out of seeing a complete mammoth, and it would be nearly a century before the opportunity to do so would arise.

In 1900 a landslide by the Baresovska River revealed a complete specimen. When a Lamut tribesman sold one of the tusks, word of the discovery soon spread to the scientific community, and the Russian Academy of Sciences sent an expedition. The party, consisting of a geologist, a zoologist, and a taxidermist took more than a year to reach the remote site. Traveling more than 2,000 miles over thawing tundra, the scientists had to bring all equipment and provisions by horseback or on pack animals. When they finally reached the mammoth, they were astounded to see the well-preserved creature in a sitting position, looking as if it were trying to get up. They could even see food between its jaws, the remains of the meal it was eating when it fell through the ice into a crevice. Because there was no way to preserve the entire mummy or to keep it frozen, the taxidermist skinned the animal and removed the flesh from its bones, and the team brought the hide and skeleton back to civilization on sleds. The Baresovska mammoth is now on display in the Leningrad Zoological Museum. It would be quite a while before another intact mammoth would be available for scientific study, but by the time it was discovered, research techniques had advanced considerably.

In July of 1977 a bulldozer operator in Magadan, Siberia, uncovered the frozen remains of a baby mammoth. Radiocarbon dating indicated that the mammoth, nicknamed "Dinna," died approximately 44,000 years ago. The cells were well preserved, but the proteins had degraded considerably. Unfortunately Russian scientists

Mammoths, mummies of The Magadan mammoth, discovered in Siberia in 1977. *Photo courtesy Eve Cockburn.*

permitted the specimen to thaw and then placed the tissues in a strong formaldehyde solution, causing additional damage. Subsequent attempts to clone the mammoth's DNA failed. Cloning could have answered questions about the form from which the mammoth evolved and its relationship to the modern elephant.

Had the standard procedure for research on frozen mummies been followed, there would have been a better chance of reproducing the DNA. This would have involved keeping the mammoth frozen and removing and thawing only a small section. Such a procedure must be carried out with great caution because live bacteria or viruses may be present. Live 10,000-year-old bacteria have been found by boring into the ice of Antarctica, and living bac-

teria more than 1,000 years old were found in the Roman fort of Vinolanda in northern England.

One year after the Magadan discovery, two better preserved mammoths were discovered in northern Siberia, one at Taimir and one at Yuribei. The Taimir mammoth died in approximately 53,000 B.C. and the other about 10,000 B.C. DNA was extracted from these two, but it was not possible to clone either sample.

MANDURUCHU TROPHY HEADS Until recently the Manduruchu Indians of Brazil took the heads of their enemies as trophies. Unlike the technique of the Jivaro Indians, these heads are preserved with the skull intact. The brains are removed and then the skin is dried over a fire. The hair and ears are decorated with feather

MOST REV. AMBROSE MARÉCHAL, D. D.,
Third Archbishop of Baltimore.

Marechal, Ambrose Archbishop of Baltimore,
Ambrose Marechal had his heart preserved in whiskey.

ornaments, and often the eye sockets are filled
with a black resinous gum and rodent teeth.

MARECHAL, AMBROSE (1768–1828)

Archbishop of Baltimore from 1817 until his
death, Marechal stipulated in his will that his
heart be removed from his body, preserved, and
kept at his beloved St. Mary's Seminary in Baltimore.

Born in France, Marechal studied both law
and theology and was ordained in the Sulpician
Society on March 25, 1792. The French Revolution had begun, and the day after his ordination
Marechal left Paris in disguise and sailed from Le
Havre for Baltimore. After missionary work he
became a professor at the Theological Seminary
associated with St. Mary's College in Baltimore.

On December 14, 1817 he was consecrated
Archbishop of Baltimore.

While traveling in Canada on a confirmation
tour, Archbishop Marechal caught a cold, returned to Baltimore, and felt better, but soon
developed symptoms of pectoral dropsy and died
on January 29, 1828. In accordance with his will,
his heart was sent to St. Mary's Seminary, where
it was kept in a glass reliquary immersed in whiskey to preserve it. For 166 years it remained in its
glass container, until June of 1993 when it was
sent to the Anatomical Service Division of the
University of Maryland School of Medicine. The
reason for transferring the heart was to preserve
it in a more stable manner than immersion in
alcohol. The heart was examined and plastinated
(see PLASTINATION) by Ronald Wade of the Anatomical Services Division. His report states:

> The 166 year old post-mortem heart specimen
> was received at the lab in June 1993. It had been
> held in a round glass container for well over 150

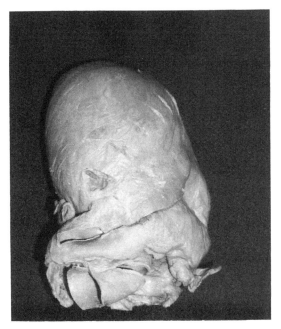

Marechal, Ambrose The 166-year-old heart of the
Archbishop, after recent conservation and plastination.
Photo courtesy Ronald Wade.

years. The specimen's appearance was dark; the tissue was hard, showing signs of shrinkage, and evidenced an odour of distilled alcohol (whiskey).

The specimen treatment began with its immersion in a bath of 5 percent hydrogen peroxide for one week. As a result the specimen appeared markedly lighter in color and hydrated to a more normal appearance and shape. The plastination process commenced with freeze substitution dehydration using acetone. Dehydration consisted of three baths of 100 percent acetone over a thirty-day period (at -28 degrees C [-18.4° F]). Forced impregnation of the S-10 silicone polymer followed and was completed in seven days. The specimen was then prepared for curing. The heart was removed from the silicone vacuum chamber and reoriented to a natural shape by packing the cavities with polyethylene plastic film. Gum rubber bands were used to hold the shape. After curing, the bands and packing were removed. Archbishop Marechal's heart was permanently preserved and returned on October 5, 1993 to be reinstalled in a new reliquary at St. Mary's Seminary.

MARQUISE OF TAI This Chinese mummy discovered in 1972 in Hunan Province is perhaps

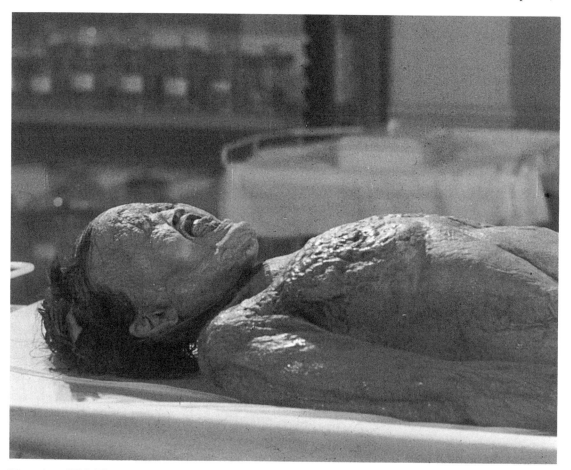

Marquise of Tai The remarkably well-preserved mummy from a Han Dynasty (207 B.C.–A.D. 220) tomb in China. *Photo courtesy Dr. Long-xiang Peng.*

McCURDY, ELMER J. 103

the best-preserved mummy in the world. Most Hunan tombs had been looted in the 1930s and 1940s, but two huge burial mounds near the capital, Changsha, remained untouched and were excavated by the Chinese government. After four months a tomb containing a series of nested coffins was found, the coffins being buried in five tons of charcoal to absorb any water that might enter the tomb.

The innermost coffin contained the body of Lady Ch'eng, wife of Litsang, the Marquis of Tai, who lived 2,100 years ago. The fifty-year-old woman had been buried and hermetically sealed in a solution containing mercury salts that was still liquid when scientists entered the tomb. Lady Ch'eng's joints were still flexible and could be easily bent; the skin was so pliable that when touched a depression formed and then rebounded so it could no longer be seen.

Because of the excellent preservation of the body, it was possible to perform a nearly normal autopsy to determine the cause of death. The internal organs were all in place and sixteen badly worn teeth remained in the mandible. In the marquise's stomach 138 mushmellon seeds were discovered, the remains of her last meal. Her death was probably the result of two factors: a gallstone completely blocked the lower end of the common bile duct and the arteries, especially the coronary artery, were clogged with plaque. The marquise probably died when the extreme biliary colic caused a heart attack.

MASPERO, GASTON, SIR (1846–1916)
Director General of the Egyptian Antiquities Service from 1881–86 and from 1899–1914. Maspero unwrapped more royal mummies than any other Egyptologist.

As an adolescent Maspero demonstrated a remarkable facility for languages, studying hieroglyphs when he was fourteen and publishing his first translation of a papyrus at the age of twenty. Early in his studies he moved to South America to study the Inca language, Quichua, but returned to France to devote his life to Egyptology.

He first went to Egypt as part of an expedition to record tomb inscriptions, and when August Mariette died in 1881, Maspero became director of the Bulaq Museum and of the Egyptian Antiquities Service. Thus he was in charge when the cache of royal mummies was discovered at Deir el-Bahri in 1881. (See DEIR EL-BAHRI.)

Because he was primarily interested in language, for the first several years after the mummies were discovered, Maspero devoted himself to translating the inscriptions on the coffins and dockets that accompanied the bodies. In 1886, eager to see the faces of the great ones of Egypt, Maspero began a program of unwrapping the royal mummies that was far too rapid for careful observation and recording. In a single day he unwrapped the mummies of Seti I, Seqenenre Tao II, and Ahmose I. In less than one month, between June 9 and July 1, 1886, he unwrapped twenty-one mummies. Because he was untrained in anatomy, little about the mummies was learned and much valuable information was lost forever.

McCURDY, ELMER J. (d. 1911)
This Oklahoma train robber was mummified with arsenic.

On October 6, 1911 Elmer McCurdy and several members of his gang attempted to rob an evening train going from Kansas to Oklahoma that was supposedly transporting several thousand dollars in Indian tribal payments. Near Okesa, Oklahoma, they robbed the train only to discover that it was the wrong one. They got away with $46.00 and a shipment of whiskey.

Drinking heavily, Elmer went to the Revard Ranch in the Osage Hills, a frequent hideout for desperadoes. There, half drunk, he went to sleep on a pile of hay in the barn. The posse chasing the gang arrived that night, surrounded the barn, and waited for daylight. The Bartlesville, Oklahoma *Daily Enterprise* for October 8, 1911 quotes one of the posse members, "We were standing around waiting for him to come out when the first shot was fired at me. It missed me and he then turned his attention to my brother, Stringer Fenton. He shot three times at Stringer when my brother got under cover he turned his attention to Dick Wallace. He kept shooting at all of us for about an hour. We fired back every time we could. We do not know who killed him."

The body was taken to the Johnson Funeral Establishment in Pawhuska, Oklahoma, where examination revealed that Elmer had been killed by a single bullet entering the chest and lodging in the abdomen—he was lying down in the hay when he was shot. Such a scenario was relatively common in the West at the turn of the century, but what makes Elmer unique is what happened to his body.

On December 10, 1976 a Universal Studio crew was filming "The Six-Million Dollar Man" at an amusement park in Long Beach, California. To film a chase through the house of horrors, a glow-in-the-dark dummy hanging from a gallows was moved by a technician to a better spot. When the arm fell off, revealing a bone, the police were called and the body was taken to the Los Angeles County coroner's office for an autopsy.

The remarkably well-preserved body had been embalmed with a great quantity of arsenic. A bullet wound was found, and a copper bullet jacket was removed from the pelvis. Ballistic tests showed the bullet was the kind produced after 1905 but discontinued before World War II. Long Beach police eventually discovered that the body had quite a career in carnival sideshows, such as Louie Sonney's Museum of Crime and Crafts Carnival Circus. In 1971 the body was in a coffin in the Hollywood Wax Museum, but when the museum defaulted on the rent, the body went to the Long Beach show. How the body began its tour is a bit of American enterprise.

When the owner of the Johnson Funeral Establishment learned that Elmer had no next of kin, rather than burying him, he preserved the bandit with extra arsenic and kept him in a back room of the parlor, where for a nickel the curious could see the "Bandit who wouldn't give up." This one-mummy sideshow continued for years until an out-of-town visitor emerged from the back room shaking; Elmer was his brother. He was given the body to be taken home to Kansas for proper burial, but years later it was learned that the "brother" was a carnival operator; the theatrical career of Elmer McCurdy had begun.

After the discovery on the set of "The Six-Million Dollar Man," the coroner's office positively identified the body as that of the late train robber. Photos obtained of Elmer at the time of death revealed that his clothes had not been changed in more than half a century. The body was scheduled for cremation but a committee of Oklahomans, hearing what was about to happen to their native son, contacted Dr. Thomas Noguchi, the Los Angeles City/County Coroner, insisting that Elmer be properly buried in Oklahoma. McCurdy now lies in the Summit View Cemetery at Guthrie, Oklahoma, under two cubic yards of concrete—to make sure he stays put.

MEDIEVAL MUMMIFICATION (A.D. **600–1500**) During the Middle Ages bodies were rarely embalmed or mummified, with the exception of those of saints or royalty. These mummifications were performed by court physicians or members of the religious orders. The chemicals used for mummification were oil of turpentine, camphor spirits, oil of lavender, oil of rosemary, vermilion, spirits of wine, resin, and saltpeter.

Toward the end of the Middle Ages, compounds of zinc, arsenic, aluminum chloride, bichloride of mercury, alcohol, and alum were used. These ingredients were introduced by alchemists, who were experimenting with a variety of chemicals and elements in their laboratories.

MEENYBRADAN BOG WOMAN, THE This 2,000-year-old bog mummy was discovered in Ireland in 1976 and was in remarkably good condition. The hair was still intact, and all the limbs were present. The woman had been obese, so adipocere had formed (see ADIPOCERE). Her mummy was taken to the National Museum of Ireland, where it was kept in a freezer at -26

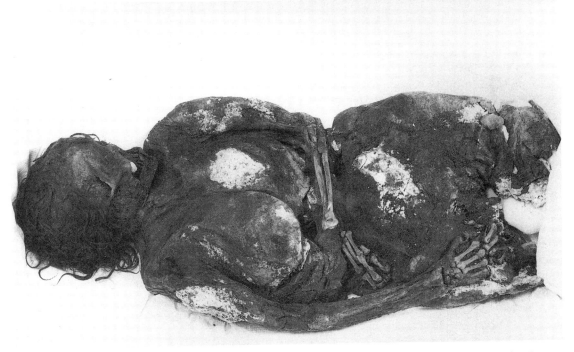

Meenybradan Bog Woman The Meenybradan woman was found in a bog in Ireland. *Photo courtesy National Museum of Ireland.*

degrees Celsius (-14.8° F). In 1985 it was transferred to the British Museum for conservation.

After experimenting with tissue samples, it was decided to soak the mummy in polyethylene glycol (PEG), which is often used by museum conservation departments for waterlogged material. The PEG is absorbed into the objects and strengthens them. Meenybradan Woman was immersed in a vat of 15 percent PEG in distilled water for four weeks. The body was then freeze-dried at -32 degrees Celsius (-25.6° F) for thirty-one days. The stabilized body was then returned to the National Museum of Ireland, where it remains today.

MENKAURE, SUPPOSED MUMMY OF
King of Egypt during the Fourth Dynasty, Menkaure (called "Mycerinus" by the Greeks) built the smallest of the three large pyramids at

Giza. A stone sarcophagus was found in each of the three pyramids, but only in Menkaure's was there a mummy.

The pyramid was first opened in modern times in 1837 by Colonel Richard Howard-Vyse, who found a beautiful basalt sarcophagus carved with a palace facade decoration. He also found human remains and the lid of a wooden anthropoid coffin with the name "Menkaure" on it. All three—the sarcophagus, the mummy, and the coffin lid—were disappointments.

Because of the style in which it is carved, the lid cannot be from the Fourth Dynasty; it is from the Saite period, almost 2,000 years later. Radiocarbon dating of the human remains showed that the mummy was from the first centuries A.D. Neither lid nor mummy are Menkaure's. Saite priests probably found Menkaure's burial chamber plundered and piously made a new coffin for the reburial. Presumably this tomb was later robbed, but in the Christian era another body was placed in the tomb.

The only object in the pyramid that was truly Menkaure's was the stone sarcophagus, but it now lies at the bottom of the ocean. In 1883 it was shipped from Egypt to the British Museum on the merchant ship *Beatrice*. The ship stopped at Malta for supplies and left that port on October 30, 1838, but neither ship nor the precious cargo was seen again. The *Beatrice* sank in deep waters somewhere near Cartagena.

MERCURY Mercury, because of its antiseptic properties, kills bacteria and thus can be used to preserve bodies. The ancient Chinese placed the bodies of their deceased in capsules containing a solution of mercury salts (see MARQUISE OF TAI), thus preserving them. In 1981 a unique example of mummification by mercury was found in Japan.

The Japanese rarely practiced artificial mummification, and since the soil of Japan is not conducive to natural mummification, rarely are ancient bodies found. In the city of Sendai, several hundred miles north of Tokyo, the lords of Sendai built their tombs beginning in the early seventeenth century. These tombs were destroyed during an air raid in 1945, but in the 1970s the local government decided to restore them. When the body of Tadamune, the second lord of the clan, was found, amazingly soft tissue from the viscera was still intact.

The body, dressed in ritual silk garments, had been placed in a seated position in a wooden tub that rested on a lacquered palanquin. Throughout the chest area scientists found droplets of mercury totaling more than two pounds. Evidently the mercury was poured into Tadamune's mouth, while he was sitting in the coffin. Following gravity, it traveled through the pharynx and larynx, into the bronchial tubes and into the lungs. There it acted as an antiseptic, preserving parts of the body.

MERENRE PHARAOH OF EGYPT, MUMMY OF (2283–2278 B.C.) Merenre's is the only complete mummy of a ruler of the Old Kingdom; the only other remains of Old King-

dom pharaohs are body parts found in their plundered tombs. Discovered by Gaston Maspero in 1881 in its pyramid, Merenre's body had been entirely unwrapped by robbers but was complete. In the early part of this century, the mummy was exhibited in the Egyptian Museum's Royal Mummies Room as No. 5250 but is not listed in the 1912 Catalogue General volume on royal mummies and has not been on exhibit for many years.

MESTI One of the four sons of the Egyptian god Horus. Mesti was associated with the south and his function was to protect mummies' internal organs. He is the only one of the four sons of Horus to be represented with the head of a human (see FOUR SONS OF HORUS).

Often there were magical spells on the four jars containing the mummy's internal organs. On the jar with the lid in the shape of Mesti's head, a typical spell reads:

Words spoken by Mesti:
I am Mesti, thy son Osiris.
I come to protect thee. I make
thy house fine as commanded by
Ptah and Re, himself.

MIZRAIM The ancient Hebrew word for Egypt. During the seventeenth century, when mummies were being ground into medicines for English apothecaries' shops, the word was used to denote powdered mummies.

MNEVIS BULL, MUMMIES OF One of the three bulls worshipped in ancient Egypt (see APIS BULL and BUCHIS BULL), the Mnevis was worshipped, mummified, and buried at Heliopolis, called "On" in the Bible. Only two burials of the Mnevis have been found, each a pit dug in the ground and lined with polished stone. Unfortunately both tombs had been flooded by ground water, destroying the remains of the bulls.

It is known that only one Mnevis bull was alive at any one time and that the bull was associated with the sun god Re. When the bull died it was buried with funerary jewels and servant statues, just like a noble of ancient Egypt. Aside from this, little is known of the cult of the Mnevis.

MODERN MUMMIFICATION (EGYPTIAN METHOD)

In 1994 a team of scientists led by Bob Brier, an Egyptologist at Long Island University, and Ronald Wade, Director of the Maryland State Anatomy Board, replicated an ancient Egyptian mummification. The procedure was performed on a human cadaver at the Medical School of the University of Maryland.

In an attempt to reproduce as closely as possible an Egyptian mummification, replicas of ancient bronze tools were forged with precisely the same metal content (88 percent copper and 12 percent tin) as Egyptian bronze instruments. Because Herodotus (see HERODOTUS OF HALICARNASSUS) said that a "sharp Ethiopian stone" (obsidian) was used to make the abdominal incision, obsidian blades were flaked for this purpose. A replica of an embalmer's table discovered in 1922 by Egyptologist Herbert Winlock was made for the cadaver to lie on. Natron (see NATRON), the dehydrating agent used by ancient Egyptian morticians, was obtained at the Wadi Natrun, the ancient source, fifty miles north of modern Cairo.

The procedure was performed on an unembalmed cadaver of a male who had died at the age of seventy-six. The brain was removed through the nose by breaking the ethmoid bone and extending a hooked rod into the cranium. The rod was then rotated until the brain was broken down to a semiliquid state. Finally the cadaver was turned face downward, so the brain could run out the nose. For the removal of the internal organs, a 3½-inch abdominal incision was made on the left side, using an obsidian blade. Only the heart was left inside the body, as was the ancient Egyptian practice.

Once the internal organs were removed, the body cavities were washed with palm wine, and both the thorax and abdominal cavity were filled with small packets of natron to absorb the body fluids. The body and separate internal organs were then placed on the embalmer's board in a small room, where the temperature (105 degrees Fahrenheit [40.5° C]) and humidity (29 percent) were controlled. Covered with natron, the body and organs remained in the room for thirty-five days. At the end of this period the natron was removed and the cadaver examined.

The body had the appearance of an ancient Egyptian mummy. The hands and feet were dark and hard to the touch. There was no smell of putrefaction, and cultures taken from the cranium and abdomen tested negative for bacteria, viruses, and fungi. The major difference between the mummy and an ancient one was that some fluids, primarily lipids, remained in the larger muscles, the quadriceps, and the gluteus maxima. When the body was placed in natron it weighed approximately 150 pounds, with the organs removed. After the thirty-five days, it weighed approximately seventy-five pounds, losing much of its water due to dehydration.

The body was anointed with cedar, palm, lotus, frankincense, and myrrh oils and wrapped in pure untreated linen. In an attempt to determine the results of tomblike conditions on a body, that is with some moisture still present, the mummy was replaced in the temperature/humidity-controlled room for nearly five months. At the end of this period, the mummy had lost an additional twenty-five pounds of fluids through evaporation. Still there was no odor of putrefaction or evidence of tissue decay. By this time the body had become rigid because of the near-total dehydration. When the researchers attempted to cross the arms on the chest, the position of royal mummies, they were unable to bend the arms. This led them to conclude that the goal of the ancient embalmers was not complete dehydration of the body. Rather, as the modern experimenters had found, after thirty-five days in natron, some moisture remains, and this would have been necessary to manipulate and position the mummy for wrapping. The final dehydration could then occur in the tomb.

The mummy has been examined by CAT scans and MRI (magnetic resonance imaging) to

Monkey Tomb Some of the mummified apes found by American excavator Theodore Davis in 1906. *Photo courtesy Dennis Forbes,* KMT *magazine.*

determine its condition; tissue is periodically sampled and analyzed to monitor the state of cell preservation. The mummy remains in storage at room temperature at the Medical School of the University of Maryland.

MONKEY TOMB A small pit tomb in the Valley of the Kings that contained numerous animal mummies. Because many of the animals were cenocephalic apes, the tomb became known as "The Monkey Tomb."

The tomb was discovered in January 1906 by Theodore Davis, a wealthy American businessman and Edward Ayrton, his excavator. One cenocephalic ape was found in a seated position, wearing a necklace of blue disc beads; another larger ape had its wrappings torn from its head, perhaps by tomb robbers looking for gold decorations. There were other mummified animals in the tomb—ibises and ducks—along with what the excavator described as "Bundles of intestines made up in the form of little human figures." There was also a small human mummy mask. The mummies in the tomb have never been fully described in any publication and raise many questions.

Baboons and ibises were identified with gods and were mummified as offerings but ducks were not, they were eaten. When ducks were buried in tombs they were intended to be food for the deceased. Thus the combination of duck mummies and those of sacred animals along with a human mummy mask is puzzling.

MOODIE, ROY L. American paleopathologist who pioneered the use of X rays in the study of mummies. In 1931 he published his landmark work, *Roentgenologic Studies of Egyptian and*

Peruvian Mummies, which reproduced seventy-six X rays of mummies in the Chicago Field Museum of Natural History. Moodie's comments on the information provided by the X rays inspired later researchers to x-ray mummies.

MORE TEUTONICO Latin for "in the German method." In the Middle Ages this meant boiling a body so the flesh could be removed and only the bones kept. This was necessary because often important people did not die at their intended places of burial, and techniques for preservation of the body had not been developed. Thus only the bones were transported to the final resting place. This technique was first used in Germany.

Saint Louis, King of France, who died while on crusade in Tunis in 1270, was transported in this manner to Saint-Denis in Paris, where he was buried. The body of Saint Thomas Aquinas was also preserved in this manner.

MOUND PEOPLE The Bronze Age (c. 1100 B.C.) inhabitants of Denmark, the mound people were buried in oak coffins and covered with huge piles of earth.

Unlike their descendants, the bog people, who lived a thousand years later and were buried nearly naked with no possessions, the mound people were buried fully clothed with grave goods. Like the bog people, oxygen-deprived water rich in tannic acid from tree remains preserved their bodies.

Throughout Denmark the plains are dotted with hundreds of large earth mounds—some more than 100 feet in diameter and several stories high—that remained virtually untouched for centuries. In the early part of the nineteenth century, farmers began spreading the rich mound soil on their fields to increase crop productivity. In the course of removing the tons of earth, burials were uncovered and a pattern emerged. Usually a heavy well-preserved oak coffin, made simply by splitting a huge log in half and hollowing out the two parts, was found surrounded by stones. Nor-

mally water had entered the coffin, become acidic from the tannin in the oak, and dissolved the bones, leaving the skin and hair. The clothes, however, were preserved, as were bronze swords and daggers and gold jewelry.

The discoveries began in 1827, when a farmer removing soil from a mound discovered an oak coffin covered by a pile of stones. The coffin, full of water, contained a woolen cap and cloak, dagger, sword, horn comb, and a lock of black human hair. The rest of the body had dissolved. For much of the nineteenth century, farmers continued to find water-filled coffins and human remains.

As knowledge of the Danish mound finds increased, treasure-seekers began digging the mounds and the number of finds increased, though often in the rush for artifacts, the sites were disturbed, the findings were not recorded, and much archaeological information was lost. In 1860 the first preserved body was found in an oak coffin at Lille Dragsoj. Fortunately the parish priest, Valdemar Thisted, heard about the discovery and asked that it remain unopened till he could be present. When he supervised the opening of the coffin, he observed that a complete human body "had sunk together into a glutinous, oily and in places fatty substance in which the forms could only be indistinctly discerned." The skull seemed to retain its thick black hair, but when the remains were studied in Copenhagen, it was revealed that the skull had actually dissolved in the acid water, and it was merely the tanned skin that remained.

When King Frederick VII became interested in the mound finds, archaeologists were sent to supervise and record the excavations, thus important information was gathered. Subsequently entire bodies were found, and the burial customs of the mound people emerged. Each coffin usually contained a single adult, stretched out on its back with hands at the sides. Buried in their daily clothes, these people took with them into the next world only a few treasured possession. Some mounds contained several coffins, probably family members, and almost always each coffin was surrounded by stones. Occasionally these oak coffins contained two bodies—an adult and a small child. Because of the poor condition of the bodies, it has not been possible to determine the causes of death, it is not known if they died at the same time of natural causes, or if the child was sacrificed to accompany the adult to the next world.

The burials of the mound people provide a glimpse into the clothing, weapons, and customs of the Danes of 3,000 years ago. At Borum Eshoj, near the east coast of Denmark, an entire family was buried in a huge mound more than 125 feet across and 30 feet high. The first indication that the mound contained burials came in 1850, when a farmer discovered a stone coffin that contained a bronze sword and some other artifacts, but no human remains. A few years later another stone coffin containing only some bronze artifacts was uncovered.

In 1871, as more soil was removed from the mound, a traditional oak coffin was discovered. The workers who found it turned it upside down, scattering the contents—bones, clothing, and bronze implements. Disappointed that there was no gold, the workers eventually turned everything over to the Historical Society, and the burial was reconstructed. The bones were those of an elderly woman, who had been buried in a wool dress with a belt terminating in elaborate tassels. On her hair was a woven hair net, so she would look attractive. Although a woman, she was buried with a dagger and also bracelets, combs, and pins for ornamentation.

The discovery of this noblewoman convinced archaeologist Conrad Engelhardt that more burials might be found in the mound. In 1875 he began excavating and soon found a nine-foot-long oak coffin in the center of the mound. Oak chips around it suggested that it had been fashioned at the burial spot itself. Inside was the body of a man, stretched out on his back, hands at his sides. He was clean shaven, and beneath his woolen cap was a full head of hair, stained black

by the tannic acid from the oak coffin. Approximately fifty-five at the time of his death, his skeleton showed that he suffered from rheumatism. He wore a woolen loincloth and had been buried with his cape and covered with a cow skin.

The same year that the man was discovered, a third coffin was found between the man's and woman's burials. This was the burial of a young man who had died in his late teens or early twenties. Dressed in a tunic with a leather belt, he had on his left arm a highly decorated wooden scabbard containing a bronze dagger. The objects and clothing in his coffin were similar in quantity and quality to those of the man and woman and it is quite possible that the three were a family, perhaps a father, mother, and son. (See EGTVED GIRL and SKRYDSTRUP GIRL.)

MUISCA MUMMIES The Muisca were complex societies that existed from the ninth to eighteenth centuries in the central Andean highlands of Colombia. The nobility were artificially mummified, but after the Spanish conquest under Jimenez de Quesada, both the culture and the practice of mummification died out. The capital of Colombia, Bogotá, stands on what was once the important Muisca city of Bacata.

The Muisca mummified only their elite political, military, and religious leaders and their families. The procedure almost always involved smoking the body over an open fire. In 1515 Gonzalo Fernandez de Oviedo reported:

> . . . when a chieftain dies in these lands, they will take his body and sit him on a log or stone . . . and they will place fire around him, very close, without the flames touching the body . . . and the fire will burn continuously until all the grease and humidity comes out from the nails of the hands and feet, and evaporates and dries in such a way that the skin adheres to the bones, and the flesh becomes completely dry; and once he is dried, without opening the body, they put him in a house next to the body of his father, who is placed in the same manner.

Although de Oviedo says the mummies were placed in a house, many were placed in caves. This is clear from a Muisca mummy brought to the British Museum in 1838 by W. Turner, England's envoy and minister to Colombia. The registration card assigns it No. 1838-11-11-1 and states " . . . it was found with thirteen others in a cave." Four years later Robert Bunch, another British envoy, returned with a second mummy. Its registration card assigns it Number 1842-11-12-1 and records " . . . found in a cave September 1842 with 27 other mummies, most of which were destroyed by the Indians."

The two examples in the British Museum are among the few Muisca mummies that survived the Spanish conquest. Because they were originally adorned with gold jewelry and bundled in

textiles, the Spanish systematically plundered the mummies. Friar Pedro Simon described the sacking of the main Muisca temple, where the mummies of the rulers were kept.

> . . . they began taking things from the dried
> bodies which were placed on scaffolds. . . .
> they must have been important people because
> they were all wrapped in very fine cotton
> blankets with fine gold jewels of different types. . . .

After the Spanish had taken what they wanted, the temple caught fire, and both the temple and the mummies were completely destroyed.

MULDBJERG CHIEFTAIN, THE   This burial of a Danish Bronze Age (c. 1100 B.C.) chieftain contained one of the most elaborate coffins of the period, but unfortunately the mummy was badly damaged. The burial is notable because the mound that covered it was a figure-eight shape, rather than the usual single mound.

The Bronze Age mound people traditionally buried their nobility in oak coffins covered by an earth mound, sometimes more than 100 feet in diameter. The mound in Muldbjerg, in west Jutland, Denmark, is unique because of its shape. The county commissioner excavated it in 1883, discovering a large oak coffin covered by a huge hollow tree trunk that formed a barrel vault. The coffin contained the remains of a man who had stood more than six feet tall. His clothes, including his short woolen coat, were well preserved, but all that remained of his body were his hair, leg bones, lower jaw, right upper arm, and fingernails. The rest had been dissolved by the water that had penetrated the burial.

Encouraged by this find, the excavator searched for more burials within the mound. Another burial of a woman was found, and it became clear that originally this mound had been separate from the first. The woman, probably the chieftain's wife, had died before him and was

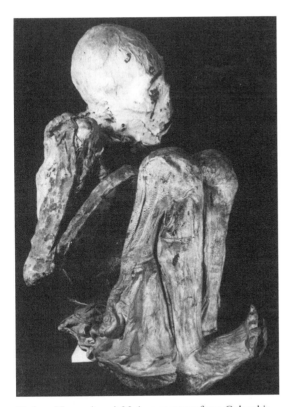

Muisca Mummies A Muisca mummy from Colombia. *Photo courtesy Dr. Félipe Cardénas-Arroyo.*

buried in a modest mound. When the chieftain died, he was buried in the second, larger mound. Excavations revealed a third burial of another woman between the two mounds, linking the other two and causing the figure-eight. The second woman may have been the chieftain's second wife, who outlived him and was eventually buried next to him.

MUMMIA Persian word meaning "bitumen," the mineral formed from pitch. It is from this word that we get the English "mummy."

In ancient times bitumen was believed to have great curative properties. The Roman naturalist Pliny the Elder, who died in the eruption of Vesuvius in A.D. 79, wrote that bitumen was good for curing leprosy, gout, toothaches, dysentery, and wounds. The Arab physicians also had faith in the medicinal properties of bitumen, and the eleventh-century physician Avicenna (Ibn Sina) used it to heal fractures, abscesses, disorders of the liver and spleen, and even to cure leprosy. Early travelers to Persia mentioned its supposed miraculous properties, and when Sir William Ousley visited Kieh Mummaiy (Mummy Mountain) he reported that the Persians valued mummia more than gold because they believed it healed cuts instantly and mended broken bones in minutes. So prized was mummia that in 1809 the king of Persia sent the queen of England a sample as a gift.

In the Middle Ages when travelers visited Egypt and saw the embalmed corpses of the ancient Egyptians, they mistook the darkened resins coating these bodies for the black bitumen they called mummia. Thus the word "mummia" came to be linked to preserved bodies. In the thirteenth century the Baghdad physician Abd Al Latif visited Cairo and reported, "In the belly and skull of their corpses is also found in great abundance a substance called mummy. The inhabitants of the country transport it to the city, where it is sold for a trifle. For half a dirham I purchased three heads filled with the substance." Soon the entire body—not just the resins that had

been used in the embalming—was called "mummia," from which we get our English "mummy." Now the resins, bones, and flesh were all ground together and sold as medicine. The confusion between the mineral bitumen and the human remains appeared in *The Physical Dictionary* of 1657—"Mummia, a thing like pitch sold at the apothecaries; some affirm its taken out of old tombs." Because Persian mummia was so rare, the more plentiful Egyptian substitute soon became the staple for European druggists.

Although it was forbidden to export mummies from Egypt, for a bribe anything was possible, and by the sixteenth century there was a brisk trade in mummies. John Sanderson, an Englishman traveling through the Levant, visited the pyramids on April 28, 1586. A few miles from the pyramids, he was lowered into a tomb containing piles of mummies. He broke off arms, legs, and heads and shipped home 600 pounds of mummies, including a complete body. Eventually even the tombs of Egypt could not meet the growing market for mummia, and Egyptian physicians and entrepreneurs began preparing recently deceased corpses for sale. As the practice became public, fresh mummies were accepted as medicine, and some European physicians began mixing alchemy and pharmacology, with the German physician Oswald Crollius suggesting the kind of corpse from which the best tincture of mummia could be produced. He required a red-haired twenty-four-year-old man who had met a violent death, preferably by hanging or stabbing. The body should be exposed to the air for twenty-four hours, cut into small pieces, then marinated in a mixture of wine, powdered myrrh, and aloes. When finally dried, the flesh would be like smoked fish, from which a red tincture could be extracted that would cure almost anything.

By the seventeenth century, European physicians were having their doubts about the efficacy of mummia. Better translations of medieval writers made clear the confusion of Persian bitumen with resin-coated bodies; chemical studies and detailed anatomical investigations were giving rise to a new science and a medicine that was empirical and left little room for untested ingredients. The ingestion of resinous cadavers became unfashionable, and by the eighteenth century mummia was rarely seen in the apothecary's shop.

MUMMIES. MUMMIES? MUMMIES! An exhibition of mummy sculptures by artist Stephen L. Auslender, held at the Tribeca 148 Gallery in New York, December 11, 1993–January 15, 1994.

Not exact representations of mummies, the sculptures included figures of pregnant women, human heads attached to abstract shapes, and other more enigmatic shapes. Almost all were constructed of layered fiberglass and wrapped in layers of hospital gauze coated with polyester resin. The "mummies" ranged in size from the eight-inch-high ten-piece Mummyman series to the eight-foot-high *Mummy 21.*

MUMMIES OF THE PHARAOHS An exhibition of wax replicas of the royal mummies of Egypt that toured Europe in 1996. Included were Ramses the Great and Seti I.

MUMMY Any cadaver that is preserved either naturally or artificially. Skeletal remains do not constitute a mummy; preservation of soft tissue is necessary to qualify as a mummy.

MUMMY, THE This paperback novel, published in 1995, was written by Barbara Steiner for Scholastic Children's Books. The story line is pure fiction and none of the Egyptological references are factual, but it is a good mystery for young teenagers.

The setting is the opening of an exhibition of Egyptian objects in the Denver Museum of Natural History. Lana Richardson, a teenage volunteer at the museum, is fervent in her interest in ancient Egypt and acts as a guide during the new exhibit of objects on loan from the Egyptian Museum in Cairo. The most notable objects on display are

Mummies. Mummies? Mummies! *Mummy 18.* A sculpture by Stephen L. Auslender. *Photo courtesy of the artist.*

the mummy and coffin of Prince Nefra, who died on the eve of his wedding day, according to legend. Also on display is the empty coffin of his bride, Princess Urbena, who is said to have committed suicide on hearing of Prince Nefra's death. Her body mysteriously disappeared from her tomb, thus her coffin is empty. Accompanying the display is the emerald necklace given to the princess by Prince Nefra.

The preexhibition reception for the museum staff and volunteers is attended by the key characters: Dr. Walters, the museum curator; Ms. Blair Vaughn, a well-known young archaeologist; Antef Raam, the young Egyptian representative who accompanied the exhibits to Denver; Darrah, the Egyptian exchange student; and Lana's friends Marge, Rondey, and Josh.

During the reception Lana feels drawn to the mummy of Prince Nefra, and while visiting him the lights in the gallery go out. She hears the voice of Prince Nefra, who has mistaken her, because of her Egyptian hair style, for his beloved Princess Urbena, who has been missing since she disappeared from her tomb. Nefra whispers to Lana, and she becomes frightened.

When she arrives home that evening, a black cat has mysteriously appeared at Lana's house. The strange cat, whose name is Seti, follows her to the museum and sometimes waits for her on the museum steps at the end of the day. Lana continues her work with great enthusiasm but is again frightened when she visits Prince Nefra, to whom she is strangely attracted, and notices that the hands of the mummy have moved, no longer being folded across his chest.

One day as the museum is closing, Lana goes to check that all the visitors have left the mummy gallery and is attacked by a stranger. When the lights go out, the display case housing the valuable emerald necklace is shattered, and the wedding necklace of Princess Urbena is stolen. When Lana decides to take a shortcut home and walks in the mist and rain through a deserted park, she is confronted by a figure who looks like the mummy of Prince Nefra and who demands

The Mummy Hammer Films' 1959 remake of the classic starred Christopher Lee in the title role.

that she return the necklace that he had presented to Princess Urbena. Lana is saved from the mummy's attack when her newly acquired black cat, Seti, appears and frightens the mummy away.

The story is interesting because the mysterious occurrences happen on two levels. First it seems that Lana has some strange connection to ancient Egypt, and second it seems that someone in the museum is trying to frighten her by dressing up as the mummy of Prince Nefra. Her black cat Seti seems to act as her guardian, warning her or defending her when she stumbles into scary situations. Woven throughout the story are the dreams of ancient Egypt that Lana has from time to time, in which she seems to be the lost princess, Urbena.

As the story unfolds Lana copes with the mysterious occurrences while keeping up with her school work and her boyfriend, who has no interest in Egyptology. She is a good role model for young teenagers, for she is caring and honest, resourceful, and very hardworking. All of these qualities pay off in the final scenes of the story, when the museum has a farewell costume party for the staff and volunteers the night before the exhibit is to be returned to Egypt. Lana, dressed in a special Egyptian costume that her mother designed for her, is accompanied to the party by Seti. During the course of the evening, it is noted that she looks like Princess Urbena, and she is persuaded, against her will, to try on Urbena's famous emerald wedding necklace that had been mysteriously returned to its case. While still wearing the priceless necklace, Lana goes to the mummy room to say a final farewell to Prince Nefra, who occasionally seems to whisper messages to her. As she approaches the coffin, she again hears the voice of Nefra and faints. When she awakens, Lana finds that she is in the coffin of Princess Urbena. The story has several twists and turns involving the museum staff and the cat, Seti. As the mystery is solved, Lana is released from the coffin, unharmed.

MUMMY, THE Hammer Film Productions' 1959 remake of Universal Pictures' 1932 classic retained the basic plot but changed the names. The mummy is now Kharis, and his lost love is the Princess Ananka. As in the 1932 version, the artifacts found in Tutankhamen's tomb served as models. The burial of Ananka features an animal-headed funerary couch, Anubis statue, model boat, and alabaster jars patterned after those of the boy-king. Indeed, when the Scroll of Life is removed from its box, Tutankhamen's cartouche is clearly visible. Although the artifacts are faithfully reproduced, the description of mummification is off the mark. Viewers are told that the high priest entered the tomb after the coffin "and behind him [is] the casket containing the heart of the princess." In Egyptian mummification, the heart is left inside the body. (See HEART.)

Another Egyptological error is that throughout the film the chief god is Karnak. Karnak was a temple where the god Amun and others were worshipped, but there was never an Egyptian god named Karnak.

Realizing that the great success of the classic was due to Karloff's brilliant portrayal of the mummy, Hammer Films used British horror film star Christopher Lee as the mummy. Lee turned in a believable performance, but in the process of crashing through windows and carrying Ananka through swamps, dislocated his shoulder and pulled his neck muscles.

MUMMY, THE   The classic Universal Pictures film was released in 1932 and became both an instant success and the most famous of all mummy movies. The role of the mummy was specifically created for Boris Karloff (see KAR-LOFF, BORIS), who was fresh from a successful appearance as the monster in *Frankenstein*. Originally called *Cagliostro*, the screenplay of the film was rewritten and retitled *Im-Ho-Tep* and only became *The Mummy* just before release. As the film neared completion, it became increasingly clear that the focus should be on the mummy as much as possible. The January 1933 issue of *Mystery* magazine contains the original story of "The Mummy," and it is interesting to compare

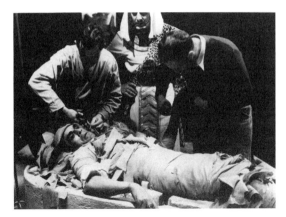

The Mummy   Acid-treated linen was used to wrap Boris Karloff for his portrayal of the mummy Im-Ho-Tep.

the story with the film to see the last-minute changes. In the magazine version the heroine, Helen, is shown to have had many lives, starting with that of the Egyptian princess Anck-es-en-Amon, but including those of a first-century Christian martyr, an eighth-century barbarian queen, a medieval lady, and a French aristocrat. These scenes were cut to make the mummy the central character, but they still exist somewhere in the vaults of Universal Pictures.

The movie rode the crest of the tremendous interest in ancient Egypt created by the discovery of Tutankhamen's tomb. Tutankhamen's actual wife's name, Anck-es-en-Amon, was used for the name of the Egyptian princess in the movie.

According to the movie, Princess Anck-es-en-Amon died and was buried by her father, the pharaoh. Her lover, the high priest Im-Ho-Tep, risked his life to steal the Scroll of Thoth, which when read aloud could magically bring her back to life. He was caught and buried alive in an unmarked grave. This grave is subsequently discovered by a team from a museum, and Im-Ho-Tep is revived when the Scroll of Thoth is read in his presence.

What is never made fully clear in the film, because explanatory scenes were dropped during the final cut, is that Helen Grosvenor, the heroine, is the reincarnation of Anck-es-en-Amon and is recognized by Im-Ho-Tep, now resurrected in the guise of Ardath Bey. When Helen is magically called to the Cairo Museum by Ardath Bey, she willingly goes, happy to be reunited with her lost lover, but she balks when he explains that she must die before she can resurrect and join him for eternity.

The film was completed in only twenty-three days, and much of the filming was done in Red Rock Canyon, a hundred miles north of Los Angeles, because it closely resembles the Valley of the Kings both in color and topography. A small crew was sent to Egypt to film background scenes, which were projected on a "process screen." The actors performed in front of this screen, while the process camera synchronized with the shoot camera so the final composite product gave the viewer the illusion that the actors were in Egypt.

MUMMY BROWN A pigment used by artists during the seventeenth and eighteenth centuries that incorporated ground mummies into the base. Even after the practice of grinding mummies stopped, a similar color was called "mummy brown."

MUMMY BUNDLES Peruvian mummies were often wrapped in large quantities of textiles, and for this reason they are called "mummy bundles."

Sometime toward the end of the Early Horizon Period (c. 300 B.C.), the inhabitants of the south coast of Peru began wrapping their dead in a seated position, creating bundles. Usually placed in a flexed position in a coiled basket, the cadaver was covered with a single cotton shroud and then enveloped in layers of cloth, often a layer of plain-weave cloth alternating with a layer of polychrome cloth. In the most elaborate mummy bundle of this period, four distinct layers were used.

In the Middle Horizon Period (A.D. 600–1000) even more elaborate bundles were created. Here too the body was seated in a basket and covered with a shroud or poncho. The bundle was built up of successive layers of cotton lint and woven textiles. Often other packing materials, such as grass, cords, and reeds, were included as filler. On top of this mass was a false head made of fibers and cloth, decorated with shell eyes, a nose, and a human-hair wig with a headband. Some of these bundles are so large and elaborate that they weigh more than 200 pounds.

After the conquest of Peru by the Spanish in 1534, the practice of mummification, and consequently the creation of mummy bundles, declined and finally ended completely when the majority of the Peruvians converted to Christianity.

MUMMY CAVE A cave in the Absaroka Mountains of northwest Wyoming, in which a mummy was found in 1963. The mummy, lying in fetal position, had been wrapped in a sheepskin blanket and placed on its right side, facing the back wall of the cave. The male, in his mid-thirties at the time of death, died around A.D. 730 and had been ceremonially buried.

The examination of this North American mummy was rather unusual as it was done with the cooperation of the Plains Indians Advisory Board. (Most Native Americans, for religious reasons, do not approve of such research.) After the body was studied nondestructively, it was returned for burial.

MUMMY CLOTH (EGYPTIAN) The cloth used to wrap Egyptian mummies was the subject of considerable debate up to the nineteenth century, with experts disagreeing as to whether it was made of cotton or linen.

The Greek traveler Herodotus noted ". . . the Egyptians wrapped their dead in cloth of the Byssus," but what plant the Byssus was, no one knew. In the eighteenth century John Reinhold Forster wrote an essay, "De Bysso Antiquorum," stating that the cloth was cotton, while Larcher said in the notes of his translation of Herodotus that "Byssus" meant cotton. This claim became near-fact, even though neither author gave evidence for the assertion. In 1821 Augustus Granville (see GRANVILLE, AUGUSTUS) had used a test that seemed to rely on the electrical properties of linen and cotton. He tested the cloth from a mummy he had unwrapped by rubbing it on glass and ivory. His claim was that cotton would be unchanged but linen would gain luster, though it is not clear why he believed this. His test "proved" that his mummy had been wrapped in cotton.

The first scientific treatise on mummy cloth was James Thomson's *On the Mummy Cloth of Egypt,* in which Thomson notes the lack of proof and presents his own. In 1822 Thomson met Giovanni Belzoni in London, when Belzoni was exhibiting the model of the tomb of Seti I. Belzoni gave him samples of mummy cloth he had brought from Egypt. Thomson noted that the quality of the cloth varied considerably—from very fine to exceedingly coarse—and resolved to determine what the samples were made of. There were several methods by which cotton could be distinguished from linen. The specific gravity of each differs, and the electrical properties of each are different. Thomson, however, did not have large enough pieces to make use of these properties in his tests.

Thomson's test was based on the common knowledge that cotton was not suitable for dressing wounds but linen was. He reasoned that this was probably due to a difference in the structure of the fibers, with cotton being more sharp and angular. Thomson found that Antonie van Leeuwenhoek, the pioneer in microscopic studies, had examined cotton and linen under a microscope in 1678 and had observed just this difference. Thomson asked Bauer, the microscopist who did drawings for the *Transactions of the Royal Society,* to examine the samples Belzoni had given him. Each one was found to be linen, and the question of the nature of mummy cloth was finally settled. Indeed, it is now well known that in antiquity Egypt did not have the cotton plant, so all the fabric was linen.

Linen is made from the flax plant, whose botanical name is *Linum usitatissimum* ("most used") because of the extensive use to which it has been put. Flax is an annual plant that in Egypt grew to a height of thirty inches. In the middle of the slender stalk is a woody core, and between this center and the outer bark are the tough flax fibers—raw linen. The Egyptians placed the harvested stalks in artificial ponds of stagnant water for up to ten days, so the fibers could easily be separated from the pithy center. The fibers were then dried and twisted together by placing a few in the palm of one hand and rubbing them on any smooth surface. Fibers could be added continually to make a thread of any length. A long ball of these twisted fibers was kept in water to maintain pliability for spinning into yarn.

The spinner would take one end of the ball and fasten it to a spindle with a hollow ring called a whorl at one end, which gave momentum to the spindle as it was revolved by hand. The fibers were thus twisted together more tightly till the yarn was ready for weaving.

The Egyptians were great weavers and some of their linen contained as many as 540 threads to the inch—the finest European linen has approximately 350. The reason the linen used to wrap mummies varies greatly in quality is that no special bandages were produced for mummy wrappings. Old clothes and sheets were used, thus there was no standard mummy bandage, either in width or quality. An ancient papyrus that tells embalmers how to wrap a mummy has a drawing of the god Horus bringing bandages to the mummy; the edges of the bandages are ragged, showing that they were torn from used linens.

MUMMY LIVES, THE This recent (1993) mummy film stars Tony Curtis as both the mummy and the mummy's alter ego, Dr. Mohassid. The film is closely modeled after Universal Pictures' 1932 classic, *The Mummy,* with Tony Curtis playing the part created by Boris Karloff.

The story lines of the two films are basically the same. In the remake the high priest of the god Zoth is buried alive for defiling a sacred concubine of the god. As in the earlier version, the mummy is discovered in its intact tomb. It reanimates and begins to kill those who have violated the tomb. Also as in the Karloff classic, the mummy is restored to a presentable appearance, in this case Dr. Mohassid, who searches for the reincarnation of his lost love of 3,000 years ago.

Most curious about this B-grade movie is that the credits say the film was inspired by Edgar Allan Poe's short story, "Some Words with a Mummy." The film has virtually no resemblance to Poe's work, which is a comedy about a mummy who is brought to life by electricity and who is unimpressed with nineteenth-century America. *The Mummy Lives* does, however, have specific scenes lifted from the 1932 *The Mummy*. When the heroine's boyfriend attempts to shake hands with Dr. Mohassid, the ancient doctor recoils, just as Ardath Bey did, "I do not like to be touched—an Eastern prejudice." Also as in the classic version, the mummy goes about killing those who entered the tomb but is finally destroyed by fire just as he is about to kill and mummify the heroine.

There are a few puzzling inconsistencies in the films. Viewers are told both that "For his terrible crimes he was mummified without having his entrails removed" and that he was buried alive. It can't be both.

The Mummy Lives deviates from the classic on one important point. This film goes into considerably more detail about mummification. As Dr. Mohassid is about to mummify one of the Egyptologists as punishment for entering the tomb, he gags him by placing in his mouth the instrument normally used for the Opening of the Mouth Ceremony, the ritual performed on a mummy at burial. The irony is not lost on the Egyptologist. Dr. Mohassid also gives a learned dissertation on how the brain was removed through the nose and even has a fairly accurate set of ancient embalming tools.

For those familiar with the details of Howard Carter's discovery of Tutankhamen's tomb, there is an insider's reference: one of the Egyptologist's pet canary is eaten by a snake. This is exactly what happened to Carter's canary and helped fuel the myth of the curse of Tutankhamen.

The Mummy Lives is a true mummy film, centering around the mummy and its curse and providing many details of the actual mummification process. It is unfortunate that the plot and dialogue leave so much to be desired.

MUMMY MOVES, THE A thinly plotted novel by Mary Gaunt, this book was one of the first (1925) mummy stories to appear after the discovery of Tutankhamen's tomb. Here we have a mummy who seems to be a killer, as she is found to have blood on her hands.

MUMMY MUSICAL, THE Author Michael Tester in 1992 created a forty-five-minute play for children, something like an MTV video with funky characters and music. The native Long Island playwright and independent producer explained his first children's play, *The Mummy Musical*, as "a journey into a child's imagination that revolves around a fantasy trip." His script, mindful of today's children's idioms and frames of reference, incorporates a colorful cast of characters including a very hip Cleopatra and the heroine Shirley, whom Tester points out is not unlike Dorothy, who traveled the yellow brick road to Oz. Set in a very happening Egyptian nightclub named the Cairocabana, The Mummy Brothers, a "5,000-year-old rap act" tap dance through their very cool routine as the journey unfolds. The production opened at the Airport Playhouse in Bohemia, New York, on Long Island.

MUMMY OR RAMSES THE DAMNED, THE Best-selling author Anne Rice combined elements from past mummy films and stories to create this extremely popular novel, which was published in 1989. As in the 1932 film *The Mummy* (see THE MUMMY), a museum expedition early in this century discovers an intact tomb, this time containing the body of Ramses the Great. Archaeologists puzzle over anachronisms, such as Greek and Latin inscriptions and references to Cleopatra. The explanation is that Ramses, who indeed lived more than a thousand years before Cleopatra, discovered an elixir that kept him alive until the Roman invasion of Egypt, when he met and fell in love with the last queen of Egypt. (The mummy in the Egyptian Museum in Cairo that tourists believe is Ramses II is a commoner substituted by Ramses.)

When Marc Antony ran himself through on his sword and was dying, Cleopatra asked Ramses to give Antony the elixir to save him, but Ramses refused. Then the queen killed herself, and Ramses, grieving for his lost love, had himself entombed far away from the sun, which was necessary to revive him. There he remained in a state of suspended animation until the museum expedition opened his tomb and the sun's rays struck him.

Unlike the film mummies, Rice's mummy is a benevolent handsome character, who adapts to modern times as Reginald Ramsey. One day while visiting the Egyptian Museum's mummy room, he recognizes an unidentified female mummy as that of Cleopatra. Pouring the elixir on the decrepit mummy, he brings her back to life, restoring Cleopatra to her former beauty. As in the film, lovers are reunited after thousands of years of separation.

There are some remarkable plot twists in *The Mummy or Ramses the Damned,* but unlike the movie there is no resolution. The reader is told that the adventures will continue in a sequel.

MUMMY'S BOYS Three Stooges film in which Maney, Moe, and Curley find themselves inside the Great Pyramid and are chased by the mummies whose sleep they have disturbed. No plot, no laughs.

MUMMY'S CURSE, THE This 1945 B-grade movie concluded Universal Pictures' mummy series. It contained many of the standard plot devises and themes of the earlier films—reincarnation, love through the centuries, forbidden arcane knowledge—but the public had seen it all, and the movie was a box office failure.

Lon Chaney, Jr. once again played Kharis, the mummy. Despite the fact that in the previous film, *The Mummy's Ghost*, Kharis and Ananka disappeared into a swamp in Massachusetts, they turn up in Cajun Louisiana! While Kharis is being studied by archaeologists, construction workers uncover his lost love, the Princess Ananka, in a swamp. Searching for Ananka, Kharis begins a reign of terror on the local inhabitants.

"MUMMY'S FOOT, THE" This nineteenth-century short story by Théophile Gautier was one of the first to explore the magical properties of mummies—or parts of them.

When a man purchases a mummy's foot in a Parisian antique shop, he is told by the wizened owner that it is the foot of Princess Hermonthis. The man, who takes the foot home to use as a paperweight, has purchased more than he expected. As the foot moves across his desk, the sad princess appears in search of her foot. After he offers to give it back, the grateful princess transports her benefactor back to ancient Egypt to meet her father.

The king asks what he would like in return for the foot, and by now the young man has fallen in love with the princess and asks to marry her. In this story, and all subsequent mummy stories

The Mummy's Curse *The Mummy's Curse* was Lon Chaney, Jr.'s last appearance as Kharis the mummy. The movie was a box office failure and concluded Universal Pictures' mummy series.

The Mummy's Ghost Although the lobby card for *The Mummy's Ghost* advertised such stars as Lon Chaney, John Carradine, and George Zucco, they could not replace Boris Karloff, and the film was only a modest success.

involving love between a modern and an ancient, it is not to be. The king explains that the age difference between the couple is too great and the young man is unceremoniously transported back to the nineteenth-century with only an amulet as a souvenir of his lost love.

MUMMY'S GHOST, THE The next to the last (1944) in Universal Pictures' mummy movie sequence. In this film John Carradine plays the young high priest who protects the mummy. By

the end of this film, Caradine and the mummy are fighting over the girl (who is the reincarnation of Kharis's forbidden love, Princess Ananka). The mummy wins, and he and his old flame sink happily into a swamp in Massachusetts.

MUMMY'S HAND, THE Universal Pictures' 1940 sequel to its classic *The Mummy*. The mummy, patterned after that of Ramses III in the Egyptian Museum, Cairo, was played by Tom Tyler. When the actor played the mummy, he was suffering from degenerative arthritis, so the mummy's twisted limbs were a necessity in this case.

The first of the mummy movies in which the mummy is named Kharis, it is also the first in which tana leaves appear. The high priest uses three of them to keep Kharis's heart beating and nine to give him life. The movie contains many archaeological errors. In one scene Professor Petrie explains that the expression on the mummy's face indicates that he was buried alive. A moment later he comments that the skin is soft and lifelike, "The most amazing example of embalming I've ever seen." This indeed was a remarkable mummy, to have been both buried alive and embalmed. The excavators also use a means not normally employed in archaeological investigations—they dynamite a mountain to uncover the hidden tomb!

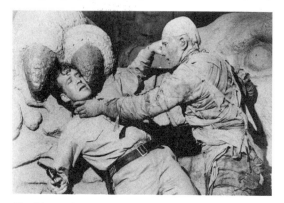

The Mummy's Hand In *The Mummy's Hand*, Universal Pictures' first sequel to *The Mummy*, the mummy's image and name was changed.

The Mummy's Tomb In *The Mummy's Tomb* Turhan Bey plays the high priest entrusted with the care of Kharis, the mummy.

Mummy Tags Mummy tags were used by Egyptian embalmers to identify mummies during the process of mummification. The mummy tag of Senkollanthes, daughter of Kollanthes, asks that "... her soul live before Osiris, Foremost of the West, the Great God, Lord of Abydos." *Photo courtesy Museum of Fine Arts, Boston.*

MUMMY'S TOMB, THE Released in 1942 this film was Universal Pictures' sequel to *The Mummy's Hand*. The plot centers around the high priests of Karnak's attempts to thwart those who wish to disturb the mummy's resting place. The mummy was played by Lon Chaney, Jr., though much of the time it was stuntman Eddie Parker beneath the wrappings. In this film the wizened high priest, played by George Zucco, passes the responsibility of protecting Kharis on to the much younger Turhan Bey.

This is the first of the mummy films in which the mummy leaves Egypt, traveling to Massachusetts to avenge the desecration of Princess Ananka's tomb. One by one the members of the original expedition are killed until the mummy and the high priest are destroyed by fire.

MUMMY TAGS During the Roman period (31 B.C.–A.D. 395) of Egyptian history, mummies were frequently provided with identity tags made of wood rectangles with a hole at one end where the corners were trimmed off, much like a modern luggage tag. These tags had both a practical and religious function.

Wrappings covered the identifying features of the mummy, and labels facilitated identification in the embalmer's shop, where there might be many mummies at one time. Frequently mummies were moved years after burial, to make room in a tomb for more recent mummies, and the tags helped keep track of who was who.

The religious function of the tags was based on the belief that to say or write the name of the deceased was to make them live again. Thus the tags gave new life to the dead, and often they bear a brief prayer to Osiris, the god of the dead, to assure the deceased's acceptance into the next world.

MUMMY! THE, OR A TALE OF THE TWENTY-SECOND CENTURY A novel written by Jane Webb Loudon (1807–58) and published in 1827, *The Mummy!* is the first mummy story in the English language.

Loudon is best known as the author of horticulture and gardening books, based on the works of her husband, John, who was famous for his gardening encyclopedias. *The Mummy!* is one of the earliest pieces of science fiction, and is set in London in 2126. Although the city is technologically advanced—electricity controls rainstorms, steam boats go sixty miles per hour, and women's hats are illuminated by "lighted gas"—the civilization is morally bankrupt and about to collapse because of political infighting.

Published soon after Mary Shelley's *Frankenstein*, Loudon capitalized on the theme of a reanimated being, but here it is the resurrected mummy of King Cheops who begins the action. Regretful of his own past corruption, the pharaoh puts all his effort into restoring economic, moral, and social stability to London.

MUMMY WHEAT The ancient Egyptians frequently buried supplies of food with their dead to sustain them in the next world. There are many stories of "mummy wheat" sprouting after 3,000 years in a tomb, but none are true. This mistake arose, however, because wheat did in fact sprout in tombs soon after they were sealed.

Along with the food supplies, the ancient Egyptians buried what are called Osiris molds—molds in the shape of the god of the dead, Osiris—that had been filled with earth, planted with wheat, and placed in the tomb at the time of burial as symbols of resurrection. Because the seeds were only a year or so old, they frequently germinated in the tomb. It is not possible for wheat to germinate after thousands of years because the wheat germ dies after only a few years, and wheat that is "only" a hundred years old cannot grow.

In the 1930s E.A. Wallis Budge, the curator of Egyptian antiquities in the British Museum, gave ancient wheat found in tombs to Dr. Wilfred Parker, director of the National Institute of Agricultural Botany at Cambridge. Microscopic examination showed that the wheat embryos were dead. Dr. Parker planted them anyway, but after sixteen days all had rotted and were covered with mold.

MURDER IN THE PLACE OF ANUBIS This 1994 novel, written by Lynda S. Robinson, is set in the time of Tutankhamen, and the story centers around a murder that is committed in the mummification workshop of Thebes.

The body of the querulous scribe, Hormin, is found buried under natron in the embalmer's shop, a ritual embalmer's knife still embedded in his throat. The primary clue is a heart amulet of extraordinary fine quality found with the body. The majority of the novel revolves around Meren, The Eyes and Ears of the Pharaoh, and his son, Kysen, as they attempt to solve the murder. The book utilizes accurate details about ancient Egyptian mummification and ritual practices.

n

NAPLES This southern Italian city has for centuries used natural mummification as part of its burial practice. Because Naples is at the base of Mount Vesuvius, its soil is rich in volcanic ash, which is ideal for natural mummification. The deceased of Naples are buried without coffins, so the bodies come in direct contact with the soil and dehydrate quickly, and are thus preserved. After eighteen to twenty-four months, the naturally mummified bodies are dug up and returned to their families for permanent burial in aboveground vaults.

NAPOLEON, BODY OF (1769–1821) Emperor of France and one of the greatest military tacticians of all time, Napoleon's preserved body lies in the Hôtel des Invalides in Paris and is still the subject of controversy, for some believe he did not die of natural causes.

Napoleon first distinguished himself when he was a captain in the army by recapturing the French port of Toulon from the British. He was promoted to the rank of brigadier general at the age of twenty-four, and in 1799 in a coup d'état, Napoleon became first consul. He declared himself emperor of France in 1804. During his rule the government was reorganized under the Code Napoleon, which guaranteed equality and liberty. As Napoleon conquered Europe, country by country, the Code Napoleon was established, and in many countries it is still the basis of the legal system.

After a series of brilliant military victories, Napoleon invaded Russia. The campaign was a complete disaster. Unprepared for the bitter Russian winter and the repeated retreats of the Russian army, Napoleon lost hundreds of thousands of men when they froze to death or died of starvation. Realizing that he was weakened, Europe united against him, and in 1814 Napoleon abdicated and was exiled to the island of Elba.

After a dramatic escape from Elba in 1815, Napoleon returned to France and reorganized his army. His brief campaign ended in defeat at the Battle of Waterloo in Belgium. Soon after, Napoleon surrendered and was exiled to the isolated island of Saint Helena in the south Atlantic Ocean.

Napoleon remained on the island, under house arrest by the British, until his death on May 5, 1821. Much controversy surrounded Napoleon's death. The French claimed the climate contributed to his decline and that the British had slowly killed him. The British claimed he had died of stomach cancer. In an autopsy performed by Dr. Antomarchi with half a dozen other doctors present, Bonaparte's liver and stomach were removed, and it was clear that the liver was diseased and the stomach cancerous and perforated. Napoleon had indeed died of stomach cancer. Antomarchi wished to return to Europe with the stomach but was refused permission to do so. Napoleon's heart and stomach were placed in a silver urn that was filled with alcohol and soldered closed. He was placed in a tin coffin lined with satin. The tin coffin was placed inside a wood coffin, and the wood coffin was placed inside a lead coffin. Finally the three coffins were to be placed inside a mahogany one. When no mahogany could be found on the island, Captain James Bennett of the Saint Helena Regiment offered his mahogany dining table for lumber. Aside from the preservation of the internal organs in spirits, no embalming of Napoleon's body is recorded. There were limited resources on the island, and it is doubtful that Antomarchi could have obtained the necessary supplies. On May 7, 1821 the body of Napoleon Bonaparte was laid to rest on Saint Helena.

Before his death Bonaparte had requested that his remains be buried among the French people. For nearly twenty years the French requested the British to return Napoleon's remains to France, but the English feared the body might be a rallying point for Bonapartists to seize power and refused. Then in 1840 the English agreed to give up Napoleon's remains to an official French delegation. On October 15, 1840, the twenty-fifth anniversary of Napoleon's arrival on the island, the grave was opened and the coffins removed. The French refused to sign a receipt until they had verified that Napoleon's body was indeed inside the innermost coffin. When the coffins were opened, those present were shocked. Rather than a corpse in the advanced stages of decay, Bonaparte looked as he did on the day of his death. His fingernails had grown a bit, as is common after death, but his skin and flesh appeared perfectly preserved, and many of those present remarked that he looked as he were sleeping. The coffins were taken in solemn procession to the waiting ship, the *Belle Paule*, which docked forty-three days later at Cherbourg. It took seven more days for Napoleon's remains to reach Paris. Wherever the ship docked there were ceremonies attended by the aging soldiers who had served under Bonaparte.

Napoleon, body of This porphyry sarcophagus at the Hôtel des Invalides, Paris, contains the remarkably well-preserved body of Napoleon.

The coffins remained on board at each port, so it was in Paris that Napoleon's body first touched French soil. A special funeral boat had been constructed, which included a temple of gilded wood from which hung drapes of purple and gold. Thousands camped on the hillsides to pay their respects. On the day of the procession, December 15, 1840, it was a bitterly cold -8 degrees F, but hundreds of thousands of people filled the streets of Paris to view Napoleon's funeral procession. An indoor spot by a window cost 100 francs ($20), and there were more buyers than sellers. Thirty-six thousand official passes were distributed by the Ministry of the Interior, but more than a quarter of a million requests were made.

At 2:00 P.M. in the afternoon the cortege made its way to the Hôtel des Invalides. The king, Louis-Philippe, descended from his throne to meet the coffin. Mozart's *Requiem* was sung, and for eight days the coffin remained on view in the church.

In February it was transferred to its tomb in the basement of the Hôtel des Invalides, where it rests today. On either side are coffins containing the bodies of his faithful comrades Bertrand and Duroc. At the entrance are the tombs of his brothers, Jérôme and Joseph. The inscription above Napoleon reads:

Let him rest in peace beneath this dome
It is a helmet made for a giant's head.

The body of Napoleon was not examined when it returned to France and has not been examined since it was exhumed on Saint Helena. The remarkable condition of the unembalmed body nineteen years after burial caused considerable debate. Recently investigators claimed that it was evidence that Napoleon had been murdered. They argue that Napoleon died of arsenic poisoning, and because arsenic is a preservative, his corpse remained intact. Most historians of Napoleon reject this theory and believe that the evidence of stomach cancer is far too compelling to reject.

Napoleon's body may be an example of natural mummification. The nested coffins holding the emperor were not merely placed in the ground. A vault 11 feet deep, 8 feet long, and 4½ feet wide was dug to receive the coffins. When those exhuming the coffins opened the grave, it was difficult to reach the coffins. Seven feet down there was a layer of cement that had been used to seal the grave, and under that were stone slabs ten inches thick bound together by iron clamps. Furthermore, the lid of the first coffin had been cemented shut. It took the group ten hours to open it.

Napoleon's coffins may have, in effect, been airtight and this would account for his having been naturally mummified. Also helping in the process was the fact that the internal organs had been removed, thus eliminating a prime source of putrefaction in the body.

NAST, THOMAS (1840–1902)

One of America's greatest political cartoonists, Thomas Nast created the familiar images of Uncle Sam, the Republican elephant, the Democratic donkey, and even our version of Santa Claus as a red-cheeked, white-bearded old man. Nast was also a political reporter, and in an attempt to point out corruption in New York's Democratic Party, he created a unique series of cartoons in which Egyptian mummies and mummy cases were the central theme.

Born in Germany in 1840, Nast emigrated to New York at the age of six with his family. As a very young child, Nast showed an amazing talent for drawing and a less amazing talent for school. His father, a musician, was tolerant of Nast's desire to draw and permitted Thomas to attend Theodore Kaufmann's drawing classes at 442 Broadway. When he was fifteen Nast brought a few of his drawings to Frank Leslie, who had just started a weekly illustrated magazine.

Leslie was impressed with the young artist's drawings and gave him an assignment—to sketch the vacationers taking the ferry at Christopher Street for the Elysian Fields, a resort near

Thomas Nast (A) Thomas Nast used the image of an Egyptian mummy in his political cartoons to draw attention to his fight against political corruption.

Hoboken. Nast spent all weekend sketching, and when Leslie saw the results, Nast landed his first job.

Leslie employed the best engraver and artists of the time and it was in this atmosphere that young Nast learned the techniques that would make him famous. Over the next few years, Nast covered such diverse events as the championship fight between Heenan and Sayers in London and the liberation of Italy by Garibaldi. During the Civil War, Nast's patriotic cartoons helped sustain the war effort in the North. Abraham Lincoln said, "Thomas Nast has been our best recruiting sergeant. His emblematic cartoons have never failed to arouse enthusiasm and patriotism, and have always seemed to come just when these articles were getting scarce."

In addition to his cartoons, Nast was sought after as a book illustrator and soon became world famous. With fame came his connection to the influential *Harper's Weekly* and his reputation as a political reformer.

One of Nast's most enduring targets was Samuel J. Tilden, the undisputed leader of the Democratic Party. Tilden was repeatedly involved in fraudulent schemes, and although he was caught trying to buy votes, he was nevertheless elected as the Democratic party candidate in 1876 along with his running mate, Governor Hendricks of Indiana. Nast supported Rutherford B. Hayes who credited Nast as "the most powerful single-handed aid we had."

One of Nast's earliest Egyptian themes appeared in *Harper's Weekly* for July 7, 1877. Tilden and Hendricks are shown as mummies in anthropoid coffins. Hendricks's name is written in rebus style on the first register of the coffin, while the second register states that he is from Indiana. Tilden's affiliation with New York is indicated by the windmill on the city's seal. Between the two mummified politicians is Anubis, the Egyptian god of embalming. Above the entire composition is a winged scarab, another Egyptian image familiar to Nast's readers (figure A).

Nast chose mummies because they conjured up the notion of eternal death, thus his caption, "Embalmed That They May Keep Until 1880 or Longer," was a hopeful understatement. Neither man ever ran again. Nast had underrated Tilden's resiliency, however, and soon after the 1876 election Tilden was involved in one of the greatest political scandals of all time, which had all the excitement of a murder mystery.

A senate committee obtained copies of telegrams which were sent during the Democratic convention by Tilden to his nephew and secretary, Colonel Pelton. These telegrams were in code but were printed by the *New York Tribune* with suggestions as to their meaning. Each day more of the code was revealed, and each day thousands of readers bought thousands of newspapers for the "next thrilling installment." Finally when the full cipher was broken, it was clear that Tilden had attempted to buy the presidency. Once again Nash went after Tilden with his pen, again depicting Tilden as a mummy. While the caption reads "Cipher Mumm(er)y," the cartoon details reveal everything (figure B).

On the central panel of the coffin are the actual cipher telegrams which had been published by the *New York Tribune*. The address on the first telegram is 15 Gramercy Park, which was Tilden's and appears as a keyhole beneath the mummy's chain.

Tilden's chief conspirators were C.W. Woolley, whose code name was "Fox," and Morton Marble, whose code name was "Moses." Both code names appear on the mummy's shoulder.

The first telegram, when deciphered, read:

Have just received a proposition to hand over at any hour required Tilden decision of board and certificate of Governor for $200,000.

While $200,000 was the amount of the payoff, other amounts had been discussed, and bargaining had occurred.

The second telegram on the coffin reads:

Board may make necessary expenses on half a hundred thousand dollars. Can you say will deposit in bank immediately as agreed?

The last telegram on the coffin is the reply:

Telegram received. Will deposit dollars agreed. (You) cannot however draw before vote (of) member (is) received.

Clearly there was not enough trust among those thieves to pay for a vote before it was received.

The details of Nast's cartoon show his development of the Egyptian motif. In his first Egyptian cartoon, he included a winged scarab above the mummies. Here the scarab has turned into a bag of money, and the wings are those of a bat. Hieroglyphs were an ideal motif in a car-

toon dealing with ciphers, and Nast gives full credit to the *New York Tribune* for the decipherment—standing next to the mummy is a key labeled "Found by the N.Y. Tribune."

Amazingly, Tilden would remain a significant political force for another decade! Nast repeatedly used the mummy image to lampoon him, but now he incorporated non-Egyptian symbols, which readers would always recognize. "Fraud" would be stamped across Tilden's forehead, and the keyhole with "15 Gramercy Park, N.Y." would be placed beneath the chin. Somewhere on the coffin readers could find "Moses" and "Fox" and the phrase "Cipher mum(er)y."

As the 1880 election approached, the Democratic Party was in trouble. They couldn't nominate

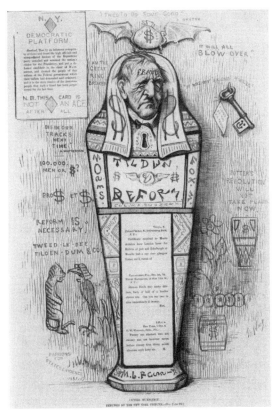

Thomas Nast (B) Political cartoon showing Samuel J. Tilden as a mummy. The hieroglyphs reveal a scandal in which he was involved.

Thomas Nast (C) Political cartoon showing Tilden as a mummy, to indicate that his career is dead.

to the convention, hoping that this would draw him nomination by acclaim. The ploy did not work; the convention elected General Hancock as its candidate. Always ready to ridicule Tilden, the familiar mummy is shown with the letter of withdrawal as a lightning rod intending to draw the nomination. The lightning just misses Tilden and strikes Hancock (figure D).

The last cartoon to use the Tilden mummy was drawn for the 1884 Democratic convention. By now Tilden was out of the picture, and the image depicted the Democratic tradition of corruption being moved to Tomb Stone Alley.

One of Thomas Nast's greatest skills was his ability to create images that said "Egypt" to the public. The most frequently used symbol was the anthropoid coffin, but another visual was the scarab, the beetle (*scarabaeus sacre*), which was ancient

Tilden because he couldn't win, but not to nominate him would look like an admission of guilt for the bribery attempt during the 1876 election. John Kelly, the leader of Tammany Hall, had declared he would rather a Republican were elected than Tilden. Under such pressure, it was rumored that Tilden would withdraw his candidacy. Calling on all the familiar images, Nast portrayed John Kelly as a Roman legionary leaning oven the Tilden mummy. "It is whispered again that Tilden has given in" (figure C). Fearful that Tilden might yet resurrect, a few weeks before the Democratic convention in Cincinnati, Nast depicted a pharaonic Democratic Party laboring under the heavy weight of Tilden's coffin.

Tilden, still very much alive and attempting to regain nomination, sent a letter of withdrawal

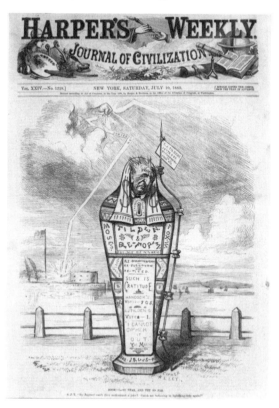

Thomas Nast (D) Political cartoon using mummies to indicate the 1880 Democratic nominee for president.

Natron Small packets of natron were placed inside the body cavities of Egyptian mummies to speed dehydration. *Photo courtesy Museum of Fine Arts, Boston.*

Egyptians' symbol of continued existence. The winged scarab was frequently inscribed on tomb and temple walls as a protective talisman, but Nast replaced the scarab with a money bag and made it the emblem of political greed. The image was familiar enough that the public would still read it as Egyptian. Hieroglyphs and mummies were also images that no one would miss as Egyptian, as was the sphinx, and Nast used them all.

NATRON A naturally occurring mixture of sodium carbonate, sodium bicarbonate, and sodium chloride—basically baking soda and salt—that was the primary ingredient in ancient Egyptian mummification. The body was covered in natron for approximately thirty-five days, which removed most of the moisture from the body and emulsified the body fats so they would run out. For these thirty-five days, small bags of natron were placed inside the abdomen and thoracic cavities to dehydrate the body from the inside as well. At times solutions of natron were used in canopic jars (see CANOPIC JARS) to preserve the internal organs. (See HETEPHERES.)

In addition to its use in the actual mummification process, natron was used in religious rituals for purification. One of the terms for natron was "divine substance." Dishes of ritual natron were found in Tutankhamen's tomb.

The two chief sources of natron in ancient Egypt were El Kab, a city in Upper Egypt, and the Wadi Natrun, an area approximately sixty miles west of Cairo.

NATURAL CURIOSITY, A **(1988)** A novel written by Margaret Drabble (b. 1939), in which the Lindow Man bog mummy is an unstated theme.

Alix Bowen, the main character of the novel, is somehow drawn to a captured serial murderer obsessed with Roman Iron Age rituals. She frequently visits Paul Whitmore in a prison outside of London, where he is serving time for beheading his victims in Iron Age style. As Alix brings him books so he can study Iron Age archaeological finds, her best friend visits the British Museum to see the newly displayed Lindow Man (see LINDOW MAN). Later the two women have a long discussion about bog mummies, P.V. Glob, the Danish expert on the mummies, and Seamus Heaney, the poet laureate of bog mummies.

Seemingly everyone in the story has a connection to bog mummies: the poet for whom Alix works has written about them, the father of a friend of her son is an excavator of burial sites, and Lindow Man is the silent leit motif throughout *A Natural Curiosity*.

NATURAL MUMMIFICATION Occasionally, without any attempt at preservation, a body is naturally mummified. No single explanation covers all natural mummification; sometimes one factor can explain it, and at other times a combination of conditions causes the phenomenon. Freezing, dehydration by dry air (see PERUVIAN MUMMIES), or dehydration caused by burial in warm dry sand can cause mummification, but there are times when these conditions are absent and mummification still takes place.

In all bodies, cells break down at the time of death. There are two major causes of bodily decomposition, putrefaction and autolysis. Putrefaction is the decay caused by bacteria acting on organic matter. Much of the early decay in cadavers is caused by bacteria in the intestines. Autolysis is the decomposition of tissues caused by enzymes within the body. During life the enzymes are bound to cells, but at death they are released, causing decay.

In natural mummification an "enzymatic equilibrium" of the tissues is reached, and the destruction of protein substances stops. It is possible for trace elements in soil, whitewash on crypt walls, or other combined environmental factors to produce a natural mummy. (See VENZONE, ITALY, MUMMIES OF.)

NAVELLI, ITALY, MUMMIES OF Navelli, a small town in central Italy, contains the Church of San Bartolomeo, which may house literally thousands of mummies.

In 1988 the floor of the rectory of the church collapsed, revealing a series of underground rooms in which the inhabitants of Navelli had been buried for centuries. The bodies had naturally mummified, and preliminary inspection indicates that the rooms may accommodate the entire population of the town from the fourteenth century to the beginning of the nineteenth century, when Napoleon Bonaparte banned the burial of bodies beneath churches. The mummies have not yet been studied scientifically, but are a very important collection because a great deal could be learned about disease and death in Italy over a period of five centuries.

"NEXT IN LINE, THE" An early (1947) Ray Bradbury story that centers around the mummies of Guanajuato, Mexico.

A couple visiting Guanajuato as tourists decide to visit the crypt where the mummies are kept. The caretaker explains that the mummies are the bodies of those inhabitants of Guanajuato whose families would not or could not pay the annual burial fee. If the family paid the burial fee for three years, the body remained in the cemetery for three years, but once the fee was not paid, the body was exhumed and placed in the aboveground crypt. As the caretaker relates who each individual mummy was and what his or her life was like, the husband takes a photo of each, while the wife who is extremely fearful of the mummies counts them to distract herself.

After the excursion the couple returns to their hotel room, but the woman is so unnerved that she convinces her husband to leave town immediately. Unfortunately their car won't start, and they are stranded for two more days. Terrified that she will somehow become one of the mummies, Marie stays up all night listening to her heart beat—a sign that she is still alive. During the day she reads old American magazines line by line, again a sign that she is alive (I read, therefore I am).

Marie is so afraid of becoming a mummy that in the evening, as her husband prepares to go to bed, she asks him to promise that if she dies that night, he will not leave her with the mummies. Joseph reassures her that everything will be all right, but he regards her request as silly and merely says, "You'll be fine tommorrow." We are never given the details, but the reader is told that the next day Joseph leaves Guanajuato alone.

NIEMAN-MARCUS MUMMY   The 1971 Christmas catalog of the Nieman-Marcus Department Store in Dallas listed "His and Hers authenticated Mummy Cases . . . Companions from the past richly adorned, but gratefully vacant." The cases were purchased for the Rosicrucian Egyptian Museum in San Jose, California, but when they were being prepared for shipping, the store discovered that one case still contained a mummy. The store called the museum to assure the curator that they would dispose of the mummy before shipping, but the curator happily told them to ship the mummy also.

The inscription on the coffin containing the mummy indicates that the original occupant was Usermontu, a priest of the god Montu at Thebes. The coffin dates from the Late Period (c.600 B.C.) and is on display, along with the mummy, at the museum.

"The Next in Line"   One of the Guanajuato mummies as described in "The Next in Line."   *Photo courtesy John Mahoney.*

North American Mummies A naturally preserved Native American mummy from Canyon del Muerto, c. A.D. 300–500. *Photo courtesy Eve Cockburn.*

NORTH AMERICAN MUMMIES Almost all of the Native American mummies found in the United States are the result of natural mummification by dry air. These mummies come from either the southwest or southern United States, and in both areas most of the mummies have been discovered in caves.

The mummies from the Southwest are of the early inhabitants of Arizona, known as the Anasazi, the Navajo word for "ancient people." The earliest of these people are known as the Basket Makers, hunter-gatherers who lived in caves between A.D. 100 and 700. They buried their dead in stone-lined pits that were originally used for food storage, and the climate frequently preserved the bodies. Because the pits, or "cists"

as they are called, were relatively small, the bodies had to be placed in a modified fetal position, which may have been the origin of the American Indian practice of burying their dead in flexed position. The bodies were usually wrapped in fur blankets and accompanied by some small objects, such as pipes or baskets, probably indicating a belief in life after death. One burial even included a brand-new pair of sandals.

Later Arizona mummies are more common and have been found in Painted Cave, Canyon Creek Ruin, McCuen Cave, Ventana Cave, and Canyon del Muerto. These mummies have usually been placed in a corner of a cave or beneath an overhang for protection and have thus dehydrated naturally. The mummies from Ventana Cave were of special interest because it was hoped that they might lead to the solution of a modern medical problem. There is a high incidence of valley fever (coccidioidomycosis) among the Papago, and it was hoped that by studying the mummies of the previous inhabitants of the area, it might be possible to determine if the disease was a modern one or if the early residents also suffered from it. The mummies were x-rayed, but no traces of the disease were found. The disease may therefore be caused by modern conditions, but more research is needed to confirm this. Forty-three of the mummies found in the Southwest are stored in the Arizona State Museum in Tempe.

Of the mummies found in the southern United States, most come from caves in Kentucky, with a few found in Tennessee. The Kentucky mummies were found in the Mammoth Cave area, mostly by early nineteenth-century saltpeter miners. One famous mummy, known as Fawn Hoof, was discovered in that area in Short Cave in 1813. Found in a stone-lined box grave in a seated position, she was wearing fine burial garments of animal skin and was accompanied by a significant number of grave goods. The extremely well preserved body was exhibited in the United States Museum in 1876, and later the body was dissected and the bones cleaned.

The skeletal remains of Fawn Hoof are now in storage in the Smithsonian Institution in Washington, D.C.

Two mummies similar to Fawn Hoof were discovered in 1810 in a cave in Warren County in west Tennessee. The mummies, one male and one female, were clothed in fine garments, accompanied by grave goods, placed in large cane baskets, and buried in a pit in the cave floor. In the woman's hand was a fan made from the tail feathers of a turkey.

The mummies of Native Americans may be an important resource for the study of the diseases and lifestyles of the earliest inhabitants of the American South and Southwest. They have not yet been studied extensively because of opposition from Native American groups, who oppose such studies on religious grounds.

O

OPENING OF THE MOUTH CEREMONY

On the day an ancient Egyptian was buried, the opening of the mouth ceremony was performed on the mummy. The officiating priest raised a ceremonial knife and touched it to the mouth of the mummy. (Sometimes an instrument resembling an adz, a woodworker's tool, was used.) This symbolic opening of the mouth would enable the mummy to speak in the next world. The ritual could also be performed on a statue of the deceased if the body was not readily available.

OSIRIS (THE MYTH OF)

The myth of Osiris is central to the ancient Egyptians' practice of mummification. No complete Egyptian copy of the myth exists, and the best ancient version is that of Plutarch, a Greek priest at Delphi, who wrote around A.D. 100.

Osiris and Isis were brother and sister and also husband and wife. Their brother, Seth, and another sister, Nephthys, were also husband and wife. Osiris brought civilization to Egypt, introducing farming and cattle-raising, thus freeing the early inhabitants of the Nile valley from misery. Then Osiris left Egypt to bring civilization to the rest of the world, leaving Isis, the powerful goddess of magic, to keep their evil brother, Seth, in check.

Upon Osiris's return Seth obtained his brother's exact body measurements by trickery and constructed a highly ornamental wooden chest to fit Osiris precisely. During a banquet Seth offered the magnificent chest as a gift to whoever could fit inside it, but guest after guest failed in their attempts. Osiris tried and succeeded. However, as soon as he settled inside the chest, Seth threw the bolts and poured molten lead over it. He then cast the chest into one of the Delta branches of the Nile. A violent storm subsequently carried the chest to Byblos in Lebanon, where it washed ashore and wedged in the branches of a tree. In time the tree grew to an extraordinary size, it's trunk enveloping the chest and Osiris. In the course of building his palace, the king of Byblos cut down the tree to use as one of the pillars.

As soon as Isis learned what had happened to her husband, she set out to recover his body. Enlisting the aid of the Queen of Byblos, Isis had the pillar cut open so she could recover the body of Osiris and bring it back to Egypt for proper burial. When Seth discovered that the body of Osiris had been returned to Egypt, he hacked it into fourteen pieces, and scattered them throughout Egypt. Isis then recovered every piece, except one, the phallus, which had been thrown into the Nile and consumed by fish. Isis reassembled her deceased husband and fashioned an artificial phallus for him. Transforming herself into a bird, Isis hovered over Osiris's body and brought him back to life by reciting magical words.

This myth reveals the origin of mummification in the cult of Osiris. The importance of a proper burial on Egyptian ground is emphasized by the efforts that Isis made to recover her husband's body. The importance of an intact corpse is shown by her search for all the parts of the body and the fact that she fashioned an artificial phallus to replace the missing member. Isis, in the form of a bird, hovers over a complete body. Finally she speaks the proper words, and the body resurrects. Osiris retains, after death, the same body he inhabited while alive. Mummification thus becomes essential to immortality; the body must be preserved for the afterlife.

P

PAABO, SVANTE Swedish biologist who was the first to successfully clone DNA from a mummy. (See CLONING.)

PACHACAMAC MUMMIES Pachacamac, a region on the coast of southern Peru, has produced a considerable number of mummies, some of which have only recently come under scientific investigation.

The settlement at Pachacamac centered around the temple, built in honor of the god Pachacamac, creator of the universe. In the eighth century A.D. Pachacamac was a thriving community, but it slowly diminished until around A.D. 1465 when the powerful Incas invaded and the inhabitants unresistingly joined them. After the alliance the population grew, and the temple was enlarged to accommodate the increased religious activity. When Francisco Pizarro arrived in 1533 in search of gold, the temple of Pachacamac was destroyed, and Christianity was forced upon the people.

Much of what we know about the Pachacamacs is due to the efforts of Professor Max Uhle, one of the pioneers of South American archaeology. He first excavated in South America in 1892 for the Prussian Government, sending back collections of artifacts and mummies from wherever he went. In 1892 his excavation at Pachacamac was funded by the University of Pennsylvania. For an entire year he excavated at the site, collecting pottery, textiles, and mummies that he sent to the university's museum in Philadelphia.

Mummification was essential to the Pachacamac belief in life after death, the preservation of the body being crucial to continued existence. Bodies were placed in a seated position and wrapped with layer after layer of textiles.

The mummies were buried with everyday objects that would be needed in the next world—needles for making fishnets, grain, and pouches containing medicines. Often a decorative feathered shawl would be wrapped around the mummy's shoulders just before burial. The most desirable place to be buried was next to the temple, near the god, so the entire area surrounding the temple was occupied by cemeteries. It was here that Max Uhle excavated and found some of the earliest Pachacamac mummies, which dated from the seventh century. Many of these mummy bundles are comprised of an elaborate superstructure built around the mummy, which rests in the center. The bundles were stuffed with leaves from local fruit trees, and were held in place by basketlike woven frames. Sometimes the bales were topped with a false head carved of wood with inlaid shell eyes. Some of the mummies that Uhle sent back to the university museum have disintegrated, but those that remain have recently been the subjects of scientific study.

The four Pachacamac mummies still in the museum were x-rayed at the University of Pennsylvania Hospital. All were shown to be children, the oldest about fifteen years old and the youngest about one year old. In two cases the cause of death could be determined from the X rays. The one-year-old had been ritually decapitated with a stone knife as a sacrifice to the gods. Infant sacrifice was rare, although older children, both boys and girls, were often sacrificed to please the gods during the month of August, when the first corn was planted. Other

Pachacamac Mummies The Pachacamac mummies of southern Peru. *Photo courtesy University of Pennsylvania Museum, Philadelphia.*

causes for sacrifice were plagues, famine, military defeats, or any communal tragedy.

The other child for whom the cause of death could be determined was a girl about twelve years old. The X ray of her skull showed that the bones forming the top of the skull were misaligned. She may have had a brain tumor that eventually caused such pressure on the skull that the bones were forced apart.

It is surprising that there was no attempt to treat the girl's illness surgically. Ancient Peruvian doctors were skilled in the art of trephination—drilling a hole to remove a small piece of bone in the skull and relieve pressure or to examine the brain and determine the cause of a problem. The young girl must have suffered from headaches and blurred vision, and we can only wonder why she was not treated by the ancient physicians.

PADIHERSHEF, MUMMY OF Padihershef, the first human mummy to be brought to America, reached Boston in 1823. The mummy had been obtained by the British consul at Alexandria for Jacob van Lennep, a Dutch merchant at Smyrna, who wished to donate it to a public establishment "as a mark of respect to the city." Thus the mummy was entrusted to the captain of the *Sally Ann*, R.B. Edes, to bring it to Boston.

The mummy, enclosed in its inner and outer anthropoid coffins, was given to the Massachusetts General Hospital, where it was examined by Drs. Warren, Jackson, and Gorham. The ultimate intention was to place the mummy on display, charge admission, and thus raise money for the hospital. The first $200 profit was to go to the Boston Dispensary, and any additional funds would be given to "such poor persons as are destitute or distressed on leaving this institution after sickness and confinement." Because the mummy had to be attractive for display, it could not be totally unwrapped. Dr. John Warren, the distinguished surgeon, declared it genuine, based on accounts he had read by travelers to Egypt who described mummies. Dr. Warren also unwrapped the head of the mummy.

The mummy was displayed at Mr. Doggett's Repository of the Arts on Market Street in a specially constructed glass case. Handbills were printed, and advertisements for the viewing of "The Egyptian Mummy" were placed in local newspapers. During the first two days, more than 500 people paid their 25¢ to see Padihershef.

The mummy remained on display for several months and was such a great fund-raiser that the trustees of the hospital decided to send Padihershef on a tour of southern cities, and this was arranged by Doggett & Co. The mummy was displayed at eleven major cities between Boston and Charleston, South Carolina but was transported only by water because it was feared that the rough roads would damage it. Padihershef's year-long tour was not the great success his Boston sojourn had been. Soon after his arrival in Boston, other mummies reached America, and by the time he was displayed in New York, Philadelphia, and Baltimore, other mummies had preceded him. The novelty had worn off. Indeed, now newspaper ads not only advertised a mummy, but claimed that "this is in more perfect preservation than any other Mummy ever brought to this country."

The mummy and its cases returned to Massachusetts General Hospital, where they remained for half a century, until they were exhibited at the Boston Museum of Fine Arts. In 1896 Padihershef and his inner coffin were returned to the hospital, while the outer coffin remained at the museum. But this was far from the last move for the peripatetic mummy. In 1932 the outer coffin became the property of the George Walter Vincent Smith Art Museum in Springfield, Massachusetts, but by that time no one remembered that it went with the mummy and the inner coffin that were at the hospital. Part of the reason for this was that when Padihershef and his coffins first came to the United States, hieroglyphic writing was just beginning to be deciphered, and although his name appeared on both coffins, no one knew this. He was merely "the mummy," and the coffins were anonymous. Thus when the coffins were separated and the memory of their belonging together was lost, the connection went unnoticed. Only later, when the coffins were translated, was it again established that they belonged to the same person. Indeed much information about Padihershef was painted on the coffins. He was a "stonecutter of the necropolis," so he probably spent a significant part of his life carving the rock-cut tombs of the wealthy. His father was Iref-Iaen-Hershef and his mother Heribes-enes. Both father and son have the name of the god Hershef incorporated in their names, which may indicate that the entire family were followers of this god. The style of the coffins and the names of the family members suggest that the family lived and died sometime during the Twenty-sixth Dynasty (663–525 B.C.).

During the period from 2 December 1984 to 20 January 1985, the mummy of Padihershef and his inner coffin were reunited with the outer coffin for an exhibition at the George Walter Vincent Smith Art Museum. At the present time the first mummy to come to America and his inner coffin are at Massachusetts General Hospital, while the outer coffin is across the state at the art museum.

PALEOPATHOLOGY The study of diseases or pathological conditions in ancient people. (Derived from the Greek words for "ancient" and "suffering" and first coined in 1892 by the German physician, R.W. Schufeldt.) The goal of paleopathology is to understand how diseases begin, spread, and die out. To understand a modern infectious disease and predict its course, it is best to know as much of its history as possible. By analyzing mummies and comparing the frequency of their pathological conditions with those of modern humans, insights can be gained into the causes of specific diseases.

Early investigations centered on bones because they are both the best-preserved parts of the body and the easiest to study. More recently, advanced technology has permitted sophisticated studies of soft tissues. The focus of paleopathology has changed considerably over the years, and even cloning of mummies has been attempted. (See CLONING and PALEOPATHOLOGY ASSOCIATION.)

PALEOPATHOLOGY ASSOCIATION Founded in 1973 to study diseases in ancient humans (see PALEOPATHOLOGY), the association pioneered the team approach in the study of mummies. Its members, primarily physicians, biologists, and Egyptologists, have conducted several carefully documented autopsies on Egyptian mummies (see PUM-II). The association publishes the *Paleopathology Newsletter* and membership information can be obtained from

Mrs. T.A. Cockburn, Secretary
Paleopathology Association
18655 Parkside
Detroit, MI 48221

PALGRAVE MUMMY, THE This novel (1924) by F.M. Pettee is one of the many mummy stories that appeared shortly after the discovery of Tutankhamen's tomb. Hastily written, the contrived plot centers around a mummy in an anthropoid coffin that has a curse in hieroglyphs running down its front.

In one scene the heroine, Olive Palgrave, seems to turn into a living mummy. The literally unbelievable explanation is that for her own amusement, she had designed a vaudeville act in which she turns into a mummy. This was made possible by using a new makeup she discovered that turns brown when hit with bright light!

PARACHISTE The term used in Egypt during the Greek occupation (332–30 B.C.) for the specialist in mummification who made the abdominal incision on the cadaver so the internal organs could be removed. Because the Egyptians were prohibited from defiling a human body, stones were ceremonially thrown at the parachistes after they had opened the body, despite the fact that their services were necessary.

PENISCHER, LOUIS (17TH CENTURY) Author of the first modern mummy story. When Penischer published his treatise on mummification, *Traité des Embaumements Selon les Anciens et Modernes*, in 1699, he included a tale of the misfortunes that can plague those who defile the tombs of Egypt. Penischer's narrative of a European traveler who returns from Egypt with two mummies set the precedent for all the similar tales that followed. The voyager's ship narrowly avoids sinking in a storm, but that is just the beginning of his misfortunes.

PEPI-ANKH, TOMB OF The scenes decorating the walls of the tomb of this high-ranking official of the Sixth Dynasty provide a rare glance into the mortuary industry of ancient Egypt, though not into the actual mummification process.

The scenes show that the body of Pepi-Ankh in its coffin was ferried across to the west bank of the Nile and taken in a procession of family, priests, and an embalmer to a "tent of purification," where funerary rituals were performed. The body purified, the procession moved on to the embalmer's workshop, where it stayed for nearly two months. The family then returned to the embalmer's shop with the empty coffin to retrieve the body. They would then return to the tent of purification for the "Opening of the Mouth" ceremony, (see OPENING OF THE MOUTH CEREMONY) before proceeding to the tomb for burial.

PERÓN, EVA DUARTE (1919–1952)

Wife of Juan Perón, president of Argentina. Born an illegitimate peasant, she became an actress and star of radio soap operas before marrying President Perón. Because of her ability to control the media and her championing of the cause of the poor and oppressed, she held great political power in Argentina and far exceeded her husband's popularity. Known popularly as "Evita" (little Eva), she had become almost a religious icon to the poor of Argentina by the time she died on July 26, 1952.

Minutes after her death Dr. Pedro Ara, a Spanish physician serving as the cultural attaché at the Spanish embassy in Buenos Aires, began mummifying her body. A skilled embalmer, Dr. Ara frequently demonstrated his abilities by displaying the head of a peasant he had embalmed many years earlier. The preliminary work on Eva Perón's body was done in less than twenty-four hours so it could be viewed in state by the people of Argentina. For six days millions of Argentines lined the streets for a twenty-second glimpse of the body in its glass-topped silver casket.

For the next several months, Dr. Ara continued to work on Eva's body in the Ministry of Employment building (Confederación General del Trabajo [CGT]). Using a technique perfected in Argentina, Ara slowly injected paraffin into the body, infusing the tissues with a protective coating of wax to create one of the most remarkable examples of mummification ever seen. Unlike most mummies, which are desiccated and do not appear lifelike, the body of Eva Perón seems to be alive. The body remained at the CGT headquarters for several years, while a multimillion dollar mausoleum was constructed to receive the final remains of Eva Perón.

In 1955 when President Juan Perón was overthrown by the military, the body of his wife was hidden for fear that it would become a rallying point for the ousted Perónists. The body was placed in a crate marked "radio sets" and shipped to the Argentine embassy in Bonn, Germany, where it was stored for several years. Later it was given the fictitious identity of an Italian widow and buried in Milan. Sixteen years later when Juan Perón was living in exile in Madrid and about to be restored as president of Argentina, Eva Perón's body was exhumed from a grave marked "Maria Maggi" in Lot 86, Garden 41, in Musocco Cemetery in Milan, Italy.

After exhumation, the body was transferred from Milan to Madrid. Even after Perón returned to Argentina, Eva's body remained in Madrid until his death on July 1, 1974, when it was flown to Buenos Aires so it could be viewed beside her husband's body. Still in its glass-topped silver casket, the body had not changed visibly. Finally on October 22, 1976, the mummy was placed in the "Familia Duarte" crypt in the Recoleta Cemetery in Buenos Aires, where it rests today.

PERUVIAN MUMMIES Frequently called "mummy bundles" because they are wrapped in yards of textiles, Peruvian mummies come primarily from the coastal desert. There are also some highland mummies, which were preserved by the cold dry air of the Andes Mountains. Mummies of the drier central and south coast of Peru are better preserved than those of the north, which experiences rain. Around A.D. 1100 a tremendous rain, or El Niño, soaked the area, damaging earlier burials. Thus pre-A.D. 1100 burials are skeletonized, with little soft tissue or textiles preserved.

During the Preceramic and Initial periods (2000–900 B.C.), no special embalming process was used for these mummies; the internal organs were left inside the body, and no oils or spices were used for its preservation. The body was often placed in a modified fetal position, sitting upright with legs drawn up under the chin, arms crossed over the chest. Often ropes were used to tie the body into this position. Frequently small symbolic objects such as feathers, shells, or coca were placed in the hands, and finally the body was swathed in cotton textiles.

Artificial mummification began when Andean society became more complex, with clearly defined rulers or chiefs, whose preserved bodies ("living corpses") became objects of veneration for the tribes. Later the mummies of Inca rulers were buried with their wives, retainers, and slaves. In the last decades of the Inca empire, the mummies of Inca rulers were served by special attendants, who knew when to give food and drink to the corpses and acted as spokespersons for the deceased. The mummies were exhibited

Peruvian Mummies Seventeenth-century drawing of the mummies of an Incan ruler and his family taken to Cuzco for burial.

at Cuzco during religious ceremonies, and in 1559 Garcilano de la Vega observed several of these mummies that had been gathered by the Spanish conquerors.

> The bodies were so intact that they lacked neither hair, eyebrows nor eyelashes. They were in clothes just as they had worn when alive. . . . I remember touching the finger of Huayna Capac. It was hard and rigid, like that of a wooden statue. The bodies weighed so little that any Indian could carry them from house to house in his arms or on his shoulders. They carried them wrapped in white shrouds through the streets and plazas, the Indians dropping to their knees, making reverences with groans and tars, and many Spaniards removing their caps.

Although there are quite a few sixteenth-century accounts of the remarkable conditions of the mummies of Inca rulers, there are few that describe the mummification procedures. One exception is Blas Valera's 1609 account, in which he states that the mummies were eviscerated and covered with balsam, and when balsam was unavailable, bitumen was used. Archaeologists have not yet discovered a body of an Inca ruler that clearly shows artificial mummification, and it is possible that their remarkable preservation was due to natural conditions. This is an area of mummification where more research is needed.

PETTIGREW, THOMAS (1791–1865) Prominent English physician (he vaccinated Queen Victoria), who became the most prolific and famous of the nineteenth-century mummy unrollers. Pettigrew became interested in mummies when he was asked by Giovanni Battista Belzoni, an early excavator (see BELZONI, GIOVANNI BATTISTA), to examine some of the mummies the Italian had recently brought from Egypt.

Pettigrew's first public unrolling took place on April 6, 1833 before a packed audience in the lecture hall of Charing Cross Hospital, where he was professor of anatomy. Over the next few decades Pettigrew unwrapped dozens of

Peruvian Mummies

mummies, often preceding the performance with a week-long series of evening lectures on ancient Egyptian history and religion.

Pettigrew's *History of Egyptian Mummies* was the first scientific work dedicated solely to mummies and was illustrated by George Cruickshank, who was to become famous as Charles Dickens's illustrator. The work is still of interest to scholars because of its detailed history of mummification and Pettigrew's careful observations of the mummies he unwrapped. He was the first to note that mummification techniques varied over the different periods of Egyptian history, and his medical training made him an astute observer of the mummies' physiological characteristics. Pettigrew was satirized in Edgar Allan Poe's "Some Words with a Mummy," which appeared in 1845. (See "SOME WORDS WITH A MUMMY.")

PHARAOH'S CURSE, THE This film is definitely not a high point for mummy cinema. Its apparent low budget, flimsy plot, stale dialogue, and appalling acting make it one of the least worthwhile movies involving mummies ever made.

Set in the early 1900s, the film begins with a group of British soldiers escorting the wife of an American archaeologist through the desert to her husband who is excavating a tomb. Along the way they meet up with a mysterious woman of the desert who warns them that they are traveling the wrong way and offers to show them a quicker route if only they will follow her. Perhaps it's the evil and menacing look she gives them while offering the group her services, but the head officer gets the subtle feeling that they should stick to their maps. They continue along their path with her accompanying them. While in her presence mysterious things occur—water goes missing, as does the medical supply kit, etc.

After arriving at the dig, the tomb is opened (despite the inevitable curse), and the lid of the sarcophagus is lifted. Inside lies the mummy in his fully wrapped glory. Quite the scientists, the members of the group decide that slicing him

open is the thing to do. Making an incision on the left side of the mummy's neck causes a young Egyptian laborer, who is in the tomb, to feel a sharp pain in the same place of his neck. The boy is rushed to the medical tent for examination. There he suddenly undergoes a rapid aging process—fifty years in a matter of hours. Soon he is little more than a decomposed skeleton, and shortly after he disappears altogether.

Naturally this is where people start dying. The mummy has transported his essence into the boy. The mummy walks, actually he lumbers, as any decent mummy should. Upon discovering a secret chamber, one member of the group is confronted by the mummy. One of the few pleasures of this movie comes from seeing the unbandaged living mummy, who looks just like Andy Rooney! And not just a little bit—he's a dead ringer (so to speak). He hobbles out of his chamber and "mummies" the scientist to death. It's really not clear how he kills people. He limps over to them and leaves the rest to the audience's imagination.

More people die. Unfortunately, enough survive for some more inane dialogue. Eventually the mummy and the chief archaeologist are buried under tons of rubble, thus sealing the tomb forever. This of course paves the way for the standard "there are some things society isn't ready to know about" ending.

One other funny aspect of the movie is the tomb itself. The walls look as if they belong in a medieval castle, not in the desert. The hieroglyphs are cute, too. It looks as though the pharaohs were busy playing tic-tac-toe, not writing curses.

PIZARRO, FRANCISCO, MUMMY OF (1476?–1541) Spanish explorer and conqueror of Peru, Pizarro is known for his great military leadership but also for his cruelty. Born an illegitimate peasant, he became a soldier of fortune, and at the age of fifty he went to Peru in search of gold. After marching with his band of 110 men to Cajamarca in the interior of Peru,

Pizarro encountered Atahualpa, the Inca king, and his army of 40,000. Unsure of what to do, Atahualpa allowed Pizarro to take possession of the citadel, while the Inca army surrounded it. Pizarro called for a meeting, but when Atahualpa and his retinue entered the citadel, the men were killed, the women raped, and Atahualpa was taken captive.

In return for his freedom, Atahualpa offered to fill with gold a room twenty-two feet long, seventeen feet wide, and seven feet high. For five months the Incas frantically collected all the gold they could find in an attempt to free their leader. When the room was nearly full, Pizarro killed Atahualpa.

In the following years Pizarro and his troops plundered, confiscated crops, and enslaved the Incas. In 1533 a rival of Pizarro, Diego de Almagro, captured Cuzco, the Inca capital, and its vast stores of gold. Pizarro's larger army soon took the gold from Almagro, and to be rid of Almagro and his men, Pizarro offered him Chile. For two difficult years Almagro explored Chile, but came to the bitter realization that Chile did not have gold like Peru and returned to Peru to fight Pizarro. In 1538 Pizarro executed Almagro and stripped his son and followers of all their land. Three years later Almagro's son and followers decided to kill Pizarro.

On June 26, 1541, Almagro's men forced their way through the palace doors and burst in on Pizarro as he was eating Sunday dinner with friends. Most of the dinner guests fled, but a few, loyal to Pizarro, stayed to fight. There are several eyewitness accounts of the battle, so most of the details are known.

Unable to get his armor on quickly, Pizarro wrapped his left arm in his cloak and entered the fight. Most of Pizarro's followers were quickly killed, and Pizarro, left alone, killed three of his attackers, but his sword became lodged in the third and as he attempted to pull it free, his throat was pierced by a rapier. Mortally wounded, Pizarro fell to the floor as his attackers repeatedly stabbed him. His last words were a request for

water, but in response one of the soldiers broke a water jar over his head, exclaiming that his next drink would be in hell.

Riots broke out as the news of Pizarro's assassination spread. That night Pizarro's body was buried behind the Lima Cathedral. In the next 100 years the body was moved four times. In 1545 the body and swords were placed in a wood box under the cathedral's altar, as Pizarro had requested in his will. In 1551 Pizarro's daughter paid to have a special chapel constructed in the cathedral to house her father's remains. In 1606 the body was moved to a new chapel, but it was damaged by an earthquake, and sometime around 1625 the body was moved inside the cathedral.

In 1661 when the remains of Saint Toribio, Peru's first saint, were being examined for verification, a record was found mentioning a box with the inscription, "Here is the head of Marquis Don Francisco Pizarro who discovered and won Peru and placed it under the royal crown of Castile." The box was not found, and Pizarro's body remained undisturbed till the cathedral, damaged by an earthquake, was rebuilt in 1778.

The year 1891 marked the 350th anniversary of the death of Pizarro, and a team of scientists examined his body and discovered that it had mummified naturally in the dry air of Lima. The mummy had no hands, and although it was clearly male, there were no genitals—a fact the investigators attributed to mutilation by his assassins. The mummy was authenticated as that of Pizarro, documents were signed in triplicate, and a beautiful sarcophagus of glass, marble, and bronze was built to house the remains of the conquistador. Since 1891 thousands of tourists have visited the mummy of Pizarro beneath the altar of Lima Cathedral, but recently it has been discovered that the mummy is not Pizarro's.

In 1977 workmen cleaning the crypt beneath the altar removed some loose bricks in a wall and discovered two niches with wooden boxes containing human remains. Included with the bones in one of the boxes, a small lead casket bore the inscription, "Here is the head of Marquis Don Francisco Pizarro. . . ." When a small team of scientists examined the bones, they declared them to be those of Pizarro, but their findings were never fully accepted. In 1984 forensic anthropologist William R. Maples went to Lima to make the definitive examination.

There were actually several bodies in the two wooden boxes—two children, an elderly female, an elderly male, and the headless skeleton of a second elderly male. The head said to be Pizarro's belonged to the headless skeleton in the other box. Examination of this skeleton proved that it was Pizarro's.

Examination of the skeleton revealed that its owner had died a violent death at the hands of several assailants. The cuts and gashes on the bones suggested numerous thrust wounds—four to the neck alone. One cut, from a double-edged sword, was probably the one described in the contemporary accounts that brought Pizarro to the ground. His vertebrae and ribs bore evidence of more than a dozen stab wounds, and the left hand and arm had been cut in Pizarro's attempts to fend off the attackers with his right hand. This was undoubtedly the body of Pizarro. Pizarro's skeleton is now in the glass and marble sarcophagus in the Lima Cathedral's chapel. The imposter mummy, its identity unknown, is buried beneath the cathedral in a crypt.

PLASTINATION The process was developed in Germany by Dr. Gunther von Hugens during the 1980s and basically involves replacing the water in tissue with a resin. Silicone is most often used, and the procedure requires the following four steps:

1. Fixation—This step is intended to stop all bacterial and enzyme activity within the specimen, so that it does not decay. Tissues

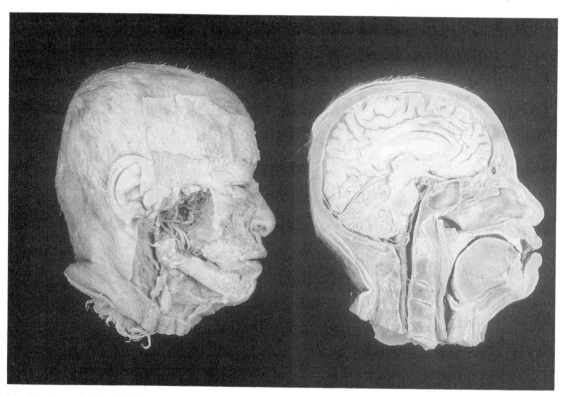

Plastination Plastinated hemisection of human head.

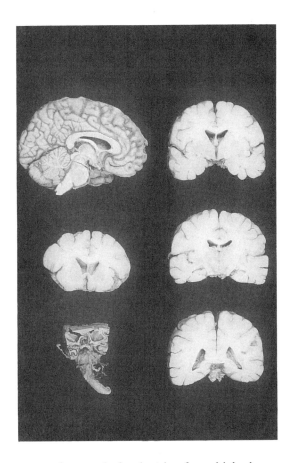

Plastination Plastinated human brain sections. *Photos courtesy Ronald Wade.*

are frequently fixed with a formaldehyde solution, although they may be injected with or immersed in the solution. (See FIXATION.)

2. Dehydration—Once the tissues are fixed so they will not decay, they must be dehydrated. This is usually accomplished by a freeze substitution technique. The specimens are submerged in containers of acetone for as long as six weeks, which draws out the water until less than 1 percent remains when measured with a hydrometer.

3. Impregnation—The specimens are immersed in a sealed chamber with a vacuum force applied. The vaporization of acetone pulls the polymer into the tissue. This enables the specimens to retain their original shape.

4. Curing—In the last stage of the procedure, the specimens are placed in a curing chamber using a chemical vapor to solidify the polymer. This is usually done at room temperature. The specimens cure from the outside first, allowing the polymer to remain locked in the deep tissues. The specimens cure thoroughly in four to six weeks. When the resin is thoroughly dry, the specimens are ready for use.

Various organs have been preserved by plastination, and the technique is now widely used for teaching purposes. Plastination has tremendous advantages over the earlier method of preserving organs in formaldehyde, because plastinated organs are dry, odorless, durable, and stiff and can be handled easily. Because of the details visible in plastinated specimens, they are far superior to plaster or plastic models of organs prepared for classroom use.

Pompeii   Cast of victim caught in the eruption of Mt. Vesuvius A.D. 79. *Photo courtesy David Moyer.*

Recently plastination has been used to prepare body sections. This technique requires the cadaver to be frozen, then a slice less than one inch thick is removed. The sample is plastinated using an epoxy or polyester resin and by following the four steps outlined above. This presents a unique teaching device because students can see the relationship between the adjacent parts of the body. For example, the spinal cord can be seen passing through the vertebrae supported by adjacent muscles. Plastination sections are also used in conjunction with CAT scans since together the two offer a view of a slice through the body.

POMPEII   This Italian city perished when Mt. Vesuvius erupted and buried 2,000 inhabitants. Commonly believed to be mummies, the bodies found at Pompeii, which were covered with stones,

ash, and mud, disintegrated under their covering of hot ash, and hollow casts remained.

The ancient Roman city of Pompeii was in the rich agricultural section of Italy known as Campania, and the comfortable lives of Pompeii's citizens came to a tragic end when the dormant volcano, Mt. Vesuvius, erupted on the morning of August 24, A.D. 79. By evening Pompeii and the nearby town of Herculaneum were half buried with ash, pumice, and mud. As the rain of lava, ash, and mud continued, the area was completely covered and remained buried and lost for sixteen centuries.

A well digger in 1709 discovered a theater in the lost city of Herculaneum, near Pompeii, and in 1738 the Bourbon royal family organized "treasure hunts" to the area, but it wasn't until the Italian government's Director of Works, Cavaliere Fiorelli, began systematic excavation of

Pompeii in 1860 that any records were kept. When a workman was removing loose debris from an excavation in Pompeii, the remains of a linen bag were found that contained coins, ornaments, and keys. While collecting this find, the workman's pick axe struck a hollow spot in the soil, and upon investigation Signor Fiorelli found a cavity. He had for some time believed that people might have been trapped in the city when the volcano erupted. When this hole was discovered, the first casualties were found. The hole was a body cavity created when the body of the deceased disintegrated under the hot ash, lava rocks, pebbles, and mud. Fiorelli poured plaster of paris into the cavity and made the first body cast of a citizen of Pompeii. He perfected a method of making casts of the hollows left by the disintegrated bodies and kept the individual casts in a small museum he opened at Pompeii.

Augustus Goldsmidt, a visitor to Pompeii during Fiorelli's work, described Fiorelli's technique.

> As soon as the cavity was filled with plaster (and the plaster was firm) the earth around it was removed. The ashes in which the bodies were buried must have fallen in a damp state, and hardened gradually by the lapse of time, and as the soft parts of the bodies decayed and shrunk a hollow was formed between the bodies and the crust of soil. This formed the cavity into which the plaster was poured . . . So intimately did these ashes penetrate, and so thoroughly had the cast been taken, that the texture of the undergarments, drawers and an inner vest with sleeves is distinctly visible.

The people of Pompeii apparently did not flee immediately but watched in amazement and horror as the mountain opened and a cloud of ash rose a thousand feet in the sky. The cloud drifted toward Pompeii, and soon rain, ash, pebbles, and boulders were falling on the town. Roofs began to collapse under the weight. When the citizens of Pompeii finally realized their danger, they fled. In one house a suckling pig was left roasting; in another bread was baking. One family in their haste neglected to unchain their guard dog, who choked itself trying to escape. Many who ran through the streets were crushed by falling buildings or suffocated by sulfurous fumes, as they ran to escape through the west gate. Many of those who reached the gate were trampled in the terror and confusion. Shells of their bodies were found in a massive pile near the gate.

Each body was found frozen in the position in which the person died, and the plaster casts so carefully taken by Fiorelli have preserved even more personal details than have been found in ancient mummies. Fiorelli noted an unusual detail on the cast of a man who had died grasping his garment as if to remove it, leaving the lower portion of his body exposed.

> A curious peculiarity still distinctly traceable is that the hair of the pubes is shaved so as to leave it in a semi-circular form, such as may be observed in the statues, and which has, I believe, been generally supposed to be merely a sculptural convention.

Another of the casts revealed that the mistress of the house must have delayed her departure to gather her jewelry before leaving. She was found collapsed in the damp ashes and pebbles in the street with her jewelry, bags of coins, and a silver mirror. Three servants died with her.

One of the most poignant scenes was discovered in a house where a family had gathered for a funeral feast in honor of a recently deceased family member. Apparently death had struck quickly, for the family had not even risen from their couches when they died mourning the passing of their relative.

POPE, PRESERVATION OF BODY Because all popes in the Catholic church may be potential saints, and the bodies of saints are often preserved, the church has specific procedures for the disposition of a pope's body. When a pope dies, the cardinal camerlengo examines the body and calls the pope's name three times. If there is no response, the pope is declared dead.

If death occurs outside the Vatican, the body is washed, shaved, and embalmed immediately. If death occurs inside the Vatican, the body is taken by the back stairs to the Chapel of Sixtus V, where it lies in state for twenty-four hours. Then it is embalmed. The body is then transported to the chapel of the Blessed Trinity, where it is on view to the faithful for three days. After the three days there is an additional embalming, and the body is placed in a lead coffin enclosed in a cypress casket. The body then lays in St. Peter's Basilica for at least one year.

Even body parts of the popes are preserved. When John Paul II was shot in 1981, part of his intestines was removed. The intestinal section was taken to the *sacra praecordia* in the Church of Santi Vincenzo ed Anastastio. According to Catholic theology, the pope's parts and their bodies will be reunited on Resurrection Day, so the parts must be preserved. Since 1590 parts of popes removed by embalmers and surgeons have been kept in terra-cotta jars.

PORPHYRY   Roman author of the first century A.D., who was the only ancient writer to mention that the Egyptians placed the internal organs in canopic chests (see CANOPIC CHEST and CANOPIC JARS). In his *De Abstinentia* he says:

There is one point which must not be passed over, namely that when they embalm the dead of the wealthy class, among other observances paid to the corpse, they privately remove the intestines and place them in a chest, which they make fast and present before the sun, while one of those occupied in embalming the body recites a prayer. And this prayer, which Ekphantas translated from his native language, is to the following effect: "O Lord Sun and all you gods who give life to men, receive me favorably and commit me to abide with the everlasting gods. For as long as I continued in that life, I have steadfastly reverenced the gods whom my parents instructed me to worship, and I have ever

honored the gods who brought my body into the world; while, as concerns my fellow men, I have done no murder, nor betrayed a trust, nor committed any other deadly sin. But, if, during my life, I have sinned in eating or drinking what was unlawful, the fault was not mine, but this" (showing the chest in which was the stomach).

PRINCE OF EL PLOMO   In February 1954 treasure hunters discovered the intact burial of an eight- or nine-year-old Inca prince. The boy had been drugged, taken up the Cerro el Plomo mountain (28 miles east of Santiago, Chile) and buried alive at an altitude of 17,700 feet. The body and grave goods were sold to the National Museum of Natural History in Santiago, and the body was kept in a freezer till it could be studied.

The cold dry mountain air had preserved the boy just as he had died, crouched in fetal position for warmth. His face painted red, he wore a tunic, a headdress made of black llama hair and condor feathers, and a silver bracelet and pendant. He had been buried with several pouches, one containing still fragrant cocoa leaves. Other bags contained his baby teeth and fingernail cuttings, gold, silver, and shell figurines of llamas, and a female idol dressed in miniature clothes and headdress.

The body was studied in 1982 by a team of pathologists, who discovered warts on the boy's hand and under an electron microscope were able to see the papilloma virus that caused them, the earliest identification of an ancient virus. The young prince, a member of the Ultimate Inca culture, had probably been sacrificed to the sun god sometime between 1480 and 1540, when the culture was disrupted by the arrival of Pedro de Valdiva.

PRINCE OF WALES, MUMMIES OF
When royalty visited Egypt in the nineteenth century, it was usually arranged that something memorable would be found. In 1868 when the Prince of Wales visited Egypt, about thirty coffins and mummies were "discovered" near the Colossi of Memnon at Thebes and given to His Highness as a souvenir of his trip. The prince returned to England with twenty of the best, and

this group was examined by Samuel Birch, keeper of Egyptian antiquities at the British Museum. Unfortunately Birch had no medical training, and little about mummification was learned. The mummies and their coffins were eventually dispersed among various museums and friends of the prince.

PROHIBITIONS AGAINST MUMMIFICATION

Many religions have viewed the preservation of the human body as unnatural and an excessive concern for the physical at the expense of the spiritual aspect of a person. Although the Hindu religion prefers cremation, other religions tend to view burial in the ground as the natural end to human existence.

In the Old Testament it is specified that Sarah, wife of Abraham, be buried in the ground (Genesis 23: 19–20). Also in Genesis is the familiar "For dust thou art and unto dust shalt thou return" (Genesis 3: 19). The Greeks also believed that the body belonged in the ground. In Euripides' *Supplicants*, Theseus says:

Now they are dead, permit them in the earth
To rest concealed. For whence at first proceeds
Each portion of our frame, thither again
Must it return—the spirit flies aloft,
And with its native ether claims alliance;
The body mingles with the dust below.

Early patriarchs of the church also spoke against mummification and to some extent this assisted in stopping the practice in Egypt during early Christian times. Saint Anthony asked his followers to assure that he would not be mummified:

And if your minds are set upon me, and yes remember me as a father, permit no man to take my body and carry it into Egypt, lest according to the custom which they have, they embalm me and lay me up in their houses, for it was [to avoid] this that I came into this desert. And ye know that I have continually made exhortation concerning this thing and begged that it should

not be done, and ye will know how much I have blamed those who observed this custom.

PSUSENNES I, KING OF EGYPT, MUMMY OF (1039–991 B.C.)

See TANIS, ROYAL MUMMIES OF.

PSYCHO

The famous shower scene in this black-and-white film directed by Alfred Hitchcock was so shocking in the 1960s when it was released that few movie-goers remember the mummy that plays a central part in the movie. *Psycho* changed Hollywood's perception of horror movies, and for the first time a feature-length film, directed by a prominent Hollywood director, touched upon society's taboos, showing nudity, bloodbaths, necrophilia, transvestism, and schizophrenia. Hitchcock was able to pull it off by claiming that the film was one huge joke. The American public, while they did not laugh, found they loved being scared to death.

The movie opens with Marion Crane (Janet Leigh) in a hotel room with her lover, Sam Loomis (John Gavin). The audience voyeuristically watches, as the camera views the scene from outside the hotel room window, and it becomes apparent that Sam cannot obtain a divorce and the affair is no longer satisfying to Marion. When she returns to the real estate office where she works, Marion is entrusted with $40,000 cash to be deposited for her employer. Unhappy and disillusioned, she sees the $40,000 as a means of escape. Marion drives her car across the state line to California, and during a rainstorm she makes a wrong turn, sees the lights of the Bates Motel, and decides to stop for the night.

Tired and hungry Marion accepts the motel owner Norman Bates's offer of a sandwich. As she sits in his parlor talking to the sensitive and lonely young man, Marion realizes that she cannot go through with her plan and decides to return the stolen money the next day. When Marion goes to her motel room, next to the office, Norman moves a picture on the wall and watches her undress. He nervously replaces the picture, leaves the office, and walks to his bleak Victorian house behind the motel. As he enters the house the camera remains outside, and the audience hears the shrill voice of an elderly woman, his insanely jealous mother, screaming at Norman for wanting to have dinner with the young woman.

In the meantime, weary from her long day, Marion is taking a shower. From behind the shower curtain, she can see a shadow entering the bathroom. The curtain is swept aside, and the dark figure of an old woman wields a large butcher's knife. Marion screams as the knife slashes her again and again, and she falls over the side of the tub, pulling the shower curtain with her.

Norman Bates, who is conveniently lurking about, is aghast at what his mother has done. He carefully wraps Marion with the shower curtain and puts the body, her suitcase, and the $40,000 which is concealed in a newspaper, in the trunk of Marion's car and pushes the car into a nearby swamp.

When Marion does not come home, her sister (Vera Miles) goes to Sam Loomis, and they begin the search. A private detective (Martin Balsam) is hired to find Marion and the missing money. He follows Marion's trail to the Bates Motel and discovers that Norman Bates has lied about Marion having stayed there, and he goes to the Victorian house to investigate. As the investigator reaches the top of the stairs, he is stabbed repeatedly by an old woman and falls to his death.

When Sam and Marion's sister do not hear from the private investigator, they too go to the Bates Motel, after talking with the local sheriff who tells them that Mrs. Bates has been dead and buried for eight years. While Sam distracts Norman Bates, the sister enters the house and finds Mrs. Bates's bedroom, where she notices a strange powder on her dressing table. When she hears footsteps she makes her way to the basement to hide and finds Mrs. Bates sitting in a chair facing the wall. When the chair is swiveled around, the audience comes face-to-face with the horrifying mummy of Mrs. Bates.

Hitchcock provided clues during the movie leading one to guess a mummy was involved, but the audience was so traumatized by the assault on their senses that the movie's subtle points were often overlooked. For example, when the unfortunate Marion Crane meets Norman Bates, one of the first things he tells her is about his hobby, taxidermy. This information hints at his interest and expertise in preserving things. The strange powder on Mrs. Bates's dressing table is perhaps a preservative.

Norman is, of course, revealed to be a schizophrenic killer, who has assumed the personality of his deceased and domineering mother. Although the audience is left believing that Norman mummified his mother, in fact, he had preserved another corpse as a stand-in for her.

Hitchcock, with his keen eye for detail, personally devised the horrifying appearance of the mummy and often used it in the many pranks he played on the good-natured Miss Leigh. On one occasion Hitchcock placed the mummy in Leigh's darkened dressing room, and when she switched the light on, she found herself face-to-face with the mummy. It is said that her loud screams were more frightening than her piercing shrieks in the shower scene.

PUM II Short for Pennsylvania University Museum, Pum II was the second of the museum's mummies to be studied. When the mummy was autopsied on the first two days of February 1973, it marked the beginning of modern scientific mummy studies. It was an early attempt at the team approach to mummy autopsies, and the participants included Egyptologists, physicians, X-ray technicians, and scientists from other disciplines.

The autopsy took place at Wayne State Medical School but was cosponsored by the division of physical anthropology at the Smithsonian Institution and the department of ancient art at the Detroit Institute of Arts. Leading the team was William H. Peck, an Egyptologist from the Detroit Institute of Arts. Peck began by unwrapping the mummy, who was covered in twelve layers of linen. The last layer had been drenched with resin that had hardened to the consistency of glass, and had to be removed with a hammer and chisel.

Finally the body was revealed to be in excellent condition; even some eyelashes remained on the eyelids. The mummy was of a man approximately thirty-five years old. The abdomen was opened, and five packages of organs were removed. The ancient embalmers had removed the organs at the time of mummification, dehydrated and wrapped them, and then returned them to the body cavity, so the deceased would be complete in the next world. His fingernails had been dyed red with henna.

As the team worked on the mummy, samples were taken to be sent to various specialists. Insect larvae found in the mummy were sent for analysis to entomologists and were found to be those of flesh-eating flies. Blood samples were sent to hematologists, resin samples to chemists, and bone samples to other specialists. For several years after the autopsy of Pum II, samples were analyzed, reports published, and new information gained. The interdisciplinary approach to the study of a mummy was firmly established by this project.

PUTREFACTION The process by which a body decays after death. Mummification is an attempt to stop putrefaction. The decaying process begins in the intestine and colon. Bacteria in the intestines help digestion by breaking down food so nutrients can be absorbed, but upon death they begin the decomposition of the body. This is why, in most forms of mummification, evisceration is essential.

One of the early signs of putrefaction is bloating of the body. This occurs when the intestinal bacteria produce gas that fills the body and causes a foul smell. This gas also flows into the blood vessels, causing the skin to turn green, then purple, and finally black.

In addition to bacterial decay, another factor in putrefaction is autolysis—cell breakdown. This happens in a predictable manner. First the energy-releasing mechanisms, the mitochondria, swell. Other structures in the cell dissolve, and the cell loses its connection to adjacent cells. Control over cellular water is lost, and destructive acids (enzymes) are released from within the cell.

Between bacterial decay and autolysis, putrefaction occurs in a specific sequence. Not all organs decay at the same rate. The uterus and prostate gland are particularly resistant to this process and are often intact months after death. Thus it is not essential in mummification that they be removed immediately.

PYRAMID TEXTS A series of magical spells placed on the walls of the pyramids of the kings and queens of Egypt during the Old Kingdom (2664–2181 B.C.). These spells were intended to protect the mummy while it was in the burial chamber, assure its safe journey to the west, and secure a place for the deceased with the gods of the next world.

The first pharaoh to have these magical inscriptions in his tomb was Unas, the last king of the Fifth Dynasty. One spell from Unas's Saqqara pyramid guarantees that the deceased king will have food.

Oh Unas, stand up, sit down to the thousand loaves of bread, the thousand jars of beer. The roast of thy double rib is from the slaughter house, thy retch-bread is from the Wide Hall. As a god is supplied with the offering meal, Unas is supplied with this his bread.

Unas's successors, the kings and queens of the Sixth Dynasty, also had magical spells carved on the interior walls of their pyramids and added new spells. After the Sixth Dynasty, however, spells to protect mummies were placed on the coffins (see COFFIN TEXTS) and pyramid texts were no longer used.

QEBHESENUEF One of the four sons of the Egyptian god Horus. Qebhesenuef was associated with the west and protected mummies' internal organs. He is represented with the body of a man and the head of a falcon.

Frequently magical inscriptions were written on the four jars holding the internal organs of a mummy (see CANOPIC JARS). On the jar whose lid was shaped like Qebhesenuef's head, a typical spell read:

Words spoken by Qebhesenuef:
I am thy son Osiris, I come to protect thee. I keep thy bones, I collect thy limbs, I bring to thee thy heart. I place it for thee in its place in the body.

R

RAMSES II (RAMSES THE GREAT)
Pharaoh of Egypt from 1279–1213 B.C. Known for his military campaigns and monumental building projects, Ramses II was one of the great kings of Egypt, ruling for sixty-seven years and leading Egypt to prosperity and expansion. Some believe him to have been the pharaoh of the Exodus.

The mummy of Ramses II was discovered in 1881 in the great Deir el-Bahri cache of royal mummies (see DEIR EL-BAHRI). His mummy is the only royal mummy ever to have left Egypt. The mummy was flown to the Musée de l'Homme (Anthropology Museum) in Paris on September 26, 1976 for treatment and restoration because of its deteriorating condition. Eighty-nine different species of fungi were found growing in and on the mummy in 370 separate colonies. The king's body was sterilized by gamma radiation during two sessions of six hours and twenty minutes each at 1.8 megarads.

X rays revealed that the heart was still in the chest, but had been sewn in place with gold threads, perhaps because it had been accidentally cut free during the mummification process. By the time of his death, Ramses was suffering from advanced atherosclerosis and an X ray of his pelvis showed calcification of both femoral arteries. For the last decade of his life, the pharaoh must have walked bent over, crippled by arthritis. All his teeth were worn down and showed great decay. In his mandible is a hole, caused by the spread of dental infection. An abscess by his teeth was serious enough to have caused death by infection, although this cannot be determined with certainty as the cause of death.

Ramses lived past the age of eighty, but his hair is strikingly blond—dyed as a final step in the mummification process so he would be young forever. Microscopic inspection of the roots of the hair revealed that Ramses was originally a redhead.

Ramses II The mummy of Ramses II (Ramses the Great) is the only royal mummy ever to have left Egypt.

Anwar Sadat's War and Peace Room at the Egyptian Museum in late 1979 but was then placed in storage until 1994. It is currently on display again in the new "Mummy Room" of the Egyptian Museum.

RAMSES III, KING OF EGYPT, MUMMY OF (1182–1151 B.C.)

Ramses III's mummy was the model for many of the Hollywood mummy movies. His mummy was discovered in the Deir el-Bahri cache (see DEIR EL-BAHRI) within an unusually large coffin. Nearly ten feet long, the coffin held two mummies, Ramses III and Queen Ahmose-Nefertari.

Ramses III is the first mummy to have artificial eyes—the eye sockets were packed with linen to give a more lifelike appearance. The face of Ramses III was coated with resins by the embalmers, so that when Gaston Maspero (see MASPERO, GASTON, SIR) unwrapped the mummy in 1886, the hardened resins had to be carefully chipped away by a sculptor.

Ramses III The mummy of Ramses III (above) was the model for American film sequels to *The Mummy.* Ancient embalmers placed linen around the neck to cover the fact that the head had fallen off. The film mummy (right) has kept the scarf.

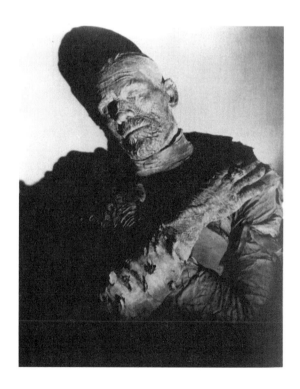

After completing the treatment of Ramses's mummy, the original linen in which he was wrapped was washed, sterilized, and used to re-wrap the king. On May 10, 1977 the mummy of Ramses the Great was returned to the Egyptian Museum, Cairo, in a sterilized display case so the fungi would not return. The refurbished mummy of Ramses II was displayed briefly in President

RAMSES V, KING OF EGYPT, MUMMY OF (1145–1141 B.C.) The mummy of the pharaoh was found by Victor Loret in 1898 in a cache of royal mummies in the tomb of Amenhotep II. It was unwrapped on June 25, 1905 in the Egyptian Museum in Cairo by G. Elliot Smith.

Although the king ruled during the Twentieth Dynasty, several aspects of his mummification are typical of the Twenty-first Dynasty. The abdominal cavity had been packed with sawdust and the internal organs were placed inside it. Also, the face had been painted red, typical of the Twenty-first Dynasty and later. This is probably because Twenty-first Dynasty embalmers repaired the damage done to the body by tomb robbers.

Small scabs on the body seemed to indicate that this pharaoh had smallpox. In 1979 President Anwar Sadat permitted minute samples to be tested. One of the scabs was examined by paleopathologists, who found particles that looked like smallpox virus, but this could not be confirmed conclusively because the radioimmune test for smallpox was negative. Recently a more sensitive test—the immunoprecipitation test—for smallpox confirmed that Ramses V did indeed have smallpox. It is quite possible that one of the biblical plagues was a smallpox epidemic.

REHYDRATION OF MUMMIFIED TISSUES To study brittle mummified tissues, it is often necessary to reintroduce water into them to make them flexible enough to be sliced thinly for viewing under a microscope. One technique is to soak the tissue in human blood serum. The undiluted serum is deactivated at fifty-six degrees Celcius for thirty minutes to stop enzymatic activity. Then it is stored at four degrees Celcius. The mummified tissue is then immersed in eight times its volume of serum for twenty-four hours. Finally it is washed in running water for five minutes and rinsed in 75 percent ethanol. It can then be imbedded in paraffin for examination under a microscope. For large tissue samples such as an entire arm, where blood serum would be too expensive, fabric softener has been used successfully.

RESURRECTION The religious belief that some time after death the physical body will reanimate and the deceased person will come to life again.

The belief in resurrection is central to many religions but was first expressed by the ancient Egyptians more than 4,500 years ago. In the Egyptian religion resurrection was the impetus for mummification. Because the Egyptians believed the body would resurrect in the next world, it was crucial to preserve the body, and mummification was the means by which this was achieved. In an attempt to ensure a pleasant afterlife for those who had lost a limb in this life, the embalmers frequently would fashion an artificial leg or arm to be buried with the mummy, so it would be complete when it resurrected.

The Egyptians never stated how long the mummy would remain in the tomb before resurrection in the place of the dead, or the west. The belief in resurrection also led to the practice of placing everyday articles in the tombs. Since the next world was expected to be a continuation of this one, objects used in this life would be needed by the resurrected mummy in the next world.

The belief in resurrection later became an important aspect of Christianity. The first example of resurrection in the New Testament is in John 11:1–45. Lazarus died in Bethany and had been buried for four days by the time Jesus arrived. Jesus proclaimed, "I am the resurrection and the life: he that believeth in me, though he were dead, yet he shall live." He then commanded "Lazarus come forth" and Lazarus, still bandaged in his burial wrappings, emerged from his cave/tomb. This is the moment of Christian triumph over death, a precursor to the resurrection of Christ from his tomb.

Even in modern Chinese thought, resurrection of the physical body plays a role. In the Forbidden City in Beijing, it was a practice of the emperors to permit only eunuchs in the women's quarters. These eunuchs were usually castrated as young boys and raised to serve the emperor. Because they believed they would resurrect in the next world, and wished their bodies to be complete, eunuchs preserved their genitals in jars to be buried with them.

RHIND PAPYRI Two of the few papyri to deal with any aspect of mummification, these scrolls of religious texts both discuss the procedure for wrapping a mummy. They are named after Alexander Rhind, a Scottish lawyer who discovered them in 1860 while excavating at Gourna, a village near the Valley of the Kings. The papyri were written for a husband and wife who had died within two months of each other in the year 9 B.C.

The couple's tomb had not been plundered, and one chamber contained an unfinished sarcophagus carved of pink Aswan granite with its lid still cemented to it. When the lid was removed, a mummy was revealed, stuck to the inside of an inner coffin by bitumen that had been poured around it. The mummy's face was encased in a gilded mask; encircling the head was a bronze wreath of gold-painted leaves. Within the wrappings Rhind found figures of gods cut from sheet gold.

The arms of the mummy rested by its sides, and on the left side was a papyrus identifying the owner as Montu-Sebef, who died at the age of fifty-nine. The papyrus was written in both the demotic and hieratic scripts of the Egyptian language. Hieratic was reserved for more formal religious documents and was used primarily by the priests. Demotic is what the literate population used for daily transactions. The papyrus describes the rituals that took place after the removal of the brain and internal organs.

The body was bathed in the "Pool of Khonsu" and then placed at rest for thirty days in the "Place of Cleansing" (natron). Also discussed are the frankincense, cedar oil, and linen used in the wrapping. The papyrus mentions that during the first thirty-six days of mummification, eight ceremonies were performed, followed by an additional nine through the seventieth day. Thus there was a total of seventeen rituals, a sacred number for mummification in ancient Egypt. There were seventeen essential openings and parts of the body: seven openings of the head, four sons of Horus (the internal organs), two legs, two arms, one front torso, and one back for a total of seventeen.

The mummy of Taani, wife of Montu-Sebef, was also found in the tomb, and it too had been buried with a papyrus inside the coffin on the left side. It repeated much of the information in her husband's papyrus. While these two papyri tell nothing about the actual procedure for the removal of the internal organs, they are among the few papyri that tell anything about Egyptian mummification practices.

RICE, ANNE (b. 1941) American writer known primarily for her novels dealing with vampires, collectively referred to as the "Vampire Chronicles." She is also the author of *The Mummy or Ramses the Damned,* which drew heavily on earlier mummy films and novels. (See THE MUMMY OR RAMSES THE DAMNED.)

RIDDLES AND MUMMIES, THE TEN BEST There are hundreds of riddles about mummies, most of them made up by school children. Here are the ten best:

1. What is the most important day in Egypt?
   Mummy's Day.
2. What do you call a mummy who wins the lottery?
   A lucky stiff.
3. What kind of underwear does a mummy wear?
   Fruit of the Tomb.
4. What kind of music do mummies like most?
   Wrap music.
5. What do you call a mummy whose wrappings are stuck together?
   A gummy mummy.

6. What is the mummy's favorite musical program?
   Name that tomb.
7. What is the mummy's favorite flower?
   Chrysanthamummies.
8. What was a favorite saying in ancient Egypt?
   A fool and his mummy are soon parted.
9. What did the waiter say to the mummy?
   Bone appétit.
10. Why don't mummies have hobbies?
    They are too wrapped up in their work.

RIGOR MORTIS A stiffening of the muscles two to four hours after death. Generally believed to be a permanent condition of the cadaver, it is actually temporary. Rigor mortis is affected by the acid level of the blood. After death the pH level becomes acidic because of increases in the lactic and carbonic acids. The stiffening usually begins with the small muscles of the eyes, the neck, and jaw and over a period of six hours spreads to the other, larger muscles. The blood of a normal person has a pH of 7.4, but during rigor mortis it drops to 6.3. This acidic period lasts only two days, then the body loses its stiffness and once again becomes flaccid. The relaxing of the body allowed the Egyptian embalmers to position the limbs of the deceased before wrapping.

RING OF THOTH, THE One of two mummy stories written by Sir Arthur Conan Doyle (see "LOT NO. 249"), "The Ring of Thoth" presents the theme of lovers united across millennia but with a reverse twist.

The story concerns an attendant in the Louvre's Egyptian department, who is actually Sosra, an ancient Egyptian who discovered a potion for immortality through medical researches while a priest at the Temple of Osiris at Avaris. He drank the potion, but the girl he loved was hesitant to meddle with such mysteries. Before she had decided whether or not to drink it, she died of the plague. Only Sosra, the priest, and one of his close colleagues, Parmes, knew the secret and took the potion. Parmes loved the girl as well, so both men

were doomed to mourn her death for eternity. Parmes devoted all his life to discovering an antidote to the potion so that he could die and join his beloved in her tomb.

Eventually he discovered the antidote and took it. He told Sosra about the antidote but not its secret, so only he would join the girl in death. He did, however, tell Sosra that one portion of the antidote remained hidden inside the ring of Thoth. For centuries Sosra, cursed with immortality, occupied his time learning the languages of the world and reading Egyptological reports in the hope of finding his beloved and the ring.

Now Sosra reads about a tomb discovered near Avaris that contains the intact mummy of a young girl on whose breast lies the ring of Thoth. He sails for Cairo to see if this mummy is his beloved, but at the Boulaq Museum, Mariette Bey tells him that everything has been shipped to the Louvre. To be reunited with the girl, Sosra takes the job of a lowly attendant in the Louvre's Egyptian department.

At the first opportunity he opens the mummy case and recognizes his long-lost love. The ring still contains the potion. He takes it and expires in the arms of the mummy.

RITUAL OF EMBALMING A religious text describing the procedure for wrapping a mummy. Known from only two very similar papyri, one in the Louvre and the other in the Egyptian Museum in Cairo, each was intended to be buried with the deceased. Both papyri stipulate that the head is to be anointed with frankincense and the rest of the body with sacred oils. Magical names are given to each bandage, and the order of wrapping the different parts of the body is specified. The Louvre papyrus mentions the final words of the bandaging ritual: "You live again, you live again, forever. You are young again, forever."

ROMANCE OF A MUMMY, THE Published in 1857, this novel by Théophile Gautier is memorable for several reasons. Displaying an impressive knowledge of ancient Egypt and providing numerous details of the customs, clothing, furniture, flowers, food, etc., of pharaonic times, it is the first historically accurate novel set in Egypt. It is also the first to touch on the theme of the living falling in love with a mummy.

The book begins with a remarkable preshadowing of Howard Carter's discovery of Tutankhamen's tomb. "I have a presentiment that we shall find a tomb intact in the Valley of Biban-el-Molouk, said a young Englishman of haughty mien to an individual of much more humble appearance. . . ." The humble individual was a hired archaeologist, and just like Carter and Lord Carnarvon, the duo discovers an intact tomb.

The mummy is a beautiful queen, Tahoser, who was buried with a papyrus that tells the sad tale of her death. This is the "romance" of the mummy. The young Lord Evondale falls in love with the deceased beauty and transports her to England, where he can protect her remains.

ROYAL MUMMIES ROOM   The mummies of the kings and queens of Egypt were discovered at the end of the nineteenth century and, apart from Ramses II having spent six months in Paris (see RAMSES II), have never left Egypt. They have been kept in what has been called the "Royal Mummies Room," first at the Boulaq Museum and later in Room 52 on the second floor of the Egyptian Museum, Cairo. The royal mummies come primarily from two sources: the 1881 discovery of the Deir el-Bahri cache (see DEIR EL-BAHRI) and the 1898 discovery of nine royal mummies in the tomb of Amenhotep II.

In 1979 President Anwar Sadat ordered the Royal Mummies Room closed to tourists, stating that it was undignified for the bodies of the former rulers of Egypt to be on public display. After Sadat's assassination the mummies remained off limits to tourists until 1994, when the mummies room was refurbished, new display cases were designed and built, and eleven royal mummies were placed on display. Among the mummies are eight kings and three queens:

Seqenenre II, Amenhotep I, Tuthmosis II, Tuthmosis IV, Seti I, Ramses II, Merneptah, Ramses V, Queen Merytamun, Queen Nedjemet, and Queen Henettowy.

A second mummies room is now under construction and is scheduled to open in 1998 with additional royal mummies on display.

ROUYER, P.C.   French pharmacist who accompanied Napoleon Bonaparte on his Egyptian campaign and was one of the first scientists to gain firsthand knowledge of excavated mummies of unquestionable authenticity. Rouyer wrote a lengthy essay in the "Memoires" section of his *Description de l'Égypte* and made some astute observations about the various methods of mummification. He correctly pointed out that dehydration was the crucial step in mummification, but falsely assumed that it was accomplished by artificially heating the bodies.

Rouyer unwrapped numerous mummies and distinguished those with abdominal incisions and those without, explaining that the internal organs of those without incisions had been dissolved by a caustic solution. He also noted the different techniques of filling the abdominal cavity—some with bitumen, some with spices, and some not at all. Rouyer found a complete papyrus with one of the mummies but didn't realize what it was because ancient Egyptian writing had not yet been deciphered. Indeed, he described uncovering various gold, bronze, and ceramic statues within the wrappings but says they " . . . have no connection to the religion of these people, but appear to be only mementos of what they cherished during life."

Although some of Rouyer's speculations were incorrect, he was a man of science and called for more research on the subject of mummies. He was especially intrigued by the animal mummies he encountered and suggested future research would determine why they had been mummified. At the end of his essay, he comments that with modern "chemical arts," someday a modern mummy could be created rivaling those of ancient Egypt.

RUFFER, SIR MARC ARMAND
(1859–1917) One of the pioneers of the scientific study of mummies. The son of a French baron, Ruffer studied medicine first at Oxford and later with the great Louis Pasteur. While researching a serum for diphtheria, he contracted the disease and went to Egypt to recuperate. He fell in love with the country and stayed, becoming a professor at the Cairo Medical School.

Ruffer was in Egypt when large numbers of mummies were being excavated and was a friend of the director of the Antiquities Service, Gaston Maspero, who asked him to apply his medical skills to the study of mummies. Ruffer's major contribution was a technique that enabled the brittle tissues of mummies to be studied under a microscope. (See RUFFER'S SOLUTION.)

In December 1916 Ruffer left Egypt for Salonika, intending to reorganize the Sanitary Service for the Greek provisional government. On the way back to Egypt, his ship was lost at sea.

RUFFER'S SOLUTION A solution of alcohol and 5 percent carbonate of soda used to soften brittle ancient tissue so that it can be sliced thinly enough to view under a microscope. Developed in 1909 by Sir Marc Armand Ruffer, it opened an entirely new field of study. Ruffer was able to soak entire limbs of mummies in his solution to rehydrate them, so he could dissect out arteries and study arterial disease in ancient Egyptians. (See RUFFER, SIR MARC ARMAND.)

RUYSCH, FREDERICK (1638–1731)
Born in The Hague, Netherlands, Ruysch became world famous for his moral tableaux that utilized preserved cadavers and body parts.

Ruysch opened an apothecary shop while a teenager, and when he came of age, he obtained a proper license. He was awarded his medical degree at the age of twenty-six from the University of Leiden, where he learned and developed techniques for preparing anatomical specimens. His specialty was blood vessels, which he dried and varnished. He also used injections of wax to preserve specimens.

In 1666 he became professor of anatomy at Leiden, a position that he kept until his death at the age of ninety-two. Two of his auxiliary positions influenced his artistic anatomical tableaux. In 1668 he was given the responsibility of training midwives, giving him access to a great deal of fetal material that he incorporated into his work. Later, in 1697, he became "Doctor to the Court" and thus gained access to the bodies of executed criminals.

Five rooms in his home were devoted to displays of the specimens he had prepared. Many of the displays were posed in bizarre postures—one skeleton was playing a violin made of dried human tissue; another wept into a handkerchief made of peritoneal membrane.

His preparation frequently had moral undertones. In one scene that is submerged in liquid, the syphilitic skull of a prostitute is kicked by the leg of a baby. Ruysch's comment was, "The reason why part of the skull is placed under the little foot need not be sought far afield, since this prostitute would not have contracted this frightful disease had she not had such a reprehensible profession!"

Ruysch never revealed what liquids he used to preserve his displays, but one ingredient in his Liquor Balsamicus was brandy.

Several of Ruysch's children helped prepare the displays. His young daughter sewed lace garments for preserved fetuses and made decorations for small severed arms floating in liquids. His creations also included imaginative sculptures—a violin made of bone with a dried artery for a bow, or a vase made from the testes. Ruysch became famous for his creations, and one admirer said, "His mummies were a revelation of life, compared with which those of the Egyptians presented but a vision of death. Man seems to continue to live, and to continue to die in the other."

The collection was purchased in 1717 by Peter the Great. The more than 2,000 items were cataloged and shipped to Russia. Only half reached their destination, many of the delicate creations having been destroyed by the hazardous journey. Some of the displays still exist in the Kunstkammer Museum in Saint Petersburg.

S

SAN DOMENICO MAGGIORE, ABBEY OF One of the most important churches in Naples, the Abbey of San Domenico Maggiore contains the mummies of twelve Aragon kings and princes and twenty-six Neapolitan nobles of the fifteenth through seventeenth centuries. These bodies are of great interest, as many seem to have been mummified in imitation of the ancient Egyptian method.

The brains were removed but not via the nostrils as in the Egyptian procedure. Instead the cranial vault was sawed open, the brain removed, and the cranium filled with a packing of resin and animal hair. Often the internal organs were removed through an abdominal incision and the

San Domenico Maggiore, abbey of A poultice tied to the right arm of Maria d'Aragona had been dipped in sulfur.

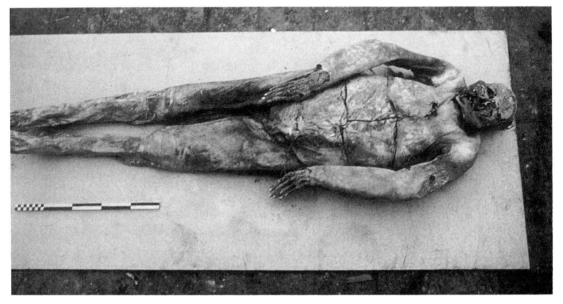

San Domenico Maggiore, abbey of The mummy of Maria d'Aragona, a noblewoman of the Renaissance known for her beauty.

cavity packed with resin and a filler. Sometimes the bodies were wrapped in linen, again in imitation of the Egyptian procedure. Beneath the bodies, in the sarcophagi, the embalmers had frequently placed limestone scraps to assist the draining of the body fluids.

A team from the Institute of Pathology of Pisa, headed by Dr. Gino Fornaciari, studied the mummies between 1984 and 1987. The mummies were x-rayed and examined in the crypt, and tissue samples were studied in the laboratory at Pisa. One of the most interesting findings was from the mummy of a two-year-old boy, whose face had been covered with pustules when he died. Tests showed that the boy had died of smallpox more than 400 years ago. This is one of the earliest documented cases of smallpox in Europe.

The mummy of Maria d'Aragona (1503–68), a noblewoman of the Italian Renaissance known for

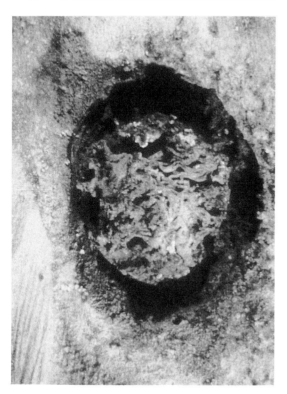

San Domenico Maggiore, abbey of The ulcer beneath the poultice was the result of syphilis.

her beauty, had the right arm bound with linen bandages intertwined with ivy leaves. Beneath the bandage was an ulcer, and inside it was a poultice of vegetable fibers that had been dipped in sulfur—a common treatment for skin diseases during the sixteenth century. Histological tests in the laboratory revealed that the noblewoman had venereal syphilis, which was known during the Renaissance as the "Neapolitan disease." This is the first case documented from soft tissues of ancient human remains.

The research team also determined that both Ferdinando Orsini, Duke of Gravina in Apulia (d. 1549), and Ferrante I of Aragon, King of Naples (d. 1492), died of cancers similar to those found today.

SAINTS, INCORRUPTIBILITY OF BODIES Although incorruptibility of the body is not adequate grounds for canonization, the Catholic Church does believe that the bodies of some saints have been miraculously preserved. The belief is that the state of these bodies is due neither to artificial means of preservation (embalming) nor the natural conditions of the soil, tombs, etc., into which the bodies were placed. It is often stated that there are cases when even after centuries, some of these bodies remain moist and flexible, unlike naturally dehydrated bodies.

The earliest saints were martyred during the reigns of the Emperors Nero, Domitian, Antonius Pius, Marcus Aurelius, Decius, and Valeriannus (A.D. 41–313). Their bodies became objects of veneration, and cults of the saints grew. Today there is still a large cult of Holy Bodies, especially in Italy. In Italy there are 315 relics of saints, including twenty-five mummies.

Most of these are natural mummies, created when the bodies were buried under conditions conducive to the natural preservation of soft tissue—often in hot dry crypts. Dr. E. Fulcheri of the Institute of Anatomical Pathology in Genoa has examined many of these mummies and has concluded that there are nineteen natural mummies of saints in Italy.

Natural Mummies:
Santa Lucia (d. 304)
San Ciriaco (d. 363)
Sant'Anselmo da Lucca (d. 1086)
Sant'Ubaldo da Gubbio (d. 1160)
Beata Beatrice d'Este (d. 1226)
Beata Elena Enselmini (d. 1231)
Beato Giordano Forzate (d. 1248)
Santa Rosa da Viterbo (d. 1252)
Santa Zita da Lucca (d. 1278)
Sant'Agnese da Montepulciano (d. 1317)
Sant' Odorico da Pordenone (d. 1331)
Santa Francesca Romana (d. 1440)
Sant' Antonio da Firenze (d. 1459)
Beata Margherita di Savoia (d. 1464)
Santa Caterina da Bologna (d. 1465)
Beata Angela Merici (d. 1540)
San Gregorio Barbarigo (d. 1627)
Beata Centurione Bracelli (d. 1651)
Savina Petrilli (d. 1923)

There are also several examples of artificially mummified saints, most of which were done in a period of less than 200 years (1297–1447) and were a product of the cultural setting of medieval Italy. Frequently holy people were venerated before they died, so at death their bodies were displayed for considerable periods of time. To make this possible, mummification was practiced. There was also a demand for relics of saints during this period, and throughout Italy sepulchers were erected to house portions of these revered people. Thus when holy people died, the bodies were sometimes divided so that segments could be sent to different cities as objects of worship. If the bodies were mummified and the internal organs removed, relics were available to send to various cities. There was even a hierarchy of body parts, with some being more desirable than others. The heart was, of course, the most valuable organ, but other *reliquiae insignes* included the head, arms, legs, and vital organs. Next in importance were the *reliquiae notables* such as the hands and feet. Minor fragments were *reliquiae exiguae*. Thus mummification served a dual purpose: it pre-

served the body so it could remain on view for a prolonged period of time, but it also provided relics for the faithful.

ARTIFICIAL MUMMIES OF SAINTS

Name	Sex	Year	Country
Santa Margherita da Cortona	F	1297	Toscana
Santa Chiara da Montefalco	F	1308	Umbria
Beata Margherita Vergine	F	1320	Umbria
Santa Catarine da Siena	F	1380	Toscana
San Bernardino da Siena	M	1444	Umbria
Santa Rita da Cascia	F	1447	Toscana

It is interesting that most of the artificially mummified saints are women, and often out of modesty the details of embalming are omitted in reports of the saints' deaths.

In 1988 the body of Saint Margaret of Cortona (1247–97) was examined and the exact method of mummification determined. Saint Margaret began her life with no signs of holiness. As a girl she was carefree and free-spirited. As a young adult she became the mistress of a young and wealthy cavalier and lived with him for nine years. One day his dog led Margaret to a spot in the woods, where she found her lover's mangled body. Margaret took this as a sign from God to change her ways, and she went to the Franciscans at Cortona who took her in. Margaret dedicated herself to nursing and established a hospital. It is said that in the last years of her life, she performed many miraculous healings.

Church records merely state that when she died in 1297, "The People of Cortona, having received the news of her glorious departure, summoned the General Council to honor and glorify the Supreme Lord, then rushing with great emotion to the church of San Basilio, they embalmed her body, dressed it with a red tunic and buried it in a new sepulchre."

Upon examination of her body, long incisions were found on the chest and abdomen, through which the internal organs had been removed. There were also incisions on her thighs, probably to remove as much tissue and fat as possible to prevent putrefaction. The incisions were sewn together with thick black thread. The body of Saint Margaret is on view in a glass coffin under the main altar of the Basilica of Cortona.

During mummification, it was frequently noted that saints' internal organs, especially the heart, exhibited signs of his or her holiness. Sometimes the heart was said to contain a figure of the crucifix formed of tissue, and other times it was said that three gallstones, representing the trinity, were found during mummification. When the heart of Saint Chiara of Montefalco (d. 1308) was being mummified, it was said that the organ exhibited the figure of the cross, the scourge, the spear, and three nails—almost a total representation of the crucifixion.

SAPONIFICATION The process by which fat in the body after death turns into adipocere, a substance closely resembling soap (see ADIPOCERE). When conditions of fat content, water, temperature, etc., are just right, saponification can be extensive, producing a natural soap mummy. (See SOAP LADY, THE.)

SCORTICATI Italian term for "flayed men." An eighteenth-century anatomical preparation in which the skin was peeled back to expose the muscles, veins, and arteries.

SCROLL OF LIFE In various mummy movies, when the mummy is brought back to life, the Scroll of Life is often read. This is probably a reference to the Book of the Dead, a collection of spells intended to protect and reanimate the mummy (see BOOK OF THE DEAD). In the 1932 film *The Mummy*, starring Boris Karloff, the papyrus is called the "Scroll of the Thoth," but on screen a real Book of the Dead, written for a scribe named Ani, is shown. This papyrus roll is now in the British Museum.

SCYTHIANS, MUMMIES OF The first true horseriders in history (eighth century

B.C.–third century A.D.), these nomadic tribes originally inhabited the Altai region of southern Siberia, bordering on China and Mongolia. Called "Scythians" by the Greeks, they mummified their dead and buried them in elaborate tombs constructed by sinking log chambers into the ground.

These fierce warriors of the Eurasian steppes fought on horseback with bows and arrows, giving them a tremendous advantage over their unmounted enemies. They were illiterate, so there are no written records of their culture, but because their tombs often froze in the cold Siberian ground, their remains have been preserved. The first written account of Scythian mummification is by Herodotus, the Greek traveler who visited the area around 450 B.C.

> . . . when the king dies, they dig a grave, which is square in shape, and of great size. When it is ready, they take the king's corpse, and having opened the belly, and cleaned the inside, fill the cavity with a preparation of chopped cypress, frankincense, parsley-seed, and anise-seed, after which they sew up the opening.
>
> (Herodotus, *Persian Wars*, Book IV, 71)

Herodotus was especially impressed by the rituals that accompanied the burial of a king. He says that all of the warriors cut off a piece of their ear, cut their hair, and put an arrow through their left hand as signs of mourning. He also mentions that one of the king's concubines, his groom, servant, and messenger were all strangled so they could be buried with their master. The most bizarre of the rituals mentioned by Herodotus took place one year after the king's burial. Fifty of the best horses were killed, mummified, and skewered on posts in the ground to form a circle, tail-to-nose, around the king's grave. Fifty young grooms were strangled and mummified, then a pole was passed through their bodies, spine to neck, by means of which they were fixed astride the horses. In this way Scythian kings were provided with ghostly horses and riders. No archaeological confirmation of Herodotus's description of this ritual has been found, but other aspects have been substantiated.

The earliest scientific excavation of Scythian tombs was conducted by A.V. Radlov in the 1860s in the Altai Mountains, but little of interest was found because of the poor condition of the graves. Most of the better-preserved (frozen) remains are of the Pazarik tribe, who dug circular tombs called "kurgins" that were mounded with stones above ground. These were first excavated in 1929 by S.I. Rudenko, who continued his work for nearly half a century. Much of what we know about Scythian mummies is due to his research, but current workers are adding pieces to the picture.

Within the below-ground chamber, the body was often placed in a hollowed log that served as the coffin. The Pazarik sacrificed their horses so they could be buried with the deceased, enabling them to continue to ride in the next world, but only the humans were mummified. The elaborate mummification technique included the removal of the brain through a hole in the back of the skull, evisceration via a long abdominal incision, and removal of portions of the larger muscles through several incisions. The body was then packed with aromatic spices and the incisions sewn closed with animal tendons.

Mummies of both men and women have been decorated with elaborate blue tattoos of real and mythological animals. There seems to have been near equality of men and women as both were tattooed and both had elaborate burials. Some women were warriors, and were called "Amazons" by the Greeks.

SEQENENRE TAO II, PRINCE OF EGYPT
(c. 1850 B.C.) The mummy of Seqenenre was discovered among the other royal mummies at Deir el-Bahri and was unwrapped by Gaston Maspero, director of the Egyptian Antiquities Service, on June 9, 1896. Everyone present was so shocked by what they saw that Maspero did not complete the unwrapping. Seqenenre had died violently. There are five serious wounds to his head. A blunt instrument delivered a blow that broke both nasal bones and broke and dislocated facial bones. In addition, a sharp weapon, perhaps a spear, penetrated the skull below the left ear.

A literary papyrus known as the "Sallier Papyrus" may contain the answer to why Seqenenre was killed. Sometime around 1650 B.C. Egypt was conquered by foreigners called the "Hyksos," or foreign kings. Seqenenre ruled at the end of the period of Hyksos domination, and the Sallier Papyrus tells of his role in Egypt's fight for freedom.

The Hyksos ruler, Apophis, ruled from his capital, Avaris, in the Delta; Seqenenre, a Theban prince, ruled from Thebes in the south. According to the papyrus, Apophis sent Seqenenre an inflammatory letter stating that the hippopotami in Thebes, 500 miles away, were keeping him awake and had to be silenced. The papyrus breaks off before we hear the result of the letter, but the condition of Seqenenre's mummy suggests an end to the story. One theory proposes that Seqenenre went north to fight Apophis, where he died in battle. In support of this theory there is evidence that he was embalmed far from the professional embalmers' workshops of Thebes. Although the viscera were removed through an incision on the left side, little else was done to preserve the body. Some aromatic sawdust was sprinkled on it and linen was placed in the abdominal cavity, but there is no evidence of traditional drying with natron. No attempt was made to straighten the legs or place the hands along the sides, and the hands remain in what seems to be a final gesture of agony. Seqenenre may well have been embalmed near or even on the battle fields, wrapped, and then brought back to Thebes for burial.

While the wounds indicate Seqenenre died violently, they do not prove that he died in battle. In fact, they are more consistent with his having been murdered in his sleep. The facial wounds are horizontal, an unusual orientation for injury if someone is fighting upright; if an axe strikes someone who is standing, the gash will be oblique or vertical. In ancient combat the bones of one's arms were often broken in an attempt to fend off blows. No such damage is seen on Seqenenre's arms.

Another possibility is that Seqenenre received the spear wound beneath his left ear during the battle, and that it either killed him or knocked him unconscious. Then the four blows to the head were delivered while he was down. Given the fact that three different weapons were used to bring about the king's demise, it appears that at least two and probably three enemies cooperated in dispatching Seqenenre to the netherworld.

SERAPEUM   The place of burial for the sacred Apis bulls (see APIS BULL). The word "Serapeum" is a corruption of a corruption based on a combination of two gods' names—Osiris and Apis. In ancient Egyptian the name of the god Osiris was pronounced "Usir." "Osiris" is the Egyptian word with the Greek ending tacked on. Apis was pronounced "Ap," but again the Greeks added the ending. During the period of Greek rule in Egypt, the two gods merged to become "Usir-Ap," and later the Romans added the "eum" to indicate the place of the Usir-Ap, the "Serapeum."

The Serapeum was discovered by August Mariette, a young Egyptologist whom the Louvre had sent to Egypt to buy Coptic manuscripts. When negotiations bogged down Mariette began visiting antiquities dealers, where he saw many stone sphinxes that had come from Saqqara. The ancient geographer Strabo had described the Serapeum when he visited it approximately 2,000 years earlier and said it was preceded by an avenue of sphinxes. Familiar with the writings of Strabo, Mariette explored Saqqara, where he discovered fifteen sphinxes half covered by the sand. Realizing that he must be near the Serapeum, he began excavating and in 1852 cleared the entrance to the Serapeum.

He soon entered a high spacious corridor about an eighth of a mile long, lined on both sides with twenty-four chambers. Each contained a huge granite sarcophagus, carved to receive the mummy of an Apis bull. The lids alone weigh approximately fifteen tons each, but still almost all the sarcophagi had been opened and plundered in antiquity. The chambers and sarcophagi had been created between the beginning of the Twenty-sixth Dynasty (663 B.C.) and the end of the Greek period (30 B.C.), but this was not the only gallery Mariette discovered.

Another gallery for the bulls of the Nineteenth through Twenty-second Dynasties was soon found. In the middle of this gallery, Mariette encountered a boulder so huge that he had to dislodge it with explosives. Under it he discovered what appeared to be the mummy of a man, its gold mask still covering the face and gold amulets suspended around the neck. Two jasper amulets bore the name Kha-em-Wase, a famous son of Ramses the Great and a patron of the Serapeum. Eighteen human-headed amulets were inscribed, "Osiris-Apis, the great god, lord of eternity." When Mariette unwrapped the mummy, he found only a mass of perfumed bitumen and a mixture of small bones. This was not the grave of Kha-em-Wase, but the remains of an Apis bull made to resemble a human.

The last gallery Mariette discovered was for the even earlier burials of the bulls of the Eighteenth Dynasty. One unplundered chamber contained two large rectangular coffins painted black. Again Mariette received a surprise when he opened them. Beneath the wrappings of what appeared to be Apis bulls lay a jumble of small bones and gold amulets bearing Kha-em-Wase's name. The meaning of these strange findings within the Serapeum are still debated by scholars today. There were also normal burials for the Apis—in which the bulls were mummified, wrapped, and placed in their sarcophagi. Some Egyptologists believe that the fragmentary burials suggest that upon death the Apis was eaten at a ritual meal and the remains buried; others believe that the curious burials indicate that in ancient times, soon after burial, some of the chambers

Serapeum   A nineteenth-century illustration of tourists visiting the Serapeum, the burial place of the sacred Apis bull.

were robbed and the bulls destroyed in the search for gold. Later the pious Kha-em-Wase had the burials restored and had his name placed with the pitiful remains to commemorate his good deed.

SHE   Authored by the famous nineteenth-century writer H. Rider Haggard, *She* introduces an immortal queen who lived during the late Egyptian period, although she herself is not an Egyptian. Throughout *She*, mummies act as props to set a bizarre mood, though they do not come to life. Drawing on the fact that mummies are highly combustible, Rider Haggard has the mysterious inhabitants of Kor use mummies as torches.

SHELDON MUSEUM MUMMY   The Sheldon Museum in Middlebury, Vermont, con-

tained one mummy, whose grave is still visited by scores of Egyptophiles each year. The mummy was purchased from G.A. Leavitt & Co. of New York in 1886 by Henry Sheldon, an eccentric collector of curiosities. Along with the mummy came the story that it was the infant prince Amum Her Kepshef, son of Pharaoh Sesostris III. The child's mummy had supposedly been found in the family pyramid at Dashur in the middle of the last century.

The truth of the mummy's claim to royal birth is uncertain, but what is documented is that the mummy reached Sheldon in Middlebury in December of 1886. A week before Christmas he wrote in his diary, "A baby mummy came to me by express in good condition." The mummy was displayed only briefly before being placed in the museum's attic where it remained, deteriorating for more than half a century. By the 1940s the mummy had so decayed that George Wolcott Mead, chairman of the museum's board of directors, decided it should be buried, declaring, "This was once a human being. It is fitting and proper that it should have a Christian burial." The mummy was cremated and buried in Mead's family plot in West Cemetery on the edge of Middlebury College. Marked by a tombstone that bears both ancient Egyptian and Christian symbols, it is perhaps the only Egyptian mummy buried in an American cemetery.

SHERLOCK HOLMES AND THE CURSE OF THE MUMMY'S TOMB
Written by Fred Fondren and Louis Ripley, this modern play was presented at the Prometheus Theater in New York from October 14 through October 31, 1994. The entire play takes place on one summer's day in 1897. The only set is the lobby of the Pharaoh's Arms Hotel in Luxor, Egypt.

SHESHONQ II, KING OF EGYPT (890 B.C.)
See TANIS, ROYAL MUMMIES OF.

SHRUNKEN HEADS
The preservation of the heads of ancestors, as well as the taking of heads as trophies of war, has been widely practiced throughout the world. Perhaps the most famous of these headhunters were the Jivaro Indians of Ecuador.

For vertebrates the head is the most important part of the body, containing the brain and the sense organs. Thus the preservation of the head is an example of the magical principle *pars pro toto*, "The part is the whole." The Jivaro believed that by preserving the head of a slain enemy, they possessed his powers.

Following are the three distinct steps in the preparation of a shrunken head:

1. Decapitation. The head is cut off close to the shoulders, preserving as much skin as possible. The head is brought back to the village, where in a solemn ceremony the chief authorizes the preparation of the trophy, or *Tsanta* as it is called.

2. Dissection. An incision down the middle of the skull to the neck facilitates the removal of the scalp. The scalp is gently separated from the top of the skull, so that the halves of the scalp hang down from the face. The most difficult part, removal of the skin from the face bones, is done with sharp bamboo splinters and flint knives. The result is a sack-like specimen that preserves all the features of the deceased, including the eyes, lips, and nose.

3. Shrinking. The eyes and lips are sewn closed to prevent evil spirits from escaping, and the scalp incision is also sewn closed, the hair hiding the suture. The head is then boiled in a liquid containing plants rich in tannin that both preserve the skin by tanning it and shrink the entire head. Finally the head is filled with hot sand or rocks in order to remove excess fat, flesh, and connective tissue, so the skull can shrink still more. While this is done the face is covered with vegetable oil and fats, and the features are modeled to retain their original characteristics.

As the procedures for the shrinking proceed, the headhunter fasts and observes other rituals to assure the success of the spiritual aspect of the process. When the process is complete, a village feast marks the introduction of the *Tsanta* into the community, for its powers now belong to the entire tribe.

SIPTAH, KING OF EGYPT, MUMMY OF (1208–1202 B.C.)
The mummy of Siptah is often claimed to exhibit the earliest known case of polio. Siptah's deformed left foot was caused by the condition *talipes equino-varus*, which is often produced by polio. It is unlikely, however, that Siptah actually had the disease, for where there is one case of polio, there are usually many. Had he suffered from the disease,

Shrunken Heads The Jivaro Indians of Ecuador removed the skin from the skulls of enemy warriors and shrank it to the size of a fist. *Photo courtesy Department of Library Services, American Museum of Natural History. Negative No. 38750, photo by Kay O. Lenskjold.*

other mummies with similar deformities should have been discovered.

Siptah's mummy is the first found to have the embalmer's incision on the left abdomen sewn together, a practice that continued into the Twentieth Dynasty. His is also the first mummy to have linen padding stuffed into the cheeks to give a lifelike appearance.

SKRYDSTRUP GIRL, THE   One of the most famous of the Danish mound people burials (Bronze Age, c. 1100 B.C.), the body of this young woman was discovered in the summer of 1935 at Skrydstrup in northeast Denmark. The mummy is most remarkable for the manner in which it naturally preserved.

As in most burials of this type, the Skrydstrup Girl was buried in an oak coffin and covered with a large earth mound—more than thirteen feet high and eighty feet in diameter. Unlike most other mound burials, however, the oak coffin totally disintegrated, leaving the body wrapped in its blanket on the bed of stones on which the coffin once rested. In spite of these seemingly adverse conditions, the body survived.

Discovered by an experienced museum excavator, the burial was not examined at the site. It was covered with tissue paper and the entire ensemble encased in 500 pounds of plaster, so it could be moved without damage to the National Museum in Copenhagen for conservation. At the museum, when the plaster was opened and the blanket removed, the head of a young woman emerged. Her strawberry-blond hair was piled high, held in place by both a headband and a hairnet. Her earrings were twisted spirals of gold, looped over the ears and tied in place by her hair. The Skrydstrup Girl had perfect, cavity-free teeth; the position of her molars on X rays taken at the museum indicate that she was approximately eighteen when she died. Tall (five feet seven inches) and slender, with fine facial features, she must have been striking. On her feet were moccasins with padding made of grass for softer walking. From the flowers that had been placed inside her coffin, it could be determined that she had died during the summer.

When first discovered, Skrydstrup Girl captured the imagination of the Danish people, and thousands lined up to view their beautiful distant ancestor.

SLEEPWALKER   A novel (1991) by Michael Cadnum, in which a bog mummy takes the place traditionally played in fiction by an Egyptian mummy.

The story takes place at an excavation site in York, England. Instead of a murdering Egyptian mummy, the fiend is the bog mummy of an Anglo-Saxon king, killed more than 1,000 years ago. In a thinly veiled takeoff of the mummy movies of the 1940s, the vengeful bog mummy wanders through the archaeologists' camp, trying to kill all the participants in the excavation.

"SMITH AND THE PHARAOHS"   A short story by H. Rider Haggard. This turn-of-the-century tale explores the romantic element of mummies. The main character, Smith, on a visit to the British Museum becomes obsessed with the cast of a statue of a woman's head. Drawn by his desire to learn about the woman, he becomes an amateur Egyptologist, traveling to Egypt repeatedly in search of information about his long-dead love.

He discovers her tomb and finds that she was an Egyptian queen named Ma-mee, but to his dismay tomb robbers have damaged the tomb and burned the mummy. Smith gathers up the tomb's pitiful contents—a woman's delicate hand, two rings, and a broken statuette—and brings them to the director of the Egyptian Museum in Cairo. When Smith is accidentally locked in the museum overnight, he see the mummies of the kings and queens of ancient Egypt; among them is his beloved Ma-mee.

Smith discovers that he is the reincarnation of an ancient Egyptian sculptor who once loved Ma-mee. As in all mummy stories of the romantic genre, the love can never be enduring. Smith ends up wondering about the reality of what he has seen.

SMITH, GRAFTON ELLIOT (1871–1937)

One of the pioneers of mummy studies, Smith was an Australian anatomist who was professor of anatomy at the Cairo School of Medicine. While in Egypt he was frequently called upon to examine mummies and was one of the first to conduct a systematic study of mummification in Egypt. In 1912 he published *The Royal Mummies*, the catalog of the royal mummies in the Egyptian Museum, Cairo. In it he makes important observations about procedures used in the mummification of the kings and queens of Egypt.

Smith's most important work was *Egyptian Mummies*, which he coauthored with W.R. Dawson in 1924. He surveyed the entire history of mummification, creating the standard work on the subject.

His ideas on cultural anthropology were eccentric and not generally accepted. He published several works suggesting that Egypt was the source of most of the civilized world's practices and customs. The most controversial of these was *Migrations of Cultures,* published in 1915.

SOAP LADY, THE

Obese woman buried during the nineteenth century. Her body fat turned to adipocere, a fatty substance produced

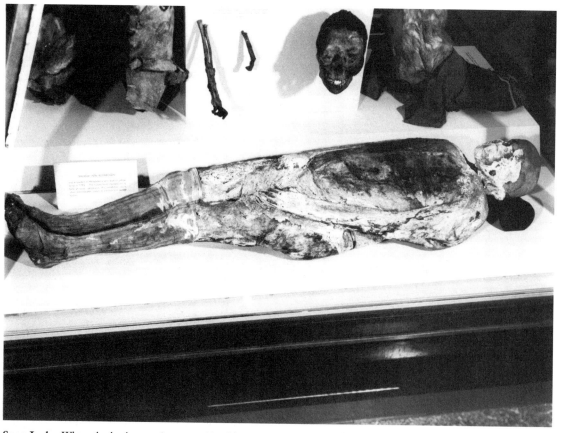

Soap Lady When the body contains a considerable amount of fat and soil conditions are just right, adipocere, a gray-white soaplike substance is produced. The Soap Lady's companion, the Soap Man, still wears the stockings with which he was buried more than a century ago.

SONGS AND MUMMIES   171

by dead bodies, preserving her body like a huge bar of soap. This natural mummy is on display in the Mutter Museum of the College of Physicians in Philadelphia.

The Soap Lady entered the museum in 1874. During that year an old Philadelphia burial ground was being moved because of construction, and the remarkable bodies of a man and a woman that seemed to have turned to soap were found. These bodies were obtained by Dr. Joseph Leidy, the foremost anatomist of the time; the Soap Lady went to the Mutter Museum and the Soap Man went first to the University of Pennsylvania's Wistar and Horner Museum and later to the Smithsonian Museum, where he is today.

For a body to be transformed into one like that of the Soap Lady, a considerable amount of fat must be present in the body at the time of death, so this is a phenomenon primarily of the obese. The fat in the body, in conjunction with water—either present in the body or in the burial ground—forms fatty acid salts. This produces adipocere, a gray-white substance with a waxy consistency. The fatty acids enter other tissues and inhibit bacterial growth, thus preserving the body. The formation of adipocere extracts water from other tissues, and this dehydration also retards bacterial growth, again preserving the body. When the factors of body fat, water in the ground or body, temperature, and amount and kind of clothing are just right, a mummy such as the Soap Lady is produced. It is months before any change can be seen, and probably years before a complete soap mummy is formed.

"SOME WORDS WITH A MUMMY"   A short story by Edgar Allan Poe that first appeared in 1845 in the *American Weekly Review*. Unlike what one might expect from Poe, this is a farce, not a horror tale. The story is a satire on the mania for unwrapping mummies that was common in Poe's day.

Several scientists gather in the night because the local museum has finally given permission to the town physician to unwrap their mummy. After the mummy is unwrapped, they decide to send a little electricity through it and zap it in the head, toe, and nose, which finally revives it. One of the men present is Mr. Gliddon, who was the American consul in Egypt and who wrote an early American work on hieroglyphs. This is fortunate since he is needed to converse with the mummy, whose name is Allamistakeo.

The mummy is somewhat bothered by being disturbed, but enjoys a lively discussion with the gentlemen who surround him. His American hosts are nonplussed because the ancient guest is not impressed with American know-how and feels that the buildings described don't compare with the Karnak temple. The scientists repeatedly try to impress the mummy with modern marvels, such as steel, artesian wells, and paved roads, but Allamistakeo can always point to Egyptian engineering feats that surpass them. In a final attempt at one-upping the recently awakened visitor, they ask if ancient Egyptians ever produced either Ponnonner's lozenges or Brandreth's pills. When the mummy replies in the negative, the session ends with the American antiquarians finally feeling superior.

SONGS AND MUMMIES   Prior to the discovery of Tutankhamen's tomb in 1922, there were quite a few songs about mummies. With titles like "The Maid and the Mummy" or "Mummy Mine," they inevitably dealt in a lighthearted way with love between a living person and a mummy.

Mummy, a million years you have been sleeping friendlessly
Mummy, a million years I've used in weeping so endlessly
I've wasted thro' the years just sighing
Oh! Can't you hear me again crying?
Waken? Your love no more denying, Mummy mine, mine.
   "Mummy Mine" 1918
   Words by Richard Coburn
   Music by Vincent Rose

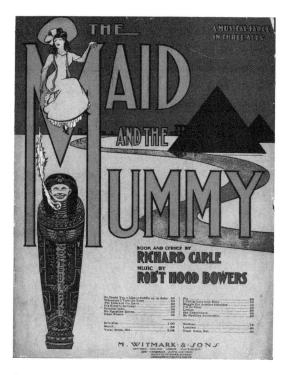

Songs and Mummies Sheet music for "The Maid and the Mummy."

After the discovery of Tutankhamen's tomb and the autopsy of his mummy, which was publicized throughout the world, the reality of a mummy as desiccated flesh and bones became fixed in the public's consciousness and mummies were no longer made light of or romanticized. After the world saw Tutankhamen's body, the mummy songs stopped.

SPIRIT CAVE MAN Named after Spirit Cave in Nevada's Churchill County where he was found, this male mummy has recently been shown to be the oldest mummy ever discovered in North America.

Excavated in 1940, Spirit Cave Man was found lying on his side, wrapped in a cloak of animal skins with moccasins on his feet. His body had been sewn into two woven mats, and the dry cave had naturally mummified his body. He was

in his forties when he died, possibly from a fractured skull. At the time of death, there were horrible abscesses at the roots of his teeth, which must have caused constant pain.

He was buried with textile bags that are woven in the diamond-plated pattern, one of the earliest patterns in North American weaving. When Spirit Cave Man was discovered, it was estimated that he was about 2,000 years old. For more than fifty years he remained in storage at the Nevada State Museum, until 1996 when a new technique—accelerator mass spectrometry—was used to recalculate his age. This technique is far more precise than earlier tests and counts individual carbon atoms in the hair. The amazing finding was that Spirit Cave Man was approximately 9,000 years old, 7,000 years older than was previously thought. To confirm the findings the textiles were dated, and they also proved to be 9,000 years old.

The skeletal features of the head of the mummy differ somewhat from modern Native Americans'. His long cranium and long small face are more closely related to Southeast Asian peoples. As further research on Spirit Cave Man progresses, new information about the earliest inhabitants of North America is expected to emerge.

SUGAR-CURED MUMMIES Prior to the nineteenth century the preparation of soft-tissue anatomical specimens for medical schools was a problem. One solution, used by the Scottish anatomist Allan Burns (1781–1813), was to sugar-cure specimens in much the same way as hams were prepared. Using this technique Burns created an extensive collection for the College Street Medical School in Glasgow. When he died the museum eventually came into the possession of Dr. Granville Sharp Pattison (1791–1851), who had been Burns's student.

The collection was an extremely valuable asset because professors at medical schools supported themselves by selling tickets to their lectures, and interesting anatomical specimens could be an important attraction. When Pattison left Scotland for the United States, he brought the 1,000 specimens with him to the University of Maryland, where he taught anatomy and surgery. In 1820 the entire collection was purchased by the university for $7,800 and at that time included examples of diseased and normal organs, body sections, and complete bodies. For a while the collection was an attraction for visitors to the university, but eventually the museum fell into disrepair and the collection was forgotten. Approximately 100 of these sugar-cured mummies, and parts of mummies, still exist in the anatomical facility of the medical school of the University of Maryland.

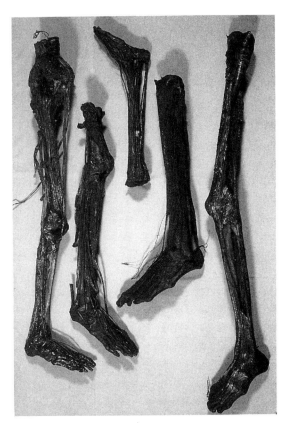

Sugar-cured Mummies Sugar-cured legs, prepared as anatomical specimens. Nineteenth century. *Photos courtesy Ronald Wade.*

Sugar-cured Mummies Sugar-cured mummy of a child. Nineteenth century.

SUMMUM A company located in Salt Lake City, Utah, that provides mummification service. Founded in the 1970s by Claude Nowell, who later changed his name to Amen Ra, the company's procedure is loosely based on ancient Egyptian mummification. For a minimum fee of $35,000, Summum will mummify and place your body in an anthropoid Egyptian-style coffin, which they call a mummiform. The process they use differs considerably from the ancient Egyptian method of dehydration. If desired, the body can first be embalmed using the normal funeral-parlor method, so it may be viewed at a traditional service. When the body is turned over to Summum, it is placed in a stainless steel vat in a liquid bath consisting of salts, oils, alcohol, and other chemicals that are a patented trade secret. Unlike the Egyptian method, the internal organs are left inside the body. The brain is removed through an opening in the skull, preserved, and then replaced in the skull. Once this is completed, the body is covered with oils, wrapped in polyurethane, then linen, and finally sealed in resin and placed inside the mummiform. The air inside the mummiform is replaced with argon, killing any bacteria that might decompose the body. When the mummiform is welded shut, the process is complete.

Summum   A mummiform into which one of Summum's customers can be placed after mummification. *Photo courtesy Gracey Ra, Summum.*

Custom-designed mummiforms are available and can cost as much as $500,000 for a jewel-encrusted model. A face mask can be made before death so the mummiform will bear your likeness, just as Tutankhamen's coffins bore his portrait. One lawyer who has subscribed to Summum's services has requested a three-piece suit for his mummiform, and another client wishes to go into eternity wearing his baseball hat. The company plans to store the mummies inside a granite mountain in Utah.

As of now, no human has been preserved by Summum. Although more than a hundred people have signed up for the service, none have yet died. So far the only mummies are pets—the owner's Doberman, Butch; his cat, Oscar; and most recently Eric, a client's pet bird.

SUM VII   Written by physician T.W. Hard, the central event of this novel (1979) is the high-tech reanimation of the mummy, SUM VII, which stands for State University Museum mummy No. 7. Dr. Reilly, a paleopathologist, is performing an autopsy on the mummy but soon realizes that SUM VII is not your ordinary mummy. The internal organs are intact, the fingers pliable, and cell samples revitalize when placed in nutrients. The decision is made to attempt to reanimate the mummy, and the description of the open-heart procedure is realistic. The book even includes arteriograms of the cerebral vessels of SUM VII and charts of his EKGs.

After reanimation an attempt is made to communicate with SUM VII, but before significant progress can be made, the mummy escapes. After a series of adventures, SUM VII succumbs to the effects of the aneurysm from which he originally died. Rather than attempt to revitalize him again, the medical team eventually reburies SUM VII in his tomb and in a secret location.

TAI, MARQUISE OF See MARQUISE OF TAI.

TAMERLANE (1336–1405) The Mongol warrior, whose empire once extended from the Mediterranean Sea to India, died in present-day Kazakhstan on his way to invade China. Medieval sources recorded that his body was sprinkled with rose water and musk and preserved in camphor. Then it was placed in a steel coffin and buried at the Gur-i-Emir mausoleum in Samarkand.

The Gur-i-Emir mausoleum was begun in 1404 at Tamerlane's command to house the body of his grandson, Mohammed Sultan, who died at the age of twenty-nine. The mausoleum was completed after Tamerlane's death and used as a crypt for his entire family.

In 1944 on the 500th anniversary of the great Uzbek poet, Alisher Navoi, the crypt of Gur-i-Emir was opened. One of the purposes of the scientific investigation, led by T.N. Kary-Nizasov of the Uzbekistan Socialist Soviet Republic Academy of Sciences, was to find out if Tamerlane was indeed mummified and if so to determine the technique used. Tamerlane's grave was in the middle of the mausoleum, and over it was a gravestone covered by a thin onyx slab bearing the following inscription:

This is the grave of the most mighty Sultan and most noble Khan preserved in safety and protection, the Emir Timur, son of the Emir Teragai, son of the Emir Barkul, son of the Emir Aklangis, son of the Emir Idshil, son of the Emir Idamchi Berlas, son of the Emir Kachulai Khan, son of the Emir Tumanai, son of the Emir Ghengis Khan, son of the Emir Kabul Khan, son of the Emir Yesukai Bahadur, son of the Emir Bartag Bahadur, son of the Emir Kabul Khan, son of the Emir Tumanai, son of the Emir Bug, his mother Alan Juva. And there was as is related no adultery on her part, but it was the fruit of pure light (radiated) from (one of the) descendants of the Lion (Asad), Allah the Conqueror, Alia the son of Abu Taliga—thus may Allah confer honor upon his visage.

Tamerlane's claim that he is related to the great Ghengis Khan is probably not true. The inscribed slab was removed, revealing a small crypt constructed of limestone blocks. It was only seven feet long, three feet high, and slightly less than three feet wide—just large enough to accommodate the wooden coffin. Over the coffin was a dark blue cloth with a verse of the Koran woven in silver thread. When the lid of the juniper wood coffin was removed, the crypt was filled with the smell of the camphor that had been used to preserve the body. The ancient accounts were correct. Tamerlane had been mummified but the process had not been a success. Although mummified muscle and skin remained on the head, neck, and hip, much of the body was merely a skeleton. In spite of the poor condition of the mummy, it was possible to confirm much of what was merely legend up until the body was examined.

The name "Tamerlane" is a European corruption of Timur Lang ("Timmer the Lame"). In a war against the Turkomans in 1362, Tamerlane received an arrow in the leg, and he limped for the rest of his life. His right hand was also injured by arrows, so by the age of thirty he was a cripple with a bad hand. Nevertheless, he retained the reputation of a man of great strength into his old age. Much of this was confirmed by the examination of his mummy.

The right leg was significantly shorter than the left as a result of the knee cap having fused to the thigh bone, so that the leg could not completely extend. The bones of the right leg were considerably thinner and weaker than those of the left leg. Tamerlane did, indeed, limp. The examination also confirmed that his right arm was impaired. The bones at the elbow joint had fused together so that the arm was permanently bent, causing stiffness. It is a sign of the greatness of the man that his disabilities never deterred him. Although his skeleton shows numerous battle wounds, this was not the body of a feeble old man. He died at the age of sixty-nine riding out to invade China.

It was said that Tamerlane was fond of riding and often spent the entire day in the saddle. This may have been compensation for his pronounced limp. On horseback he was the equal of anyone. Tamerlane's hair, wooden coffin, and a bust reconstructed from his skull are in the Navoi Literature Museum of the Uzbek Republic Academy of Sciences in Tashkent.

TANA LEAVES Leaves boiled into a potion during the cycle of the full moon to keep a mummy alive. In Universal Pictures' *The Mummy's Hand* (1940), it is specified that three keep the mummy's heart beating and nine give "life and motion." But the high priest cautions never to give more than nine or an uncontrollable monster will result. Tana leaves are purely fictional.

TANIS, ROYAL MUMMIES OF The only pharaohs' mummies discovered after Tutankhamen's (1922) were those of three kings of the Third Intermediate Period: Psusennes I (1039–991 B.C.), Amenenope (993–984 B.C.), and Sheshonq II (d. 890 B.C.). Discovered at Tanis in 1939 by French excavator Pierre Montet, a series of connecting limestone tombs contained

the intact remains of these pharaohs and a few other members of their courts.

Sheshonq II had been buried in a gold face mask paralleling Tutankhamen's, and as in the boy-king's burial four miniature coffins held the internal organs. The body had been badly damaged by water that had entered the coffin—the bones of the mummy's legs were covered with tiny rootlets that had grown around them like vines. Examination of the skull revealed that the ethmoid bone had been pierced so the brain could be removed through the nose in the traditional manner. From the degree of ossification of the ribs and from the degree of skull-suture closure, it was determined that Sheshonq II was past the age of fifty when he died. His skull also revealed the cause of death as an injury to the head, which developed into a massive infection that spread to much of the cranium. There is no evidence of healing; Sheshonq II died of septic infection.

In a chamber adjoining Sheshonq II's, Montet found the burial of Psusennes I. He had been buried in a solid silver coffin containing a gold mask and jewelry, again the equal of Tutankhamen's. The king's fingers and toes had been enclosed in gold stalls, and he was buried with gold sandals. Unfortunately the mummy had been badly damaged by water infiltrating the tomb, but some information could be obtained from the bones that remained. The pharaoh's teeth were in horrible condition—worn down and abscessed. His vertebrae were arthritic and the bones of his feet deformed. Psusennes I must have been crippled during the last years of his reign.

The third and final king's tomb that Montet discovered in the complex was that of Amenenope. Again there was an exquisite face mask and royal jewelry, but the mummy had been destroyed by water, and little could be learned from what remained.

TAPPING THE ADMIRAL A British naval term for drawing a glass of rum from a keg;

derived from the method by which Horatio Nelson (1758–1805) was preserved after his death.

Nelson's entire career was as a naval man. He entered the British navy when he was twelve years old. By the age of twenty-one, he was a captain and he went on to distinguish himself at numerous sea battles. In 1794 he was instrumental in taking Corsica from the French. In the battle he lost his right eye. In 1798 he sank Napoleon's fleet as it was anchored at Abukir Bay in Egypt and was promoted to vice admiral. In 1805 at Cape Trafalgar, Spain, Nelson defeated the combined French and Spanish fleets, but toward the end of the engagement, he was killed by a French sharpshooter.

Rather than bury their famous admiral at sea, as would have been customary, his officers decided to return Nelson's body to England for burial. To preserve it, the body was immersed in a large vat containing the ship's supply of brandy. The sailors, not wanting to be deprived of their alcohol on the voyage home, periodically siphoned off and drank the brandy, thus the term "tapping the Admiral." The body of Admiral Nelson is buried at Saint Paul's Cathedral in London.

TATTOOS   The practice of decorating the body by tattooing is thousands of years old and has been practiced by many cultures. Mummies with preserved skin are often found with the tattoos still distinguishable.

In ancient Egypt, tattooing was practiced primarily by women. In women the tattoos were almost always geometric designs composed of dots. Often these took the form of dotted lines around the arms.

One of the oldest tattooed mummies is that of the famous Iceman discovered in the European Alps (see ICEMAN). The Iceman's tattoos may not have been purely decorative. The tattoos were in unusual areas—by his spine, on his ankles, etc. X rays showed that the tattoos were in areas where there was arthritic bone, so they may have been therapeutic, intended to relieve the pain, much like acupuncture.

In 1994 Russian excavators discovered in Ukok in southern Siberia the frozen tomb of a Scythian princess, who had died approximately 2,000 years ago. On her upper left arm was an intricate blue tattoo of a mythical creature. It is believed that the tattoo was a sign of her high status.

THAY, TOMB OF   Tomb No. 23 in the Valley of the Nobles (Qurna, Egypt) was prepared for Thay, the scribe responsible for writing the dispatches of the pharaoh Merneptah (1212–1202 B.C.).

The Egyptians rarely depicted the process of mummification, but painted on one of the walls of Thay's tomb is a scene of an Egyptian embalmer's shop, in which the mummy of Thay is shown being wrapped. In one scene embalmers hold cups from which they brush a coating of resin on the wrapped mummy. Beneath the mummy stands a two-handled pan for refilling the small cups. The body rests on two supports, so the bandages can be passed all around it.

TIYE, QUEEN   The mummy of Queen Tiye, grandmother of the pharaoh Tutankhamen may have recently been identified by scientific detective work. Victor Loret, Director of the Egyptian Antiquities Service, discovered three unwrapped, unidentified mummies in a side chamber off Amenhotep II's tomb in 1898. One of the mummies was called "the Elder Lady." Her right hand was extended at her side and the left lay across the chest, a pose associated with royal women of the Eighteenth Dynasty.

Edward Wente, a University of Chicago Egyptologist, suggested in the 1970s that the Elder Lady might be Queen Tiye, the wife of the pharaoh Amenhotep III. There is no ancient Egyptian word for "queen," only one for "wife." Pharaohs had several wives, but only one was designated as "great wife," and this phrase is usually translated as "queen." Tiye, the great wife of the pharaoh, was also the mother of a pharaoh, the monotheist Akhenaten, and the grandmother of a pharaoh, Tutankhamen.

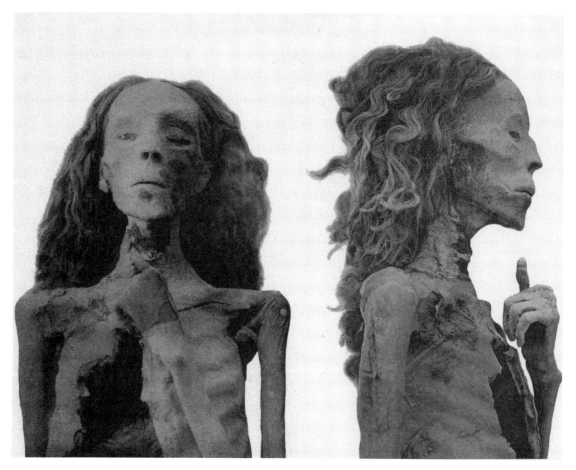

Queen Tiye The Elder Lady was found in the tomb of Amenhotep II. The position of her arms suggests that she was royalty. *Photo courtesy Egyptian Museum, Cairo.*

A find from Tutankhamen's tomb may suggest that the Elder Lady is Queen Tiye. Howard Carter, the discoverer of Tutankhamen's tomb, found a miniature coffin inscribed for Tutankhamen. It contained a miniature gilded anthropoid coffin, again inscribed for Tutankhamen. Inside the gilded coffin Carter found a curious assortment of objects: a very small painted wood anthropoid coffin, some scraps of cloth, and a tightly bundled linen parcel containing a solid gold statuette of a kneeling king that is usually identified as Amenhotep III in his "juvenile" phase but that may be Tutankhamen. Inside the small painted coffin was an even smaller one, inscribed with the name of Tutankhamen's grandmother, Queen Tiye, and containing a lock of hair.

Often the tombs of the pharaohs included heirlooms from previous rulers or family members. Sometimes a jar used by an ancestor or a scarab inscribed with his or her name was placed in the tomb as a keepsake. The plait of Queen Tiye's hair may have been Tutankhamen's memento of a beloved grandmother. Like fingerprints, hair is unique. If the hair of Queen Tiye matched that of the Elder Lady, then the Elder Lady was probably Queen Tiye. The Egyptian Supreme Council of Antiquities is, however, extremely hesitant to permits samples from the royal mummies—even a few hairs—to be removed for study. The authorities first had to be convinced that the project had a good chance of

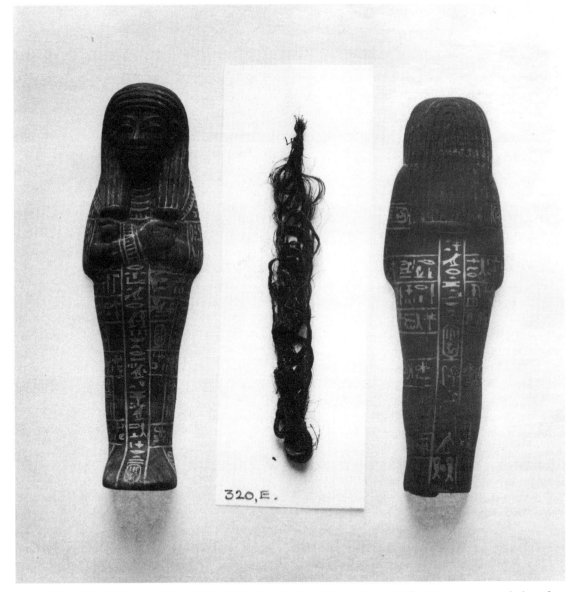

Queen Tiye The miniature coffin and lock of hair found in Tutankhamen's tomb. The hair seems to match that of the Elder Lady. *Photo courtesy Metropolitan Museum of Art.*

identifying the Elder Lady as the venerable Queen Tiye.

Permission was finally granted in 1975 for Dr. James Harris, the author of *X-raying the Pharaohs*, to take a cephalogram of the Elder Lady. This X-ray technique permits a precise plotting of cranial measurements. The side chamber in the tomb of Amenhotep II that held the Elder Lady was unsealed and the cephalogram taken. The computerized data from the Elder Lady were compared with those of Thuya, Queen Tiye's mother, to determine if the two women were similar enough to suggest a mother-daughter relationship. The test showed a remarkable similarity between Thuya and the Elder Lady. Permission then was granted for hair samples to be taken from the head of the Elder Lady and the plait of Queen Tiye's hair.

Both samples were scanned by electron microprobes to chart their chemical composition. The scan suggests that the hair found in Tutankhamen's tomb had come from the head of the Elder Lady. Queen Tiye may have been found, but the final word on the subject is yet to be written. A more recent study of the Elder Lady suggest that she probably wasn't the daughter of Thuya.

TOLLUND MAN   One of the best-preserved of the Danish bog mummies, Tollund Man was found in Tollund Fen (Thor's land) on 8 May 1950 by peat cutters. The body was so well preserved that they called the police, thinking they had found a recent murder victim. The corpse had only a cap on its head, a leather girdle around its waist, and a rope around its neck. The police brought with them curators from the local museum, who quickly realized that Tollund Man had died in approximately 220 B.C. during Denmark's Iron Age.

The face was remarkably well preserved, showing a bit of stubble around the chin. The entire body and the peat on which it rested were removed from the bog by building a wooden box around and under the man. The entire ensemble, weighing more than a ton, was transported by cart and then rail to the National Museum in Copenhagen for preservation and analysis.

Tollund Man had died by hanging, perhaps a sacrifice to the gods or a criminal executed for some crime we will never know. His internal organs were well enough preserved to determine when he had eaten his last meal and what it had consisted of. The stomach and small intestines were empty, but the large intestine contained a considerable amount of food. Tollund Man had eaten his last meal between twelve and twenty-four hours before his death. The meal was a vegetarian gruel made from barley, linseed, chamomile, and many other plants and seeds.

Tollund Man   The rope by which he was hanged is still around the neck of Tollund Man, who died c. 220 B.C.

Tollund Man   The face of Tollund Man.   *Photos courtesy Dr. Christian Fischer, Silkeborg Museum, Denmark.*

Once removed from the preservative waters of the bog, Tollund Man began to deteriorate. It was unfortunately impossible to preserve the body, but the head was preserved by soaking it for six months in a solution of water, formalin, and acetic acid. This was then changed to a 30 percent alcohol solution and then to 99 percent alcohol. Finally the head was infused with bee's wax. The head, with a reconstructed body, is on view at the Silkeborg Museum in Denmark, just a few miles from where it was discovered, and is perhaps the best likeness of an ancient man in the world today.

TOLU   A salve that was said to be rubbed on the skin of Inca mummies to protect the body. Probably used only on the very wealthy.

TOMB 55   This tomb in the Valley of the Kings contained one of the most discussed royal mummies of all time and was discovered in 1907 by the wealthy American businessman Theodore Davis and his excavator Edward Ayrton.

Many of the objects in this plundered tomb were inscribed for Queen Tiye, mother of Akhenaten, the heretic pharaoh who attempted to change the pluralistic religion of Egypt to a monotheistic one. A preliminary examination of the damaged mummy inside the royal coffin concluded that the body was of a woman—almost certainly Queen Tiye. Subsequently the bones were removed from the tomb and sent to Dr. G. Elliot Smith, professor of anatomy at the Cairo School of Medicine. His more thorough analysis established that the body was of a male who probably died in his twenties. This finding started a debate about the identity of the occupant of Tomb 55. Many favored Akhenaten, but the problem was that he lived well past his twenties. Some believed, however, that he suffered from Froelich's Syndrome, a glandular disorder that causes an elongated head, underdeveloped genitals, and a feminizing of the physique—just as Akhenaten is depicted in statues. The disease also retards bone development, so that the bones of a man of thirty-five or so could seem to be those of a man in his twenties. Thus the body in Tomb 55 could be Akhenaten's. The one problem with the Froelich's Syndrome theory is that the condition causes sterility, and Akhenaten had six daughters. With the exception of this problem, the explanation fit the data so perfectly that many Egyptologists were willing to assume that the daughters born to Nefertiti, Akhenaten's wife, were not fathered by Akhenaten. Others preferred to say that the daughters were Akhenaten's and that the bones belonged to Semenkare, a member of Akhenaten's family.

After Elliot Smith's examination of the body, the mummy of Tutankhamen was discovered and Smith's successor, Dr. D.E. Derry, reexamined the bones and compared the skull with that of Tutankhamen. He confirmed that the bones were of a male in his twenties at the time of death. He also noted a remarkable similarity between the two skulls, but this did not help establish the mummy's identity; Tutankhamen, Akhenaten, and Semenkare may all have been half brothers.

As the controversy continued, Dr. R.G. Harrison, a professor of anatomy at the University of Liverpool, performed the first and only modern examination of the remains. Because the skeleton is almost complete, with only a portion of the sternum missing, it was possible to analyze many of its anatomical features. Careful measurements and X rays of the skeleton to reveal the internal structure of the bones established that there is no evidence of either a deformed skull or a glandular disorder as had

been suggested. The body is that of a normal male with no significant abnormalities.

It was also possible to obtain a reliable age estimate. Throughout the twentieth century anatomists have been gathering empirical data about the normal range of measurements for physical features, such as the cephalic index (ratio of width to length of skull), ages at which epiphyseal union (when cartilage at the ends of the bones turns to bone) occurs, normal angle of the pelvic bones for each sex, etc. Such data permit precise determination of sex, age, and abnormalities if any exist.

As we age, our cartilage turns to bone, and bones near each other fuse. This is one reason we become less flexible as we grow older. In the case of the body in Tomb 55, based on the fusion of the bones in the sternum, the age at the time of death was between nineteen and twenty years. From the collarbone the estimate is twenty to twenty-two years, and from the sacrum the estimate is less than twenty-three years. Teeth are also a good indication of age. The third molar had not fully erupted, which indicates an age between eighteen and twenty-two. These findings are confirmed by the pelvic bones, which suggest an age of twenty to twenty-one. Given all the evidence, it is clear that this is a normal male who died very near the age of twenty and thus cannot have been Akhenaten. This leaves Semenkare as the leading candidate.

TOMB, THE This 1985 film centers around the immortal mummy of the evil princess Nefratis. As in many other mummy films, her tomb is robbed and the majority of the film is taken up with the evil queen destroying those who stole the treasures from her tomb.

Although *The Tomb* does include some well-known actors (John Carradine and Cameron Mitchell), it has little in the way of either plot or sets to recommend it. There are several references to the Universal Pictures' series of mummy films. The adventurer who steals the treasures is named Banning (Steve Banning was a character in *The*

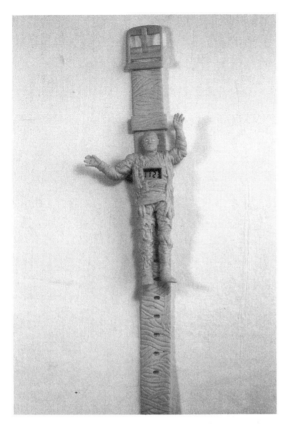

Toys and Mummies A mummy watch shows the time through a window in its chest.

Mummy's Hand), while the kindly professor is Dr. Andoheb (in *The Mummy's Tomb* Dr. Andoheb was both evil professor and high priest). In *The Mummy's Ghost* we also see John Carradine, but in a role quite different from the one he portrays in *The Tomb*.

TOYS AND MUMMIES Mummy toys fall into two categories—those designed for children and those designed for adults who are mummy aficionados. Among the latter are expensive plastic models, produced by Universal Studios, of the mummies in their sequels to *The Mummy*. Also in Universal Studios' line of toys is a plastic puzzle of Boris Karloff as the Mummy and a collection

of small "bendable, poseable" plastic mummy figures. Universal even has a mummy water pistol.

Expensive latex masks, designed with a number of different mummy faces, are available year-round in novelty and costume shops. Plastic mummified hands are also available but are usually easier to find around Halloween.

For younger and less sophisticated mummy fans, there is a more generic line of mummy toys that usually appears each year around Halloween. Included are mummy flashlights, lapel pins, and earrings with glowing eyes, mummies that attach to shoelaces to keep them from becoming untied (called "Moccasin Mummies"), and mummy

Toys and Mummies A winsome mummy waves from atop a pencil.

wristwatches with a window in the chest to show the time.

There are several mummy toys that are tied to other themes, such as the troll doll wrapped as a mummy. One of the most bizarre of these derives from the cult film *Attack of the Killer Tomatoes.* The toy is called "Mummato" and is a tomato-head wrapped like a mummy with a person in its jaws—a mummy killer tomato!

Goosebumps also produce their own line of toys related to the Goosebumps books. (See GOOSEBUMPS.)

TRUE OF VOICE   A phrase that in ancient Egyptian meant "dead." It derives from the belief that after the deceased was mummified, he or she would be judged in the Hall of the Double Truth by a tribunal of gods. In order to convince the gods that he or she had done no harm, killed no person, diverted no irrigation ditch, etc., the deceased had to make a speech in front of the tribunal. If the gods believed the plea and declared the speaker to be "true of voice," then permission to enter into the next world was granted. Thus "true of voice" became a euphemism for "deceased."

TUTANKHAMEN, MUMMY OF   King of Egypt (1355–1242 B.C.). The only pharaoh's mummy found undisturbed in the Valley of the

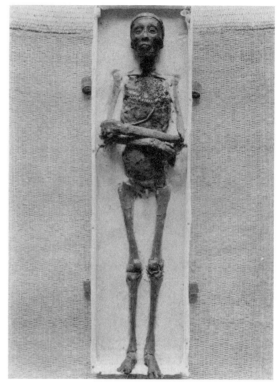

Tutankhamen   The mummy of Tutankhamen was badly damaged by the sacred oils poured over it at the time of burial.   *Photo courtesy Egyptian Expedition, The Metropolitan Museum of Art.*

Kings. Tutankhamen was a minor king who ruled for only about ten years.

U

UNIVERSAL PICTURES This Hollywood film company established itself as the premiere producer of horror movies in the 1930s with classics such as *Dracula* (1930), *Frankenstein* (1931), and *Dr. Jekyll & Mr. Hyde* (1932). In 1932 they introduced *The Mummy*, which was so successful that it was followed with *The Mummy's Hand* (1940), *The Mummy's Tomb* (1942), *The Mummy's Ghost* (1944), and *The Mummy's Curse* (1945). Universal's last tango with a mummy was *Abbott and Costello Meet the Mummy* (1955). (See entries under each film title.)

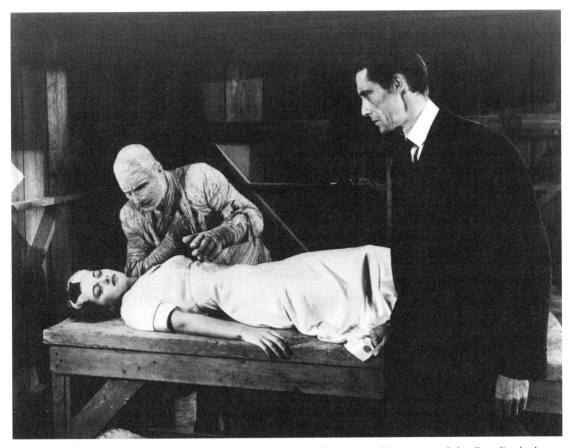

Universal Pictures Universal Pictures produced four sequels to *The Mummy*. Here a young John Carradine looks on as Lon Chaney, Jr. prepares to do his evil in *The Mummy's Ghost*.

UNLUCKY MUMMY OF THE BRITISH MUSEUM One of the most persistent and inaccurate mummy stories involves British Museum No. 22542, the inner coffin cover of a Priestess of Amun.

The story was initiated early in this century by Douglas Murray and T.W. Stead, two Englishmen who claimed they knew of a mummy brought to England and placed in a drawing room of an acquaintance. The morning after the mummy arrived, everything breakable in the room was found destroyed. The mummy was moved to several rooms in the house, each time with the same result. Soon after these supposed events, Murray and Stead visited the First Egyptian Room of the British Museum, where they saw the coffin lid of the Priestess of Amun. They decided that the face depicted on the lid was that of a tormented soul and told this to the newspapers, which were eager to print sensational stories.

Soon the coffin lid became identified with the destructive mummy, and the story acquired a life of its own and continued to grow. It was reported that the British Museum staff were so eager to be rid of the mummy (it never was a mummy, merely a coffin lid) that they sold it to an American, who attempted to transport it to the United States on the *Titanic*, the ill-fated ship that struck an iceberg and sank.

The truth is that there never was such a mummy on the *Titanic*. BM No. 22542 never left the British Museum and can currently be seen in the Second Egyptian Room. Despite several published accounts debunking the story, it persists today, and versions of it still appear in newspapers and magazines, and on television shows.

URBANIA, ITALY, MUMMIES OF The Church of the Dead in Urbania, Italy, contains many natural mummies. First built in 1380, the church's 1836 reconstruction included a semicircular wall with eighteen niches for the well-preserved remains of the former inhabitants of Urbania. The oldest mummy dates from the fourteenth century and the most recent from 1835. All were naturally preserved because of a fungus that quickly dehydrated the tissues of the deceased.

USHABTI In ancient Egyptian the word *ushabti* meant "answerer." Small ushabti statues were placed inside the tomb with the mummy to answer for it if it was called upon to do any work in the next world. These statues, made out of clay, wood, or stone, were all fashioned in the shape of a mummy, with feet bandaged together and hands protruding from the wrappings. Often the hands hold farm implements because farming was believed to be the primary kind of work in the netherworld.

Approximately 365 of these servant statues were placed in the tomb, perhaps one for each day of the year. Pharaohs had considerably more of these servants than commoners, and King Taharqa had more than a thousand. On the front of the statues, the deceased's name was usually carved or written, and on the more elaborate *ushabtis*, a magical spell was inscribed to assure that it did the work:

> Oh ushabti, if the deceased is called upon to do work in the next world, answer "Here I am!" Plough the fields, fill the canals with water and carry the sand of the east to the west.

VANDERBILT MUMMY, THE   Purchased in Egypt in 1931 by William K. Vanderbilt, this anonymous mummy was shipped to Eagle's Nest, Vanderbilt's Centerport, Long Island, estate, where it remains today. Although Egyptologists knew nothing of this mummy for more than half a century, current research is uncovering much of its history.

The mummy came with a wood anthropoid coffin, the style of which can be dated to the Twenty-first Dynasty (1080–945 B.C.). The coffin painting are so distinctive that it may even be possible to specify the tomb from which it came—the Bab el-Gusus tomb discovered in 1891, which contained the coffins and mummies of the high priests and priestesses of Amun and their families (see BAB EL-GUSUS TOMB). It is not certain, however, that the Vanderbilt mummy was the original occupant of the coffin. Frequently antiquities dealers in Egypt obtained a coffin with its mummy, but the purchaser did not want the mummy. The coffin might be sold and the mummy placed in an empty coffin, waiting to be sold to someone who wanted both coffin and mummy. Thus one can rarely be certain if a mummy and coffin belong together.

In an attempt to find out if the mummy and coffin belong together, the Vanderbilt mummy was transported in the Centerport Fire Department's ambulance to the Huntington Hospital for X rays and a CAT scan on October 30, 1995. One of the goals of the examination was to determine if the mummification procedure was consistent with that practiced during the Twenty-first Dynasty. During that period the internal organs were removed through an incision in the left side of the abdomen, dehydrated, wrapped, and then replaced in the abdominal cavity. If the X rays or CAT scan indicated such a procedure, it would support the belief that the mummy and coffin belong together.

The X rays revealed that beneath the wrappings, the mummy was in poor condition. No soft tissue or skin remained, so the bones had disarticulated. The vertebrae no longer supported the head and had fallen into two piles in the chest area. Teeth that had fallen from the jaw could be seen in the area of the knees, indicating that at some point the mummy had been placed upright. Of the teeth still remaining in the mandible, one was a molar, so the mummy was past the age of eighteen or so at the time of death. The quality and density of the bone showed that during life the person had an ample diet, with sufficient minerals and vitamins for strong bones. The spongy internal bone matrix indicated that the person was probably no more than thirty-five at the time of death and perhaps considerably younger.

Because the pelvis had shifted, it was not easy to determine if the Vanderbilt mummy was male or female, but the wide angle of the greater sciatic notch of the pelvic bone indicated the mummy was a female. As the X rays and CAT scans were examined, the profile of a young woman in her twenties, robust and healthy, emerged. The skeleton contained no traces of trauma or illness, yet the woman had died suddenly, possibly from an infection or some other ailment for which the ancient Egyptians had no treatment, but because all the soft tissue is gone, the cause of death will probably never be known.

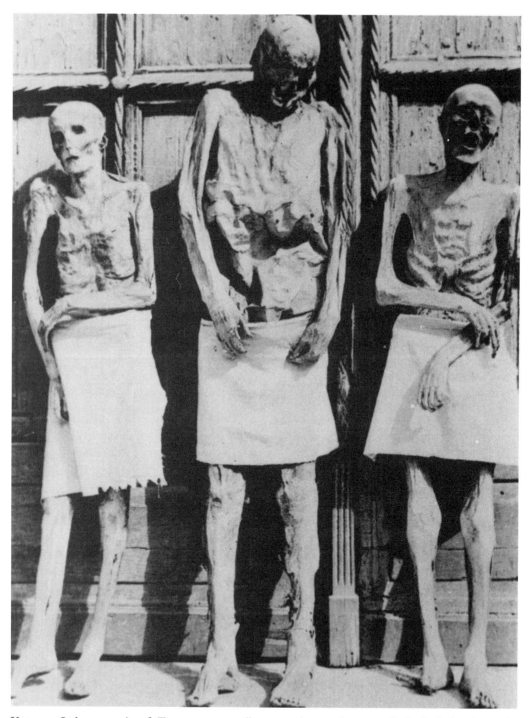

Venzone, Italy, mummies of Twenty-two naturally preserved mummies are on display in the baptistery of Venzone, Italy. *Photo courtesy Dr. Ekkehard Kleiss.*

The most intriguing finding concerned the mummification procedure. The brain was no longer in the skull, which is consistent with Twenty-first Dynasty mummification practices. From the Eighteenth Dynasty on, the brain was removed via the nose by breaking through the ethmoid bone and into the cranial vault. Although the brain was gone, CAT scans of the ethmoid bone showed that it was intact, raising the puzzle of how the brain was removed. Another anomaly was that the heart was missing. The heart in Egyptian mummies was usually left untouched inside the body. The researchers concluded that perhaps in this case the embalmers had not performed their work as conscientiously as they should have. They may not have removed either internal organs or the brain and perhaps did not properly dehydrate the body in natron. If they merely wrapped the body and returned it to the woman's unknowing family for burial, bacteria would have attacked the soft tissue, destroying it and perhaps even the brain.

The Vanderbilt mummy is now on display at the Vanderbilt Museum, Centerport, New York. Funds are now being raised to restore its coffin, and a major exhibition of mummy, coffin, and a full-scale reproduction of an ancient Egyptian embalmer's workshop is planned for 1998.

VANISHING MAN, THE   This 1911 detective novel by R. Austin Freeman was later republished under the title *The Eye of Osiris*. Like many of Freeman's novels, it features Dr. Thorndyke, a brilliant sleuth and lecturer in forensic medicine at Saint Margaret's Hospital, London.

In this novel John Bellingham, an Egyptologist and collector of antiquities, disappears mysteriously, leaving behind an Eighteenth Dynasty lapis lazuli scarab of Amenhotep that he wore on his watch chain. Foul play is suspected, but the body cannot be found.

When body parts are discovered in ponds around London, Dr. Thorndyke is able to prove that they do not belong to the Egyptologist but rather to a mummy Bellingham intended to do-nate to the British Museum. The climax of the book takes place in the British Museum, where Thorndyke produces the missing body. Bellingham had been mummified, wrapped, and placed in the coffin that was donated to the museum. This was done by Bellingham's lawyer, Mr. Jellicoe, who stood to benefit from Bellingham's will if the body was not buried as stipulated in the will.

To establish that the body in the anthropoid coffin is indeed that of the murdered Egyptologist, Thorndyke x-rays the mummy. The description of the process provides fascinating details of the early x-raying of mummies.

VENZONE, ITALY, MUMMIES OF   A small town in northern Italy, Venzone's fourteenth-century baptistery houses the mummified remains of its citizens, who died between the fourteenth and seventeenth centuries. As they died the people of Venzone were buried in vaults under the floor of the cathedral. In the nineteenth century several of these vaults were opened, and the bodies were found to have mummified naturally. The skin was dry and white, a result of the white mould fungus that formed on the bodies, quickly dehydrating them and causing the natural mummification. Twenty-two of these bodies are now on display in glass cases in the baptistery.

VIENNA, MUMMIES OF   Beneath the churches of Saint Francis and Saint Michael in the center of Vienna are catacombs that served until the year 1784 as burial places for their parishioners. Interring the dead beneath the churches of Vienna began probably in the sixteenth century and ended with an order of the Emperor Joseph II. Although these crypts were extensive, they were not adequate to house all the dead, so they were emptied several times to make room for the newer dead.

Because the crypts had excellent ventilation, and a thick layer of wood shavings placed under the bodies in the coffins absorbed the body fluids, many of these cadavers mummified naturally. When studying these bodies there was no bad

Vienna, mummies of One of the mummies in the crypts beneath the Church of Saint Michael in Vienna. *Photo courtesy Dr. Ekkehard Kleiss.*

odor, nor were there any traces of rats or vermin. Only the clothes had been destroyed by moths, which had given rise to the mistaken belief that the dead had been buried naked in some sections of the catacombs.

VODNJAN, MUMMIES OF In the cellar of the church in Vodnjan, in the former Yugoslavia,

are four of the best-preserved European mummies. They are called *Corpi Santi* because all of the bodies are of Christian saints. The bodies include a nun, Nicoletta, and Leon Zimbo, who was a bishop from Istanbul.

The oldest of the four bodies is approximately 1,300 years old. All four bodies mummified naturally.

W

WESTERNER In ancient Egypt the word "westerner" meant someone who was dead. From the earliest times the west was associated with the dead, probably because the sun was born in the east and died in the west every day. Consequently the Egyptians lived primarily on the east bank of the Nile and buried their dead on the west bank. This is why almost all the pyramids and tombs are on the west. When someone died, it was said that he or he "went west."

WRESTLING WOMEN VS. THE AZTEC MUMMY (1986) This Mexican film is a bizarre variation on the classic 1932 movie The Mummy. In this version an Aztec princess is to be sacrificed to the gods, but a sorcerer who loves her tries to use his powers to save her. Like Imhotep in the original film, he is discovered by the priests and buried alive. Now his sole purpose is to protect the body of his sacrificed love and the treasure with which she was buried. Like most mummies he is afraid of fire, but this one can change into a bat, thus combining the features of both a mummy and a vampire.

When a team of archaeologists discovers a codex that gives the location of the princess and treasure, they are killed one by one by a sinister Oriental master, whose sisters are black belt judo experts. Conveniently the last surviving archaeologist's fiancée is a professional tag team wrestler, and she and her partner wrestle the sisters to decide who gets the treasure.

This film features an interesting rock-and-roll score and the following description of the crucial tag team match: "No time limit, no disqualifications, and the losers must watch this movie again."

X

XINJIANG, MUMMIES OF The Xinjiang Uygur autonomous region in northwest China is a plain surrounded by mountains. The climate—brutally hot and extremely dry—makes natural mummification a common occurrence.

In addition to the climate, the high salt content of the soil assists in the preservation of bodies. In arid regions rains frequently leech salt from the soil, which pools in solution in the low areas. With rapid evaporation the salts build up in the shallow depressions and the top layers of soil. If a body is buried in salt-permeated layers, it will dehydrate quickly, and the salt will inhibit bacterial activity. Several hundred mummies have been found, most dating from between 100 B.C. and A.D. 800.

These naturally preserved mummies have been known for hundreds of years, but the first extended excavation was conducted between 1959 and 1975 by the Xinjiang Institute of Archaeology and the Xinjiang Museum. More than 300 mummies were unwrapped, most of which had come from shallow graves. Many were wrapped in fur clothes.

One remarkable discovery was made in an abandoned gold mine in the Qi-tai district. At the bottom of a shaft several well-preserved mummies of miners were found. They were still in their clothes, tools by their sides. Even their written permissions to mine the gold were there. Some were tied up. Apparently there had been a quarrel which led to murder, and the bodies were simply left behind in the mine. The moist soil at the bottom of the shaft contained a high percentage of salt, which naturally mummified the miners.

In 1978 a group of mummies with Caucasian or European features was discovered at a site called Qizilchoqa, "Red Hill." Since then more than a hundred such mummies have emerged from brick-lined tombs at the site. They are usually in the same position—on their backs, knees

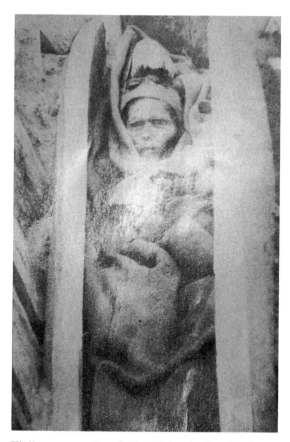

Xinjiang, mummies of The "Bohemian Burgher," one of the Caucasian mummies found in China. *Photo courtesy Dr. Victor H. Mair.*

drawn up, and fully clothed. These people had light brown or blond hair, which the women wore in braids. Some Chinese texts of the second century B.C. mention nomads who came from outside of China. These people may have migrated from as far away as Germany and Austria, but more likely they came from a closer region such as Kazakhstan. Soon the mummies' DNA will be compared with that of current populations, and their origins will probably be determined.

Nine of these mummies are exhibited in the museum in the region's capital city of Urumqi, and others are in the nearby Turpan Museum.

X RAYS The first X ray of a wrapped mummy was published by Sir Flinders Petrie in an 1898 report of his excavations at Dashasheh, eighty miles south of Cairo. The first royal mummy x-rayed was that of Tuthmosis IV in 1924. The mummy had to be taken from the Egyptian Museum to the only hospital in Cairo that owned an X-ray machine, and G. Elliot Smith and Howard Carter, the discoverer of Tutankhamen's tomb, transported the mummy by cab.

The great virtue of X rays is that they are nondestructive, and considerable information can be gained without unwrapping the mummy. From good X rays one can often determine sex, age at time of death, and sometimes the cause of death. In spite of their usefulness, X rays did not become a standard procedure for the investigation of mummies until 1931, when Dr. Roy Moodie x-rayed the entire collection of Egyptian and South American mummies in the Chicago Field Museum, demonstrating the value of the systematic application of this technique.

In the 1960s Dr. James Harris, an orthodontist, and Dr. Kent Weeks, an Egyptologist, x-rayed nearly all of the royal mummies in the Egyptian Museum in Cairo. Based on the facial features indicated by the X rays, they made suggestions about family relationships among the mummies. X-ray technology as applied to mummies was extended considerably in the 1980s by CAT scans. (See CAT SCAN.)

Y

YE OLDE CURIOSITY SHOP   This store, located on Pier 54 of the Alaskan Way in Seattle, has on permanent display two natural mummies called "Silvester" and "Sylvia."

The male mummy was approximately forty-five years old at the time of death, which was caused by a gunshot wound to the stomach. Found in 1895 half buried in the sand of Arizona's Gila Band Desert, the body had dehydrated quickly due to the low humidity of the air and the hot sands.

Sylvia was found in the nineteenth century in the highlands of Central America and is in a remarkable state of preservation, with hair, skin, and internal organs in good condition.

Ye Olde Curiosity Shop   "Silvester" died of a gunshot wound in the nineteenth century but was naturally preserved by Arizona's desert sands.

Z

ZENKER'S FLUID A fixative used in the preservation of tissue for anatomical specimens and composed of the following:

Mercuric chloride, 5 g
Potassium dichromate, 2.5 g
Sodium sulphate, 1 g
Distilled water, 100 ml
Glacial acetic acid, 5 ml

ZER, MUMMY OF King of Egypt during the First Dynasty (c. 3010 B.C.). His partial mummy discovered at Abydos is the earliest royal mummy.

In 1900 one of the workmen of Sir Flinders Petrie, the founder of scientific Egyptology, found part of an arm in the tomb of Zer. It was wrapped in linen, and under the cloth were four gold and ceramic bracelets. The arm and jewelry were delivered to the museum in Cairo, where a curator kept the bracelets but threw out the arm and linen, prompting Petrie to later write, "A museum is a dangerous place." (See photo on page 196.)

ZITA, SAINT, MUMMY OF (1218–1278)
The naturally mummified body of Saint Zita lies in the Basilica of San Frediano in Lucca, Italy.

As a girl of twelve Zita was sent to the town of Lucca to work for a wealthy family, with whom she stayed for the next forty-eight years. She led an extremely religious life, often praying in the middle of the night and fasting so she could give her food to the poor. Because of her occupation and life of service to others, she is the patron saint of domestic workers.

When she died she was buried in a simple manner in the church at Lucca, and when the casket was first opened in 1466, it was discovered that the body had not decayed. The mummy was studied in 1988 by a team of scientists who discovered that the internal organs were still in place and remarkably well preserved after 700 years. The body is on display as an object of veneration.

ZUMBO, GAETANO (1656–1701) An Italian sculptor who became famous for his wax representations of anatomical details. It has recently been revealed that his sculptures included actual body parts.

Working in Florence under the patronage of Grand Duke Cosimo III and his son Ferdinando de' Medici, Zumbo decorated tombs with elaborately sculpted scenes of plague victims—piles of corpses and babies suckling at their dead mother's breasts. He called it the *Transience of Human Glory.*

He later became involved in anatomical sculptures for educational purposes, with his masterpiece being the head of a man. Many of his sculptures survived in Florence until a flood in 1966 destroyed most of them. A modern study of the "wax" head of a man revealed it to be a human head coated with wax, on which anatomical details were carved.

Zer, Mummy of Only the arm of King Zer was found, but it is the earliest (c.3010 B.C.) Egyptian royal mummy ever found.

APPENDIX I

mummy films

The Mummy of King Ramses   (France, 1909)

The Mummy   (France, 1911)

The Mummy   (England, 1911)

The Mummy   (U.S.A., 1911)

The Eyes of the Mummy Ma   (Germany, 1922)

Mummy Love   (Germany, 1926)

The Mummy   (U.S.A., 1932)[1]

Mummy's Boys   (U.S.A., 1936)

The Mummy's Hand   (U.S.A., 1940)[1]

The Mummy's Tomb   (U.S.A., 1942)[1]

The Mummy's Ghost   (U.S.A., 1944)[1]

The Mummy's Curse   (U.S.A., 1945)[1]

Haram Alek   (Egypt, 1953)

Abbott and Costello Meet the Mummy   (U.S.A., 1955)[1]

The Pharaoh's Curse   (U.S.A., 1956)

The Aztec Mummy   (Mexico, 1957)

The Robot vs. the Aztec Mummy   (Mexico, 1959)

The Curse of the Aztec Mummy   (Mexico, 1959)

The Mummy   (England, 1959)[2]

The Curse of the Mummy's Tomb   (England, 1964)[2]

The Mummy's Shroud   (England, 1967)[2]

The Mummy and the Curse of the Jackals   (U.S.A., 1967)

Santo & Blue Demon contra los Monstruos   (Mexico, 1970)

Santo en la Venganza de la Momia   (Mexico, 1971)

Blood from the Mummy's Tomb   (England, 1971)[2]

La Venganza de la Momia   (Spain, 1973)

The Mummies of Guanajuato   (Mexico, 1975)

Theft of the Mummies of Guanajuato   (Mexico, 1975)

The Awakening   (U.S.A., 1980)

Wrestling Women vs. the Aztec Mummy   (Mexico, 1986)

I Was a Teenage Mummy   (U.S.A., 1992)

The Mummy Lives (U.S.A., 1993)

---

[1]Universal Pictures

[2]Hammer Film Productions

APPENDIX II

WHERE THE MUMMIES ARE: COLLECTIONS

EGYPTIAN MUMMIES

Ashmolean Museum, Oxford, England

The collection includes eight complete mummies, the head of a woman, and a hand with a scarab ring. There are also several other human parts and numerous animal mummies. The complete mummies include several with Fayoum mummy portraits bound into the wrappings and one mummy from the second Deir el-Bahri cache.

British Museum, London, England

Probably the largest collection of Egyptian mummies in Europe, the British Museum houses seventy-eight mummies. Unlike the Egyptian Museum's mummies, the origins of these mummies are rarely known. The first mummy to enter the collection was No. 6696, donated by Colonel William Lethieullier in 1755. His will merely mentioned that it was "found in its coffin among the ancient catacombs, about three leagues from Cairo, in the year 1721."

The seventy-eight mummies in the collection have been studied extensively, and when the Egyptian Department of the British Museum began to issue its new series of catalogs, the first was on the mummies. (*Mummies and Human Remains* by Warren R. Dawson and P.H.K. Gray, 1968.)

Brooklyn Museum, New York, United States

The museum has six mummies and three cartonage envelopes, one of which certainly contains a mummy. Only one mummy is on display.

Egyptian Museum, Cairo, Egypt

By far the largest collection in the world of Egyptian mummies is housed in the Egyptian Museum in Cairo. The collection includes hundreds of anonymous mummies, but also those of the two finds at Deir el-Bahri. There are thirty-one royal mummies, of which the following eleven are displayed in Room 52, the "Royal Mummies Room": Seqenenre Tao II, Amenhotep I, Queen Meritamun, Tuthmosis II, Tuthmosis IV, Seti I, Ramses II, Merneptah, Ramses V, Queen Nedjemet, and Queen Henettowy.

Of special interest is the mummy of Seqenenre Tao II because it shows evidence of his violent death. His many head wounds appear to have been inflicted by axes, daggers, and spears and have led Egyptologists to speculate that he was killed in battle.

The mummy of Queen Henettowy is the only one to have been restored. When she was mummified, the embalmers apparently inserted a fatty substance as packing material under her skin in the hope of creating a more lifelike mummy. When her mummy was moved from her tomb to Cairo, the higher humidity caused the mummy to rehydrate. The packing material expanded, giving Henettowy a bloated appearance, and the skin around her face split. Now restored by the Egyptian Museum, Queen Henettowy is on display.

A second room of royal mummies is scheduled to open in 1998. No catalog of the royal mummies has been published since G. Elliot Smith's *Royal Mummies* in 1912, but a booklet on the royal mummies displayed is now available.

In addition to human mummies, the Egyptian Museum houses the largest collection of animal mummies. These are on display in a special room on the second floor and include fish, birds, cats, baboons, crocodiles, etc.

The great advantage of the mummy collection in the Egyptian Museum, Cairo, is that the provenance of virtually all of the mummies is known, which increases their scientific value considerably. Although the royal mummies have been x-rayed, few other studies have been permitted on them.

Egyptian Museum, University of Leipzig, Germany

The collection contains five human mummies.

Egyptian Museum, Turin, Italy

The Egyptian Museum in Turin contains approximately thirty-five mummies, many of which are anonymous. Among the known mummies are Kha, chief architect for Amenhotep III, and Kha's wife, Merit, who were found in their intact tomb.

The collection has been x-rayed and studied, and twenty-six of the mummies were discussed in the museum's catalog, *Le Mummie del Museo Egizio di Torino* by Enzo Delorenzi and Renato Grilletto in 1987.

This study revealed that the mummy of Merit received very rough treatment at the hands of the embalmers. The X rays showed that the body had been broken in two at the thorax, and the head of one of her femurs was dislocated during mummification. All of the damage to her body was concealed by the embalmers when Merit was wrapped.

Other mummies in the collection also attest to poor workmanship on the part of the ancient embalmers. Mummy #13013 was found by the excavator Schiaparelli at the beginning of the century in a tomb belonging to children of Ramses III. The mummy was a child, apparently six years old, and although the wrappings were neatly done, the mummy inside is completely disarticulated.

The collection also includes some rare examples of excavated mummies of the Old Kingdom.

Field Museum of Natural History, Chicago, United States

The largest American collection of Egyptian mummies, the Field Museum has thirty-three complete mummies and five heads. The collection was one of the first to be studied by X ray and the results were published in 1931 by Roy L. Moodie in *Roentgenologic Studies of Egyptian and Peruvian Mummies.*

Institute for Anthropology and Human Genetics, University of Tübingen, Germany

This collection contains approximately twenty Egyptian mummies excavated at Abusir during the early part of this century. In addition there are four other human mummies and several animal mummies, including a cat, monkey, crocodile, and bird.

Liverpool Museum, Liverpool, England

The collection consists of eighteen complete human mummies, eight hands, six heads, five feet, two headless bodies, one leg, and one arm. Eight of the mummies are in the coffins in which they were originally buried. Four of the mummies are from controlled excavations, thus their historical context is known. All of the mummies are of the Twenty-first Dynasty or later.

Sixteen of the mummies were x-rayed in 1966 and the results were published in *Egyptian Mummies in the City of Liverpool Museums* by P.H.K. Gray and Dorothy Slow in 1968.

In addition to the human mummies, there are seventeen cat mummies, sixteen hawk mummies, fifteen crocodile mummies plus two heads, seven ibises, two kestels, two rats, one snake, one fish, one ram, and one jackal.

Lowie Museum, University of California, Berkeley, United States

The Lowie Museum, containing fifteen Egyptian mummies and two heads, is one of the largest collections in the United States. No catalog of the collection has been issued.

Manchester Museum, Manchester, England

This carefully studied collection contains seventeen human and thirty-one animal mummies. Many of the mummies have provenance, having been excavated by Sir Flinders Petrie, the Egypt Exploration Society, or John Garstang. Most of the mummies have been x-rayed and No. 1770 was unwrapped and studied by the Egyptian Mummy Research Team. The heads of several of the mummies have been reconstructed by forensic sculptors. The collection is published in Rosalie A. David's *The Manchester Mummy Project,* 1979.

Metropolitan Museum of Art, New York, United States

The Metropolitan Museum of Art has eleven complete mummies and one head. Most were acquired via excavations and thus have provenance. Because the museum is an art museum rather than a natural history institution, the mummies are not generally on display. Most have, however, been x-rayed, and the collection is currently being reexamined using both X rays and CAT scans.

Musée d'Histoire Naturelle, Lyon, France

The collection of the Museum of Natural History at Lyon contains a very important and extensive collection of Egyptian mummies. There are thirty-nine complete human mummies, thirty-four heads, seventeen feet, and ten hands.

In addition to the human mummies, the collection includes the greatest number of animal mummies outside of Egypt. There are approximately 1,500 mummified animals and the collection includes almost every species mummified by the ancient Egyptians—birds, cats, crocodiles, fish, gazelles, rams, bulls—and many are in perfect condition. It is these mummies that were the basis of the work produced by Loret and Gaillard at the beginning of the century—*La Faune Momifiée de l'Ancienne Egypt.*

Musée du Louvre, Paris, France

The collection of the Musée du Louvre in Paris includes twelve human mummies. Most of them come from excavations and their provenance is known. Five of the mummies are from Gayet's 1906–07 excavations at the Roman site of Antinoe in Egypt. These mummies are wrapped and their Fayoum portraits are still in place (see FAYOUM PORTRAITS). There are also two undecorated mummies in this collection.

Three mummies from the Ptolemaic period are also included in the collection, each with either a cartonage covering or wooden coffins. Of particular interest is the mummy of the Lady Henettowy, which is still covered with its faience bead net and is in its original coffin.

The fragments of human remains in the collection are two heads and a hand.

In addition to the Egyptian mummies, there are three Peruvian mummies in the collection.

Museum of Fine Arts, Boston, United States

This collection contains eleven complete mummies and three heads. Almost all the mummies were either x-rayed or CAT-scanned in the 1980s and represent almost all mummification techniques, from the Old Kingdom to the Roman Period. Included in the collection is a unique specimen, the head of Djehuty-Nakht, from el-Bersha, which exhibits that may be the earliest example of brain removal during mummification.

National Museum of Ireland, Dublin, Ireland

The collection of mummies in the National Museum of Ireland consists of four Egyptian mummies and one bog mummy. The Egyptian mummies are still in their coffins and date from the Twenty-second Dynasty, the Twenty-sixth Dynasty, and the Late Period. The fourth Egyptian mummy is from the Roman Period and its Fayoum portrait is still in place (see FAYOUM PORTRAIT). The bog body is the Meenybradan Bog Woman.

Niagara Falls Museum, Niagara Falls, United States

Like the Rosicrucian Egyptian Museum, this museum houses one of the largest private collections. In the 1860s the museum's owner, Colonel Sydney Barnett, returned from Egypt with seven coffins and six mummies. Currently on display are four mummies, including a child of the Roman Period (c. A.D. 100) and a woman with braided hair of the Late Period (c.600 B.C.). The mummy of a man with a full beard and red hair may not be an Egyptian mummy. These mummies have not been studied and some of the museum's labels are incorrect.

Oriental Institute Museum, University of Chicago, Chicago, United States

The Oriental Institute owns six complete mummies and one head. Most are excavated mummies with provenance. No catalog is available.

Rijksmuseum van Oudheden/National Museum of Antiquities, Leiden, the Netherlands

The collection contains twenty-eight complete human mummies, twenty-two human fragments, and sixty-two animal mummies. Of the human mummies eighteen can be traced to 1824 and came from the collection of Giovanni d'Athanasi, an early Greek excavator and collector. Most of the human mummies are from the Late, Ptolemaic, and Roman periods and have either cartonage coverings or wooden coffins. The collection was studied in the 1960s by P.K.H. Gray, and X rays are available for most of the mummies. In 1993 many of the mummies were on display in Leiden for the exhibit *Mummies Onder Het Mes,* with a catalog of the same title.

Among the animal mummies are twenty-one cats, thirteen ibises, many still in their original clay pots, and seven crocodiles.

Romer und Pelizaeus Museum, Hildesheim, Germany

The Pelizaeus Museum was founded in 1907 by William Pelizaeus, who donated his private collection of Egyptian antiquities to the town where he was born. The museum opened in 1911, and thus is a relatively new collection.

The mummies in the collection include three complete males, two children, and several body parts. One of the mummies (No. 19026) has its cartonage and two wooden coffins. Purchased in 1885 by Pelizaeus, it is probably from Akhmim and dates from the Third Intermediate Period.

Of particular interest is an Old Kingdom mummy that is in very poor condition (primarily a skeleton). The mummy was excavated by Junker at Giza and dates from the Sixth Dynasty (c. 2345–2181 B.C.). Old Kingdom mummies are very rare, this being one of the few examples from that period.

The mummy fragments in the collection include four hands, two feet, and two heads.

None of the mummies are currently on display as the museum in closed for remodeling and is not scheduled to reopen for several years.

Rosicrucian Egyptian Museum, San Jose, United States

One of the largest private collections of Egyptian mummies is housed in the Rosicrucian Museum, which owns seven complete mummies and one head, all unprovenanced. The mummies were not studied until 1995, when a team from Brigham Young University extracted tissue samples for DNA studies from six of the mummies.

Royal Ontario Museum, Ontario, Canada

Canada's largest collection of mummies, the Royal Ontario Museum has seven complete mummies and ten heads.

State Collection, Munich, Germany

The collection of mummies in Munich is one of the oldest in Europe. In 1818 the merchant Daniel Dumreischer, who had businesses in Alexandria and Cairo, presented the Bavarian King Max Joseph with a mummy in its painted coffin. The king donated it to the Bavarian

Academy of Science and thus the state mummy collection began.

Other mummies were later donated by Egyptologists Sir Flinders Petrie and F.W. Von Bissing. The collection grew and by 1935 was exhibited in the rooms of the Egyptian State Collection in the royal residence. Unfortunately, during World War II the mummies had to be relocated to unsuitable basements, and they suffered considerable damage; others were more deliberately damaged and some were lost. Today the collection contains seven human mummies and eighteen animal mummies. Four of the human mummies are in coffins, but it is impossible to determine if these are their original coffins.

Mummy 16d is the one given by Dumreischer to the king in 1818, and a demotic inscription on the wrappings indicates it is of the Late Period (c. 600 B.C.). The coffin in which the mummy rests gives the name Wer-Bik-Seta, but it is not certain that the mummy and the coffin go together.

Three of the human mummies were purchased in 1820 from Dr. F. Sieber of Prague who returned with them from Egypt, where he had traveled to collect exotic plants. It is not known if these three are in their original coffins.

One of the mummies, 73b, had a gold face mask, but it was destroyed during the war. Inscriptions on the bandages give the name as Djehuti-Irdis and indicate that the mummy dates from the third century B.C.

Perhaps the most interesting of the human mummies is the one that bears a Fayoum mummy portrait of a child (see FAYOUM PORTRAITS). This mummy was donated by Sir Flinders Petrie in 1912. It was found at Hawara in the Fayoum region and dates from the second century A.D. and, unlike most of the mummies in the collection, it is on display.

Other human remains in the mummy collection include one upper torso, a lower body, and five heads.

Included are quite a few animal mummies. Five small crocodile mummies have been part of the collection since 1820 and undoubtedly come from Sieber's natural history collection, although no further provenance for them is known. The mummies of two snakes, three well-preserved cats, and seven birds can also be seen, but again their provenance is unknown. By far the most important animal mummy in the collection is inventory number AS60, a bovine mummy.

This was the gift of Dr. F.S.V. Prunner-Bey, who was chairman of the department of anatomy and physiology at the University of Cairo from 1833–37. He was also the personal physician of the Khedive at the court in Cairo. The mummy was donated to the collection in 1846, and in 1865 it was described as "the mummy of a sacred cow, mother of the Apis, presumably from the Serapium at Saqqara." In 1983 the mummy was x-rayed, and was revealed to be a bull, probably dating from about 300 B.C. It may be a rare surviving example of an Apis bull.

In an attempt to create a central collection of mummies in Munich, most of the mummies in the State Collection are on permanent loan to the Institute for Anthropology and Human Genetics of the University of Munich.

University Museum, University of Pennsylvania, Philadelphia, United States

The museum contains thirteen complete Egyptian mummies and ten heads. Several of the mummies were studied extensively in the 1970s when the museum made four mummies (PUM I–IV) available for autopsy by teams of scientific researchers.

NON-EGYPTIAN MUMMIES

American Museum of Natural History, New York, United States

This collection includes seventy-one mummies, mostly pre-Colombian and Native American.

Anthropology Department, University of Colorado, Boulder, United States

By far the largest collection of mummies in the United States is housed in the University of Colorado's anthropology department in Boulder. Although not on display, this research collection of more than 400 Sudanese burials has been studied.

Field Museum of Natural History, Chicago, United States

In addition to its Egyptian mummies, the Field Museum has 128 non-Egyptian mummies, including more than sixty pre-Colombian Peruvian mummies. Fifty-three of the Peruvian mummy bundles were x-rayed and the findings were published in 1931 in Roy L. Moodie's *Roentgenologic Studies of Egyptian and Peruvian Mummies.*

Human Identification Laboratory, University of Arizona, Tucson, United States

The remains of seventeen Native Americans are housed in this study collection.

National Museum of the American Indian, New York, United States

There are seventeen complete mummies in this collection, though none are displayed. The museum's collection is not restricted to North American Indians and includes Jivaro shrunken heads as well as two unique examples of complete shrunken people.

National Museum of Natural History, Washington D.C., United States

This collection of forty non-Egyptian mummies includes several unique examples, such as the Soap Man, and among its animal mummies, an Apis bull.

Peabody Museum of Archaeology and Ethnology, Cambridge, Mass., United States

There are more than thirty pre-Colombian mummies in this collection.

University Museum, University of Pennsylvania, Philadelphia, United States

There are twenty-four non-Egyptian mummies in the collection, mostly pre-Colombian.

South American Collections

Anthropology Laboratory, Bogota, Colombia

Research collection of nine unwrapped mummies and ten bundle mummies.

Cuzco Museum, Cuzco, Ecuador

Pre-Colombian mummies on display.
Department of Anthropology, University of Tarapaca, Arica, Chile
Extensive study collection of hundreds of natural and artificial mummies.

Ica Museum, Ica, Peru

Pre-Colombian mummies on display.

Museum of Archaeology & Anthropology, Lima, Peru

Collection of South American mummies displayed.

National Museum, Bogota, Colombia

Pre-Colombian mummies on display

National Science Museum, Caracas, Venezuela

Several mummies of various periods.

Paleopathology Museum, Lima, Peru

Collection of Peruvian mummies, some on display.

San Pedro Museum, San Pedro, Chile

Hundreds of pre-Spanish conquest mummies excavated from the Atacama Desert.

European Collections

Basilica of San Domenico, Naples, Italy

Beneath the Abby of San Domenico Maggiore are thirty-eight wooden coffins containing the mummies of the kings, queens, and nobility of Aragon. They date from the fifteenth to nineteenth centuries and many have been artificially mummified.

British Museum, London, England

In addition to its Egyptian mummies, the British Museum has thirteen South American mummies: eight Peruvian, two Colombian, one Chilean, and two unknown.

Catacombs of Altavilla-Irpina, Italy

These are the most recent of the naturally preserved mummies of Italy, dating only from the eighteenth century. No exact count has been made, but there are hundreds.

Catacombs of the Capuchin Friars, Palermo, Italy

Perhaps the largest collection of mummies in the world, the Palermo catacombs contain thousands of naturally mummified Capuchins. These mummies span the sixteenth to nineteenth centuries.

Catacombs of Savoca, Savoca, Italy

Recently discovered in catacombs are approximately thirty naturally preserved mummies of the seventeenth to eighteenth centuries.

Cathedral of Venzone, Venzone, Italy

There are fifteen naturally preserved mummies of the fourteenth to eighteenth centuries beneath Venzone's cathedral.

Church of the Dead, Urbania, Italy

In the church's crypt are eighteen naturally preserved bodies of the seventeenth to nineteenth centuries.

Church of San Bartolomeo, Navelli, Italy

Beneath the church are hundreds of naturally preserved bodies of the inhabitants of Navelli that date from the thirteenth to nineteenth centuries.

Church of San Stefano, Ferentillo, Italy

Beneath the church are sixteen naturally mummified bodies from the eighteenth to nineteenth centuries.

Church of Santa Maria delle Grazie, Comiso, Italy

Beneath the church are fifty eighteenth- to nineteenth-century naturally preserved mummies.

Medici Mausoleum, Florence, Italy

Thirty-nine bodies of the Medici family dating from the sixteenth to eighteenth centuries are preserved here. Some have been artificially preserved.

Asian Collections

Gur-i-Emir Mausoleum, Samarkand, Uzbekistan

This mausoleum contains the mummies of the Timurids, the rulers of Transoxania and Iran from the fourteenth to sixteenth centuries A.D. The mummies include those of Tamerlane (1336–1405); his youngest son, Shah-Rukh (1377–1447); his grandson Ulug-Beg (1394–1499); and Miran-Shah (1366–1402), another of Tamerlane's sons. The mummies were examined in 1941 and found to be in poor condition, with only small sections of soft tissue preserved.

BIBLIOGRAPHY

EGYPT

History

Bakry, H.S.K. *A Brief Study of Mummies and Mummification.* Cairo: Al-Takaddum Press, 1965. Photographs of most of the royal mummies.

Balabanova, S. et al. "First Identification of Drugs in Egyptian Mummies." *Naturwissenschaften* 79 (1992): 358. Surprising finding of cocaine and hashish traces in Egyptian mummies.

Balout, D.L. "Gamma Rays Halt Deterioration of Mummy of Ramses II." *Biblical Archaeology Review* 9 (1983): 54–55.

Banks, Miriam A. "The Mummy of Nes-min; The Coffin of Nes-min." *Bulletin of the Rhode Island School of Design* 27, no. 1 (1939): 21–35.

Barraco, R.A. et al. "Paleobiochemical Analysis of an Egyptian Mummy." *Journal of Human Evolution* 6 (1977): 533–546.

Batrawi, A. "The Pyramid Studies: Anatomical Reports." *Annales du Service des Antiquités* 47 (1947): 97–111.

Belon, Pierre. *Petri Bellonii Cenomani De Amirabili Operum Antiquorum et reum suspiciendum Praeslantia.* Paris: William Caullot, 1553. An early work describing Egyptian, Jewish, Ethiopian, and other mummification practices. The end of the book discusses resins used.

Belzoni, Giovanni. *Narrative of the Operations and Recent Discoveries in Egypt and Nubia.* London: John Murray, 1820. Colorful account of the discovery of mummies in Egypt.

Bianchi, Robert S. "Egyptian Mummies: Myth and Reality." *Archaeology,* 35 (1983): 8–35. A good popular article.

Birch, Samuel. "Account of the Coffins and Mummies Discovered in Egypt on the Occasion of the Visit of H.R.H. The Prince of Wales in 1868–1869." *Transactions of the Royal Society of Literature,* New Series (1870): 1–29. More on the coffins than the mummies. Saite Period.

———. *The Mummies of Deir-el-Bahari.* London: Kelly & Co., 1881.

———. "Notes upon a Mummy of the Age of the XXVIth Dyn." *Archaeological Journal* 7 (1850): 273–280. Actually a mummy of the Twenty-first Dynasty with internal organs in packets in the body.

———. "On a Mummy opened at Stafford House." *Transactions of the Society of Biblical Archaeology* 5 (1887): 122–126. More description of the coffin than the mummy. The mummy was given to the Museum of Royal College of Surgeons by the Duke of Sutherland.

Blackman, Aylward. "On the Name of an Unguent Used for Ceremonial Purposes." *Journal of Egyptian Archaeology* 6 (1920): 58.

Bohleke, Briant and G. Scott. "Judge Barringer and the Deir el-Bahri Cache of Royal Mummies. Preparation for Egyptian Exhibit at Peabody Museum Results in Surprising Discovery." *Discovery* 17, no. 1 (1984–84): 13–15.

Bonfils, P. et al. "Flexible Fiberendoscopy: New Approaches and First Findings in Egyptian Mummies." *OSSA* 13 (1986): 61–73. Early use of the endoscope for examining mummies.

Boudet, Jacques. "Les secrets de l'embaumement." *Aesculape* (1955): 224–232.

Brears, P.C.D. "Mummies in Leeds Museums." In A. Rosalie David and Edmund Tapp, eds. *The Mummy's Tale*, New York: St. Martin's Press, 1993. History of how mummies came to Leeds in the nineteenth century.

Brouqui, M. et al. "Traitment par rayonnement gamma de la momie de Ramses II." *Revue Générale Nucléaire* 1 (1978): 10–14. Preservation of the mummy of Ramses II by gamma-ray irradiation.

Bucaille, Maurice. *Mummies of the Pharaohs.* New York: St. Martin's Press, 1989. Some interesting information and a highly speculative theory that the mummy of Ramses II proves that he was the pharaoh of the Exodus.

Caminos, Ricardo. *Ancient Egyptian Mummy Bandages in Madrid.* Madrid: Ministerio de Culturo, 1983.

———. "The Rendells Mummy Bandages." *Journal of Egyptian Archaeology,* 68 (1982): 145–155.

Castillos, J.J. "A Late Egyptian Mummy at the National Natural History Museum of Montevideo." *Revue d'egyptologie,* no. 28 (1976): 48–60.

Caylus, Compte de. "Des embaumements des egyptiens." *Histoire de l'Académie des Inscriptions et Belles-Lettres* 23 (1756): 119–136. Early survey of mummification, much of it inaccurate.

Cejka, J. "Contribution to the Chemical Research of Egyptian Mummies." *Zeitschrift für Ägyptische Sprache* 103 (1976): 128–139.

Chassinet, Émile. "La mise à mort rituelle d'Apis." *Recueil de Traveaux relatifs à la philologie. . . .* 38 (1926): 33–60. Suggests that the Apis bull was drowned before being mummified.

Clayton, Peter A. "Mizraim Cures Wounds and Pharaoh Is Sold for Balsams." *Popular Archaeology* 4, no. 5 (1982): 40–43.

Clendennin, F.J. "Skiagram of the Hand of an Egyptian Mummy Showing an Abnormal Number of Sezamoid Bones." *Intercolon. Medical Journal Australasia* 3 (1898): 106–107. A very early application of X rays to the study of mummies.

Cockburn, Eve. "Autopsy Team Seeks a Mummy's Medical Secrets." *Smithsonian* 4 (1973): 80–89. Popular account of a scientific team's study of a mummy that led to the founding of the Paleopathology Association.

Corcoran, Lorelei. *Portrait Mummies from Roman Egypt.* Chicago: Oriental Institute, 1995. The definitive work.

Cooney, John. "Cleveland's First Egyptian Mummy." *Cleveland Ohio Historical Society News* 23, no. 7 (1969): 2–3.

Danforth, M.S. "Report on X-ray Films of an Egyptian Mummy." *Bulletin of the Museum of Art, Rhode Island School of Design* 27 (1939): 36–37.

Dannenfeldt, Karl H. "Egyptian Mumia: The Sixteenth Century Experience and Debate." *Sixteenth Century Journal* 16, no. 2 (1985): 163–180.

Daressy, George. "Les cercueils des pretres d'Ammon (deuxième trouvaille de Deir el-Bahri)." *Annales du Service des Antiquités* 3 (1907): 3–38. Inventory of finds of the second cache of mummies found at Deir el-Bahri. Descriptions of the wrappings.

———. "Observations prises sur la momie de Mahepra." *Annales du Service des Antiquités Egyptien* 4 (1903): 74–75.

——— and C. Gaillard. *La Faune Momifiée de l'Antique Égypte.* Cairo: Egyptian Museum, 1905. Important early work on animal mummification.

D'Auria, Sue, et al. *Mummies & Magic.* Boston: Museum of Fine Arts, 1988. Exhibition catalog with much information on mummification.

David, A. Rosalie. "The Discovery and 1828 Autopsy of Natsef-Amun." In *The Mummy's Tale,* A. Rosalie David and Edmund Tapp, eds. New York: St. Martin's Press, 1993, 55–64. Historical account of an early investigation of a mummy.

———. "Early Investigations of Mummies." In *The Mummy's Tale*, A. Rosalie David and Edmund Tapp, eds. New York: St. Martin's Press, 1993, 11–19.

———. "The History of Mummification." In *The Mummy's Tale*, A. Rosalie David and Edmund Tapp, eds. New York: St. Martin's Press, 1993. A good, concise account.

———. "The Manchester Mummy Project." In *The Mummy's Tale*, A. Rosalie David and Edmund Tapp, eds. New York: St. Martin's Press, 1993. A brief description of the beginning of modern scientific team investigation of mummies in England.

Davidson, John. *An Address on Embalming Generally Delivered at the Royal Institution on the Unrolling of a Mummy*. London: James Ridgway, 1833. An early mummy unrolling, assisted by Dr. Pettigrew.

Dawson, Warren R. *A Bibliography of Works Relating to Mummification in Egypt*. Cairo: Institut français, 1929. Good reference for early works, but does not include animal mummies.

———. "Contributions to the History of Mummification." *Proceedings of the Royal Society of Medicine* 20 (1927): 832–854. An important general survey even though some of the observations have been corrected by later research.

———. "A Mummy from the Torres Straits." *Annals of Archaeology and Anthropology* 11 (1924): 87–94. A mummy from the Torres Straits is compared with Twenty-first Dynasty Egyptian mummies to suggest a diffusion of knowledge from Egypt to the rest of the world.

———. "A Mummy of the Persian Period." *Journal of Egyptian Archaeology* 11 (1925): 76–77. The famous Granville mummy.

———. "A Note on the Egyptian Mummies in the Castle Museum, Norwich." *Journal of Egyptian Archaeology* 15 (1929): 186–189.

———. "Pettigrew's Demonstrations upon Mummies." *Journal of Egyptian Archaeology* 20 (1934): 170–182. History of mummy unrollings.

———. "A Rare Vignette from the Book of the Dead." *Journal of Egyptian Archaeology* 10 (1924): 40. The only ancient Egyptian depiction of an unwrapped mummy.

———. "On Two Mummies formerly belonging to the Duke of Sutherland." *Journal of Egyptian Archaeology* 13 (1927): 155–161. A reexamination of a mummy first unwrapped by Samuel Birch and of another in the British Museum.

———. "References to Mummification by Greek and Latin Authors." *Aegyptus* 9 (1928): 106–112.

——— and P.H.K. Gray. *Catalogue of Egyptian Antiquities in the British Museum. I. Mummies and Human Remains*. London: British Museum, 1968. Important descriptions of all the mummies in the British Museum.

Dedekind, A. "A Novel Use for the Röntgen Rays." *British Journal of Photography* 43 (1896): 131. Discusses one of the earliest uses of X rays for the study of a mummy.

DeLorenzi, E. and R. Grilletto. *Le Mummie del Museo Egizio de Torino*. Milan: Instituto Editoriale Cisalpino, 1989. Photographs, X rays, and descriptions of twenty-six mummies in the Turin Egyptian Museum collection.

Derry, D.E. "An examination of the bones of King Psusennes I." *Annales du Service des Antiquités*, 40 (1940): 967–970. Little remained of this pharaoh.

———. "The 'mummy' of Sitamun." *Annales du Service des Antiquités*, 39 (1939): 411–416. Little remained of this pharaoh.

———. "Notes on the Remains of Sheshonq." *Annales du Service des Antiquités* 39 (1939): 549–551.

———. "Notes on the Skeleton hitherto Believed to Be that of King Akhenaten." *Annals du Service des Antiquités* 31 (1931): 115.

———. "Report on the Examination of Tutankhamen's Mummy." In Howard Carter, ed. *The Tomb of Tutankhamen*, New York: Cooper Square Publishers, 1963. The primary report on the autopsy of Tutankhamen that took place in the tomb. Still basically correct.

———. "Report on the Human Remains from the Granit Sarcophagus Chamber in the Pyramid of Zoser." *Annales du Service des Antiquités* 39 (1935): 411–416. Possibly Zoser's foot.

———. "Report on the Skeleton of King Amenenopet." *Annales du Service des Antiquités Egyptien* 41 (1942): 149–150. Little remained of the king's mummy.

Deiver, L. "A Human-masked and Doll-shaped Hawk-mummy." *Chronique d'Égypte* 58, no. 95 (1973): 60–65.

Diamond, Hugh Welch. "Description of an Egyptian Mummy and of the Hieroglyphics on its Case, Supposed to Be of the Time of Psammetici, Opened in 1843." *Archaeologia* 31 (1846): 408–411.

Doxiadis, Euphronsyne. *The Mysterious Fayoum Portraits.* New York: Abrams, 1995. Excellent photographs of mummy portraits.

Drenkhohn, Rosemarie and Renate Germer. *Mumie und Computer.* Hanover: Kestner-Museum, 1991. Catalog of an exhibition showing the use of computers in mummy studies.

Dunand, Françoise and Roger Lichtenberg. "Les Momies de la Nécropole de Douch." *Archeologia* 240 (1988): 30–42.

———. *Mummies. A Voyage Through Eternity.* New York: Abrams, 1994. Remarkable photographs of the mummies from a recent excavation at Duch in Egypt.

Dyson, S. "The Mummy of Middletown." *Archaeology* 32 (1979): 57–59. Popular article on the examination of a mummy at Wesleyan University in Middletown Connecticut.

Dzierzykray-Rogalski, Tadevsz. "Mummy of a Male of the Late Epoch Discovered at Deir el-Bahri in 1963/4." *Africana Bulletin* 13 (1970): 25–30.

Edwards, E.I.S. *A Handbook of the Egyptian Mummies and Coffins Exhibited in the British Museum.* London: British Museum, 1938. More on coffins than mummies, but still some important information.

Egyptian Antiquities Organization. *Mummification in Ancient Egypt and the Celebration of the Hundredth Anniversary of the Discovery of the Royal Mummies in the Valley of the Kings at Thebes.* Cairo: Egyptian Museum, 1973.

———. *The Royal Mummies.* Cairo: Ministry of Culture, 1994. Catalog prepared for the reopening of the "Mummies Room" of the Egyptian Museum.

Engelbach, Rex and D.E. Derry. "Mummification." *Annales du Service des Antiquités* 41 (1942): 233–269. An important historical survey.

Fiori, M.D. and M.G. Nunzi. "The Earliest Documented Applications of X-rays to Examination of Mummified Remains and Archaéological Material." *Journal of the Royal Society of Medicine* 88 (1995): 67–69.

Flemming, Stuart and David O'Conner. *The Egyptian Mummy Secrets and Science* (University of Pennsylvania Museum: Philadelphia) 1980. An exhibition catalog with a great amount of information.

Fouquet, D. "Note pour servir a l'Histoire de l'Embaumement en Égypte." *Bulletin de l'Institut Egyptien* 7 (1897): 89–97. Many inaccuracies in this article.

———. "Note sur les Cranes de Dachour." In *Fouilles à Dahchour*, J. De Morgan, ed. Vienna: Adolphe Holzhausen, 1895. Many incorrect observations.

———. "Notes sur les momies des pharons Ramses II et Ramses III." In *Momies Royales de Deir el-Bahri*, Gaston Maspero, Cairo: Mission Archéologique Française, 1889.

———. "Note sur la Momie d'un Anonyme." In *Momies Royales de Deir el-Bahri*, Gaston Maspero, ed. Cairo: Mission Archéologique Française, 1889.

———. "Note sur la Momie de Soqnounri." In *Momies Royales de Deir el Bahri*, Gaston Maspero, ed. Cairo: Mission Archéologique Française, 1889.

⸻. "Observations relevées sur quelques mommies royales d'Égypte." *Bulletin du Société Anthropologique* 3 (1886): 578–586.

Garstang, John. *The Burial Customs of Ancient Egypt.* London: Archibald Constable, 1907. Photos of mummies and discussions of excavations where they were found.

Germer, Renate. *Mumien.* Munich: Artemis, 1991. Good general survey of mummies.

Goyon, Jean-Claude. *Rituels funéraires de l'ancienne Égypte.* Paris: Cerf, 1972. Considerable material on mummification rituals.

Grayham, Daniel. "The Mummy at Glasgow Kelvingrove Art Galleries and Museum." *Radiology* 43 (1977): 218–222.

Gray, P.H.K. "An Account of a Mummy in the County Museum and Art Gallery, Truro." *Journal of Egyptian Archaeology* 56 (1970): 132–134.

⸻. "Embalmers' 'Restorations'." *Journal of Egyptian Archaeology,* 52 (1966): 138–140. Interesting descriptions of unusual examples of the embalmers' art.

⸻. "Notes Concerning the Position of Arms and Hands of Mummies with a View to Possible Dating of the Specimen." *Journal of Egyptian Archaeology* 58 (1972): 200–204.

⸻. "Radiological Aspects of the Mummies of Ancient Egyptians in the Rijksmuseum van Oudheden." *Oudherdkundije Mededelingen vit het Riksmuseum van Odheden te Leiden* 47 (1966): 1–30.

⸻. "Radiography of Ancient Egyptian Mummies." *Medical Radiology* 43 (1967): 34–44.

⸻. "The Radiography of Mummies of Ancient Egyptians." In *Population Biology of the Ancient Egyptians,* D.R. Brothwell and B.A. Chisrelli, eds. London: Academic Press, 1973.

⸻. "Recent Work on the Radiographic Study of Egyptian Mummies." In *Science and Archaeology,* D.R. Brothwell and E.S. Higgs, eds. London: Thames and Hudson, 1969.

⸻. "Two Mummies of Ancient Egyptians in the Hancock Museum, Newcastle." *Journal of Egyptian Archaeology* 53 (1967): 75–78.

⸻ and D. Slow. "Egyptian Mummies in the City of Liverpool Museum." *Liverpool Bulletin* 15 (1968): 1–74.

Grdseloff, Bernhard. "Nouvelle dennees concernment la tente de purification." *Annales du Service des Antiquités* 51 (1951): 129–140. Interesting material on the rituals of purification.

Greenhill, Thomas. *NEKPOKHΔEIA: or the Art of Embalming.* London: privately printed, 1705. A very important early work on the subject and the first book devoted solely to mummification.

Grew, Nehemiah. *Musaeum Regalis Societatis, or a Catalogue and Description of the Natural and Artificial Rareties Belonging to the Royal Society and preserved at Gresham College.* London: W. Rawlins, 1681. Only one mummy and the author suggests that the Egyptians boiled their dead to preserve them.

Grilletto, R. *La Splendida Vita delle Mummie.* Milan: SugarCo, 1987. Popular account with much information on the history of mummification and paleopathology.

Hadley, John. "An Account of a Mummy, Inspected at London 1763." *Philosophical Transactions of the Royal Society* 54 (1764): 1–14. This mummy had an onion wrapped next to its foot.

Haigh, T. and T.A. Flaherty. "Blood Grouping." In *The Mummy's Tale,* A. Rosalie David and Edmund Tapp, eds. New York: St. Martin's Press, 1993.

Hamilton-Paterson, James and Carol Andrews. *Mummies: Death and Life in Ancient Egypt.* London: British Museum, 1978. Good general survey, but a bit dated.

Hanzak, J. "Egyptian Mummies of Animals in Czechoslovak Collections." *Zeitschrift für Ä gyptische Sprache* 104 (1977): 86–88.

Harris, James E. "Secrets of the Pharaohs." *New Scientist* 59 (1973): 10–13.

——— and Kent Weeks. *X-Raying the Pharaohs.* New York: Charles Scribner's Sons, 1973. The first systematic X-ray study of the kings of Egypt.

Harrison, R.G. "An Anatomical Examination of the Pharonic Remains Purported to be Akhenaten." *Journal of Egyptian Archaeology* 52 (1966): 95–119.

——— et al. "Kinship of Smenkhkare and Tutankhamen Demonstrated Serologically." *Nature* 224 (1969): 325–326.

——— and A.B. Abdalla. "The Remains of Tutankhamen." *Antiquity* 46 (1972): 8–14.

Headley, John. "An Account of a Mummy inspected at London in 1763." *Philosophical Transactions of the Royal Society* 54 (1764): 1–14. This is the mummy examined by Nehemiah Grew, above.

Hertzog, Christian. *Mumio-Graphie.* Goth: Jean Reyher, 1718. An early discussion of mummification and the description of the unwrapping of a mummy that contained seventy-four amulets.

Herzberg, G. and R. Perrot. "Paléopathologie de 31 cranes égyptiens momifiés du Museum d'Histoire Naturelle de Lyon." *Paleobios* 1 (1983): 91–108. X rays of thirty-one mummified heads from Egypt.

Holt, Frank L. "Mystery Mummy: Unraveling the Remains of Ankh-hap the Egyptian." *Archaeology* 44, November/December (1991): 44–51.

Jarco, S. "Some Historical Problems Connected with the Study of Egyptian Mummies." *Bulletin de l'Institut d'Égypte* 58–9 (1981): 106–122.

Jomard, E. "Momies Humaines." In *Description de l'Égypte, Vol. III.* Paris: Pancoucke, 1821. Description of mummies found by Napoleon's scientists.

Jonckheere, F. *Autour de l'Autopsie d'une Momie.* Brussels: Foundation Égyptologique Reine Élisabeth, 1942.

Kleiss, E. "X-rays of the Heads of Egyptian Mummies." *Proceedings of 10th International Congress of Anatomy.* Tokyo: Science Council of Japan, 1975.

Lanzoni, Joseph. *Tractatus de Balsamatione Cadaverum.* Geneva, 1696. An early general description of mummification.

Lauer, J.-P. and D.E. Derry. "Decouverte a Saqqarah d'une partie de la momie du Roi Zozer." *Annales du Service des Antiquités* 35 (1935): 25–30.

——— and Z. Iskander "Donnees Nouvelles sur la Momification dans l'Égypte Ancienne." *Annales du Service des Antiquités* 53 (1955): 167–194. An important survey of the subject.

Leca, A.P. *Les Momies.* Paris: Hachette, 1976.

Ledrain, E. *La Momie.* Paris: Le Clerc, 1876. General treatment but discusses the ritual of embalming.

Leek, F. Filce. "An Ancient Mummified Fish." *Journal of Egyptian Archaeology* 62 (1976): 131–133.

———. *The Human Remains from the Tomb of Tutankhamen.* Oxford: Oxford University Press, 1972.

———. "The Problem of Brain Removal During Embalming of the Ancient Egyptians." *Journal of Egyptian Archaeology* 55 (1969): 112–116.

Lewin, Peter K. "Mummy Dearest!" *Explorers Journal*, September (1982): 110–111. Popular account of investigations of Egyptian mummies.

——— et al. "Three-Dimensional Reconstruction from Serial X-Ray Tomography of an Egyptian Mummified Head." *Clinical Anatomy* 3 (1990): 215–218.

Loret, Victor. "Les tombeaux de Toutmes III et d'Amenophis II, et la cachette royale de Biban-el-Molouk." *Bulletin de l'Institut Égyptien* 9 (1898): 91–112. The account of Loret's discovery of the royal mummies in the tomb of Amenhotep II, with photos.

Lortet, L.C. and C. Gaillard. "Sur les Oiseaux Momifiés." *Annales du Service des Antiquités* 3 (1903): 18–21.

———. *La Faune Momifiée de l'Ancienne Égypte. Vol. 9.* Lyon: Archives du Museum d'Histoire Naturelle, 1907. Important work on animal mummification.

———. *La Faune Momifiée de l'Ancienne Égypte. Recherches Antropologiques III–V Vol. 10.* Lyon: Archives du Musée d'Histoire Naturelle, 1909. Important work on animal mummification.

Lortet, L.C. and M. Hugounenq. "Sur les Poissons Momifiés." *Annales du Service des Antiquités* 3 (1902): 15–18.

Lucas, A. "The Occurrence of Natron in Ancient Egypt." *Journal of Egyptian Archaeology* 18 (1932): 62–66.

———. "A Preliminary Note on Preservative Materials Used by the Ancient Egyptians in Embalming." *Cairo Scientific Journal* 2 (1908): 133–146.

Macalister, A. "Notes on Egyptian Mummies." *Journal of the Anthropological Institute* 23 (1893): 101–121. Examination of mummies at Cambridge.

Maekawa, S. and N. Valentin. "Development of a Prototype Storage and Display Case for the Royal Mummies of the Egyptian Museum in Cairo." In *Human Mummies*, Konrad Spindler, et al., eds. New York: Springer, 1996.

Mariette, August. *Le Serapeum de Memphis.* Paris: Gide, 1882. Discovery of the mummies of the Apis bulls.

Maspero, Gaston. "Mémoire sur quelque Papyrus du Louvre." *Notice et Extracts des Manuscripts* 24 (1875): 14–104. Translation of a papyrus dealing with the ritual of embalming.

———. *Les momies royales de Deir el-Bahari.* Cairo: Mission Archéologique française, 1889. Official report on the finding of the royal mummy cache.

———. "Proces-verbal du Corps du Pharon Amenothes II." *Annales du Service des Antiquités* 3 (1902): 120–121.

———. "La pyramide du Roi Mirinri 1er." *Receuil de Traveaux Relatifs à la Philologie. . . .* 9 (1908): 177–191. Possibly the only complete mummy of an Old Kingdom pharaoh.

———. *La Trouvaille de Deir el-Bahari.* Cairo: Imprimerie française, 1881. The first account of the Deir el-Bahri royal mummy cache.

———. "The Unwrapping of Seti I." *American Journal of Archaeology* 2 (1886): 331–333.

Migliarini, E. "Account of the Unrolling of a Mummy belonging to the Grand Duke of Tuscany." *Archaeologia* 36 (1855): 161–174. Detailed description of magical bandages and amulets.

Moller, Georg. *Die Beiden Totenpapyrus Rhind.* Leipzig: 1913. Translation of a papyrus that deals with mummification rituals, especially bandaging.

Montague, Montague. "Restoration of an Egyptian Mummified Foot." *American Journal of Physical Anthropology* 20, no. 1 (1935): 95–103.

Morrison-Scott, T.C. "The Mummified Cats of Ancient Egypt." *Proceedings of the Zoological Society, London* 121 (1952): 861–867.

Neave, R. "Facial Reconstruction of Skeletal Remains: Three Egyptian Examples." *MASCA Journal* Mummification Supplement (1980): 175–177.

Osburn, William. *An Account of an Egyptian Mummy presented to the Museum of the Leeds Philosophical and Literary Society by the Late John Blayds Esq.* Leeds: Robinson & Hernaman, 1828. The first scientific team approach to examining a mummy.

Pace, Mildred Mastin. *Wrapped for Eternity.* New York: McGraw-Hill, 1974.

Parcelly, Dr. *Étude Historique et Critique des Embaumements avec la Description d'une Nouvelle Méthode.* Paris: 1891.

Partridge, Robert B. *Faces of Pharaohs.* London: Rubicon Press, 1995. Photographs and brief comments on royal mummies and their coffins.

Passalacqua, Joseph. *Catalogue raisonné et historique des Antiquités découverts en Égypte.* Paris: Galerie d'Antiquités Égyptiennes, 1826. Description of mummies in Passalacqua's collection, including an anencephalic monster.

Pellegrin, J. "Radiographie appliquee à la détermination de momie de poissons." *Bulletin Musée Historic Natural Paris* 6 (1990): 175–176. Early use of X rays for the study of fish mummies.

Penicker, Louis. *Traite des Embaumements selon les Anciens et les Modernes.* Paris: Berthelmy, 1699. An early general account of mummification.

Pettigrew, Thomas. "Account of the Examination of the Mummy of Pet-Maut-Ioh-Mer brought from Egypt by the late John Gosset, Esq." *Archaeologia* 27 (1837): 263–273. The brain of this mummy had been removed in an unusual manner.

———. *A History of Egyptian Mummies.* North Hollywood: North American Archives, reprint of 1834 edition. The first scientific book devoted to mummification.

———. "Observations on the practice of Embalming amongst the Ancient Egyptians illustrated by the unrolling of a Mummy from Thebes presented to the Association by Thomas Aeden, Esq." *Journal of the British Archaeological Association* 4 (1849): 337–348.

———. "On the Dieties of Amente as found on Egyptian Mummies." *Archaeologia* 34 (1852): 392–393.

Pickering, R.B. "Three-Dimensional Computed Tomography of the Mummy Wenuhotep." *American Journal of Physical Anthropology* 83 (1990): 49–55.

Raven, Maarten. *Mummies Ouder Het Mes.* Amsterdam: Bataafsche Lieuw, 1993. Catalog of a 1993 exhibition on mummies; in Dutch but many unique photos.

Reymond, E.A.E. *Catalogue of Demotic Papyri in the Ashmolean Museum, Volume I. Embalmers' Archives from Hawara.* Oxford: Oxford University Press, 1973. Records of a guild of embalmers.

Rhind, A. Henry. *Thebes its Tombs and Their Tenants.* London: Longmans, 1862. Discoveries of mummies and embalmers' caches.

Romano, James F. *Death, Burial and Afterlife in Ancient Egypt.* Pittsburgh: Carnegie Museum of Natural History, 1990.

Rouelle, Guillaume François. "Sur les embaumements des Égyptiens." *Histoire de l'Academie Royale des Sciences* (1750): 123–150. Mentions a mummy with the brain removed through the orbit.

Rouyer, P.C. "Notice sur les embaumements des anciens égyptiens." In *Description de l'Égypte*, Vol. VI. Paris: Pancoucke, 1821. Rouyer, a pharmacist on the Napoleonic expedition to Egypt, suggests that mummies were dried over a fire.

Ruffer, Marc Armand. "Notes on Two Mummies dating from the Persian Occupation of Egypt." *Bulletin de la Société Archaeologique d'Alexandrie* 14 (1912): 1–18.

Russell, William et al. "Radiographic Techniques in the Study of the Mummy." In *An X-Ray Atlas of the Royal Mummies*, James E. Harris and Edward F. Wente, eds. Chicago: University of Chicago Press, 1980.

Saint-Hilaire, Étienne Geoffroy. "Une Monstre Anecephale." *Memoires de l'Academie Royale des Sciences* 9 (1826): 153. Description of an unusual mummy, born with only a brain stem.

Sandison, A.T. "The Use of Natron in Mummification in Ancient Egypt." *Journal of Near Eastern Studies* 22 (1963): 259–267.

Seipel, W. "Research on Mummies in Egyptology. An Overview." In *Human Mummies*, Konrad Spindler et al., eds. New York: Springer, 1966.

Silor, J. "Radiocarbon Dating of Some Mummy and Coffin Samples." *Zeitschrift fur Agyptische Sprache* 106 (1979): 82–87.

Sluglett, J. "Mummification in Ancient Egypt" in *MASCA Journal: Mummification Supplement* (1980): 163–167. Unusual survey article discussing the price of mummification and the history of mummy unwrappings.

Smith, G. Elliot. "An Account of a Mummy of a Priestess of Amen supposed to be Ta-Usert-em Suten-Pa, with which is incorporated a detailed account of the wrappings by A.C. Mace and some Archaeological Notes by G. Daressy." *Annales du Service des Antiquités* 3 (1906): 153–182.

———. "The Antiquity of Mummification." *Cairo Scientific Journal* 2 (1908): 204–205. Discussion of the arm of King Zer, perhaps the oldest royal mummification.

———. "The Earliest Evidence of Attempts at Mummification in Egypt." In *Report of the British Association*. Dundee, 1912.

———. "Egyptian Mummies." *Journal of Egyptian Archaeology* 1 (1914): 189–196.

———. "Heart and Reins." *Journal of Manchester Oriental Society* 1 (1911): 189–196. Discussion of what was done with internal organs.

———. "History of Mummification in Egypt." In *Proceedings of the Royal Philosophical Society of Glasgow*. Glasgow: Royal Philosophical Society of Glasgow, 1908.

———. *The Migration of Early culture; A Study of the significance of the Geographical Distribution of the Practice of Mummification as Evidence of the Migrations of Peoples. . . .* London: Manchester University Press, 1915. Presents the rather eccentric theory that other cultures learned mummification from the Egyptians.

———. "The Mummies of Yuaa and Thuiu." In *The Tomb of Yuaa and Thuiu*, J.E. Quibell, ed. Cairo: Institut français, 1908.

———. "A Note on the Mummies in the Tomb of Amenhotep II at Biban al-Molok." *Bulletin de l'Institut Égyptien* 5th series, 1 (1908): 221–228. Discusses the second cache of royal mummies discovered.

———. "On the Natural Preservation of the Brain in the Ancient Egyptians." *Journal of Anatomy and Physiology* 36 (1902): 375–380.

———. "On the Significance of the Geographical Distribution of the Practice of Mummification. A Study in the Migration of Peoples and the Spread of certain Customs and Beliefs." In *Memoirs of the Manchester Literary and Philosophical Society*, 49, no. 10, 1915. Smith's belief that other cultures learned mummification from the Egyptians.

———. "The Physical Characters of the Mummy of Toutmosis IV." *Annales du Service des Antiquités* 4 (1904): 112–115.

———. "Report on Four Mummies [of the XXI Dyn.]." *Annales du Service des Antiquités* 5 (1904): 13–17. Unwrapping of mummies from the second Deir el-Bahri cache.

———. "Report on the Mummy of Senebtisi." In *The Tomb of Senebtisi*, A.E. Mace and H. Winlock, eds. New York: Metropolitan Museum of Art, 1916.

———. "Report on Two Mummies of the Middle Kingdom." In Quibell, J.E., *Excavations at Saqqara*. Cairo: Institut français, 1908.

———. "Report on the Unrolling of the Mummies of the Kings Siptah, Seti II, Ramses IV, Ramses V and Ramses VI." *Bulletin de l'Institut Égyptien* 5th series 1 (1907): 45–67.

———. "Report on the Unwrapping of the Mummy of Meneptah." *Annales du Service des Antiquités* 8 (1907): 108–112.

———. *The Royal Mummies*. Cairo: Institut français, 1912. The most important description of the royal mummies and their unwrapping.

Strouhal, Eigen, and L. Vyhnanek. "Survey of Egyptian Mummies in Czechoslovak Collections." *Zeitschrift für Agyptische Sprache* 103 (1976): 114–118.

Sudhoff, Karl. "Agyptische Mumienmacher-Instrumente." *Archiv für Geschichte der Medizin* 5 (1912): 161–171. A rare discussion of the tools used by Egyptian embalmers.

Spiegleberg, Wilhelm. "Ein Beslattungsuertag aus de Zeit des Ptolemaios Philadelphos." *Zeitschrift für Agyptische Sprache* 54 (1918): 111–114. Translation of a papyrus dealing with embalming.

Strouhal, E. "Princess Khekeretnebty and Tisethor: Anthropological Analysis." *Anthropologie* 22 (1984): 171–183.

Thompson, David L. *The Artists of the Mummy Portraits.* Malibu: J. Paul Getty Museum, 1976. Study of the Fayoum portraits.

Thomson, James. *The Mummy Cloth of Egypt.* London: R. Taylor, 1834. First scientific analysis of linen from mummies.

Warren, John C. "Description of an Egyptian Mummy presented to the Massachusetts General Hospital, with an account of the Operation of Embalming in Ancient and Modern Times." *Boston Journal of Philosophy and Arts* 2 (1823): 164–178. First mummy in the United States.

Weigall, A.E. "The Mummy of Akhenaten." *Journal of Egyptian Archaeology* 8 (1922): 193–199. There is a good possibility that the mummy described is not that of Akhenaten.

Winlock, H.E. "A Discovery of Egyptian Jewelry by X-Ray." *Bulletin of the Metropolitan Museum of Art* 31 (1936): 274–278.

———. "A Late Dynastic Embalmer's Table." *Annals du Service des Antiquités* 30 (1930): 102–106.

———. *Materials Used at the Embalming of King Tut-Ankh-Amun.* New York: Metropolitan Museum of Art, 1941.

Yahey, T. and D. Brown. "Comely Wenuhotep: Computed Tomography in Egyptian Mummy." *Journal of Computer Assisted Tomography* 8 (1984): 992–997.

Paleopathology

Abbate, O.P. "Contribution a l'histologie des momies." *Bulletin de l'Institut d'Égypte* 5th series, no. 4 (1910): 65–68. An early study on soft tissue of mummies.

Aldred, C. and A.T. Sandison. "The Pharaoh Akhenaten: A Problem in Egyptology and Pathology." *Bulletin of the History of Medicine,* 36 (1962): 293–316.

Balout, Lionel and C. Rouhet. *La momie de Ramses II.* Paris: CNRS, 1978. The definitive work on the treatment of the mummy of Ramses the Great.

Barraco, R.A. "Preservation of Proteins in Mummified Tissues." *American Journal of Physical Anthropology* 48 (1978): 487–492. Proteins degraded considerably in Egyptian mummies, but less in those treated with natron.

———, T.A. Reyman, and T.A. Cockburn. "Paleobiochemical Analysis of an Egyptian Mummy." *Journal of Human Evolution* 6 (1977): 533–546. Lipids were found to be better preserved than proteins in the Egyptian mummy known as PUM-II. The best preserved tissues were those impregnated with natron.

Benassi, E. and G. Rayni. "The Amount of Information Which can be Derived from the Radiographic Study of Mummies. . . ." In *Population Biology of the Ancient Egyptians,* D.R. and B.A. Chiarelli, eds. London: Academic Press, 1973.

Benitez, J.T. and G.E. Lynn. "Temporal Bone Preservation in a 2600-Year-Old Egyptian Mummy." *Science* 183 (1974): 200–202.

Berg, K. et al. "Blood Groupings of Old Egyptian Mummies." *Homo* 26 (1975): 148–153.

Bertoletti, M. "Une Vertèbre Lombaire Surnumeraire Complète chez un Momie Égyptienne de la XIe Dynastie." *Travaille Radiographique,* 26 (1913): 63–65. Early use of X rays that detected an extra vertebra in a mummy.

Bloomfield, J.A. "Radiology of an Egyptian Mummy." *Australasian Radiology* 29 (1985): 64–66.

Borgognini-Tarli, S.M. and G. Paoli. "Biochemical and Immunological Investigations on early Egyptian Remains." *In Population Biology of the Ancient Egyptians,* D.R. Brothwell and B.A. Chiarelli, eds. London: Academic Press, 1973.

Bourke, J.B. "The Pathology of the Vertebral Column in Ancient Egypt and Nubia." *Medical History* 15 (1971): 363–375.

———. "Trauma and Degenerative Disease in Ancient Egypt and Nubia." *Journal of Human Evolution* 1 (1972): 225–232.

Boyd, W.C. and L.G. Boyd. "An Attempt to Determine the Blood Groups of Mummies." *Proceedings of the Society for Experimental Medicine* 31 (1934): 671.

———. "Blood Grouping Tests on 300 Mummies." *Journal of Immunology* 32 (1937): 307–319.

Braustein, E.M. et al. "Paleoradiologic Evolution of the Egyptian Royal Mummies." *Skeletal Radiology* 17 (1988): 348–352.

Brothwell, D.R. and A.T. Sandison, eds. *Disease in Antiquity.* Springfield: Charles C. Thomas, 1967.

Bucaille, Maurice et al. "Intérét actuel de l'étude radiologique des momies pharoniques." *Annales de Radiologie* 19, no. 5 (1976): 475–480.

Chiarelli, B. et al. "Note preliminare sulla ultrastruttura dei Capelli de Mummia Egiaiana al Microscopio Elettrano a Sansione." *Revista di Antropologia* 57 (1970–71): 275–278. Early use of the electronmicroscope for mummy studies.

——— and E. Robino Massa. "Conservazione dei Globuli in Tessuti di Mummie Egiziane." *Archivo per l'Antrop. e l'Ethnologia* 98 (1967): 181–182.

Christensen, O. "Un examen radiologique des momies Égyptiènnes des musées danois." *La Semaine des Hôpitaux* 45 (1969): 1990–1998.

Cockburn, Aidan. "Ancient Parasites on the West Bank of the Nile." *Lancet* 8249 (1981): 938.

——— et al. "Autopsy of an Egyptian Mummy." *Science* 187 (1975): 1155–1160. The study of this mummy led to the founding of the Paleopathology Association.

Conolly, R.C., R.G. Harrison, and Ahmad Soheir. "Serological Evidence of the Parentage of Tutankhamen and Smenkhkare." *Journal of Egyptian Archaeology* 62 (1976): 184–186.

Conti, Furman A. and E. Rabino Massa. "Preliminary Note on the Ultrastructure of the Hair from an Egyptian Mummy using the Scanning Electron Microscope." In *Population Biology of the Ancient Egyptians*, D.R. Brothwell and B.A. Chiarelli, eds. London: Academic Press, 1973.

Coughlin, E.A. "Analysis of PUM-II Mummy Fluid." *Paleopathology Newsletter* 17 (1977): 7–8.

David, A.R. *Science in Egyptology.* Manchester: Manchester University Press, 1986.

de Boni, U. "Autopsy of an Egyptian Mummy (Nakht-ROM-I)." *Canadian Medical Association Journal* 117 (1977): 461–476.

Deelder, A.M. et al. "Determination of Schistosome Antigen in Mummies." *Lancet* 335 (1990): 724–725.

Delorenzi, E. and M. Mancini. "Radiological Observations on the Mummies of the Egyptian Museum of Turin." In *Population Biology of the Ancient Egyptians*, D.R. Brothwell and B.A. Chiarelli, eds. London: Academic Press, 1973.

Derry, D.E. "An X-ray Examination of the Mummy of King Amenophis I." *Annales du Service des Antiquités* 34 (1934): 47–48.

Dzierzykray-Rogalski, T. "Paleopathology of the Ptolemaic Inhabitants of the Dakhleh Oasis." *Journal of Human Evolution* 9 (1980): 71–74. Several skulls indicated leprosy, leading the author to suggest that Dakhleh contained a leper colony.

Finnegan, M. and G.C. Steyskal. "Trace Element Analysis of Tissue and Resin from the Egyptian Mummy PUM-II." *Paleopathology Newsletter* 14 (1976): 1–9.

Fodor, J. et al. "The Radiographic Investigation of two Egyptian Mummies." *Radiology Technology* 54 (1987): 443–448.

Gardner, W.A. and C.N. Griffin. "A Paleopathologic Exercise—The Charleston Museum Mummy." *Journal of the South Carolina Medical Association* 67 (1971): 269–270.

Giacometti, L. and B. Chiarelli. "The Skin of Egyptian Mummies." *Archives of Dermatology* 97 (1968): 712–716.

Graf, W. "Preserved Histological Structures in Egyptian Mummy Tissues and Ancient Swedish Skeletons." *Acta Anatomy* 8 (1949): 236–250.

Gray, P.H.K. "Bone Infraction in Antiquity." *Clinical Radiology* 19 (1968): 436–437.

———. "Calcinosis Intervertebralis with Special Reference to Similar Changes found in Mummies of Ancient Egyptians." In *Diseases in Antiquity*, D.R. Brothwell and A.T. Sandison. Springfield: Charles C. Thomas, 1967.

———. "A Case of Osteogenesis Imperfecta Associated with Dentinogneisis Imperfecta, Dating from Antiquity." *Clinical Radiology* 21 (1970): 106–108.

Harris, James E. "The Teeth of the Pharaohs." *Dental Dimensions* 1 (1977): 2–6.

——— et al. "Dental disease in the Royal Mummies." In *An X-Ray Atlas of the Royal Mummies*, James E. Harris and Edward F. Wente, eds. Chicago: University of Chicago Press, 1980.

——— and Edward F. Wente, eds. *An X-Ray Atlas of the Royal Mummies.* Chicago: University of Chicago Press, 1980. An important anthology on various topics.

Hart, G.B. et al. "Blood Group Testing of Ancient Material with Particular Reference to the Mummy of Nakht." *Transfusion* 18 (1978): 474–478.

Harwood-Nash, D.C.F. "Computed Tomography of Ancient Egyptian Mummies." *Journal of Computer Assisted Tomography* 3 (1979): 768–773.

Hunt, D.R. and L.M. Hopper. "Non-Invasive Investigations of Human Mummified Remains by Radiographic Techniques." In *Human Mummies*, Konrad Spindler et al., eds. New York: Springer, 1996.

Isherwood, Ian and C.W. Hart. "The Radiological Investigation." In *The Mummy's Tale*, A. Rosalie David and Edmund Tapp, eds. New York: St. Martin's Press, 1993. X rays and CAT scans of the mummy of Natsef-Amun.

Jonckheere, Frans. *Autour de l'Autopsie d'une Momie.* Brussels: Foundation Égyptologique Reine Élisabeth, 1942. Detailed study of the mummy of the royal scribe, Boutehamon.

Krogman, Wilton Marion and Melvyn J. Baer. "Age at Death of Pharaohs of the New Kingdom, Determined from X-Ray Films." In *An X-Ray Atlas of the Royal Mummies*, James E. Harris and Edward F. Wente, eds. Chicago: University of Chicago Press, 1980.

Kukis, A. et al. "Bile Acids of a 3200-Year-Old Egyptian Mummy." *Canadian Journal of Biochemistry* 56 (1979): 1141–1148. Study of the mummy of Nakht showed that bile acids were essentially the same as in modern humans.

Lee, S.L. and F.F. Stenn. "Characterization of Mummy bone Ochronotic Pigment." *Journal of the American Medical Association* 240 (1978): 135–138. A possible case in an Egyptian mummy of the disease alkaptonuria, which causes a gray pigment to accumulate (ochronosis) in the connective tissue.

Leek, F. Filce. "Observations on the Dental Pathology seen in Ancient Egyptian Skulls."

Journal of Egyptian Archaeology 52 (1966): 59–64.

———. "Reisner's Collection of Human Remains from the Mastaba Tombs of Giza." *Zeitschrift für Ägyptische Sprach* 111 (1984): 11–68. Most observations are on dentition.

Leigh, R.W. "Notes on the Somatology and Pathology of Ancient Egypt." *University of California Publications on American Archaeological Ethnology* 34 (1934): 1–35.

Lewin, P.K. "Current Technology in the Examination of Ancient Man." In *Human Mummies*, Konrad Spindler et al., eds. New York: Springer, 1996.

———. "Mummified Frozen Smallpox: Is it a Threat?" *Jour. Am. Med. Assn.* 253 (1985): 3095.

———. "Mummy Riddles Unraveled." *Bull. Microscopical Soc. Can.* 12 (1984): 4–8.

———. "Paleo-electron Microscopy of Mummified Tissue." *Nature* 213 (1967): 416–417.

——— et al. "Three Dimensional Reconstruction from Serial X-ray Tomography of an Ancient Egyptian Mummified Head." *Clinical Anatomy* 3 (1990): 215–218.

———. "The Ultrastructure of Mummified Skin Cells." *Canadian Medical Association Journal* 98 (1968): 1011–1012.

——— and Harwood-Nash, D.C. "X-ray Computed Axial Tomography of an Ancient Egyptian Brain." *Med. Sci.* 5 (1977): 78.

——— and E. Cuty. "Electron Microscopy of Ancient Egyptian Skin." *British Journal of Dermatology* 94 (1976): 573–576.

Llagostera, Cuenca E. *Estudia Radiologico de las Monias Egipicas del Museo Arqueologico Nacional de Madrid.* Monografias Arqueologicos No. 5. Madrid: Museo Arqueologico Nacional, 1978.

Manialawi, M. et al. "Endoscopic Examination of Egyptian Mummies." *Endoscopy* 10 (1978): 191–194. Describes the use of an endoscope to examine the mummies of Ramses II, Merneptah, and Ramses V.

Marro, G. "Contributo alla Patologia del Sisteme Osseo negli Egiziani Antichi." *Memorie della Reale Accademia della Scienze di Torino* 70 (1946): 119–140.

Marx, M.D. and S.H. D'Auria. "CT Examination of Eleven Egyptian Mummies." *Radio Graphics* 6 (1986): 321–330.

———. "Three-Dimensional Reconstruction of an Ancient Human Egyptian Mummy." *American Journal of Radiology* 150 (1988): 147–149.

Masso E. Rabino. "Arterio-sclerotic Change in the Carotid Artery of a Mummy of New Kingdom Date." *Paleopathology Newsletter* 17 (1977): 12–13.

Michelin-Lausarot, P. et al. "Preservation and Amino Acid Composition of Egyptian Mummy Structure Proteins." In *Population Biology of the Ancient Egyptians*, D.R. Brothwell and B.A. Chiarelli, eds. London: Academic Press, 1973.

Miller, Judith and Catherine Asher-McDade. "The Dental Examination of Natsef-Amun." In *The Mummy's Tale*, A. Rosalie David and Edmund Tapp, eds. New York: St. Martin's Press, 1993.

Millet, N.B. et al. "Lessons Learned from the Autopsy of an Egyptian Mummy." *Canadian Medical Association Journal* 117, no. 5 (1977): 461–476.

Moodie, Raymond L. *Paleopathology. An Introduction to the Study of Ancient Evidences of Disease.* Urbana: University of Illinois Press, 1923.

———. *Roentgenologic Studies of Egyptian and Peruvian Mummies.* Chicago: Field Museum of Natural History, 1931. The first systematic X-ray study of a collection of mummies.

Morse, D. et al. "Tuberculosis in Ancient Egypt." *American Review of Respiratory Diseases* 90 (1964): 524–541, 1964.

Mouchacca, J. "Eléments biodetercogenes de la momie de Ramses II." *Bulletin Société Mycologie Medicale* 3 (1978): 5–10. More than eighty aspects of fungi were identified on the mummy of Ramses the Great.

Neave, R.A.H. "The Facial Reconstruction of Natsef-Amun." In *The Mummy's Tale*, A. Rosalie David and Edmund Tapp, eds. New York: St. Martin's Press, 1993.

Nemeckova, A. "Histology of Egyptian Mummified Tissues from Czechoslovak Collections." *Zeitschrift für Ägyptische Sprache* 104 (1977): 142–144.

Nerlich, A.C. et al. "Osteopathological Findings in Mummified Baboons from Ancient Egypt." *International Journal of Osteoarchaeology* 3 (1992): 189–198, 1992. Diseases found in mummified baboons.

Pahl, W.M. "Computed tomography—a New Radiological Technique Applied to Medico-Archaeological Investigation in Egyptian Mummies." *OSSA* 7 (1980): 189–198. An early paper on what has now become standard procedure.

Parnigotto, P.P. et al. "Trace Element Analysis of Egyptian Mummy Hair by X-ray Fluorescence Spectrometry." *Journal of Human Evolution* 2 (1982): 591–596.

Peck, William H. et al. "Preliminary Reports on the Autopsy of Pum IV." *Paleopathology Newsletter* 16 (1976): 3–6.

Pickering, Robert B. et al. "Three-Dimensional Computed Tomography of the Mummy Wenuhotep." *American Journal of Physical Anthropology* 83 (1990): 49–55.

Post, P.W. "Ancient and Mummified Skin." *Cutis* 2 (1973): 779–781.

Prepenbrink, H. et al. "Nuclear Magnetic Resonance Imaging of Mummified Corpses." *American Journal of Physical Anthropology* 70 (1986): 27–28.

Robbins, Gay. "The Stature and Physical Proportions of the brothers Nakhtankh and Khnumnakht (Manchester Museum nos. 21470–1)." *Zeitschrift für Ägyptische Sprach* 112 (1985): 44–48.

Riddle, J.M. et al. "Peripheral Blood Elements Found in an Egyptian Mummy: A Three Dimensional View." *Science* 192 (1976): 374–5.

Rogers, L. "Meningiomas in Pharaoh's People." *British Journal of Surgery* 36 (1968): 423–424.

Rowling, J.T. and R.J. Thomson. "Pathological Changes in Mummies." *Proceedings of the Royal Society of Medicine* 54 (1961): 409–415.

Ruffer, Marc Armand. "Arterial Lesion in Egyptian Mummies." *Journal of Pathology and Bacteriology* 15 (1911): 453–462.

———. "Histological Studies on Egyptian Mummies." *Memoires Presentes à l'Institut Égyptien* 6, fascicle (1911): 3.

———. "Note on the Presence of Bilharzia Haematobia in Egyptian Mummies of the XXth Dynasty." *British Medical Journal* (1960): 16.

———. "Osseous Lesions in Egyptian Mummies." *Journal of Pathology and Bacteriology* 16 (1912): 439–465.

———. "Pathological Lesions found in Coptic Bodies." *Journal of Pathology and Bacteriology* 18 (1913): 149–162.

———. "Pathological Notes on the Royal Mummies of the Cairo Museum." *Mitteilungen zur Geschichte der Medizin und der Naturwissenschaften* 13 (1914) 239–268.

———. "Remarks on the Histology and Pathological Anatomy of Egyptian Mummies." *Cairo Scientific Journal* 4 (1910): 11–17.

———. *Studies in the Paleopathology of Egypt*. Chicago: University of Chicago Press, 1921. A very important collection of all of Ruffer's articles on the subject.

——— and A.R. Ferguson. "An Eruption Resembling Variola in an Egyptian Mummy of the XXth Dynasty." *Journal of Pathology and Bacteriology* 15 (1911): 1–3.

Salib, P. "Orthopaedic and Traumatic Skeletal Lesions in Ancient Egyptians." *Journal of Bone and Joint Surgery* 44–B (1962): 944–947.

———. "Trauma and Disease of the Post-Cranial Skeleton in Ancient Egypt." In *Diseases in Antiquity*, D.R. Brothwell and A.T. Sandison, eds. Springfield: Charles C. Thomas, 1967.

Sandison, A.T. "Degenerative Vascular Disease in the Egyptian Mummy." *Medical History* 6 (1962): 77.

———. "The Histological Examination of Mummified Tissue." *Stain Technology*, 30 (1955): 277–283.

———. "The Study of Mummified and Dried Human Tissue." In *Science in Archaeology*, D.R. Brothwell and E. Higgs, eds. London: Thames and Hudson, 1963.

Satinoff, M.I. and Calvin Wells. "Multiple Basal Cell Naevus Syndrome in Ancient Egypt." *Medical History* 13 (1969): 294–297.

Shattock, S.G. "Microscopic Sections of the Aorta of King Merneptah." *Lancet* 1 (1909): 318.

———. "A Report Upon the Pathological Condition of the Aorta of King Merneptah." *Proceedings of the Royal Society of Medicine* (Pathological Section) 2 (1909): 122.

Shaw, A.F.B. "Histological Study of the Mummy of Har-Mose, the singer of the Eighteenth Dynasty (circa 1490 B.C.)." *Journal of Pathology and Bacteriology* 47 (1938): 115.

Simandl, E. "A Contribution to the History of the Skin and of the Muscle of an Egyptian Mummy." *Anthropologie* 6 (1928): 56–60.

Simon, G. and P.A. Zorab. "The Radiographic Changes in Alkaptonuric Arthritis." *British Journal of Radiology* 34 (1961): 384–386.

Smith, G.E. "The Causation of the Symmetrical Thinning of the Parietal Bones in Ancient Egyptians." *Journal of Anatomical Physiology* (London) 41 (1906–7): 232.

Steinbock, R.T. "Studies in Ancient Calcified Soft Tissues and Organic Concretions III: Gallstones (Cholelichiosis)." *Journal of Pathology* 3 (1990): 95–106. Mummy gallstones.

Strouhal, Eigen. "Ancient Egyptian Carcinoma." *Bulletin of the New York Academy of Medicine* 54 (1978): 290–302. Possible evidence for cancer in an ancient Egyptian skull.

———. "Multidisciplinary Research on Egyptian Mummies in Czechoslovakia." *Zeitschrift für Agyptische Sprache* 103 (1976): 113.

——— and L. Vyhnanek. "Radiographic Examination of the Mummy of Qenamun the Sealbearer." *Zeitschrift für Agyptische Sprache* 100 (1974): 125–129.

Swinton, W.E. "Sir Marc Armand Ruffer: One of the First Paleopathologists." *Canadian Medical Association Journal* 124 (1981): 1388–1392.

Tapp, Edmund. "The Histological Examination of Mummified Tissue." In *The Mummy's Tale*, A. Rosalie David and Edmund Tapp, eds. New York: St. Martin's Press, 1993.

——— and K. Wildsmith. "The Autopsy and Endoscopy of the Leeds Mummy." In *The Mummy's Tale*, A. Rosalie David and Edmund Tapp, eds. New York: St. Martin's Press, 1993.

Titlbachova, S. and Z. Titlbach. "Hair of Egyptian Mummies." *Zeitschrift für Agyptische Sprache* 104 (1977): 79–85.

Vyhnanek, L. and Eigen Strouhal. "Arteriosclerosis in Egyptian Mummies." *Anthropologie* 13 (1975): 219–221.

———. "Radiography of Egyptian Mummies." *Zeitschrift für Agyptische Sprache* 103 (1976): 118–128.

Waldron, T. "A Note on a Mummy from Theban Tombs 253, 254, and 294." *Journal of Pathology* 3 (1991): 89–94. A mummy that was killed by a blow to the head.

Walker, R. et al. "Tissue Identification and Histologic Study of Six Lung Specimens from Egyptian Mummies." *American Journal of Physical Anthropology* 72 (1987): 43–48. Six lungs from bundles in the abdomens of mummies or from canopic jars were studied.

Wells, Calvin. "Ancient Egyptian Pathology." *Journal of Laryngology. Otology* 77 (1963): 262–265.

———. "The Radiological Examination of Human Remains." In *Science in Archaeology*, D.R. Brothwell and E. Higgs, eds. London: Thames and Hudson, 1963.

——— and B.M. Maxwell. "Alkaptonuria in an Egyptian Mummy." *British Journal of Radiology* 35 (1962): 679–682.

Whitehouse, Walter M. "Radiologic Findings in the Royal Mummies." In *An X-Ray Atlas of the Royal Mummies*, James E. Harris and Edward F. Wente, eds. Chicago: University of Chicago Press, 1980.

Zimmerman, Michael R. "An Experimental Study of Mummification Pertinent to the Antiquity of Cancer." *Cancer* 40 (1977): 1538–1562.

———. "Histological Examination of Experimentally Mummified Tissues." *American Journal of Physical Anthropology* 37 (1972): 271–280.

———. "The Mummified Heart: A Problem in Medicological Diagnosis." *Journal of Forensic Science* 23 (1978): 750–753. Modern hearts were mummified to see what abnormalities and diseases could be identified.

———. "The Mummies of the Tomb of Nebuenef: Paleopathology and Archaeology." *Journal of the American Research Center in Egypt* 14 (1977): 33–36.

———. "A Possible Histiocytoma in an Egyptian Mummy." *Archives of Dermatology* 117 (1981): 364–365.

———. "Pulmonary and Osseous Tuberculosis in an Egyptian Mummy." *Bulletin of the New York Academy of Medicine* 55 (1979): 604–608.

——— and W.H. Clark. "A Possible Case of Subcorneal Pustular Dermatosis in an Egyptian Mummy." *Archives of Dermatology* 112 (1976): 204–205.

Zugibe, F.T. and J.T. Costello. "A New Method for Softening Mummified Fingers." *Journal of Forensic Science* 31 (1986): 726–731.

The Mummification Process

Baumann, Bill B. "The Botanical Aspects of Ancient Egyptian Embalming and Burial." *Economic Botany* 14 (1960): 84–104.

Black, J.J. "A Stitch in Time." *Nursing Times* 78 (1982): 619–623. Ancient sutures.

Blumenthal, Johann. "Observations on some Egyptian Mummies Opened in London." *Philosophical Transactions of the Royal Society* 84 (1794): 177–195. An early realization that some mummies were fakes.

Bourriou, J. and J. Bashford. "Radiological Examination of Two Mummies of the Roman Era." *MASCA Journal: Mummification Supplement* (1980): 168–171. X rays showed deformation of body caused by embalmers.

Brier, Bob. *Egyptian Mummies.* New York: William Morrow, 1994.

——— and M.V.L. Bennett. "Autopsy of an Egyptian Fish Mummy." *Post Library Association Report* 5 (1977): 8–11. Discussion of how fish were mummified.

——— and Ronald Wade. "The Use of Natron in Egyptian Mummification." *Paleopathology Newsletter* 89 (1995): 7–9. An experimental mummification of a human cadaver.

Budge, E.A. Wallis. *Prefatory Remarks on Egyptian Mummies, on the Occasion of Unrolling the Mummy of Bak-Ran.* London: Harrison & Sons, 1890. A rare mummy with the abdominal incision on the right side.

———. *The Mummy: A Handbook of Egyptian Funerary Archaeology.* New York: Causeway Books, 1974. Reprint of an 1894 work. Many sections are dated, but still there is much useful information.

Daressy, G. "Les sepultures des Pretres d'Amon a Deir el Bahari." *Annales du Service des Antiquités* 1 (1900): 141–148.

The mummies of the high priests of Amun from the second find at Deir el-Bahri.

———. "Proces-verbal d'ouverture de la momie no. 29207." *Annales du Service des Antiquités* 3 (1903): 151–157. Examination of one of the mummies from the second Deir el-Bahri cache.

——— and G.E. Smith. "Ouvertures des momies provenant de la seconde travaille de Deir el-Bahri." *Annales du Service des Antiquités* 4 (1903): 150–160. Examination of the mummies of the high priests of Amun found in the second Deir el-Bahri cache.

David, A. Rosalie, ed. *Mysteries of the Mummies.* New York: Charles Scribner's Sons, 1978.

——— and Edmund Tapp, eds. *The Mummy's Tale.* New York: St. Martin's Press, 1993. Anthology of articles on various topics, but much on the mummification process itself.

Davidson, John. "An Address on Embalming Generally, delivered at the Royal Institution, on the Unrolling of a Mummy." London, 1833.

Dawson, Warren R. "Making a Mummy." *Journal of Egyptian Archaeology* 13 (1927): 40–49. Presents the theory that mummies were soaked in natron.

———. "Two Egyptian Mummies Preserved in the Museums of Edinburgh." *Proceedings of the Society of Antiquaries of Scottland* 61 (1928): 290–296.

Forbes, Robert James. "Bitumen in Magic, Medicine, Agriculture and Mummification." In *Bitumen and Petroleum in Antiquity,* Leiden: E.J. Brill, 1936.

Gmelin, Johan Friederich. "Experimenta Nonnulla cum Mumiis Instituta." *Commentationes So cietatis Regiae Gollingensis* 4 (1781): 3–25. An early discussion of resins and chemistry of mummification.

Granville Augustus. "An Essay on Egyptian Mummies with Observations on the Art of Embalming among the Ancient Egyptians." *Philosophical Transactions of the Royal Society* (1825): 269–316. A careful, early autopsy of a mummy by a physician.

Iskander, Zaki. "Mummification in Ancient Egypt: Development, History, and Techniques." In *An X-Ray Atlas of the Royal Mummies,* James E. Harris and Edward F. Wente. Chicago: University of Chicago Press, 1980. An important article with unique photographs.

——— et al. "Temporary Stuffing Material Used in the Process of Mummification in Ancient Egypt." *Annales du Service des Antiquités* 58 (1964): 197–208.

Lewin, Peter K. "A Unique Ancient Egyptian Mummified Head, Demonstrating Removal of the Brain from the Foramen Magnum." *Paleopathology Newsletter* 57 (1987): 12–13.

Lucas, A. "'Cedar' Tree Products Employed in Mummification." *Journal of Egyptian Archaeology* 18 (1931): 13–21.

———. "Chemical Report on Samples of Various Materials found in Nubia during the Progress of the Archaeological Survey." In *The Archaeological Survey of Nubia, Part II, Report on the Human Remains.* Cairo: National Printing Dept., 1910.

———. "Mummification." in *Legacy of Ancient Egypt,* J.R. Harris, ed. London: Oxford University Press, 1962.

———. "The Nature of the Preservative Bath used by the Ancient Egyptian Embalmers." *Cairo Scientific Journal* 2 (1908): 421–424. The author later discarded his theory that a bath was used in mummification.

———. "Preliminary Note on some Preservative Materials used by the Ancient Egyptians in Embalming." *Cairo Scientific Journal* 2 (1908): 133–147.

———. "The Preservative Materials used by the Ancient Egyptians in Embalming." *Cairo Scientific Journal* 4 (1910): 66–68.

———. "The Question of the Use of Bitumen or Pitch by the Ancient Egyptians in Mummification." *Journal of Egyptian Archaeology* 1 (1914): 241–245.

———. "The Results of the Chemical Analysis of Materials from the Mummies found in the Tomb of Amenophis II." *Cairo Scientific Journal* 2 (1908): 273–278.

———. "The Use of Natron by the Ancient Egyptians in Mummification." *Journal of Egyptian Archaeology* 1 (1914): 119–123.

———. "The Use of Natron in Mummification." *Journal of Egyptian Archaeology* 18 (1932): 125–140.

Mariette, A. "Le ritual de l'embabuement" Vol. 1. In *Les Papyrus Égyptiens du Musée de Boulaq*. Paris: A. Franck, 1871.

Murray, Margaret A. *The Tomb of the Two Brothers, with Reports on the Anatomy of the Mummies by Dr. John Cameron, etc.* Manchester: Manchester Museum, 1910.

Nicolaeff, L. "Quelques donnée au suject des méthodes d'Excérébration par les Égyptiens anciens." *L'Anthropologie* 40 (1930): 77–92.

Sauneron, Serge. *Rituel de l'embaumement: pap. Boulaq III, pap. Louvre 5.158.* Cairo: Imprimerie Nationale, 1952. Ritual for wrapping a mummy.

Schmidt, W.A. "Chemische und biologische Untersuchungen von ägyptischen Mummienmaterial." *Zeitschrift für allgemeine Physiologie* 7 (1907): 369–392. Chemistry of fatty acids found in mummy tissues.

———. "Chemical and Biochemical Examination of Egyptian Mummies including some observations on the Embalming Process of the Ancient Egyptians." *Cairo Scientific Journal* 2 (1908): 147–149.

Silverman, Martin. *Mummies.* Chicago: Field Museum of Natural History, 1967.

Smith, G. Elliot. "A Contribution to the Study of Mummification in Egypt, with special reference to the methods adopted during the time of the XXIst Dynasty for Moulding the Form of the Body." *Memoires presentés à l'Institut egyptien* 5 (1906): 1–53.

———. "Notes on Mummies." *Cairo Scientific Journal* 2 (1908): 41–46.

——— and Warren R. Dawson. *Egyptian Mummies.* London: Kegan Paul, 1991. Reprint of a 1924 work, but still important.

——— and F. Wood-Jones. *The Archaeological Survey of Nubia, Report on the Human Remains. Report for 1907–1908. Vol. II.* Cairo: Egyptian Ministry of Finance, 1910.

Spielmann, Percy E. "To What Extent did the Ancient Egyptians Employ Bitumen for Embalming?" *Journal of Egyptian Archaeology* 18 (1932): 177–180.

Sudhoff, Karl. "Ägyptische Mumienmacher-Instrumente" *Archiv für Geschichte der Medizin* 5 (1911): 161–171. A rare discussion of instruments used in mummification.

Zaki, A. and Z. Iskander. "Materials and Method Used for Mummifying the Body of Amentefnekht, Saqqara 1941." *Annales du Service des Antiquités* 42 (1943): 223–256. Details of an unusual mummification.

Mummy Fiction

Freeman, R. Austin. *The Vanishing Man.* New York: Dodd, Mead & Co., 1918. Also published under the title *The Eye of Osiris*; includes an early description of x-raying a mummy in the British Museum.

———. *The Eye of Osiris.* New York: Dodd, Mead & Co., 1929. Also published under the title *The Vanishing Man.*

Gaunt, Mary. *The Mummy Moves.* New York: Edward J. Clode, 1925. The killer mummy is a *she.*

Gautier, Théophile. *The Romance of a Mummy.* Augusta McC. Wright, trans. Philadelphia: J.B. Lippincott & Co., 1882. A wealthy Englishman falls in love with a mummy he discovers.

Hard, T.W. *Sum VII.* New York: Harper & Row, 1979. A mummy is revived by modern technology.

Greenberg, Martin H. *Mummy Stories.* New York: Ballantine, 1980. Mostly ghoulish rather than classic mummy fiction.

Morrah, Dermot. *The Mummy Case Mystery.* New York: Harper & Brothers, 1933. Oxford University is the setting for this moving mummy.

Pettee, F.M. *The Palgrave Mummy.* New York: Payson & Clarke, 1929. Highly contrived plot without a true mummy.

Pratt, Ambrose. *The Living Mummy.* New York: Stokes, 1910.

Pronzini, Bill. *Mummy!* New York: Arbor House, 1980. Anthology of mummy short stories, including classics by Conan Doyle, Poe, and Gautier.

Rice, Anne. *The Mummy or Ramses the Damned.* New York: Ballantine Books, 1989. Romance between Cleopatra and Ramses the Great, by the author of the best-selling vampire novels.

Robinson, Lynda S. *Murder in the Place of Anubis.* New York: Walker and Co., 1994. A murder in an embalmer's workshop.

Smith, H.S. *A Visit to Ancient Egypt.* Warminster: Aris & Phillips, 1974. Contains a fictional account of the burial of the mummy of an Apis bull.

Stoker, Bram. *The Jewel of Seven Stars.* New York: Zebra Books, 1978. Reprint of the 1912 classic, by the author of *Dracula.*

Webb, Jane. *The Mummy! A Tale of the Twenty-Second Century.* London: Colburn, 1827. The revived mummy of Cheops saves society.

The Mummy in Film

Anon. "Blood from the Mummy's Tomb" *Famous Monsters of Filmland* no. 98, pp. 26–31, 1973. Complete plot summary and many photos from the film.

———. "The Curse of the Mummy's Tomb" *Famous Monsters of Filmland* no. 41, pp. 12–15, 1966. Brief plot summary of the film.

———. "How to Make a Mummy" *Famous Monsters of Filmland* no. 94, pp. 26–27, 1972. How Lon Chaney, Jr. was wrapped for his mummy role.

———. "Mummies of the Screen" *Terror* no. 5, pp. 29–31, N.D. c.1960. Brief history of mummy films.

———. "The Mummy" *Terror* no. 5, pp. 11–24, N.D. c. 1960. The script for the opening scenes of the Boris Karloff 1932 film.

———. "The Mummy" *Famous Monsters of Filmland* no. 58, pp. 34–39, 1969. Brief comic strip version of the Boris Karloff film.

———. "The Mummy" *Monster Fantasy* no. 2, pp. 28–35, 1975. The 1959 Christopher Lee film told with still photographs.

———. "The Mummy" *Famous Monsters of Filmland* no. 143, pp. 14–30, 1978. Plot summary and many photos of the classic film; concludes in the following issue.

———. "The Mummy: Im-Hotep" *Famous Monsters of Filmland* no. 144, pp. 16–25, 1978. Concludes the previous issue's plot summary of the Boris Karloff film.

———. "The Mummy's Curse" *Horror Monsters* no. 4, pp. 2–11, 1962. The film told in photos.

———. "The Mummy Story" *Modern Monsters* no. 3, pp. 34–46, 1966. History of mummy films.

———. "The Mummy's Ghost" *Famous Monsters of Filmland* no. 36, pp. 24–34, 1965. Plot and photos of the Hammer Film Production film.

———. "The Mummy's Tomb" *Famous Monsters of Filmland* no. 82, pp. 6–12, 1971. Plot summary and many photos of the film; concludes in the following issue.

———. "The Mummy's Tomb" *Famous Monsters of Filmland* no. 83, pp. 6–13, 1971. Concludes the plot of the film begun in the previous issue.

Avenell, Donne and David Jackson. "The Mummy's Shroud" *The House of Hammer* no. 15, pp. 5–10, 1977. Comic strip version of the film.

Brown, Florence V. "The Mummy's Curse" *Monster Fantasy* no. 2, pp. 12–16, 1975. Discussion of the curse in mummy films.

Dello Stritto, Frank J. "The Epic Saga of Kharis the Mummy" *Cult Movies* no. 15, pp. 36–38, 1995. Detailed analysis of the sequels to the Boris Karloff film.

Frank, Alan. *Horror Films* (London: Spring Books) 1977. Places the mummy films within a broader genre.

———. "In the Shadow of the Sphinx" *The House of Hammer* no. 15, pp. 37–40, 1977. History of the mummy in film.

Gerani, Gary. "Beginnings" *Monster Fantasy* no. 2, pp. 17–27, 1975. History of the mummy films.

Glut, Don. "The Mummy's Hammer" *Monsters of the Movies* no. 6, pp. 64–71, 1975. History of Hammer Film Productions mummy films.

Haydock, Ron. "Abbott and Costello Meet the Mummy" *Terror* no. 5, pp. 6–7, n.d. c.1960. Plot summary and photos of the film.

———. "The Mummy Chronicles" *Monsters of the Movies* no. 6, pp. 5–18, 1975. History of the mummy in film, with many photos.

Jones, Ron, and Joe Orlando. "Mummy's Hand" *Monster World* no. 2, pp. 34–40, 1964. A well-done comic strip version of the film, reprinted in *Famous Monsters of Filmland*, no. 40, 1966.

——— and Wallace Wood. "The Mummy" *Monster World* no. 1, pp. 36–41, 1964. Brief but well-done comic strip version of the Boris Karloff film; reprinted in *Famous Monster*, no. 58, 1969.

Martin, John. "I Want my Mummy" *The Dark Side* no. 41, pp. 33–37, 1994. History of the mummy in film; includes several foreign movies.

Mitchel, Lisa. "Mummy Dearest" *Cult Movies* no. 12, pp. 33–35, 1994. Discussion of Karloff's role in the classic film.

Moore, Steve and David Jackson. "The Mummy" *Halls of Horror* no. 22, pp. 5–10, 1978. Comic strip version of the Hammer 1959 film.

Rigby, Jonathan. "The Curse of the Mummy's Shroud" *Hammer Horror* no. 3, pp. 20–32, 1995. Lengthy description and photos of the film.

Riley, Philip J., ed. *The Mummy* MagicImage Filmbooks: Absecon, N.J., 1989. The definitive work on the 1932 film; it includes the complete script and interviews with the cast.

Children's Books (Fiction)

Arthur, Robert. *The Mystery of the Whispering Mummy*. New York: Random House, 1965. For preteens.

Bates, Diane and Caroline Magerl. *The Curse of King Nefertrustme*. Sydney: Harper Collins, 1995. Humorous book for preteens that explores the mummy's curse theme. Most unusual in that the children are killed by the curse!

Dixon, Franklin W. *The Mummy Case*. New York: Simon & Schuster, 1980. Hardy Boys novel for preteens.

Edwards, Leo. *Jerry Todd and the Whispering Mummy*. New York: Grosset & Dunlap, 1923. For preteens.

Hutchins, Pat. *The Curse of the Egyptian Mummy*. New York: Greenwillow, 1983. Cub Scouts solve a mystery; for preteens.

Pond, Roy. *The Mummy King's Realm*. Claremont: Albatross, 1994. For preteens.

———. *The Mummy Monster Game*. Norwood, South Australia: Omnibus, 1993. For ages 7–10 years.

———. *The Mummy Rescue Mission*. Norwood, South Australia: Omnibus, 1995. For ages 7–10 years.

———. *The Mummy Tomb Hunt*. Norwood, South Australia: Omnibus, 1994. For ages 7–10 years.

———. *Tomb Travellers*. Claremont: Albatross, 1991. For preteens.

Rosen, Heather. *Mummy Jokes and Puzzles*. New York: Scholastic, 1979.

Steiner, Barbara. *The Mummy*. London: Scholastic, 1995. For early teens.

Stine, R.L. *The Curse of the Mummy's Tomb*. New York: Scholastic, 1993. For preteens.

———. *Return of the Mummy.* New York: Scholastic, 1994. For preteens.

Children's Books (Nonfiction)

Cohen, Daniel. *The Tomb Robbers.* New York: McGraw-Hill, 1980. Much material on mummies; for preteens and early teens.

Dicks, Ian and David Hawcock. *Unwrap the Mummy!* New York: Dutton, 1995. A pull-out mummy for ages 9 and up.

Deary, Terry and Peter Hepplewhite. *The Awesome Egyptians.* London: Scholastic, 1993. Mostly mummies, for preteens.

Glubok, Shirley and Alfred Tamarin. *The Mummy of Ramose.* New York: Harper & Row, 1978. An account of the life and burial of Ramose; for preteens and teens.

Harris, Jack C. *101 Wacky Facts about Mummies.* New York: Scholastic Inc., 1991.

Lauber, Patricia. *Tales Mummies Tell.* New York: Thomas Y. Crowell, 1985. Includes non-Egyptian mummies; for young adults.

Comic Books

Anon. *The Mummy.* New York: Dell Publishing, 1962. Authorized by Universal Pictures, which produced the classic film, this version deviates considerably from the movie and features a mummy with the modern Arabic name Ahmed.

Blair, Barry and Jim Somerville. *The Mummy's Curse,* Nos. 1–4. Newbury, Calif.: Aircel Comics, 1990–91. More ghoul than Egyptian mummy.

Beaderstadt, Scott. *The Mummy,* Nos. 1–4. Seattle: Monster Comics, 1991. Well-done take-off of the Boris Karloff film.

Crane, Walter D. *Sheba.* Assonet, Massachusetts: Sick Mind Press, 1996. A mummified Egyptian cat comes back to life and complains to Anubis, god of mummification.

Isabella, Tony and Val Mayerik. *The Living Mummy.* New York: Marvel Comics, 1984–1994. Adventures of N'Kantu, the warrior-king who was buried alive in ancient Egypt.

Jolley, Dan, and Tony Harris. *The Mummy.* Milwaukie: Dark Horse Comics, 1993. Authorized by Universal Studios, this version of the 1933 film stays close to the original script.

Milligan, Peter and Glyn Dillon. *Egypt. The Book of the Remains.* New York: DC Comics, 1995. Tale of an ancient Egyptian embalmer.

Rice, Anne. *The Mummy,* nos. 1–12. Tampa: Millennium Publications, 1990–1. Comic book version of the novel, *The Mummy or Ramses the Damned.*

SOUTH AMERICA

History

Allison, M.J. "Chile's Ancient Mummies." *Natural History* 94 (1985) 74–81. Good survey of Chilean mummies.

———. "Early Mummies from Coastal Peru and Chile." In *Human Mummies,* Konrad Spindler, et al., eds. New York: Springer, 1996.

———. "Tatuajes y Pintura Corporal de los Indigenos Precolumbinos de Peru y Chile." *Chungara* 7 (1981): 218–236. Body painting and tattooing on mummies from Chile and Peru.

——— et al. "Chinchorro Momias de Preparacion Complicada: Metodos de Momificacion." *Chungara* 13 (1984): 155–173. History of mummification in Chile.

———. "The pre-Columbian Dog from Arica, Chile." *American Journal of Physical Anthropology* 59 (1982): 299–304. Studies of mummified dogs showed they are the same as modern Chilean dogs.

Arriaza, Bernardo T. *Beyond Death: The Chinchorro Mummies of Ancient Chile.* Washington: Smithsonian, 1995. The definitive work on the subject.

———. "Preparation of the Dead in Coastal Andean Pre-ceramic Populations." In *Human*

Mummies, Konrad Spindler, et al., eds. New York: Springer, 1996.

Aufderheide, A.C. "Secondary Applications of Bioanthropological Studies on South American Andean Mummies." *Human Mummies*, Konrad Spindler et al., eds. New York: Springer, 1996.

—— et al. "Seven Chinchorro Mummies and the Prehistory of Northern Chile." *American Journal of Physical Anthropology* 91 (1993): 189–201.

Berrizbeitia, E.L. "Momias de Venezuela." *Natura* 92 (1990): 9–15. Five mummies are described, one of which had been dried by smoking it over a fire.

Cardénas-Arroya, J. Félipe. "The Colombian Mummy Project." *Paleopathology Newsletter* 63 (1988): 7–8. A proposal to preserve and identify insects infecting Colombian mummies.

——. "La momificacion indigena en Colombia." *Boletin Museo del Oro* 25 (1990): 120–123. Survey of Colombian mummies.

Comas, J. "Origines de la Momificacion Prehispanica en America." *Anales de Antropologia* 2 (1974): 357–382.

Culin, S. "An Archaeological Application of the Roentgen Rays." *University of Pennsylvania Free Museum of Science and Art Bulletin* 4 (1898): 180–183. Early X rays of a Peruvian mummy.

Engel, F. "Early Holocene Funeral Bundles from the Central Andes." *Paleopathology Newsletter* 19 (1977): 7–8.

Holden, Tim. "Preliminary Work on South American Mummies Held at the British Museum." *Paleopathology Newsletter* 65 (1989): 5–9. Thirteen of the thirty South American mummies in the British Museum's collection were selected for study.

Horne, P.D. "The Prince of El Plomo: A Frozen Treasure." In *Human Mummies*, Konrad Spindler et al., eds. New York: Springer, 1996.

—— and S. Quevedo Kawasaki. "The Prince of El Plomo: A Paleopathological Study." *Bulletin of the N.Y. Academy of Medicine* 60 (1984): 925–931. Study of an Inca prince sacrificed to the sun god around 1500 B.C.

Kleiss, Ekkhard. "Der Kopf ist Sitz der Seele." *Forschritte der Medizin* 110 (1992): 110–113. Preservation of human heads, especially Amazon headhunters.

——. "Mummien: Die lebendigen Toten." *Fortschrftte der Medizen* 109 (1991): 55–59. Much on bundle mummies of South America.

Poinar, G.O. Jr., and R. Hess. "Ultrastructure of 40-million-year-old Insect Tissue." *Science* 215 (1982): 1241–2. Lipids, cell organelles, muscle fibers, etc., were recognizable in a fossil fly. The start of *Jurassic Park*.

Rae, A. "Dry Human and Animal Remains—Their Treatment at the British Museum." In *Human Mummies*, Konrad Spindler et al., eds. New York: Springer, 1996. Preservation of South American mummies, and some others.

Schobinger, Juan. "Sacrifices of the High Andes." *Natural History* 4/91 (1991): 62–69. Report on an Inca mummy.

Vreeland, J.M. "Prehistoric Andean Mortuary Practices." *Current Anthropology* 19 (1978): 212–214.

Paleopathology

Allison, M.J. et al. "ABO Blood Groups in Peruvian Mummies." *American Journal of Physical Anthropology* 44 (1976): 55–62.

——. "ABO Blood Groups in Chilean and Peruvian Mummies II. Results of Agglutination—Inhibition Technique." *American Journal of Physical Anthropology* 49 (1978): 139–142. Although close neighbors, Peruvian and Chilean mummies have different blood group distributions.

——. "Generalized Connective Tissue Disease in a Mummy from the Huari Culture."

Bulletin of the New York Academy of Medicine 53 (1977): 292–301. Study of a mummy of a Peruvian girl with diseased connective tissue.

——— and E. Gerszten. *Paleopathology in Peruvian Mummies.* Richmond: Virginia Commonwealth University, 1977. Thorough review of Peruvian mummies.

Cardénas Arroyo, Félipe. "The Application of Computer Assisted Tomography in a Mummy Bundle from Colombia." *Paleopathology Newsletter* (1990): 13–14.

Ferreira, L.F. et al. "The Finding of Helminth Eggs in a Brazilian Mummy." *Transactions of the Royal Society of Tropical Medical Hygiene.* 77 (1983): 65–67.

Gerszten, P.C. and A.J. Martinez. "The Neuropathology of South American Mummies." *Neurosurgery* 36 (1995): 756–761.

Heinemann, S. "Xeroradiology of a pre-Columbian Mummy." *Journal of the American Medical Association* 230 (1974): 1256. Examination of the mummy of a three-year-old hydrocephalic child.

Mead, Charles Williams. *Peruvian Mummies and What they Teach.* New York: Museum of Natural History, 1907.

Munizaga, J. "Diaphragmatic Hernia Associated with Strangulation of the Small Bowel in an Atacamena Mummy." *American Journal of Physical Anthropology* 48 (1978): 17–20. A Chilean mummy c. A.D. 300 that died due to a strangulated hernia.

Nerlich, A.G. et al. "Immunohistochemical Detection of Interstitial Collagens in Bone and Cartilage Tissue Remnants in an Infant Peruvian Mummy." *American Journal of Physical Anthropology* 91 (1993): 279–285. New method of extracting collagen from mummies.

Rothhammer, F. et al. "Chagas' Disease in Pre-Columbian South America." *American Journal of Physical Anthropology* 68 (1985): 495–498. Disease detected in 35 Chilean mummies c. 500 B.C.–A.D. 600.

Scott, E.C. and B.R. DeWalt. "Subsistence and Dental Pathology Etiologies from Prehistoric Coastal Peru." *Medical Anthropology* 4 (1980): 263–290. Increased carbohydrates in the diet increased caries in ancient Peruvians.

Stastny, P. "HL-A Antigens in Mummified Pre-Columbian Tissue." *Science* 183 (1974): 864–866. Pre-Columbian antigens are similar to those of modern populations in the same area.

Stout, S.D. "The Use of Bone Histomorphometry in Skeletal Identification: The Case of Francisco Pizarro." *Journal of Forensic Sciences* 31 (1986): 296–300.

Tyson, Rose A. and Elizabeth S. Dyer Alcauskas. *Catalogue of the Hrdlicka Paleopathology Collection.* San Diego: San Diego Museum of Man, 1980. More than 1,000 South American pre-Columbian specimens, most skeletal.

Weinstein, R.S. "Ancient Bone Disease in a Peruvian Mummy. . . ." *American Journal of Physical Anthropology* 54 (1981): 321–326.

Zimmerman, M.R. et al. "Trauma and Trephination in a Peruvian Mummy." *American Journal of Physical Anthropology* 55 (1981): 497–501. A young male died shortly after his skull had been drilled.

EUROPE

Archaeological and Ethnographical Museum of Tenerife. *Momias—Los Secretos del Pasado.* Palmas: Museo Arqueologico y Ethnografico de Tenerife, 1992.

Artamanonov, Mickail I. "Frozen Tombs of the Scythians." *Scientific American* 212 (1965): 101–109.

Ascenzi, A. et al. "The Roman Mummy of Grottarossa." In *Human Mummies,* Konrad Spindler, et al., eds. New York: Springer, 1996.

Aufderheide, A.C. "Soft Tissue Paleopathology—An Emerging Subspecialty." *Human Pathology* 12 (1981): 865–867. A history of the subject with suggestions for the preservation and study of mummies.

Aufderheide, Mary and Arthur C. Aufderheide. "Guanche Mummies. The Bioanthropology Project." *Paleopathology Newsletter* 66 (1989): 7–8.

Barfield, L. "The Iceman Reviewed." *Antiquity* 69 (1994): 10–26. Survey article on the frozen mummy known as "The Iceman."

Barnhardt, Marion. "Update on the Magadan Mammoth's Tissue Vestiges: Skeletal Muscle Identification." *Paleopathology Newsletter* 29 (1980): 9–10. Siberian mammoth study.

Bereuter, T.L. et al. "Post-mortem Alterations of Human Lipids—Part I: Evaluation of Adipocere Formation and Mummification by Desiccation;" "Part II: Lipid Composition of a Skin Sample from the Iceman." In *Human Mummies*, Konrad Spindler et al., eds. New York: Springer, 1996.

Capasso, Luigi and Gabriella Di Tota. "The Human Mummies of Navelli: Natural Mummification at New Site in Central Italy." *Paleopathology Newsletter* 75 (1991): 7–8. Hundreds of naturally mummified bodies discovered under the flooring of the rectory of the church of San Bartolomeo.

Cruz, Joan Carrol. *The Incorruptibles*. Rockford, Ill: Tan Books, 1974. A listing and discussion of the Catholic saints whose bodies have been declared incorruptible.

Derobert, L. and H. Reichlen. *Les Momies*. Paris: Orion, n.d. c. 1950. A geographical treatment of mummification around the world with many unusual illustrations.

Dogo, G. "The Saint's Hand." *Journal of Trauma* 14 (1974): 9–19. The mummified hand of Saint Vincent indicates that he was tortured by roasting and that death occurred nine to twelve days after the torture.

Fornaciari, Gino. "The Mummies of the Abbey of Saint Domenico Maggiore in Naples: A Plan of Research." *Paleopathology Newsletter* 45 (1984): 9–10. The mummies of the kings of Aragon.

———. "The Mummies of the Abbey of Saint Domenico Maggiore in Naples: A Preliminary Report." *Archaeologie Antropologie e Etnologie* 115 (1985): 215–226. Fifteen royal and noble mummies of the eleventh century were studied; some had been artificially mummified.

———. "Natural Mummies in Central Italy: A Preliminary Survey." *Paleopathology Newsletter* 40 (1982): 11–12.

——— et al. "Adenocarcinoma in the Mummy of Ferrante I of Aragon, King of Naples (1431–1494) AD." *Paleopathology Newsletter* 83 (1993): 5–8.

———. "Analysis of Pulmonary Tissue from a Natural Mummy of the XIII Century (Saint Zita, Lucca, Tuscany, Italy) by FT-IR Microspectroscopy." *Paleopathology Newsletter* 68 (1989): 5–8.

———. "Syphilis in a Renaissance Italian Mummy." *Lancet* (1989): 614.

——— and L. Capasso. "Natural and Artificial 13th–19th Century Mummies in Italy." In *Human Mummies*, Konrad Spindler et al., eds. New York: Springer, 1996.

——— and Susanna Gambo. "The Mummies of the Church of S. Maria Della Grazia in Comiso, Sicily (18th–19th Century)." *Paleopathology Newsletter* 81 (1993): 7–10. Fifty naturally mummified bodies are discussed.

Fulcheri, E. "Mummies of Saints: A Particular Category of Italian Mummies." In *Human Mummies*, Konrad Spindler et al., eds. New York: Springer, 1996.

Glob, P.V. *The Mound People*. Ithaca: Cornell University Press, 1970.

Gonzalez-Crussi, F. *Suspended Animation*. New York: Harcourt Brace, 1995. Six essays on the preservation of bodily parts, including early anatomical specimens.

Hopfel, Frank et al., eds. *Der Mann im Eis*. Innsbruck: University of Innsbruck, 1992. Anthology of scientific papers on Iceman.

Horne, P.O. and R.R. Ireland. "Moss and a Guanche Mummy: An Unusual Utilization."

The Bryologist 94 (1991): 407–408. Moss used to preserve a Canary Islands mummy.

Iserson, Kenneth. *Death to Dust*. Tucson: Galen Press, 1995. General treatment of what happens to bodies after death.

Kaumann, B. "The Corpse from the Porchabella-Glacier in the Grisons, Switzerland." In *Human Mummies*, Konrad Spindler, et al., eds. New York: Springer, 1996.

———. "Mummification in the Middle Ages." In *Human Mummies*, Konrad Spindler et al., eds. New York: Springer, 1996.

Kleiss, Ekkhard. "Algunoa Casos de Momificacion Natural." *Ciencias Morfologicas en America* 2, no. 2 (1980): 5–18. Survey of European mummies, mostly from Italy and Vienna.

———. "La Momification Natural y Artificial." *Arquivos de Anatomia e Antropologia* 1 (1975): 37–54. Broad survey of mummification including much on European mummies.

———. "Some Examples of Natural Mummies." *Paleopathology Newsletter* 20 (1977): 5–6.

Kralik, C. et al. "Trace Element Contents of the Iceman's Bones. Preliminary Results." In *Human Mummies*, Konrad Spindler, et al., eds. New York: Springer, 1996.

Makristathis, A. "Comparison of the Lipid Profile of the Tyrolean Iceman with Bodies Recovered from Glaciers." In *Human Mummies*, Konrad Spindler et al., eds. New York: Springer, 1996.

Maples, William. *Dead Men Do Tell Tales*. New York: Doubleday, 1994. Not specifically on mummies, but contains a good chapter on the supposed mummy of Francisco Pizarro.

Meneghelli, V. and A. Poppi, eds. *Ricognizione del Corpo di S. Antonio di Padova* Padua: Messagero, 1981. Examination of the body of Saint Anthony of Padua.

Mokhnilov, M.I., et al. "Electron Microscopy of the Intestinal Content of a Mammoth." *Lancet* 2 (1984): 111–112. Virus-like particles in the intestines of a 10,000-year-old Siberian mammoth.

Nedden, Dieter and Klaus Wicke. "The Similaun Mummy as Observed from the Viewpoint of Radiological and CT Data." In *Der Mann im Eis*, Frank Hopfel et al., eds. Innsbruck: University of Innsbruck, 1992.

Polosmak, Natalya. "Postures of Heaven." *National Geographic* 186, no. 4 (1994): 80–103. Excellent popular article on a frozen Siberian mummy.

Reyman, T.A. "The Histology of Ancient Mammoth Tissue." *Paleopathology Newsletter* 33 (1981): 13–15.

Rodriguez-Martin, C. "Guanche Mummies of Tenerife (Canary Islands): Conservation and Scientific Studies in the CRONOS Project." In *Human Mummies*, Konrad Spindler, et al., eds. New York: Springer, 1996.

Rollo, Franco. "Molecular Investigations on Mummified Seeds and Other Plant Remains." In *Der Mann im Eis* Frank Hoppel et al., eds. Innsbruck: University of Innsbruck, 1992.

Rudenko, S.I. *Frozen Tombs of Siberia*. Berkeley: University of California Press, 1970. Scythian mummies.

Seipel, W. "Mummies and Ethics in the Museum." In *Human Mummies*, Konrad Spindler et al., eds. New York: Springer, 1996.

Sjovold, Torstein. "Frost and Found. The Melting of an Alpine Glacier Brings Scientists Face to Face with the Stone Age." *Natural History* 4 (1993): 60–64.

———. "The Stone Age Iceman from the Alps: The Find and the Current Status of Investigation." *Evolutionary Anthropology* 1 (1992): 117–124.

Spindler, Konrad, et al. *Human Mummies*. New York: Springer, 1996. Important collection of articles on mummies around the world.

Spindler, Konrad. "Iceman's Last Weeks." In *Human Mummies*, Konrad Spindler, et al., eds. New York: Springer, 1996.

————. *The Man in the Ice*. New York: Harmony Books, 1995. The popular account of The Iceman.

Weisgram, J. et al. "Remarks on the anatomy of a Mummified Cat Regarding the Extent of Preservation." In *Human Mummies*, Konrad Spindler et al., eds. New York: Springer, 1996.

Wells, Calvin. *Bones, Bodies and Diseases: Evidence of Disease and Abnormality in Early Man*. London: Thames and Hudson, 1964.

Bog Mummies

Balguy, C. "An Account of the Dead Bodies of a Man and a Woman which were Preserved 49 years in the Moors in Derbyshire." *Philosophical Transactions of the Royal Society* 38 (1734): 413–415.

Bennike, P. et al. "Early Neolithic Skeletons from Bolkilde Bog, Denmark." *Antiquity* 60 (1986): 199–209. One specimen had a rope around his neck, possibly a ritual sacrifice.

Brandt, J. "Plant Remains in an Early Iron Age Body." *Aarbog for Nordisk Oldkyndig og Historie* (1950): 347–351.

Brothwell, D. "European Bog Bodies: Current State of Research and Preservation." In *Human Mummies*, Konrad Spindler et al., eds. New York: Springer, 1996.

Connolly, R.C. "Lindow Man: Britain's Prehistoric Bog Body." *Anthropology Today* 5 (1985): 15–17.

Cowell, A.P. "The Lindow Man." *The Photographic Journal* 124 (1985): 101–106.

Daniels, V. "Selection of a Conservation Process for Lindow Man." In *Human Mummies*, Konrad Spindler et al., eds. New York: Springer, 1996.

Drabble, Margaret. *A Natural Curiosity*. New York: Penguin, 1987. The famous bog mummy, Lindow Man, plays a recurring role in this novel.

Glob, P.V. *The Bog People*. Ithaca: Cornell University Press, 1967.

Hunt, J. "On the Influence of some kinds of Peat in Destroying the Human Body, as shown by the Discovery of Human Remains Buried in Peat in the Shetland Islands." *Memoirs of the Anthropological Society of London* 2 (1866): 364–372.

Levanthes, Louise. "Mysteries of the Bog." *National Geographic* 171, no. 3 (1987): 397–420.

Mann, L. "Notes on the Discovery of a Body in a Peat Moss at Cambusnethan." *Transactions of the Glasgow Archaeological Society* 9 (1937): 44–55.

Munksgaard, E. "Bog Bodies—A Brief Survey of Interpretations." *Journal of Danish Archaeology* 3 (1984): 120–123.

Parker Pearson, M. "Lindow Man and the Danish Connection—further light on the mystery of the Bogman." *Anthropology Today* 1 (1986): 15–18.

Petrie, G. "Account of a Human Body in a Singular Costume, Found in a High State of Preservation in a Bog on the lands of Gallagh, in the County of Galway." *Dublin Philosophical Journal and Scientific Review* 1 (1825): 433–435.

Pyatt, F.B. et al. "An Examination of the Mobilization of Elements from the Skin and Bone of the Bog Body Lindow II and a Comparison with Lindow III." *Environmental Geochemistry and Health* 13 (1991): 153–159.

Scarfe, N. "The Body of St. Edmund: An Essay in Necrobiography." *Proceedings Suffolk Institute of Archaeology* 31 (1970): 303–317. The body believed to be Saint Edmund could have been confused with a bog body.

Stead, I.M. et al., eds. *Lindow Man, the Body in the Bog*. Ithaca: Cornell University Press, 1986.

———— and R.C. Turner. "Lindow Man." *Antiquity* 59 (1985): 25–29.

Stovin, G. "A Letter from Mr. T.G. Stovin to his Son, concerning the Body of a Woman and an Antique Shoe found in a Morass in the Isle of Axholme in Lincolnshire." *Philosophical Transactions of the Royal Society* 44 (1747): 571–576.

Tinsley, H.M. "A Record of Preserved Human Remains from Blanket Peat in West Yorkshire." *The Naturalist* 931 (1974): 134.

Whitelock, D. "Fact and Fiction in the Legend of St. Edmund." *Proceedings Suffolk Institute of Archaeology* 31 (1970): 217–233. The body believed to be Saint Edmund could have been confused with a bog body.

Wilde, W.R. "On the Antiquities and Human Remains found in the County of Down, in 1780, and described by the Countess of Moira, in *Archaeologia* vol. VII." *Proceedings of the Riyal Irish Academy* 9 (1864): 101–104.

NORTH AMERICA

Bradbury, Ray. "The Next in Line." In *The Mummies of Guanajuato.* New York: Abrams, 1978. Science fiction writer's early story about the famous Mexican mummies.

Clauser, C.J. et al. "Little Salt Spring Florida: A Unique Underwater Site." *Science* 203 (1979): 609–614. Preserved brain tissue more than 6,000 years old.

Cotten, G.E. et al. "Preservation of Human Tissue Immersed for five years in Fresh Water of Known Temperature." *Journal of Forensic Sciences* 32 (1987): 1125–1130. Preserved bodies of two people trapped in a car in Lake Superior in Minnesota.

El-Najjar, M.Y. et al. "Autopsies on two Native American Mummies." *American Journal of Physical Anthropology* 53 (1980): 197–202.

———. "Preserved Human Remains from the Southern Region of the North American Continent: Report of Autopsy Findings." *Human Pathology* 16 (1985): 273–276. Analysis of six naturally mummified bodies.

Gill, G.W. and D.W. Owsley. "Electron Microscopy of Parasite Remains on the Pitchfork Mummy and Possible Social Implications." *Plains Anthropology* 30 (1985): 45–50. A speculative article, attempting to draw social conclusions from the findings of lice eggs in the hair of Plains Indians.

Lieberman, Archie and Ray Bradbury. *The Mummies of Guanajuato.* New York: H.N. Abrams, 1978. Photos of Mexican mummies and short story by Bradbury.

Matson, G.A. "A Procedure for the Serological Determination of Blood—Relationships of Ancient and Modern Peoples with special reference of American Indians. II Blood Groupings of Mummies." *Journal of Immunology* 30 (1936): 459–470. An early study of blood in mummies.

Paabo, S. et al. "Mitochondral DNA Sequences from a 7,000 year old Brain." *Nucleic Acids Research* 16 (1989): 9775–9787. DNA extracted from the brain of a mummy found in a Florida swamp.

Saul, Frank P. and Julie M. Saul, et al. "The Mummy from Mummy cave: Preliminary Reports." *Paleopathology Newsletter* 60 (1987): 4–10. A native American mummy c. A.D. 700 was studied by a team with the cooperation of the Plains Indian Advisory Board.

Snow, Clyde and Theodore A. Reyman. *The Life and Afterlife of Elmer J. McCurdy.* Detroit: Paleopathology Association, September, 1977. The travels of the mummy of the American outlaw, Elmer McCurdy.

Tyson, R.A. and D.V. Elerick, eds. *Two Mummies from Chihuahua, Mexico: A Multidisciplinary Study.* San Diego: San Diego Museum of Man, 1985. An extensive study of two mummies.

ARCTIC

Arctic Anthropology. Madison: University of Wisconsin Press, 1984. Reports on five frozen mummies found in a house crushed by an ice fall.

Beatie, O.B. et al. "Anatomy of an Arctic Autopsy." *Medical Post*, 20 (1985): 1–2. The Franklin Expedition.

———— and J.M. Savelle. "Discovery of Human Remains from Sir John Franklin's Lost Expedition." *Historical Archaeology* 17 (1983): 100–105.

———— and John Geiger. *Frozen in Time*. New York: E.P. Dutton, 1987. The story of the Franklin Expedition with a detailed description of the frozen mummies of three of the expedition members.

Bresciani, J. et al. "Head Louse (*Pediculus humanus suscp. capitis deGeer*) from Mummified Corpses of Greenland, A.D. 1460 (+/- 50)." *Acta Entomologica Fennia* 42 (1983): 24–27.

Hart Hansen, J.P. and J. Nordqvist. "The Mummy find from Qilakitsoq in Northwest Greenland." In *Human Mummies*, Konrad Spindler, et al., eds. New York: Springer, 1996.

Hansen, H.E. and H. Gurtler. "HLA Types of Mummified Eskimo Bodies from the 15th Century." *American Journal of Physical Anthropology* 61 (1983): 447–452. Blood types of two families of frozen mummies.

Masters, P.M. and M.R. Zimmerman. "Age Determination of an Alaskan Mummy: Morphological and Biochemical Correlation." *Science* 201 (1978): 811–812.

Notman, D.N.H. et al. "Arctic Paleoradiology: Portable Radiographic Examination of Two Frozen Sailors from the Franklin Expedition (1845–1848)." *American Journal of Roentgenology* 149 (1989): 347–350.

———— and O. Beattie. "The Palaeoimaging and Forensic Anthropology of Frozen Sailors from the Franklin Arctic Expedition Mass Disaster (1845–1848): A Detailed Presentation of Two Radiological Surveys." In *Human Mummies*, Konrad Spindler, et al., eds. New York: Springer, 1996.

Smith, G.S. and Zimmerman, M.R. "Tattooing Found on a 1600 year old Frozen, Mummified Body from St. Lawrence Island, Alaska." *American Antiquity* 40 (1975): 434–437.

Zimmerman, M.R. "Mummies of the Arctic Regions." In *Human Mummies*, Konrad Spindler, et al., eds. New York: Springer, 1996.

ASIA

Cheng, T.O. "Glimpses of the Past from the Recently Unearthed Ancient Corpses in China." *Annals of Internal Medicine* 101 (1984): 714–715.

Cuong, N.L. "About the Dead Bodies of two Buddhist Monks Preserved in the form of Statues at the Dau Pagoda." *OSSA* 9/11 (1984): 105–110.

Hadingham, E. "The Mummies of Xinjiang." *Discover* (April 1994): 68–77.

Kao, Jeffrey and Yang Zuosheng. "On Jade Suits and Han Archaeology." *Archaeology* 36, no. 6 (1983): 30–37. Jade suits used to preserve the bodies of the nobility of the Han Dynasty.

Kamberi, D. "Three Thousand Year Old Charchan Man Preserved at Zaqhunluq." *Sino-Platonic Papers* 44 (January, 1994).

Mair, Victor H. "Mummies of the Tarim Basin." *Archaeology* 48 (1994): 28–35.

Wang, B.-H. "Excavation and Preliminary Studies of the Ancient Mummies of Xinjiang in China." In *Human Mummies*, Konrad Spindler et al., eds. New York: Springer, 1996.

Yamada, T.K. et al. "Collagen in 300-Year-Old Tissue and a Short Introduction to the Mummies of Japan." In *Human Mummies*, Konrad Spindler, et al., eds. New York: Springer, 1996.

Yang, K.-L. et al. "Skin Changes of 2,100 year old Changsha Female Corpse." *Chinese Medical Journal* 95 (1982): 765–776.

INDEX

Page numbers in **boldface** indicate article titles. *Italic* page numbers indicate illustrations.

Clackamas County Library
16201 S.E. McLoughlin Blvd
Oak Grove, OR 97267

DEC   9 1997